Course	Business Process - Management
Course Number	**BA302**
	Oregon State University
	College of Business

http://create.mheducation.com

ISBN-10: 1121950620   ISBN-13: 9781121950627

Contents

Credits

Chapter 1

The Role of Services in an Economy

Learning Objectives

After completing this chapter, you should be able to:

1. Identify traits that all services have in common.
2. Describe the central role of services in an economy.
3. State the Clark-Fisher hypothesis concerning the evolution of an economy.
4. Identify and differentiate the five stages of economic activity.
5. Describe the features of preindustrial, industrial, and postindustrial societies.
6. Describe the features of the new experience economy.
7. Contrast the push versus pull theories of innovation.
8. Identify the sources of service sector growth.

We are witnessing the greatest labor migration since the industrial revolution. This migration from agriculture and manufacturing to services is both invisible and largely global in scope. The migration is driven by global communications, business and technology growth, urbanization, and low-cost labor. Service industries are leaders in every industrialized nation, they create new jobs that dominate national economies, and have the potential to enhance the quality of life of everyone. Many of these jobs are for high-skilled knowledge workers and have the greatest projected growth in professional and business services. For the top ten postindustrial nations the extent of the migration to services over the past 40 years is captured in Table 1.1.

TABLE 1.1   **Percent Employment in Services for the Top Ten Postindustrial Nations, 1965–2005**

Source: http://www.bls.gov/fls/flscomparelf.htm
Table 6: Civilian Employment Approximating U.S. Concepts by Economic Sector

Country	1965	1975	1985	1995	2005
United States	59.5	66.4	70.0	74.1	78.6
United Kingdom	51.3	58.3	64.1	71.4	77.0
The Netherlands	52.5	60.9	68.3	73.4	76.5
Sweden	46.5	57.7	66.1	71.5	76.3
Canada	57.8	65.8	70.6	74.8	76.0
Australia	54.6	61.5	68.4	73.1	75.8
France	43.9	51.9	61.4	70.0	74.8
Japan	44.8	52.0	57.0	61.4	68.6
Germany	41.8	n/a	51.6	60.8	68.5
Italy	36.5	44.0	55.3	62.2	65.5

Chapter Preview

In a discussion of economic development, we learn that modern industrialized economies are dominated by employment in the service sector industries. This represents a
natural evolution of economies from preindustrial to industrial and finally to postindustrial societies. Furthermore, the economic activity of society determines the nature of
how people live and how the standard of living is measured. The nature of the service
sector is explored in terms of employment opportunities, contributions to economic sta-
bility, and source of economic leadership. The observation that our postindustrial society
is now evolving into an experience economy is discussed for both consumer and business
services. The growth of the service sector is attributed to innovation, social trends, and
information technology (e.g., Internet). We begin with a selection of service definitions.

Service Definitions

Many definitions of service are available but all contain a common theme of intangibility
and simultaneous consumption. The following represent a sample of service definitions:

> Services are deeds, processes, and performances. (Valarie A. Zeithaml and Mary Jo Bitner,
> *Services Marketing,* New York: McGraw-Hill, 1996, p. 5.)
>
> A service is an activity or series of activities of more or less intangible nature that nor-
> mally, but not necessarily, take place in interactions between customer and service employees
> and/or physical resources or goods and/or systems of the service provider, which are provided
> as solutions to customer problems. (Christian Gronroos, *Service Management and Marketing,*
> Lexington, Mass: Lexington Books, 1990, p. 27.)
>
> Most authorities consider the services sector to include all economic activities whose output is
> not a physical product or construction, is generally consumed at the time it is produced, and pro-
> vides added value in forms (such as convenience, amusement, timeliness, comfort, or health) that
> are essentially intangible concerns of its first purchaser. (James Brian Quinn, Jordan J. Baruch,
> and Penny Cushman Paquette, *Scientific American,* vol. 257, no. 2, December 1987, p. 50.)
>
> Services are economic activities offered by one party to another, most commonly employing
> time-based performances to bring about desired results in recipients themselves or in objects
> or other assets for which purchasers have responsibility. In exchange for their money, time, and
> effort, service customers expect to obtain value from access to goods, labor, professional skills,
> facilities, networks, and systems; but they do not normally take ownership of any of the physi-
> cal elements involved. (Christopher Lovelock and Lauren Wright, *Services Marketing: People,
> Technology, Strategy,* 6th ed., Upper Saddle River, NJ: Prentice-Hall, 2007, p. 6.)
>
> A service system is a value-coproduction configuration of people, technology, other internal
> and external service systems, and shared information (such as language, processes, metrics,
> prices, policies, and laws). (Jim Spohrer, Paul Maglio, John Bailey, and Daniel Gruhl, *Computer,*
> January 2007, p. 72.)
>
> A service is a time-perishable, intangible experience performed for a customer acting in the
> role of co-producer. (James Fitzsimmons)

Facilitating Role of Services in an Economy

As shown in Figure 1.1, services are central to the economic activity in any society.
Infrastructure services, such as transportation and communications, are the essential links
among all sectors of the economy, including the final consumer. In a complex economy,
both infrastructure and distribution services function as intermediaries and as the channel of distribution to the final consumer. Infrastructure services are a prerequisite for an
economy to become industrialized; therefore, no advanced society can be without these
services.

In an industrialized economy, specialized firms can supply business services to manufacturing firms more cheaply and efficiently than manufacturing firms can supply these

FIGURE 1.1
Role of Services in an Economy

Source: After Bruce R. Guile and James Brian Quinn, eds., *Technology in Services: Policies for Growth, Trade, and Employment,* Washington, D.C.: National Academy Press, 1988, p. 214.

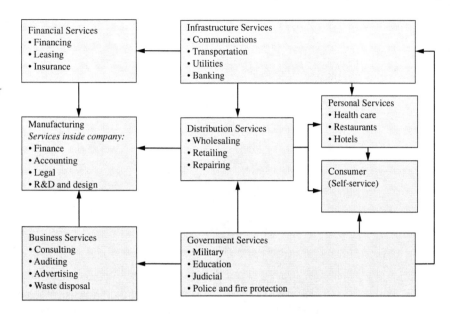

services for themselves. Thus, more and more often we find advertising, consulting, and other business services being provided for the manufacturing sector by service firms.

Except for basic subsistence living, where individual households are self-sufficient, service activities are absolutely necessary for the economy to function and to enhance the quality of life. Consider, for example, the importance of a banking industry to transfer funds and a transportation industry to move food products to areas that cannot produce them. Moreover, a wide variety of personal services, such as restaurants, lodging, cleaning, and child care, have been created to move former household functions into the economy.

Government services play a critical role in providing a stable environment for investment and economic growth. Services such as public education, health care, well-maintained roads, safe drinking water, clean air, and public safety are necessary for any nation's economy to survive and people to prosper.

Increasingly, the profitability of manufacturers depends on exploiting value-added services. For example, automobile manufacturers have discovered that financing and/or leasing automobiles can achieve significant profits. Otis Elevator long ago found that revenues from after-sales maintenance contracts far exceed the profits from elevator equipment sales. As personal computers become a commodity product with very low margins, firms turn to network and communication services to improve profits.

Thus, it is imperative to recognize that services are not peripheral activities but rather integral parts of society. They are central to a functioning and healthy economy and lie at the heart of that economy. Finally, the service sector not only facilitates but also makes possible the goods-producing activities of the manufacturing sectors. Services are the crucial force for today's change toward a global economy.

Economic Evolution

In the early 1900s, only 3 of every 10 workers in the United States were employed in the services sector. The remaining workers were active in agriculture and industry. By 1950, employment in services accounted for 50 percent of the workforce. Today, services employ about 8 out of every 10 workers. During the past 90 years, we have witnessed a major evolution in our society from being predominantly manufacturing-based to being predominantly service-based.

6   Part One *Understanding Services*

FIGURE 1.2
Stages of Economic Activity

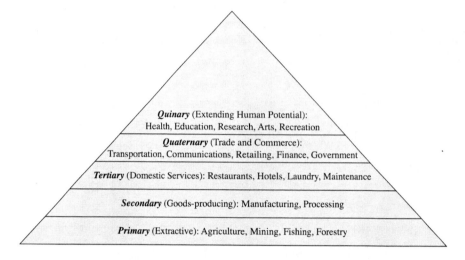

Quinary (Extending Human Potential):
Health, Education, Research, Arts, Recreation

Quaternary (Trade and Commerce):
Transportation, Communications, Retailing, Finance, Government

Tertiary (Domestic Services): Restaurants, Hotels, Laundry, Maintenance

Secondary (Goods-producing): Manufacturing, Processing

Primary (Extractive): Agriculture, Mining, Fishing, Forestry

Economists studying economic growth are not surprised by these events. Colin Clark argues that as nations become industrialized, there is an inevitable shift of employment from one sector of the economy to another.[1] As productivity increases in one sector, the labor force moves into another. This observation, known as the *Clark-Fisher hypothesis,* leads to a classification of economies by noting the activity of the majority of the workforce.

Figure 1.2 describes a hierarchy of economic activity. Many economists, including Clark, limited their analyses to only three stages, of which the tertiary stage was simply services. We have taken the suggestion of Nelson N. Foote and Paul K. Hatt and subdivided the service stage to create a total of five stages.[2]

Today, an overwhelming number of countries are still in a primary stage of development. These economies are based on extracting natural resources from the land. Their productivity is low, and income is subject to fluctuations based on the prices of commodities such as sugar and copper. In much of Africa and parts of Asia, more than 70 percent of the labor force is engaged in extractive activities.

Figure 1.3 shows the rapid increase in service employment in the United States over the past century and illustrates the almost mirror image decline in agriculture employment. Note that the "industrial revolution" began in the United States about 1850 with a percentage of manufacturing employment about equal to that projected for 2010. This sector employment trajectory is repeated for all of the nations represented in Table 1.1. Although not included in Table 1.1, the emerging economies of India, China, and Brazil already approach 50 percent service employment. We can observe that migration to services is a predictable evolution in the workforce of all nations, and successful industrial economies are built on a strong service sector. Furthermore, competition in services is global. Consider the growth of call centers in India and commercial banking by the Japanese. Trade in services remains a challenge, however, because many countries erect barriers to protect domestic firms. India and Mexico, for example, prohibit the sale of insurance by foreign companies.

Stages of Economic Development

Describing where our society has been, its current condition, and its most likely future is the task of social historians. Daniel Bell, a professor of sociology at Harvard University, has written extensively on this topic, and the material that follows is based on his work.[3] To place the concept of a postindustrial society in perspective, we must compare its features with those of preindustrial and industrial societies.

FIGURE 1.3
Trends in U.S. Employment by Sector, 1850–2010

Source: U.S. Department of Commerce, Bureau of the Census, *Historical Statistics of the United States*, 1975, p. 137, and http://www.bls.gov/fls/flscomparelf.htm

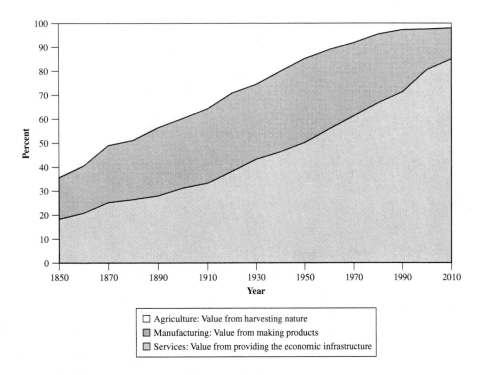

☐ Agriculture: Value from harvesting nature
▨ Manufacturing: Value from making products
▨ Services: Value from providing the economic infrastructure

Preindustrial Society

The condition of most of the world's population today is one of subsistence, or a *pre-industrial society*. Life is characterized as a game against nature. Working with muscle power and tradition, the labor force is engaged in agriculture, mining, and fishing. Life is conditioned by the elements, such as the weather, the quality of the soil, and the availability of water. The rhythm of life is shaped by nature, and the pace of work varies with the seasons. Productivity is low and bears little evidence of technology. Social life revolves around the extended household, and this combination of low productivity and large population results in high rates of underemployment (workers not fully utilized). Many seek positions in services, but of the personal or household variety. Preindustrial societies are agrarian and structured around tradition, routine, and authority.

Industrial Society

The predominant activity in an *industrial society* is the production of goods. The focus of attention is on making more with less. Energy and machines multiply the output per labor-hour and structure the nature of work. Division of labor is the operational "law" that creates routine tasks and the notion of the semiskilled worker. Work is accomplished in the artificial environment of the factory, and people tend the machines. Life becomes a game that is played against a fabricated nature—a world of cities, factories, and tenements. The rhythm of life is machine-paced and dominated by rigid working hours and time clocks.

An industrial society is a world of schedules and acute awareness of the value of time. The standard of living becomes measured by the quantity of goods, but note that the complexity of coordinating the production and distribution of goods results in the creation of large bureaucratic and hierarchic organizations. These organizations are designed with certain roles for their members, and their operation tends to be impersonal, with persons treated as things. The individual is the unit of social life in a society that is considered to be the sum total of all the individual decisions being made in the marketplace. Of course, the unrelenting pressure of industrial life is softened by the countervailing force of labor unions.

TABLE 1.2   Comparison of Societies

			Features				
Society	Game	Predominant Activity	Use of Human Labor	Unit of Social Life	Standard of Living Measure	Structure	Technology
Pre-industrial	Against nature	Agriculture Mining	Raw muscle power	Extended household	Subsistence	Routine Traditional Authoritative	Simple hand tools
Industrial	Against fabricated nature	Goods production	Machine tending	Individual	Quantity of goods	Bureaucratic Hierarchical	Machines
Post-industrial	Among persons	Services	Artistic Creative Intellectual	Community	Quality of life in terms of health, education, recreation	Inter-dependent Global	Information

Postindustrial Society

While an industrial society defines the standard of living by the quantity of goods, the *postindustrial society* is concerned with the quality of life, as measured by services such as health, education, and recreation. The central figure is the professional person, because rather than energy or physical strength, information is the key resource. Life now is a game played among persons. Social life becomes more difficult because political claims and social rights multiply. Society becomes aware that the independent actions of individuals can combine to create havoc for everyone, as seen in traffic congestion and environmental pollution. The community rather than the individual becomes the social unit.

Bell suggests that the transformation from an industrial to a postindustrial society occurs in many ways. First, there is a natural development of services, such as transportation and utilities, to support industrial development. As labor-saving devices are introduced into the production process, more workers engage in nonmanufacturing activities, such as maintenance and repair. Second, growth of the population and mass consumption of goods increase wholesale and retail trade, along with banking, real estate, and insurance. Third, as income increases, the proportion spent on the necessities of food and home decreases, and the remainder creates a demand for durables and then for services.

Ernst Engel, a Prussian statistician of the 19th century, observed that as family incomes increase, the percentage spent on food and durables drops while consumption of services that reflect a desire for a more enriched life increases correspondingly. This phenomenon is analogous to the Maslow hierarchy of needs, which says that once the basic requirements of food and shelter are satisfied, people seek physical goods and, finally, personal development. However, a necessary condition for the "good life" is health and education. In our attempts to eliminate disease and increase the span of life, health services become a critical feature of modern society.

Higher education becomes the condition for entry into a postindustrial society, which requires professional and technical skills of its population. Also, claims for more services and social justice lead to a growth in government. Concerns for environmental protection require government intervention and illustrate the interdependent and even global character of postindustrial problems. Table 1.2 summarizes the features that characterize the preindustrial, industrial, and postindustrial stages of economic development.

FIGURE 1.4

Percent Distribution of U.S. Employment by Industry, 2006

Source: http://www.bls.gov/news.release.ecopro.t01.htm

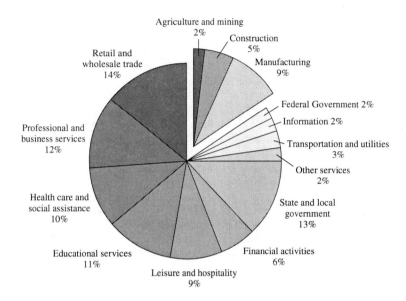

Nature of the Service Sector

For many people, *service* is synonymous with *servitude* and brings to mind workers flipping hamburgers and waiting on tables. However, the service sector that has grown significantly over the past 50 years cannot be accurately described as composed only of low-wage or low-skill jobs in department stores and fast-food restaurants. Instead, as Figure 1.4 shows, employment in 2006 was divided among a number of high-skill service categories such as professional and business services, health care and social assistance, and educational services.

Changes in the pattern of employment will have implications on where and how people live, on educational requirements, and, consequently, on the kinds of organizations that will be important to that society. Industrialization created the need for the semiskilled worker who could be trained in a few weeks to perform the routine machine-tending tasks. The subsequent growth in the service sector has caused a shift to white-collar occupations. In the United States, the year 1956 was a turning point. For the first time in the history of industrial society, the number of white-collar workers exceeded the number of blue-collar workers, and the gap has been widening since then. The most interesting growth has been in the managerial and professional-technical fields, which are jobs that require a college education.

Today, service industries are the source of economic leadership. During the past 30 years, more than 44 million new jobs have been created in the service sector to absorb the influx of women into the workforce and to provide an alternative to the lack of job opportunities in manufacturing. The service industries now account for approximately 70 percent of the national income in the United States. Given that there is a limit to how many cars a consumer can use and how much one can eat and drink, this should not be surprising. The appetite for services, however, especially innovative ones, is insatiable. Among the services presently in demand are those that reflect an aging population, such as geriatric health care, and others that reflect a two-income family, such as day care.

The growth of the service sector has produced a less cyclic national economy. During the past four recessions in the United States, employment by service industries has actually increased, while jobs in manufacturing have been lost. This suggests that consumers are willing to postpone the purchase of products but will not sacrifice essential services like education, telephone, banking, health care, and public services such as fire and police protection.

Several reasons can explain the recession-resistant nature of services. First, by their nature, services cannot be inventoried, as is the case for products. Because consumption and production occur simultaneously for services, the demand for them is more stable than that for manufactured goods. When the economy falters, many services continue to survive. Hospitals keep busy as usual, and, while commissions may drop in real estate, insurance, and security businesses, employees need not be laid off.

Second, during a recession, both consumers and business firms defer capital expenditures and instead fix up and make do with existing equipment. Thus, service jobs in maintenance and repair are created.

The 21st Century Career

As shown in Figure 1.5, health care and social assistance and professional and business services have the largest projected change in employment in the coming decade. These high-skill careers will exhibit the following characteristics according to Michelle L. Casto:[4]

- More career opportunities for everyone.
- Freedom to choose from a variety of jobs, tasks, and assignments.
- More flexibility in how and where work is performed (i.e., working from home or telecommuting).
- More control over your own time.
- Greater opportunity to express yourself through your work.
- Ability to shape and reshape your life's work in accordance with your values and interests.
- Increased opportunity to develop other skills by working in various industries and environments.
- Self-empowerment mindset.
- Allows one to create situations or positions where one can fill a need in the world that is not being filled.
- Opportunity to present oneself as an independent contractor or vendor with services to offer.

FIGURE 1.5
Projected Percent Change in U.S. Employment by Industry, 2006–2016

Source: http://www.bls.gov/news.release/ecopro.t01.htm

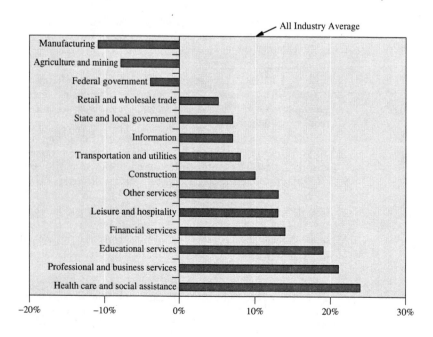

New Experience Economy[5]

The nature of the service economy has moved past the transactional nature of services to one of experience-based relationships. Consider how Starbucks and Disney World have defined their respective services as an experience. Table 1.3 describes the features of different economies in the historical evolution from agrarian to experience. To appreciate the subtle differences, pay particular attention to the words used to describe each economy. Note that the *experience economy* is further divided into consumer services and business services.

Consumer Service Experience

Experiences create added value by engaging and connecting with the customer in a personal and memorable way. As businesses explicitly charge for the memorable encounters they stage, we transition from a service economy to the new experience economy. Figure 1.6 displays four types of consumer experiences characterized by the level of customer participation and level of interaction with the environment. Entertainment (e.g., watching a movie) is the least involved level of experience and escapist (e.g., scuba diving) requires the most commitment from the customer.

Consumer service experience design is based on five principles. *Theme the experience* is illustrated by the Forum Shops in Las Vegas that are decorated with Roman columns and where salespeople wear togas. An example of *harmonize impressions with positive cues* is found at the O'Hare Airport Parking Garage where each floor is painted with a distinctive color and unique music is played to help returning travelers find their parked automobiles (e.g., hard rock on the first floor and classical on the second). *Eliminate negative cues* is illustrated creatively by the use of talking trash containers (i.e., the container says "thank you" when an item is discarded) at a Cinemark Theater in Austin,

FIGURE 1.6
**The Four Realms
of an Experience**

Source: Reprinted by permission of *Harvard Business Review.* Exhibit adapted from "Welcome to the Experience Economy," by B. Joseph Pine II and James H. Gilmore, July–August 1998, p. 102. Copyright © 1998 by the President and Fellows of Harvard College: all rights reserved.

		Customer participation	
		Passive	*Active*
Environmental relationship	*Absorption*	Entertainment (movie)	Education (language)
	Immersion	Estheticism (tourist)	Escapism (scuba diving)

TABLE 1.3 Economic Evolution

Economy	Agrarian	Industrial	Service	Experience	
				Consumer services	Business services
Economic Offering	Food	Packaged goods	Commodity service	Consumer services	Business services
Function	Extract	Make	Deliver	Stage	Co-create
Nature	Fungible	Tangible	Intangible	Memorable	Effectual
Attribute	Natural	Standardized	Customized	Personal	Growth
Method of Supply	Stored in bulk	Inventoried	Delivered on demand	Revealed over time	Sustained over time
Seller	Trader	Producer	Provider	Stager	Collaborator
Buyer	Market	Customer	Client	Guest	Collaborator
Expectation	Quantity	Features	Benefits	Sensations	Capability

Scuba divers escape to an underwater world that requires special equipment for survival.
Royalty-Free/CORBIS

Texas. An example of *mix in memorabilia* is providing group pictures of vacationers to Club Med. *Engage all five senses* is found at the Rainforest Café in Las Vegas (e.g., jungle sounds and mist in the air).

Business Service Experience

For business-to-business (B2B) services, value is derived from the coproduction or collaborative nature of the relationship such as we see in a consultancy engagement. The new business service experience has three dimensions:

Co-creation of value
- The customer is a coproducer of the value extracted from the relationship.
- The customer is an input to the service process.

Relationships
- The relationship with the customer is of paramount importance because it is a source of innovation and differentiation.
- Long-term relationships facilitate the ability to tailor the service offerings to customers' needs.

Service capability
- Provide service capacity to meet fluctuations in demands while retaining quality of service.
- Quality of service is measured primarily from the perspective of the customer.

The core experience of B2B service is one of creating, enabling, problem solving, and innovative use of information that is not consumed in the exchange, but is enhanced and remains available for further use by others.

Table 1.4 presents a complete listing of both consumer and business service experiences to be found in the 21st century, all of which rely heavily on a skilled knowledge-based workforce.

TABLE 1.4
Typology of Services in the 21st Century

Source: Adapted from Bryson, J. R., P. W. Daniels, and B. Warf. *Service Worlds: People, Organizations, Technologies.* New York: Routledge, 2004, p. 33.

Core Experience	Essential Feature	Examples
Creative	Present ideas	Advertising, theater
Enabling	Act as intermediary	Transportation, communications
Experiential	Presence of customer	Massage, theme park
Extending	Extend and maintain	Warranty, health check
Entrusted	Contractual agreement	Service/repair, portfolio mgt.
Information	Access to information	Internet search engine
Innovation	Facilitate new concepts	R&D services, product testing
Problem solving	Access to specialists	Consultants, counseling
Quality of life	Improve well-being	Health care, recreation, tourism
Regulation	Establish rules and regulations	Environment, legal, patents

Sources of Service Sector Growth

Service sector growth is fueled by advances in information technology, innovation, and changing demographics that create new demands. Information technology has a substantial impact on the growth of digital services. Figure 1.7 shows how information (digital) services have grown to the point that this "information sector" dominates the U.S. economy, contributing 53 percent to the GDP (Gross Domestic Product). The arrows on the two axes show the direction of projected growth in the services and information components of the economy. Notice how information services (quadrant D) is growing at the expense of physical products (quadrant A).

Information Technology

The drive to miniaturize information technology equipment such as the Blackberry for Internet connectivity removes the need for physical proximity for service delivery and permits alternative delivery formats. Banking, for example, has become an electronic service with online access to personal accounts for transfer of funds or payment of bills. In health care, X-rays are digitized and transmitted off-shore for interpretation by a radiologist. Information technology has thus impacted the process of service delivery and

FIGURE 1.7
Distribution of GDP in the U.S. Economy

Source: Karmarkar, Uday and Uday M. Apte. "Operations Management in the Information Economy: Information Products, Processes, and Chains," *Journal of Operations Management* 25 no. 2 (March 2007), p. 440.

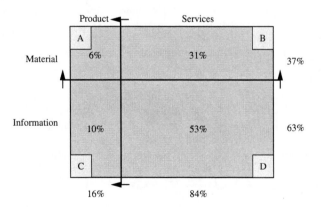

Sector	Description	Example
A	Physical Products	Automotive, Steel, Chemicals
B	Physical Services	Transportation, Retailing
C	Digital Products	Computers, DVDs, HDTV
D	Information Services	Finance, Telecommunications

created new service value chains with new business opportunities as creative intermediaries. Uday Karmarkar and Uday Apte make the following three propositions:[6]

- In the future, the major part of the United States GDP is going to be generated by "information chains" and not supply chains, and most managers are going to be employed in the information sectors.
- The management of these information chains and sectors has a great deal to do with process economics and its impact on the configuration and operation of information chains and processes.
- Technological developments underlie and drive the economics of processes and value chains.

Innovation

The product development model that is driven by technology and engineering could be called a *push theory of innovation.* A concept for a new product germinates in the laboratory with a scientific discovery that becomes a solution looking for a problem. The 3M experience with Post-it notes is one example of this innovation process. The laboratory discovery was a poor adhesive, which found a creative use as glue for notes to be attached temporarily to objects without leaving a mark when removed.

The introduction of new product technology, however, does have an ancillary effect on service innovation. For example, the DVD player spawned a video rental business and created a renewed demand for old movies. The next innovation was the creation of Netflix to deliver the DVD to your home by mail. The Internet and World Wide Web were developed as a robust network of linked computers for military and scientific file sharing. It became the essential enabler for e-commerce and more recently the platform for social networks such as Facebook and LinkedIn and, of course, the ability to search the world with Google.

For services, the Cash Management Account introduced by Merrill Lynch is an example of the *pull theory of innovation.* During the period of high interest rates in the 1980s, a need arose to finance short-term corporate cash flows because individual investors were interested in obtaining an interest rate that was higher than those currently available on passbook bank deposits. A new service concept often originates with an observant contact employee who identifies an unmet customer need. For example, a hotel might institute an airport shuttle service because the concierge noticed a high demand for taxi service.

Service innovation also can arise from exploiting information available from other activities. For example, records of sales by auto parts stores can be used to identify frequent failure areas in particular models of cars. This information has value both for the manufacturer, who can accomplish engineering changes, and for the retailer, who can diagnose customer problems. In addition, the creative use of information can be a source of new services, or it can add value to existing services. For example, an annual summary statement of transactions furnished by one's financial institution has added value at income tax time.

Service innovators face a difficult problem in testing their service ideas. The process of product development includes building a laboratory prototype for testing before full-scale production is initiated. One example of an effort in this direction is provided by Burger King, which acquired a warehouse in Miami to enclose a replica of its standard outlet. This mock restaurant was used to simulate changes in layout that would be required for the introduction of new features such as drive-through window service and a breakfast menu.

Changing Demographics

The French Revolution provides an interesting historical example of how a social change resulted in a new service industry. Before the revolution, only two restaurants were in existence in Paris; shortly afterwards, there were more than 500. The deposed nobility had been forced to give up their private chefs, who found that opening their own restaurants was a logical solution to their unemployment.

Service Benchmark

WALMART IS NUMBER ONE ON THE *FORTUNE* 500 LIST

Walmart achieved a remarkable first in spring 2002—it made the top of the *Fortune* 500 list. This accomplishment marks the first time that a service business leads the hallowed list.

Although Walmart position is unprecedented in the seven years since *Fortune* admitted service industries to its 500, it is not a big surprise given the position of services in today's economy. In fact, 51 of the top 100 companies on the list for 2009 are service enterprises. Consumers now spend more on services than on manufactured goods, so many manufacturers have turned to providing services in addition to durable goods. General Electric, for example, has entered the financing market, and so have American automakers. The line between manufacturing and providing services has blurred.

A major influence on future service needs is the aging of the U.S. population. As the baby boom generation enters retirement demand for health care and financial services will increase. People are living longer and placing increased demand on health care services to maintain active life styles. The replacement of pension plans with defined contribution plans (401K) creates a demand for investment counseling and financial management services. Finally, the available time for leisure activities will be reflected in demand for airline travel, ocean cruises, restaurants, and hotel rooms.

Summary

We have discovered that the modern industrial economies are dominated by employment in the service sector. Just as farming jobs migrated to manufacturing in the 19th century under the driving force of labor-saving technology, manufacturing jobs in due time migrated to services. Now as we begin the new millennium, an experience economy is emerging to satisfy rising expectations for services. Chapter 2 develops new managerial skills by arguing that the distinctive characteristics of services require an approach to management that is significantly different from that found in manufacturing.

Key Terms and Definitions

Clark-Fisher hypothesis a classification of economies according to the activity of the majority of the workforce. *p. 6*

New experience economy a stage of economic evolution in which added value is created by engaging and connecting with the customer in a personal and memorable way. *p. 11*

Industrial society a society dominated by factory work in mass-production industries. *p. 7*

Postindustrial society a service society in which people are engaged in information, intellectual, or creative-intensive activities. *p. 8*

Preindustrial society an agrarian society structured around farming and subsistence living. *p. 7*

Pull theory of innovation service innovations that are driven by customer needs. *p. 14*

Push theory of innovation product innovations that originate in scientific laboratories. *p. 14*

Topics for Discussion

1. Illustrate how the type of work he or she does influences a person's lifestyle. For example, contrast a farmer, a factory worker, and a schoolteacher.
2. Is it possible for an economy to be based entirely on services?
3. What is the value of self-service in an economy?

16   Part One *Understanding Services*

4. Go on the Internet and find the percent employment in services over the past 40 years for a country not listed in Table 1.1

5. Go to Wikipedia.com and search under the topic of "service economy." What do you make of the data plotted on the world map?

6. Determine if the service sector is currently expanding or contracting based upon the Non-Manufacturing Index (NMI) found at the ISM Report on Business on the Institute of Supply Management Web site "http://www.ism.ws/pubs/ismmag/"

Interactive Exercise

The class breaks into small groups. Each group identifies service firms that should be listed in the top *Fortune* 100 and places them in rank order of estimated annual revenue.

Selected Bibliography

Bryson, J. R.; P. W. Daniels; and B. Warf. *Service Worlds: People, Organizations, Technologies*. New York: Routledge, 2004.

Chase, Richard B., and Uday M. Apte. "A History of Research in Service Operations: What's the Big Idea?" *Journal of Operations Management* 25, no. 2 (March 2007), pp. 375–386.

Heineke, Janelle, and Mark M. Davis. "The Emergence of Service Operations Management as an Academic Discipline." *Journal of Operations Management* 25, no. 2 (March 2007), pp. 364–374.

Karmarkar, Uday. "Will You Survive the Service Revolution?" *Harvard Business Review,* June 2004, pp. 101–107.

Endnotes

1. Colin Clark, *The Conditions of Economic Progress,* 3rd ed. (London: Macmillan Co., 1957).
2. N. N. Foote and P. K. Hatt, "Social Mobility and Economic Advancement," *American Economic Review,* May 1953, pp. 364–378.
3. Daniel Bell, *The Coming of Post-Industrial Society: A Venture in Social Forecasting,* (New York: Basic Books, 1973).
4. http://www.quintcareers.com/career_success.html
5. Joseph Pine and James Gilmore, "Welcome to the Experience Economy," *Harvard Business Review,* July–August 1998, pp. 97–105.
6. Uday Karmarkar and Uday M. Apte, "Operations Management in the Information Economy: Information Products, Processes, and Chains," *Journal of Operations Management* 25, no. 2 (March 2007), pp. 438–453.

Chapter 2

The Nature of Services

Learning Objectives

After completing this chapter, you should be able to:

1. Explain what is meant by a service-product bundle.
2. Identify and critique the five distinctive characteristics of a service operation and explain the implications for managers.
3. Explain how services can be described as customers renting resources.
4. Describe a service using the five dimensions of the service package.
5. Use the service process matrix to classify a service.
6. Explain how a strategic classification of services can be helpful to managers.
7. Explain the essential features of the service-dominant logic.
8. Explain the role of a service manager from an open-systems view of service operations.

In this chapter, we explore the distinctive features of services. The service environment is sufficiently unique to allow us to question the direct application of traditional manufacturing-based techniques to services without some modification, although many approaches are analogous. Ignoring the differences between manufacturing and service requirements will lead to failure, but more importantly, recognition of the special features of services will provide insights for enlightened and innovative management. Advances in service management cannot occur without an appreciation of the service delivery process that creates the experience for the customer.

The distinction between a *product* and a *service* is difficult to make, because the purchase of a product is accompanied by some facilitating service (e.g., installation) and the purchase of a service often includes facilitating goods (e.g., food at a restaurant). Each purchase includes a bundle of goods and services as shown in Table 2.1.

Our examples each have a principal focus or core activity that is either a product (i.e., business suits) or service (i.e., room for the night). However, peripheral goods and services augment the bundle offered to the customer. Finally, a variant often is used to differentiate the bundle from that of competitors.[1]

The ability to bundle services with a product has not been lost on manufacturers seeking to capture service revenue when their product has become a commodity with thin margins. For example, Otis Elevator is willing to take a sharp pencil in its bid for escalators

TABLE 2.1
Service-Product Bundle

Element	Core *Goods* Example	Core *Service* Example
Business	Custom clothier	Business hotel
Core	Business suits	Room for the night
Peripheral goods	Garment bag	Bathrobe
Peripheral service	Deferred payment plans	In-house restaurant
Variant	Coffee lounge	Airport shuttle

in a new shopping center knowing full well that the after-sales maintenance contract represents a predictable cash flow for the life of the facility. This revenue enhancement strategy by manufacturers of deliberately coupling a service with their product is referred to as *servitization*.

Chapter Preview

We begin the chapter by answering the question *Why study services?* with a discussion of the distinctive characteristics of service operations. The non-ownership nature of services is illustrated with implications for management. The question *What is a service?* can be answered with the service package, explicit and implicit benefits performed within a supporting facility using facilitating goods and information. Services from diverse industries can be grouped into categories that share similar operations challenges when the delivery process is defined by degree of customization and degree of labor intensiveness. Finally, services are classified into five categories to obtain strategic insights.

Based on these observations, the role of the service manager is viewed from an open-system perspective. That is, the service manager must deal with an environment in which the customers are present in the delivery system. This contrasts with manufacturing operations that are isolated or "buffered" from the customer by an inventory of finished goods. Thus, manufacturing traditionally has operated as a cost center, focusing on process efficiency. Service managers, who often operate as profit centers, must be concerned with both efficient and effective delivery of services.

Distinctive Characteristics of Service Operations

In services, a distinction must be made between *inputs* and *resources*. For services, inputs are the customers themselves, and resources are the facilitating goods, employee labor, and capital at the command of the service manager. Thus, to function, the service system must interact with the customers as participants in the service process. Because customers typically arrive at their own discretion and with unique demands on the service system, matching service capacity with demand is a challenge.

For some services, such as banking, however, the focus of activity is on processing information instead of people. In these situations, information technology, such as electronic funds transfer, can be substituted for physically depositing a payroll check; thus, the presence of the customer at the bank is unnecessary. Such exceptions will be noted as we discuss the distinctive characteristics of service operations. It should be noted here that many of the unique characteristics of services, such as customer participation and perishability, are interrelated.

Customer Participation in the Service Process

The presence of the customer as a participant in the service process requires an attention to facility design that is not found in traditional manufacturing operations. That automobiles are made in a hot, dirty, noisy factory is of no concern to the eventual buyers because they first see the product in the pleasant surroundings of a dealer's showroom. The presence of the customer on-site requires attention to the physical surroundings of the service facility that is not necessary for the factory. For the customer, service is an experience occurring in the *front office* of the service facility, and the quality of service is enhanced if the service facility is designed from the customer's perspective. Attention to interior decorating, furnishings, layout, noise, and even color can influence the customer's perception of the service. Compare the feelings invoked by picturing yourself in a stereotypical bus station with those produced by imagining yourself in an airline terminal. Of course, passengers are not allowed in the terminal's *back office* (e.g., the luggage-handling area), which is operated in a factory-like environment. However, some innovative services have opened the back office to public scrutiny to promote confidence in the service (e.g., some restaurants provide a view into the kitchen, some auto repair bays can be observed through windows in the waiting area).

An important consideration in providing a service is the realization that the customer can play an active part in the process. A few examples will illustrate that the knowledge, experience, motivation, and even honesty of the customer all directly affect the performance of the service system:

1. The popularity of supermarkets and discount stores is predicated on the idea that customers are willing to assume an active role in the retailing process.
2. The accuracy of a patient's medical record can greatly influence the effectiveness of the attending physician.
3. The education of a student is determined largely by the student's own effort and contributions.

This strategy is best illustrated by the fast-food restaurants that have significantly reduced the typical number of serving and cleaning personnel. The customer not only places the order directly from a limited menu but also is expected to clear the table after the meal. Naturally, the customer expects faster service and less expensive meals to compensate for these inputs, but the service provider benefits in many subtle ways. First, there are fewer personnel who require supervision and such things as fringe benefits. Second, and more importantly, the customer provides the labor just at the moment it is required; thus, service capacity varies more directly with demand rather than being fixed by the size of the employed staff. The customer acts like a temporary employee, arriving just when needed to perform duties to augment the work of the service staff.

This strategy has received great acceptance in a society, such as the United States, where self-reliance is valued. Instead of being a passive buyer, the customer becomes a contributor to the gross national product.

Taking the customer out of the process, however, is becoming a common practice. Consider retail banking, in which customers are encouraged to use telephone or computer transactions, direct deposit, and automatic-debit bill paying instead of actually traveling to the bank. Moreover, the advent of Internet commerce gives new meaning to the phrase "window shopping."

Simultaneity

The fact that services are created and consumed simultaneously and, thus, cannot be stored is a critical feature in the management of services. This inability to inventory services precludes using the traditional manufacturing strategy of relying on inventory as a buffer to absorb fluctuations in demand. An inventory of finished goods serves as a convenient system boundary for a manufacturer, separating the internal operations of planning and control from the external environment. Thus, the manufacturing facility can be operated at a constant level of output that is most efficient. The factory is operated as a *closed system,* with inventory decoupling the productive system from customer demand. Services, however, operate as *open systems,* with the full impact of demand variations being transmitted to the system.

Inventory also can be used to decouple the stages in a manufacturing process. For services, the decoupling is achieved through customer waiting. Inventory control is a major issue in manufacturing operations, whereas in services, the corresponding problem is customer waiting, or "queuing." The problems of selecting service capacity, facility utilization, and use of idle time all are balanced against customer waiting time.

The simultaneous production and consumption in services also eliminates many opportunities for quality-control intervention. A product can be inspected before delivery, but services must rely on other measures to ensure the quality of services delivered. We address this important topic of service quality in Chapter 6.

Perishability

A service is a perishable commodity. Consider an empty airline seat, an unoccupied hospital or hotel room, or an hour without a patient in the day of a dentist. In each case, a lost opportunity has occurred. Because a service cannot be stored, it is lost forever when not used. The full utilization of service capacity becomes a management challenge, because customer demand exhibits considerable variation and building inventory to absorb these fluctuations is not an option.

Consumer demand for services typically exhibits very cyclic behavior over short periods of time, with considerable variation between the peaks and valleys. The custom of eating lunch between noon and 1 PM places a burden on restaurants to accommodate the noon rush. The practice of day-end mailing by businesses contributes to the fact that 60 percent of all letters are received at the post office between 4 and 8 PM.[2] The demand for emergency medical service in Los Angeles was found to vary from a low of 0.5 call per hour at 6 AM to a peak of 3.5 calls per hour at 6 PM.[3] This peak-to-valley ratio of 7 to 1 also was true for fire alarms during an average day in New York City.[4]

For recreational and transportation services, seasonal variation in demand creates surges in activity. As many students know, flights home are often booked months in advance of spring break and the year-end holiday.

Faced with variable demand and a *time-perishable capacity* to provide the service, the manager has three basic options:

1. Smooth demand by:
   a. Using reservations or appointments.
   b. Using price incentives (e.g., giving telephone discounts for evening and weekend calls).
   c. Demarketing peak times (e.g., advertising to shop early and avoid the Christmas rush).
2. Adjust service capacity by:
   a. Using part-time help during peak hours.
   b. Scheduling work shifts to vary workforce needs according to demand (e.g., telephone companies staff their operators to match call demand).
   c. Increasing the customer self-service content of the service.
3. Allow customers to wait.

The last option can be viewed as a passive contribution to the service process that carries the risk of losing a dissatisfied customer to a competitor. By waiting, the customer permits greater utilization of service capacity. The airlines explicitly recognize this by offering standby passengers an unsold seat on the departing flight.

Intangibility

Services are ideas and concepts; products are things. Therefore, it follows that service innovations are not patentable. To secure the benefits of a novel service concept, the firm must expand extremely rapidly and preempt any competitors. Franchising has been the vehicle to secure market areas and establish a brand name. Franchising allows the parent firm to sell its idea to a local entrepreneur, thus preserving capital while retaining control and reducing risk.

The intangible nature of services also presents a problem for customers. When buying a product, the customer is able to see it, feel it, and test its performance before purchase. For a service, however, the customer must rely on the reputation of the service firm. In many service areas, the government has intervened to guarantee acceptable service performances. Through the use of registration, licensing, and regulation, the government can assure consumers that the training and test performance of some service providers meet certain standards. Thus, we find that public construction plans must be approved by a registered professional engineer, a doctor must be licensed to practice medicine, and the power company is a regulated utility. In its efforts to "protect" the consumer, however, the government may be stifling innovation, raising barriers to entry, and generally reducing competition.

Heterogeneity

The combination of the intangible nature of services and the customer as a participant in the service delivery system results in variation of service from customer to customer. The interaction between customer and employee in services, however, creates the possibility of a more satisfying human work experience. In services, work activity generally is oriented toward people rather than toward things. There are exceptions, however, for services that process information (e.g., communications) or customers' property (e.g., brokerage services). In the limited customer-contact service industries, we now see a dramatic reduction in the level of labor intensiveness through the introduction of self-service technology.

Even the introduction of automation may strengthen personalization by eliminating the relatively routine impersonal tasks, thereby permitting increased personal attention to the remaining work. At the same time, personal attention creates opportunities for variability in the service that is provided. This is not inherently bad, however, unless customers perceive a significant variation in quality. A customer expects to be treated fairly and to be given the same service that others receive. The development of standards and of employee training in proper procedures is the key to ensuring consistency in the service provided. It is rather impractical to monitor the output of each employee, thus, customers play a role in quality control through their feedback.

The direct customer–employee contact has implications for service (industrial) relations as well. Autoworkers with grievances against the firm have been known to sabotage the product on the assembly line. Presumably, the final inspection will ensure that any such cars are corrected before delivery. A disgruntled service employee, however, can do irreparable harm to the organization because the employee is the firm's sole contact with customers. Therefore, the service manager must be concerned about the employees' attitudes as well as their performance. J. Willard Marriott, founder of the Marriott Hotel chain, has said, "In the service business you can't make happy guests with unhappy employees."[5] Through training and genuine concern for employee welfare, the organizational goals can be internalized.

Non-ownership Characteristic of Services[6]

From a marketing perspective, services, unlike goods, do not involve transfer of ownership. If customers do not receive ownership when they purchase a service, then what are they buying? One view is that customers gain access or rental of resources for a period of time such as a hotel room for the night or a seat on an airplane. Service industries share their resources among customers by allocating the use of them. Customers do not purchase an asset but, instead, have use of the asset for a specific time, whether it is the use of human labor (e.g., dentist), technology (e.g., cellular network), or a physical asset (e.g., theme park). Notice that in each example, customers often share the service provider's asset concurrently with other customers. Table 2.2 lists the five classes of non-ownership services with examples.

Sharing resources among customers presents management challenges. In the case of goods rental, convenience of a rental office location for pickup and drop-off is essential. Car rentals, for example, are found at airports. However, Enterprise is an exception, because it began delivering vehicles to the local population instead of catering primarily to travelers. Maintenance of the rental good and returning the good to acceptable condition between customer rentals is a necessary and ongoing activity. In the case of place and space rental, customers are able to participate in the economies of scale derived from sharing a larger space with many users while enjoying some degree of separation and privacy. For airlines, the extra large seats and leg room in business class partially explains the relatively high ticket price. For any shared facility, housekeeping is a routine activity performed between periods of customer usage (e.g., trash pickup upon landing

22 Part One *Understanding Services*

TABLE 2.2   **Non-ownership Classification of Services**

Type of Service	Customer Value	Examples	Management Challenge
Goods rental	Obtain temporary right to exclusive use	Vehicles, tools, furniture, equipment	Site selection and maintenance
Place and space rental	Obtain exclusive use of defined portion of a larger space	Hotel room, seat on airplane, storage unit	Housekeeping and achieving economies of scale
Labor and expertise	Hire other people to do a job	Car repair, surgery, management consulting	Expertise is a renewable resource, but time is perishable
Physical facility usage	Gain admission to a facility for a period of time	Theme park, camp ground, physical fitness gym	Queuing and crowd control
Network usage	Gain access to participate	Electric utility, cell phone, Internet	Availability and pricing decisions

for an airline flight and changing linen upon departure of a hotel guest). The challenge facing management of labor and expertise resources is, first, keeping the resource skill current through training and, second, avoiding idle periods when hours are not billable. Management of queues and crowd control is a challenge for managers of physical facilities that are shared by a large population of customers. Disney, for example, has made a science of controlling waiting lines using multiple techniques that include diversions and allowing guests to reserve time slots for rides hours in advance. Uptime is critical for network services because customers depend upon and expect access 24–7 (24 hours per day, 7 days per week). Thus, continuous availability is essential, but because usage varies depending on time-of-day and day-of-week, pricing for the service must be creative and flexible.

The Service Package

Service managers have difficulty describing their product. This problem is partly a result of the intangible nature of services, but it is the presence of the customer in the process that creates a concern for the total service experience. Consider the following examples. For a sit-down restaurant, atmosphere is just as important as the meal because many diners regard the occasion as a way to get together with friends. A customer's opinion of a bank can be formed quickly on the basis of a teller's cheerfulness or the length of the waiting line.

The *service package* is defined as a bundle of goods and services with information that is provided in some environment. This bundle consists of five features as shown in Figure 2.1 in the shape of an onion with the service experience at the core.

1. *Supporting facility.* The physical resources that must be in place before a service can be offered. Examples are a golf course, a ski lift, a hospital, and an airplane.
2. *Facilitating goods.* The material purchased or consumed by the buyer, or the items provided by the customer. Examples are golf clubs, skis, food items, replacement auto parts, legal documents, and medical supplies.
3. *Information.* Data that is available from the customer or provider to enable efficient and customized service. Examples include electronic patient medical records, airline Web site showing seats available on a flight, customer preferences from prior visits, GPS location of customer to dispatch a taxi, and Google map link on a hotel Web site.
4. *Explicit services.* The benefits that are readily observable by the senses and that consist of the essential or intrinsic features of the service. Examples are the absence of

FIGURE 2.1
Service Package

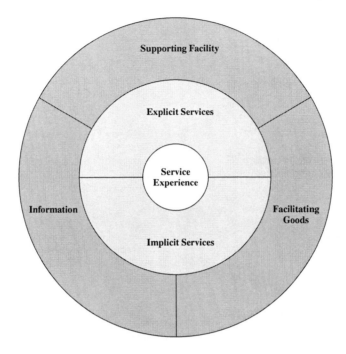

pain after a tooth is repaired, a smooth-running automobile after a tuneup, and the response time of a fire department.

5. *Implicit services.* Psychological benefits that the customer may sense only vaguely, or the extrinsic features of the service. Examples are the status of a degree from an Ivy League school, the privacy of a loan office, and worry-free auto repair.

All of these features are experienced by the customer and form the basis of his or her perception of the service. It is important that the service manager offer a total experience for the customer that is consistent with the desired service package. Take, for example, a budget hotel. The supporting facility is a concrete-block building with austere furnishings. Facilitating goods are reduced to the minimum of soap, towels, and tissue paper. Information on room availability is used to book a reservation. The explicit service is a comfortable bed in a clean room, and implicit services might include a friendly desk clerk and the security of a well-lighted parking area. Deviations from this service package, such as adding bellhops, would destroy the bargain image. Table 2.3 lists criteria (with examples) for evaluating the service package.

The importance of facilitating goods in the service package can be used to classify services across a continuum from pure services to various degrees of mixed services. For example, psychiatric counseling with no facilitating goods would be considered a "pure" service. Automobile maintenance usually requires more facilitating goods than a haircut does.

Making general statements about service management is difficult when there are such variations in the nature of services. However, an appreciation of the unique features of the service environment is important for understanding the challenges facing service managers.

Grouping Services by Delivery Process

Concepts of service management should be applicable to all service organizations. For example, hospital administrators could learn something about their own business from the restaurant and hotel trade. Professional services such as consulting, law, and medicine have special problems because the professional is trained to provide a specific clinical service (to use a medical example) but is not knowledgeable in business management.

TABLE 2.3   **Criteria for Evaluating the Service Package**

Supporting Facility

1. *Location:*
   Is it accessible by public transportation?
   Is it centrally located?
2. *Interior decorating:*
   Is the proper mood established?
   Quality and coordination of furniture.
3. *Supporting equipment:*
   Does the dentist use a mechanical or air drill?
   What type and age of aircraft does the
      charter airline use?

4. *Architectural appropriateness:*
   Renaissance architecture for university campus.
   Unique recognizable feature of a blue tile roof.
   Massive granite facade of downtown bank.
5. *Facility layout:*
   Is there a natural flow of traffic?
   Are adequate waiting areas provided?
   Is there unnecessary travel or backtracking?

Facilitating Goods

1. *Consistency:*
   Crispness of french fries.
   Portion control.
2. *Quantity:*
   Small, medium, or large drink.

3. *Selection:*
   Variety of replacement mufflers.
   Number of menu items.
   Rental skis available.

Information

1. *Accurate:*
   Up-to-date customer addresses.
   Correct credit report.
2. *Timely:*
   Severe storm warning.

3. *Useful:*
   X-ray to identify a broken bone.
   Inventory status.

Explicit Services

1. *Training of service personnel:*
   Is the auto mechanic certified by the National
   Institute for Automotive Service Excellence
      (NIASE)?
   To what extent are paraprofessionals used?
   Are the physicians board certified?
2. *Comprehensiveness:*
   Discount broker compared with full service.
   General hospital compared with clinic.

3. *Consistency:*
   Airline's on-time record.
   Professional Standards Review Organization
      (PSRO) for doctors.
4. *Availability:*
   Twenty-four-hour ATM service.
   Is there a Web site?
   Is there a toll-free number?

Implicit Services

1. *Attitude of service:*
   Cheerful flight attendant.
   Police officer issuing traffic citation with tact.
   Surly service person in restaurant.
2. *Atmosphere:*
   Restaurant decor.
   Music in a bar.
   Sense of confusion rather than order.
3. *Waiting:*
   Joining a drive-in banking queue.
   Being placed on hold.
   Enjoying a martini in the restaurant bar.

4. *Status:*
   College degree from Ivy League school.
   Box seats at sports event.
5. *Sense of well-being:*
   Large commercial aircraft.
   Well-lighted parking lot.
6. *Privacy and security:*
   Attorney advising client in private office.
   Magnetic key card for hotel room.
7. *Convenience:*
   Use of appointments.
   Free parking.

Thus, managing professional service firms offers attractive career opportunities for business school graduates.

A service classification scheme can help to organize our discussion of service management and break down the industry barriers to shared learning. As suggested, hospitals can learn about housekeeping from hotels. Less obviously, dry-cleaning establishments can learn from banks—cleaners can adapt the convenience of night deposits enjoyed by banking customers by providing laundry bags and after-hours dropoff boxes. For professional firms, scheduling a consulting engagement is similar to planning a legal defense or preparing a medical team for open-heart surgery.

To demonstrate that management problems are common across service industries, Roger Schmenner proposed the *service process matrix* in Figure 2.2. In this matrix, services are classified across two dimensions that significantly affect the character of the service delivery process. The vertical dimension measures the degree of labor intensity, which is defined as the ratio of labor cost to capital cost. Thus, capital-intensive services such as airlines and hospitals are found in the upper row because of their considerable investment in plant and equipment relative to labor costs. Labor-intensive services such as schools and legal assistance are found in the bottom row because their labor costs are high relative to their capital requirements.

The horizontal dimension measures the degree of customer interaction and customization, which is a marketing variable that describes the ability of the customer to affect personally the nature of the service being delivered. Little interaction between customer and service provider is needed when the service is standardized rather than customized. For example, a meal at McDonald's, which is assembled from prepared items, is low in customization and served with little interaction occurring between the customer and the service providers. In contrast, a doctor and patient must interact fully in the diagnostic and treatment phases to achieve satisfactory results. Patients also expect to be treated as individuals and wish to receive medical care that is customized to their particular needs. It is important to note, however, that the interaction resulting from high customization creates potential problems for management of the service delivery process.

The four quadrants of the service process matrix have been given names, as defined by the two dimensions, to describe the nature of the services illustrated. *Service factories* provide a standardized service with high capital investment, much like a line-flow manufacturing plant. *Service shops* permit more service customization, but they do so in a high-capital environment. Customers of a *mass service* will receive an undifferentiated service in a labor-intensive environment, but those seeking a *professional service* will be given individual attention by highly trained specialists.

Managers of services in any category, whether service factory, service shop, mass service, or professional service, share similar challenges, as noted in Figure 2.3. Services with high capital requirements (i.e., low labor intensity), such as airlines and hospitals, require close monitoring of technological advances to remain competitive. This high

FIGURE 2.2
The Service Process Matrix

Source: From "How Can Service Businesses Survive and Prosper?" by Roger W. Schmenner, *Sloan Management Review*, vol. 27, no. 3, Spring 1986, p. 25, by permission of publisher. Copyright 1986 by the Sloan Management Review Association. All rights reserved.

Degree of interaction and customization

	Low	High
Low	*Service factory:* • Airlines • Trucking • Hotels • Resorts and recreation	*Service shop:* • Hospitals • Auto repair • Other repair services
High	*Mass service:* • Retailing • Wholesaling • Schools • Retail aspects of commercial banking	*Professional service:* • Physicians • Lawyers • Accountants • Architects

Degree of labor intensity

26 Part One *Understanding Services*

FIGURE 2.3
Challenges for Service Managers

Source: From "How Can Service Businesses Survive and Prosper?" by Roger W. Schmenner, *Sloan Management Review,* vol. 27, no. 3, Spring 1986, p. 27, by permission of publisher. Copyright 1986 by the Sloan Management Review Association. All rights reserved.

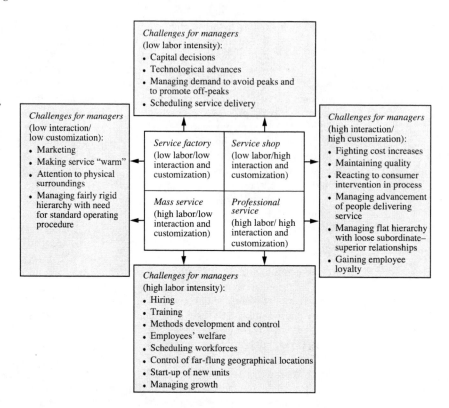

capital investment also requires managers to schedule demand to maintain utilization of the equipment. Alternatively, managers of highly labor-intensive services, such as medical or legal professionals, must concentrate on personnel matters. The degree of customization affects the ability to control the quality of the service being delivered and the perception of the service by the customer. Approaches to addressing each of these challenges are topics that will be discussed in later chapters.

Classifying Services for Strategic Insights[7]

A general discussion of service strategy is complicated by the diversity of service firms in the economy and their differing customer relationships. However, strategic insights that transcend industry boundaries are needed to avoid the myopic view, which is prevalent among service managers, that concepts do not translate from one industry to another. For example, competitive strategies used by banking services could find an application in laundry services because both deal with a customer's property. The new laundry drop-off and pick-up service available at commuter rail stations is similar in concept to bank automatic teller machines in supermarkets. The following classification schemes developed by Christopher Lovelock provide us with an appreciation of possible strategic dimensions that transcend industry boundaries.

Nature of the Service Act

As Figure 2.4 shows, the service act can be considered across two dimensions: who or what is the direct recipient of the service, and the tangible nature of the service. This creates four possible classifications: (1) tangible actions directed to the customer, such as passenger transportation and personal care; (2) tangible actions directed at the customer's possessions, such as laundry cleaning and janitorial services; (3) intangible actions directed at the customer's intellect, such as entertainment; and (4) intangible actions performed on the customer's assets, such as financial services.

FIGURE 2.4

Nature of the Service Act

Source: Adapted with permission of the American Marketing Association: Christopher H. Lovelock, "Classifying Services to Gain Strategic Marketing Insights," *Journal of Marketing,* vol. 47, Summer 1983, p. 12.

Direct recipient of the service

	People	Property
Tangible	*People's bodies:* Health care Passenger transportation Beauty salons Exercise clinics Restaurants	*Physical possessions:* Freight transportation Repair and maintenance Laundry and dry cleaning Veterinary care
Intangible	*People's minds:* Education Broadcasting Information services Theaters Museums	*Intangible assets:* Banking Legal services Accounting Securities Insurance

(Vertical axis label: Nature of the service act)

This classification scheme raises questions about the traditional way in which services have been delivered. For example, does the customer need to be present physically throughout the service, only to initiate or terminate the transaction, or not at all? If customers must be present, then they must travel to the service facility and become part of the process, or the server must travel to the customer (e.g., ambulance service). This has significant implications for facility design and employee interaction, because the impressions that are made on the customer will influence his or her perceptions of the service. In addition, questions are raised concerning the impact of facility location and business hours on customer convenience. It is not surprising that retail banks have embraced ATMs and other electronic communication alternatives to personal interaction.

Thinking creatively about the nature of the service may identify more convenient forms of delivery or even a product that can substitute for the service. For example, movie DVDs and CD recordings of concerts represent a convenient substitute for physical attendance, and they also serve as permanent library records of the events.

Relationship with Customers

Service firms have the opportunity to build long-term relationships because customers conduct their transactions directly with the service provider, most often in person. In contrast, manufacturers traditionally have been isolated from the eventual end user by a distribution channel consisting of some combination of distributors, wholesalers, and/or retailers. Figure 2.5 contrasts the nature of the customer's "membership" with the nature of the service delivery. The value to the firm of customer membership is captured in this figure; however, a number of changes have occurred since it was first published in 1983. For example, car rental firms and major hotel chains have joined airlines in offering specials through frequent user programs. In addition, some private toll highways offer annual passes, which can be attached to one's car. These passes electronically trigger a debit so that the driver need not stop to pay a toll.

Knowing your customers is a significant competitive advantage for a service organization. Having a database of customers' names and addresses and their use of the service permits targeted marketing and individual treatment of customers. Customers benefit from membership because of the convenience of annual fixed fees and the knowledge that they are valued customers who will receive occasional perks (e.g., frequent flyer awards).

Customization and Judgment

Because services are created as they are consumed and the customer is often a participant in the process, an opportunity exists to tailor a service to the needs of the customer.

FIGURE 2.5

Relationships with Customers

Source: Adapted with permission of the American Marketing Association: Christopher H. Lovelock, "Classifying Services to Gain Strategic Marketing Insights," *Journal of Marketing*, vol. 47, Summer 1983, p. 13.

Type of relationship between service firm and its customers

		"Membership" relationship	No formal relationship
Nature of the service delivery	Continuous delivery	Insurance Telephone subscription Electric utility Banking	Radio station Police protection Lighthouse Public highway
	Discrete transactions	Long-distance phone calls Theater series tickets Transit pass Wholesale buying club Airline frequent flyer	Toll highway Car rental Movie theater Public transportation Restaurant

Figure 2.6 shows that customization proceeds along two dimensions: either the character of the service permits customization, or the service personnel have the discretion to modify the service.

Selecting the quadrant of Figure 2.6 in which to position a service is a strategic choice. For example, traditional movie theaters offer only one screen; thus, they are appropriately located in the low-low quadrant. Most new movie theaters, however, are built with multiple screens, allowing some degree of customization. Among fast-food restaurants, Burger King advertises "Have it your way," permitting some customization of its "Whopper." Within a particular industry, every quadrant could be occupied by different segments of that industry, as illustrated by the various types of food-service operations in Figure 2.6. A strategic choice of offering more customization and allowing service personnel to exercise judgment, however, has implications for the service delivery system.

Nature of Demand and Capacity

We have noted that the time perishability of service capacity creates a challenge for service managers because these managers lack the option of producing and storing inventory for future sale. Even so, the extent of demand and supply imbalances varies across service industries, as shown in Figure 2.7.

To determine the most appropriate strategy in each case, it is necessary to consider the following questions:

1. What is the nature of the demand fluctuation? Does it have a predictable cycle (e.g., daily meal demand at a fast-food restaurant) that can be anticipated?
2. What are the underlying causes of these fluctuations in demand? If the causes are customer habits or preference, could marketing produce a change?
3. What opportunities exist to change the level of capacity or supply? Can part-time workers be hired during peak hours?

Because managing capacity and demand is a central challenge to the success of a service firm, Chapter 11, Managing Capacity and Demand, is devoted entirely to this topic.

Method of Service Delivery

As Figure 2.8 shows, the method of service delivery has both a geographic component and a level-of-customer-interaction component.

Services with multiple sites have significant management implications for ensuring quality and consistency in the service offering. Detailed strategic implications of facility location are discussed in Chapter 10. With advances in electronic communications, arm's-length transactions are becoming more common because they offer customer convenience and

FIGURE 2.6

Customization and Judgment in Service Delivery

Source: Adapted with permission of the American Marketing Association: Christopher H. Lovelock, "Classifying Services to Gain Strategic Marketing Insights," *Journal of Marketing,* vol. 47, Summer 1983, p. 15.

Degree of customization

		High	Low
Extent to which customer contact employees exercise judgment in meeting customer needs	**High**	Surgery Taxi service Gourmet restaurant	Education (large classes) Preventive health programs Family restaurant
	Low	Telephone service Hotel services Retail banking Cafeteria	Public transportation Movie theater Spectator sports Institutional food service

FIGURE 2.7

Nature of Demand for the Service Relative to Capacity

Source: Adapted with permission of the American Marketing Association: Christopher H. Lovelock, "Classifying Services to Gain Strategic Marketing Insights," *Journal of Marketing,* vol. 47, Summer 1983, p. 17.

Extent of demand fluctuations over time

		Wide	Narrow
Extent to which demand exceeds capacity	Peak demand met without major delay	Electricity Telephone Hospital maternity unit Police emergencies	Insurance Legal services Banking Laundry and dry cleaning
	Peak demand regularly exceeds capacity	Tax preparation Passenger transportation Hotels and motels	Fast-food restaurant Movie theater Gas station

FIGURE 2.8

Method of Service Delivery

Source: Adapted with permission of the American Marketing Association: Christopher H. Lovelock, "Classifying Services to Gain Strategic Marketing Insights," *Journal of Marketing,* vol. 47, Summer 1983, p. 18.

Availability of service outlets

		Single site	Multiple sites
Nature of service delivery	Customer travels to service firm	Theater Barbershop	Bus service Fast-food chain
	Service firm delivers	Pest control service Taxi	Mail delivery AAA emergency repairs
	Transaction at arm's length	Credit card company Local TV station	National TV network Telephone company

efficient service delivery. For example, using the Internet UPS allows customers to prepare shipping labels and track packages from home, and thus decreases the amount of physical interaction between the customer and a human service provider. The strategic implications of the design of a service delivery system and its effect on the interaction between customer and service organization are topics in Part Two: Designing the Service Enterprise.

Service-Dominant Logic[8]

Service-dominant logic is a service-centered alternative to the traditional goods-centered paradigm for describing economic exchange and value creation. The central idea is that service is the fundamental basis of value creation when defined as the application of competencies for the benefit of another through exchange. As a component of the service package, facilitating goods may be involved in the exchange, but value-in-use (value as realized and determined by the customer) is the important feature.

Table 2.4 contains the 10 foundation premises (FP) of service-dominant logic with a brief explanation/justification of each. We provide further elaboration below:

- FP1: Service is seen as an activity or process (thus singular), not an intangible unit of output (plural in the goods analogy), derived from applying (operant rather than operand) competencies (knowledge and skills) for the benefit of another party.
- FP2: The process of value creation in a postindustrial society is complex with many intermediary systems (e.g., Internet) facilitating the process of exchange.
- FP3: Although goods are a store of energy, material, and labor costs, they realize a value only upon use (e.g., a car providing the service of transportation).
- FP4: Competitive advantage is captured in a firm's intellectual capital, skills, and knowledge that can be applied to creating value for the customer.
- FP5: If service is the application of competencies for the benefit of others, then all economic activity is essentially service no matter whether the economy is considered agrarian, industrial, or postindustrial.
- FP6: If value is co-created with the customer, then the service activity must involve the customer in some capacity (e.g., mind, body, belongings, information) in an interactive relationship.

TABLE 2.4   **Foundational Premises (FP) of Service-Dominant Logic**

Source: Stephen L. Vargo and Melissa Archpru Akaka, "Service-Dominant Logic as a Foundation for Service Science: Clarifications," Service Science 1(1), Table 1 pp. 35, 32–41, 2009.

FP	Premise	Explanation/Justification
1	Service is the fundamental basis of exchange.	The application of operant resources (knowledge and skills), "service," is the basis for all exchange. Service is exchanged for service.
2	Indirect exchange masks the fundamental basis of exchange.	Goods, money, and institutions mask the service-for-service nature of exchange.
3	Goods are distribution mechanisms for service provision.	Goods (both durable and non-durable) derive their value through use—the service they provide.
4	Operant resources are the fundamental source of competitive advantage.	The comparative ability to cause desired change drives competition.
5	All economies are service economies.	Service (singular) is only now becoming more apparent with increased specialization and outsourcing.
6	The customer is always a co-creator of value.	Implies value creation is interactional.
7	The enterprise cannot deliver value, but only offer value propositions.	The firm can offer its applied resources and collaboratively (interactively) create value following acceptance, but can not create/deliver value alone.
8	A service-centered view is inherently customer oriented and relational.	Service is customer-determined and co-created; thus, it is inherently customer oriented and relational.
9	All economic and social actors are resource integrators.	Implies the context of value creation is networks of networks (resource-integrators).
10	Value is always uniquely and phenomenologically determined by the beneficiary.	Value is idiosyncratic, experiential, contextual, and meaning laden.

- FP7: Just as a product has no intrinsic value until used, a service is only a capacity to create value upon customer activation (e.g., a seat on an airplane has no value if empty upon takeoff).
- FP8: Because a service is co-created with the customer, the service exchange naturally becomes customer-focused.
- FP9: Value is created when the customer integrates and applies the resources of the service provider along with other resource-integrators to achieve the exchange (e.g., purchase on eBay using PayPal).
- FP10: Each customer determines the value or quality of the service based on personal needs at the specific time (e.g., fast lunch or dinner date) and in the particular context (e.g., alone or group) as an experience.

Service-dominant logic has become the foundation of a new field of study called "service science" championed by the IBM Almaden Research Center and called Service Science, Management, and Engineering (SSME). SSME is the application of scientific, management, and engineering disciplines to tasks that one organization beneficially performs for and with another organization or individual. The objective is to make productivity, quality, performance, compliance, growth, and learning improvements more predictable in work-sharing and risk-sharing (coproduction) relationships. The heart of service science is the transfer and sharing of resources within and among service systems. The normative function of service systems is to connect people, technology, and information through value propositions with the aim of co-creating value for the service systems participating in the exchange of resources within and across systems.

An Open-Systems View of Services

Service organizations are sufficiently unique in their character to require special management approaches that go beyond the simple adaptation of the management techniques found in manufacturing a product. The distinctive characteristics suggest enlarging the system view to include the customer as a participant in the service process. As Figure 2.9 shows, the customer is viewed as an input that is transformed by the service process into an output with some degree of satisfaction.

FIGURE 2.9
Open-Systems View of Service Operations

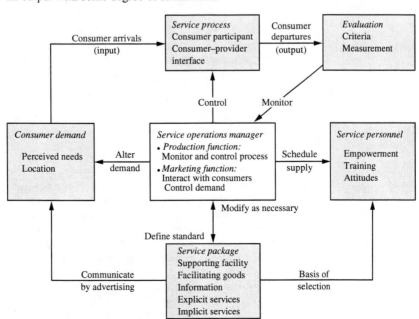

Service Benchmark

You might think Herb Kelleher, founder and former CEO of Southwest Airlines, has all the answers. His company is the most successful airline in the United States by almost every measure—on-time departures, fewest bags lost, most passenger miles, and highest customer satisfaction.

Southwest Airlines didn't obtain this lofty position, however, simply by having board meetings and brainstorming sessions within the privacy of its own walls. Company planners also went "outside the box." For example, to improve the turnaround time of flights, they went to the races—the Indianapolis 500 in particular. Instead of watching the race, however, they watched the pit crews fuel and service the competing cars. Their observations gave them insights into equipment, handling parts, and teamwork that translated into better on-time service. These were insights that could not be gained just by observing the operations of other airlines. Oftentimes the race is won in the pits.

The role of the service operations manager includes the functions of both production and marketing in an open system with the customer as a participant. The traditional manufacturing separation of the production and marketing functions, with finished-goods inventory as the interface, is neither possible nor appropriate in services. Marketing performs two important functions in daily-service operations: (1) educating the consumer to play a role as an active participant in the service process and (2) "smoothing" demand to match service capacity. This marketing activity must be coordinated with scheduling staff levels and with both controlling and evaluating the delivery process. By necessity, the operations and marketing functions are integrated for service organizations.

For services, *the process is the product*. The presence of the customer in the service process negates the closed-system perspective that is taken in manufacturing. Techniques to control operations in an isolated factory producing a tangible good are inadequate for services. No longer is the process machine-paced and the output easily measured for compliance with specifications. Instead, customers arrive with different demands on the service; thus, multiple measures of performance are necessary. Service employees interact directly with the customer, with little opportunity for management intervention. This requires extensive training and empowerment of employees to act appropriately in the absence of direct supervision.

Further, customer impressions of service quality are based on the total service experience, not just on the explicit service that is performed. A concern for employee attitudes and training becomes a necessity to ensure that the implicit service is also appreciated by the customer. When viewed from the customer's perspective, the entire service process raises concerns ranging from the aesthetic design of the facility to pleasant diversions in waiting areas.

An open-system concept of services also allows one to view the customer as a co-producer. Permitting the customer to participate actively in the service process (e.g., providing a salad bar at a restaurant) can increase productivity, which in turn can create a competitive edge.

Summary

The management of an open system requires techniques and sensitivities different from those of a closed system. Service managers are faced with nonroutine operations in which only indirect control is possible. In services, it is the human element that is central to effective operations. For example, the unavoidable interaction between service provider and consumer is a source of great opportunity, as in direct selling. However, this interaction seldom can be fully controlled; thus, service quality may suffer. For this reason, the attitude and appearance of personnel in service organizations are important considerations. For a service, the presence of the customer in the process allows for co-creation of value. In many respects, the service manager adopts a style of management that incorporates the functions of marketing and operations.

Key Terms and Definitions

Back office the service delivery activities *not* observable to the customer (e.g., restaurant kitchen). *p. 18*

Explicit services the essential or intrinsic features readily observable by the senses (e.g., on-time departure, quality of meal). *p. 22*

Facilitating goods material purchased or consumed by the buyer, or items provided by the customer (e.g., food, golf clubs). *p. 22*

Front office the service delivery activities observable to the customer (e.g., dining area of a restaurant). *p. 18*

Implicit services psychological benefits or extrinsic features the customer may sense only vaguely (e.g., security of a well-lighted parking lot, privacy of a loan office). *p. 23*

Service-dominant logic is a view that all economies are service economies in which value is always co-created in the exchange of doing something for another party. *p. 30*

Service package five components describing a service: supporting facility, facilitating goods, information, explicit service, and implicit service. *p. 22*

Service process matrix a classification of services based on the degree of interaction and customization and the degree of labor intensity that results in four categories: service factory, service shop, mass service, and professional service. *p. 25*

Service science a field of study of the transfer and sharing of resources within and among service systems. *p. 31*

Servitization revenue enhancement by bundling service with sale of a product (e.g., financing new car sale). *p. 18*

Supporting facility the physical resources that must be in place before a service can be offered (e.g., golf course, hospital building, airplane). *p. 22*

Time-perishable capacity a service that is not used during some period of time and, therefore, is lost forever (e.g., an empty seat on an airplane). *p. 20*

Topics for Discussion

1. What are the characteristics of services that will be most appropriate for Internet delivery?

2. When does collecting information through service membership become an invasion of privacy?

3. What are some of the management problems associated with allowing service employees to exercise judgment in meeting customer needs?

4. Illustrate the "distinctive characteristics of service operations" for a service with which you are familiar.

5. What factors are important for a manager to consider when attempting to enhance a service firm's image?

6. Critique the "Distinctive Characteristics of Service Operations" by arguing that the characteristics of customer participation, simultaneity, perishablity, intangibility, and heterogeneity may apply to goods as well.

Interactive Exercise

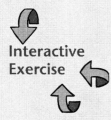

The class breaks into five groups and each group is assigned one of the service classifications (e.g., nature of act, relationship with customer, customization, nature of demand, or method of delivery) to come up with an example for each quadrant in the matrix.

36   Part One *Understanding Services*

Selected Bibliography

Chase, Richard B. "The Mall Is My Factory: Reflections of a Service Junkie." *Production and Operations Management* 5, no. 4 (Winter 1996), pp. 298–308.

Cook, David; Chon-Huat Goh; and Chen H. Chung. "Service Typologies: A State of the Art Survey." *Production and Operations Management* 8, no. 3 (Fall 1999), pp. 318–38.

Kwortnik, Robert Jr., and Gary M. Thompson. "Unifying Service Marketing and Operations with Service Experience Management," *Journal of Service Research* 11, no. 4 (May 2009), pp. 389–406.

Largo, Stephen L., and Robert F. Lusch. "The Four Service Marketing Myths: Remnants of a Goods-Based Manufacturing Model." *Journal of Service Research* 6, no. 4 (May 2004), pp. 324–35.

Laroche, Michael; Gordon H.G. McDougall; Jasmin Bergeron; and Zhiyoug Yan. "Exploring How Intangibility Affects Perceived Risk." *Journal of Service Research* 6, no. 4 (May 2005), pp. 373–89.

Sampson, Scott E., and Craig M. Froehle. "Foundations and Implications of a Proposed Unified Services Theory." *Production and Operations Management* 15, no. 2 (Summer 2006), pp. 329–42.

Spohrer, Jim, and Paul P. Maglio. "The Emergence of Service Science: Towards Systematic Service Innovations to Accelerate Co-creation of Value." *Production and Operations Management* 17, no. 3 (May-June 2008), pp. 238–246.

Endnotes

1. Based on "Customer Benefit Package" found in David A. Collier, *The Service/Quality Solution,* (Burr Ridge, Ill: Irwin, 1994), pp. 63–68.
2. R.C. Cohen, R. McBridge, R. Thornton, and T. White, *Letter Mail System Performance Design: An Analytical Method for Evaluating Candidate Mechanization,* Report R-168 (Washington, D.C.: Institute for Defense Analysis, 1970).
3. James A. Fitzsimmons, "The Use of Spectral Analysis to Validate Planning Models," *Socio-Economic Planning Sciences* 8, no. 3 (June 1974), pp. 123–28.
4. E. H. Blum, *Urban Fire Protection: Studies of the New York City Fire Department,* R-681 (New York: New York City Rand Institute, 1971).
5. G. M. Hostage, "Quality Control in a Service Business," *Harvard Business Review* 53, no. 4 (July–August 1975), pp. 98–106.
6. From Christopher Lovelock and Evert Gummesson, "Whither Services Marketing? In Search of a New Paradigm and Fresh Perspectives," *Journal of Service Research* 7, no.1 (August 2004), pp. 34–36.
7. Adapted from Christopher H. Lovelock, "Classifying Services to Gain Strategic Marketing Insights," *Journal of Marketing* 47 (Summer 1983), p. 920.
8. From Stephen L. Vargo and Melissa Archpru Akaka, "Service-Dominant Logic as a Foundation for Service Science: Clarifications," *Service Science* 1, no. 1 (2009), pp. 32–41.
9. Prepared by Rich Ellis, Thomas Prudhomme, and Marly Yanaza under the supervision of Professor James A. Fitzsimmons.

Chapter 3

Service Strategy

Learning Objectives

After completing this chapter, you should be able to:

1. Critically discuss the competitive environment of services.
2. Formulate a strategic service vision.
3. Describe how a service competes using the three generic service strategies.
4. Perform a SWOT and Five Forces Analysis.
5. Explain what is meant by qualifiers, service winners, and service losers.
6. Discuss the competitive role of information in services.
7. Explain the concept of the virtual value chain and its role in service innovation.
8. Identify potential limits in the use of information as part of a competitive strategy.
9. Categorize a service firm according to its stage of competitiveness.

As machine technology once changed an agricultural economy into an industrial economy, today's information technology is transforming our industrial economy into a service economy. The availability of computers and global communication technologies has created industries for collecting, processing, and communicating information. Today everyone on the globe can be in instant communication with everyone else, and this revolution is changing world society in many ways. Consider the impact of the emerging private satellite network industry, which provides uplinks and downlinks for personnel training, product introductions, credit checks, billing, financial exchanges, and overall telecommunications.

Kmart was among the first retail giants to establish a private satellite network using the new small-dish antenna VSAT (Very Small Aperture Terminal) placed on store roofs to receive and transmit masses of data. The VSAT at each Kmart is linked to the company's Troy, Michigan, data center via a satellite transponder leased from GTE Spacenet. The communication network has allowed Kmart to coordinate its multisite operations better and to realize substantial benefits, such as improved data transmission about the rate of sales, inventory status, product updates, and, most important, credit authorizations for customers. The instant accessibility of credit histories can significantly lower the risk of nonpayment that credit card companies face, thus lowering the discount rate that reverts back to the retailer. This savings alone eventually will pay for the cost of the satellite network.[1]

Chapter Preview

Service strategy must begin with a vision of the place and purpose of the enterprise. A strategic service vision is formulated by addressing questions about the target market, service concept, operating strategy, and delivery system. However, the competitive environment of services presents challenges such as low entry barriers, product substitution, and limited opportunities for economies of scale that must be overcome.

Three generic strategies have been found successful in formulating strategies that allow a firm to outperform competitors. The strategies of overall cost leadership, differentiation, and market focus are approaches that service firms have adopted in various ways to gain competitive advantage. With each of these strategies, however, management must not lose sight of the fact that only a focus on the customers and on satisfying their needs will result in a loyal customer base.

Before entering a market, an analysis of a company's position relative to its competitors and other players is advisable. Such an analysis begins with the well-known *five forces* model to gain an appreciation of the competitive nature of the industry. A SWOT analysis to assess strengths, weakness, opportunities, and threats follows.

Winning customers in the marketplace means competing on several dimensions. Customers base their purchase decisions on many variables, including price, convenience, reputation, and safety. The importance of a particular variable to a firm's success depends on the competitive marketplace and the preferences of individual customers.

A framework for viewing the contribution of information to the competitive strategy of the service firm also is presented. Using the dimensions of strategic focus both external and internal and competitive use of information both online and offline four strategic roles of information are identified: creation of barriers to entry, revenue generation, database asset, and productivity enhancement. Industry examples for each role illustrate how firms have used information effectively.

Service product innovation is driven by an appreciation of the virtual value chain that assembles information on customer needs based on changing demographics and lifestyles. This database can be mined to develop new service offerings targeted at an existing customer base. However, there are limits to the use of information including questions of privacy, fairness, reliability, and data accuracy.

The chapter concludes with a framework that categorizes service firms according to their level of competitiveness with respect to key operational dimensions.

The Strategic Service Vision

The purpose and place of a service firm in the market begins with an entrepreneur's idea and an unmet need. Table 3.1 presents a framework in the form of questions one should ask in formulating a *strategic service vision*. The basic categories presented from left to right are: service delivery system, operating strategy, service concept, and target market segments. Within each category questions are offered to help in the development of the category. As one moves between categories a question is posed to assess how well the category has achieved the strategic service vision. For example, the between-category question "does the service delivery system support the operating strategy?" addresses the appropriateness of the service delivery system for the intended operating strategy. Table 3.1 is limited to a domestic service. Additional questions are necessary to account for cultural elements when applied in a global context. The international elements that need to be added to the strategic service vision shown here can be found in Table 14.1 in the Globalization of Services chapter.

To demonstrate the effectiveness of this framework, Table 3.2 illustrates the initial strategic service vision of Southwest Airlines when it served only three cities in Texas (i.e., Dallas, Houston, and San Antonio). With startup firms such as Southwest Airlines, it is best to apply the strategic service vision from right to left beginning with the target market.

TABLE 3.1 Elements of the Strategic Service Vision

Source: Adapted and reprinted by permission of J. L. Heskett, W. E. Sasser, and L. A. Schlesinger, *The Service Profit Chain* (New York: The Free Press, 1997), p. 9.

Service Delivery System	Operating Strategy	Service Concept	Target Market Segments
What are important features of the service delivery system including: The role of people? Technology? Equipment? Layout? Procedures?	What are important elements of the strategy? Operations? Financing? Marketing? Organization? Human resources? Control?	What are important elements of the service to be provided, stated in terms of results produced for customers?	What are common characteristics of important market segments? What dimensions can be used to segment the market? Demographic? Psychographic?
What capacity does it provide? Normally? At peak levels?	On which will the most effort be concentrated? Where will investments be made?	How are these elements supposed to be perceived by the target market segment? By the market in general? By employees? By others?	How important are various segments? What needs does each have?
To what extent does it: Help ensure quality standards? Differentiate the service from competition? Provide barriers to entry by competitors?	How will quality and cost be controlled? Measures? Incentives? Rewards?	How do customers perceive the service concept?	How well are these needs being served? In what manner? By whom?
	What results will be expected versus competition in terms of: Quality of service? Cost profile? Productivity? Morale/loyalty of servers?	What efforts does this suggest in terms of the manner in which the service is: Designed? Delivered? Marketed?	

Arrows: Does the service delivery system support the operating strategy? ↔ To what extent is the value of results and process quality for customers leveraged over cost to the service provider? ↔ How well is the service concept positioned in relation to customers' needs and competitors' offering? ↔

TABLE 3.2   **Southwest Airlines Strategic Service Vision**

Service Delivery System	Operating Strategy	Service Concept	Target Market Segment
• Fun cabin atmosphere to differentiate service • Use only Boeing 737 aircraft to control maintenance and operating costs • Hire cabin crew based on attitude	• Quick turnaround at gate results in high utilization of aircraft • No assigned seating rewards punctuality and promotes on-time performance	• Short flights with frequent departures • Serves peanuts and soft drinks only • Use of inner-city or low traffic airports avoids congestion • Carry-on luggage	• State of Texas residents • Business traveler who drives because of inadequate service • Inexpensive family travel on weekends

Understanding the Competitive Environment of Services

In general, service firms compete in a difficult economic environment, and there are many reasons for this difficulty:

• *Relatively low overall entry barriers.* Service innovations are not patentable, and in most cases, services are not capital-intensive. Thus, innovations can easily be copied by competitors. However, other types of entry barriers exist, such as locating a resort hotel on the best beach of an island (e.g., the Club Med location on the island of Moorea in French Polynesia).

• *Minimal opportunities for economies of scale.* The necessity of physical travel for many services limits the market area and results in small-scale outlets. Franchised firms can realize some economies of scale by sharing purchasing or advertising costs; in other instances, using the Internet can be a substitute for physical travel (e.g., ordering from Amazon.com).

• *Erratic sales fluctuations.* Service demand varies as a function of the time of day and the day of the week (and sometimes seasonally), with random arrivals. Can you think of some exceptions?

• *No advantage of size in dealing with buyers or suppliers.* The small size of many service firms places them at a disadvantage in bargaining with powerful buyers or suppliers. Many exceptions should come to mind, however, such as McDonald's buying beef and Marriott's buying mattresses.

• *Product substitution.* Product innovations can be a substitute for services (e.g., the home pregnancy test). Thus, service firms must not only watch other service competitors but also anticipate potential product innovations that might make their services obsolete.

• *Customer loyalty.* Established firms using personalized service create a loyal customer base, which becomes a barrier to entry by new services. For example, a hospital supply firm may place its own ordering computer terminals at customers' sites. These terminals then facilitate the placement of new orders to the extent that competitors are effectively excluded.

• *Exit barriers.* Marginal service firms may continue to operate despite low, or even nonexistent, profits. For example, a privately held firm may have employment of family members rather than maximizing profit as its goal. Other service firms, such as antique stores or scuba diving shops, have a hobby or romantic appeal that provides their owners with enough job satisfaction to offset low financial compensation. Thus, profit-motivated competitors would find it difficult to drive these privately held firms from the market.

For any particular service industry, there are firms that have overcome these competitive difficulties and prospered. For example, McDonald's has achieved a dominant position in the fast-food industry by overcoming many of the difficulties listed here. New entrants, however, must develop a service strategy that will address the important competitive features of their respective industries. Three generic strategies have been successful in providing a competitive advantage, and illustrations of how service firms have used these strategies will be our next topic.

Competitive Service Strategies[2]

Michael Porter has argued persuasively that three generic competitive strategies exist: overall cost leadership, differentiation, and focus.[3] Each strategy will be described in turn, with examples of how service firms use them to outperform their competition.

Overall Cost Leadership

An *overall cost leadership* strategy requires efficient-scale facilities, tight cost and overhead control, and often innovative technology as well. Having a low-cost position provides a defense against competition, because less efficient competitors will suffer first from competitive pressures. Implementing a low-cost strategy usually requires high capital investment in state-of-the-art equipment, aggressive pricing, and start-up losses to build market share. A cost leadership strategy sometimes can revolutionize an industry, as illustrated by the success of McDonald's, Walmart, and Federal Express. Moreover, service firms have been able to achieve low-cost leadership using a variety of approaches.

Seeking Out Low-Cost Customers

Some customers cost less to serve than others, and they can be targeted by the service provider. For example, United Services Automobile Association (USAA) occupies a preeminent position among automobile insurers because it serves only military personnel and their families. This group also entails lower cost because its members, who are relatively nomadic, are accustomed to and willing to do business by telephone, mail, or online. Consequently, USAA is able to eliminate any need for the extensive sales force employed by traditional insurers. Another example of this strategy is provided by low-cost retailers such as Sam's Wholesale Club and Costco, which target customers who are willing to buy in quantity, do without frills, and serve themselves.

Standardizing a Custom Service

Typically, income tax preparation is considered to be a customized service. H & R Block, however, has been successful in serving customers nationwide when only routine tax preparation is required. Also, storefront legal services and family health care centers are attractive means of delivering routine professional services at low cost. The key word here is *routine*. However, product substitution is always a danger (e.g., Turbo Tax).

Reducing the Personal Element in Service Delivery

The potentially high-risk strategy of reducing the personal element in service delivery can be accepted by customers if increased convenience results. For example, convenient access to ATMs has weaned customers from personal interaction with live tellers and, consequently, has reduced transaction costs for banks.

Reducing Network Costs

Unusual start-up costs are encountered by service firms that require a network to knit together providers and customers. Electric utilities, which have substantial fixed costs in transmission lines, provide the most obvious example. Federal Express conceived a unique approach to reducing network costs by using a hub-and-spoke network. By locating a hub in Memphis with state-of-the-art sorting technology, the overnight air-package carrier was able to serve the United States with no direct routes between the cities that it served. Each time a new city is added to the network, Federal Express only needs to add one more route to and from the hub instead of adding routes between all the cities served.

The efficiency of the hub-and-spoke network strategy has not been lost on passenger airline operators, either.

Taking Service Operations Offline

Many services, such as haircutting and passenger transportation, are inherently "online," because they can only be performed with the customer present. For services in which the customer need not be present, the service transaction can be "decoupled," with some content performed "offline." For example, a shoe repair service could locate dispersed kiosks for customer drop-off/pick-up, thus consolidating orders for delivery to an off-site repair factory, which even could be located offshore. Performing services offline represents significant cost savings because of economies of scale from consolidation, low-cost facility location (e.g., American Airlines has one of its 800-number reservations centers located in the Caribbean), and absence of the customer in the system. In short, the decoupled service operation is run like a factory.

Differentiation

The essence of the *differentiation* strategy lies in creating a service that is perceived as being unique. Approaches to differentiation can take many forms: brand image (e.g., McDonald's golden arches), technology (e.g., Sprint's fiberoptics network), features (e.g., American Express's complete travel services), customer service (e.g., Nordstrom's reputation among department stores), dealer network (e.g., Century 21's nationwide real estate presence), and other dimensions. A differentiation strategy does not ignore costs, but its primary thrust lies in creating customer loyalty. As illustrated here, differentiation to enhance the service often is achieved at some cost that the targeted customer is willing to pay.

Making the Intangible Tangible

By their very nature, services often are intangible and leave the customer with no physical reminder of the purchase. Recognizing the need to remind customers of their stay, many hotels now provide complimentary toiletry items with the hotel name prominently affixed. The Hartford Steam Boiler Inspection and Insurance Company writes insurance on industrial power plants, but this company has enhanced its service to include regular inspections and recommendations to managers for avoiding potential problems.

Customizing the Standard Product

Providing a customized touch may endear a firm to its customers at very little cost. A hotel operator who is able to address a guest by name can make an impression that translates into repeat business. Hair salons have added many personalizing features (e.g., personal stylist, juice bar, relaxed surroundings, mood music) to differentiate themselves from barbershops. Burger King's efforts to promote a made-to-order policy is an attempt to differentiate itself from McDonald's classic make-to-stock approach to fast-food service.

Reducing Perceived Risk

Lack of information about the purchase of a service creates a sense of risk-taking for many customers. Lacking knowledge or self-confidence about services such as auto repair, customers will seek out providers who take the extra time to explain the work to be done, present a clean and organized facility, and guarantee their work (e.g., Village Volvo). Customers often see the "peace of mind" that is engendered when this trusting relationship develops as being worth the extra expense.

Giving Attention to Personnel Training

Investment in personnel development and training that results in enhanced service quality is a competitive advantage that is difficult to replicate. Firms that lead their industries are known among competitors for the quality of their training programs. In some cases, these firms have established collegelike training centers (e.g., McDonald's Hamburger University in Oak Brook, Illinois, near Chicago).

Controlling Quality

Delivering a consistent level of service quality at multiple sites with a labor-intensive system is a significant challenge. Firms have approached this problem in a variety of ways, including personnel training, explicit procedures, technology, limits on the scope of the service, direct supervision, and peer pressure, among others. For example, to ensure consistency, the Magic Pan chain of restaurants designed a foolproof machine to produce its famous crêpes. The question of service quality is further complicated by the potential gap between customer expectations and experiences. Influencing customer quality expectations thus becomes an issue, which is explored in Chapter 6, Service Quality.

Focus

The *focus* strategy is built around the idea of servicing a particular target market very well by addressing customers' specific needs. The market segment could be a particular buyer group (e.g., USAA and the military community), service (e.g., Shouldice Hospital and patients with inguinal hernias, Motel 6 and budget travelers, Federal Express and people who need guaranteed overnight package delivery), or geographic region (e.g., community college or neighborhood restaurant). The focus strategy rests on the premise that the firm can serve its narrow target market more effectively and/or efficiently than other firms trying to serve a broad market. As a result, the firm achieves competitive advantage in its market segment by meeting specific customer needs and/or by lower costs through specialization. Thus, the focus strategy is the application of differentiation and/or overall cost leadership to a particular market segment rather than the entire market.

Davidow and Uttal argue how important customer selection is to achieving a successful focus strategy.[4] They relate how one bank in Palo Alto, California, targets wealthy individuals and discourages others by policies such as closing an account after two checks have bounced. Davidow and Uttal's three-step approach to focus includes segmenting the market to design core services, classifying customers according to the value they place on service, and setting expectations slightly below perceived performance.

Strategic Analysis

Strategic analysis begins with a stated objective, such as "should we enter an industry with a new service offering?" Two popular planning tools include (1) Porter's five forces analysis of the target industry structure and (2) a SWOT analysis to assess the organization's strengths, weaknesses, opportunities, and threats in a market.

Porter's Five Forces Analysis[5]

The five forces model is used at the industry level (e.g., airlines) to determine the competitive intensity and, therefore, attractiveness of a market. The five forces affect the ability of a firm to attract customers and make a profit. Figure 3.1 shows a model of the five forces with example issues to consider in each case.

Consider Netflix as an example firm entering the video rental industry. Our discussion begins with the center block (Competitive Rivalry within Industry) upon which the external forces act.

- *Competitive Rivalry within Industry.* Often this factor is the major determinant of industry competitiveness. Rivals might be aggressive price competitors or they might use nonprice strategies such as innovation, branding, or superior quality. Industry capacity relative to total customer demand is an important indicator of whether a new entrant will find customers. An exception was Southwest Airlines, which entered the Texas market offering low-cost fares and frequent departures that tapped a latent

FIGURE 3.1

Porter's Five Forces Model

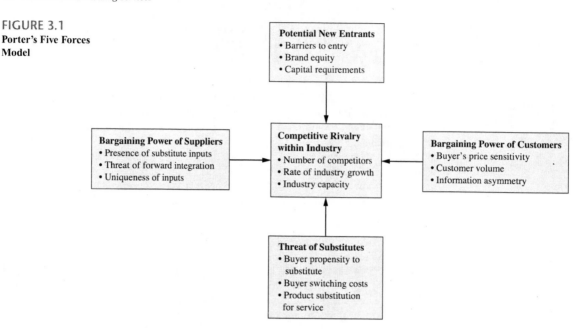

demand of business commuters who usually traveled by car. When Netflix entered the market offering DVDs exclusively by mail, its only rivals were rental stores such as Blockbuster.

- *Potential New Entrants.* Profitable markets that yield high returns invite new competitors. For example, at one time Walmart challenged Netflix, but subsequently left the field because it was unable to overcome Netflix's established brand.
- *Threat of Substitutes.* For services, substitutes often take the form of a product. For example, TurboTax software is a substitute for the services of a tax accountant. Netflix is faced with competition from cable companies that allow customers to download videos direct to their television using Tivoli.
- *Bargaining Power of Suppliers.* Suppliers of inputs can be a source of power over the firm because of product uniqueness or monopoly source. The most important suppliers to Netflix are the DVD distributors, but Netflix has considerable leverage because of volume purchases.
- *Bargaining Power of Customers.* Netflix customers might be able to exert price pressure and, thus, restrict high margins. In the travel industry the use of Priceline.com and Hotwire.com have shifted the information asymmetry to the advantage of the customer. However, Netflix uses information about customer purchases to recommend other movies with similar themes, thereby stimulating demand.

SWOT Analysis: Strengths, Weaknesses, Opportunities, Threats

A *SWOT analysis* identifies an organization's internal strength and weakness as well as threats and opportunities in the external environment. The aim of the analysis is to reveal competitive advantages, analyze prospects, prepare for problems, and allow for development of contingency plans. A SWOT analysis begins with a stated objective and concludes with a summary of strengths to be maintained, built upon, or leveraged; weaknesses to be remedied; opportunities to be prioritized, captured, or built upon; and threats to be countered, minimized, or managed. A SWOT analysis is subjective, and two people often arrive at different final versions, thus emphasizing the value of collaboration. Table 3.3 presents a sample of typical questions that might be asked in each of the four quadrants of a SWOT analysis.

TABLE 3.3 SWOT Analysis

Strengths	Weaknesses
• What are your company's advantages?	• What could you improve?
• What do you do better than anyone else?	• What should you avoid?
• What unique resources do you have?	• What factors lose sales?
• What do people in your market see as your strengths?	• What are people in your market likely to see as a weakness?
Opportunities	**Threats**
• What are your competitors' vulnerabilities?	• What obstacles do you face?
• What are the current market trends?	• What are your competitors doing?
• Does technology offer new service options?	• Is changing technology threatening your position?
• Are there niches in the market your organization can fill?	• Do you have cash-flow problems?

Winning Customers in the Marketplace

Depending on the competition and personal needs, customers select a service provider using criteria listed here. This list is not intended to be complete, because the very addition of a new dimension by a firm represents an attempt to engage in a strategy of differentiation. For example, initiation of the frequent flyer program "AAdvantage" by American Airlines was an attempt to add the dimension of customer loyalty to competition among airlines.

- *Availability.* How accessible is the service? The use of ATMs by banks has created 24-hour availability of some banking services (i.e., service beyond the traditional "banker's hours"). Use of 800-numbers and Web sites by service firms facilitate access to information and personal accounts 24/7.
- *Convenience.* The location of the service defines convenience for customers who must travel to that service. Gasoline stations, fast-food restaurants, and dry cleaners are examples of services that must select locations on busy streets if they are to succeed.
- *Dependability.* How reliable is the service? For example, once the exterminator is gone, how soon do the bugs return? A major complaint regarding automobile repair services is the failure to fix the problem on the first visit. For airlines, on-time performance is a statistic collected by the FAA.
- *Personalization.* Are you treated as an individual? For example, hotels have discovered that repeat customers respond to being greeted by their name. The degree of customization allowed in providing the service, no matter how slight, can be viewed as more personalized service.
- *Price.* Competing on price is not as effective in services as it is with products, because it often is difficult to compare the costs of services objectively. It may be easy to compare costs in the delivery of routine services such as an oil change, but in professional services, competition on price might be considered counterproductive because price often is viewed as being a surrogate for quality.
- *Quality.* Service quality is a function of the relationship between a customer's prior expectations of the service and his or her perception of the service experience both during and after the fact. Unlike product quality, service quality is judged by both the process of service delivery and the outcome of the service.
- *Reputation.* The uncertainty that is associated with the selection of a service provider often is resolved by talking with others about their experiences before a decision is made. Unlike a product, a poor service experience cannot be exchanged or returned for a different model. Positive word-of-mouth is the most effective form of advertising.

- *Safety.* Well-being and security are important considerations because in many services, such as air travel and medicine, the customers are putting their lives in the hands of the service provider.
- *Speed.* How long must I wait for service? For emergency services such as fire and police protection, response time is the major criterion of performance. In other services, waiting sometimes might be considered a trade-off for receiving more personalized services, or in reduced rates.

Writing about manufacturing strategy, Terry Hill used the term *order-winning criteria* to refer to competitive dimensions that sell products.[6] He further suggested that some criteria could be called *qualifiers,* because the presence of these dimensions is necessary for a product to enter the marketplace. Finally, Hill said that some qualifiers could be considered *order-losing sensitive.*

We will use a similar logic and the service criteria listed earlier to describe the service purchase decision. The purchase decision sequence begins with qualifying potential service firms (e.g., must the doctor be on my PPO list?), followed by making a final selection from this subset of service firms using a service winner (e.g., which of the PPO doctors has the best reputation?). After the initial service experience, a return will be based on whether a "service loser" has occurred (e.g., the doctor was cold and impersonal).

Qualifiers

Before a service firm can be taken seriously as a competitor in the market, it must attain a certain level for each service-competitive dimension, as defined by the other market players. For example, in airline service, we would name safety, as defined by the airworthiness of the aircraft and by the rating of the pilots, as an obvious *qualifier.* In a mature market such as fast foods, established competitors may define a level of quality, such as cleanliness, that new entrants must at least match to be viable contenders. For fast food, a dimension that once was a service winner, such as a drive-in window, over time could become a qualifier because some customers will not stop otherwise.

Service Winners

Service winners are dimensions such as price, convenience, or reputation that are used by a customer to make a choice among competitors. Depending on the needs of the customer at the time of the purchase, the service winner may vary. For example, seeking a restaurant for lunch may be based on convenience, but a dinner date could be influenced by reputation. Note that a service winner can become an industry qualifier (e.g., ATM use by banks).

Service Losers

Failure to deliver at or above the expected level for a competitive dimension can result in a dissatisfied customer who is lost forever. For various reasons, the dimensions of dependability, personalization, and speed are particularly vulnerable to becoming *service losers.* Some examples might be failure of an auto dealer to repair a mechanical problem (i.e., dependability), rude treatment by a doctor (i.e., personalization), or failure of an overnight service to deliver a package on time (i.e., speed).

The Competitive Role of Information in Services[7]

For service management, information technology is helping to define the competitive strategy of successful firms. Figure 3.2 illustrates the different roles in which information technology can support a service firm's competitive strategy. We shall explore each of these roles in turn with illustrations from successful applications.

Creation of Barriers to Entry

As noted earlier, many services exist in markets that have low entry barriers. James L. Heskett, however, has argued that barriers to entry can be created by using economies

FIGURE 3.2
Strategic Roles of Information in Services

Source: Adapted from James A. Fitzsimmons, "Strategic Role of Information in Services," in Rakesh V. Sarin (ed.), *Perspectives in Operations Management: Essays in Honor of Elwood S. Buffa.* Norwell, Mass: Kluwer Academic Publisher, 1993, p. 103.

Competitive use of information

	Online (Real time)	Offline (Analysis)
External (Customer)	*Creation of barriers to entry:* Reservation system Frequent user club Switching costs	*Database asset:* Selling information Development of services Micromarketing
Internal (Operations)	*Revenue generation:* Yield management Point of sales Expert systems	*Productivity enhancement:* Inventory status Data envelopment analysis (DEA)

of scale, building market share, creating switching costs, investing in communications networks, and using databases and information technologies to strategic advantage.[8] We will discuss three uses of information for creating barriers to entry: reservations systems, frequent flyer or similar programs to gain customer loyalty, and development of customer relationships to increase switching costs.

Reservation Systems

A barrier to entry can be created by investing in online reservations systems that are provided to sales intermediaries such as travel agents. American Airline's SABRE System is an example of the kind of subtle barrier to entry that is created by a comprehensive information system. United and Delta have duplicated this reservations system at great cost, but most smaller carriers use these existing systems for a fee. The competitive importance of online reservations systems became evident in late 1982. At this time, the Civil Aeronautics Board (CAB) and the U.S. Department of Justice began a joint investigation of possible antitrust violations by airline reservations systems. In this investigation, Frontier Airlines filed charges accusing United of unfairly restricting competition in the use of its Apollo computerized reservations system.[9]

Frequent User Club

It was a small step for American Airlines, given its massive reservations system, to add passenger accounts to accumulate travel credit for frequent flyer awards. These programs, which award free trips and several ancillary benefits, create strong brand loyalty among travelers, particularly business travelers who are not paying their own way. Thus, the discount fares of a new competitor have no appeal to these travelers, as People Express learned. A travel consultant has been quoted as saying, "It's one of the most anticompetitive programs ever erected."[10]

Alfred Kahn, the father of deregulation, headed the CAB in the late 1970s and did not foresee how airlines would create reservations systems and frequent flyer plans to stifle competition. He is quoted as saying, "Nobody recognized all the ways in which a carrier could insulate itself from competition."[11]

Switching Costs

Establishing customer relationships creates a cost in the form of an inconvenience for the customer to switch to another provider. Think of the hassle of changing your bank after you have arranged for automatic bill payment from your checking account.

Information technology in the form of online computer terminals has been used in the medical supplies industry to link hospitals directly to the suppliers' distribution networks. Both American Hospital Supply and McKesson, the drug distributor, have installed their online terminals in hospitals so that supplies and drugs can be purchased as the need arises. Significant switching costs are built into this arrangement, because the hospital is able to reduce inventory-carrying costs and has the convenience of online ordering for replenishments. The supplier benefits by a reduction in selling costs because it is difficult for a competitor to entice away a customer who is already coopted into its system.[12]

Revenue Generation

Real-time information technologies with a focus on internal operations can play a competitive role in increasing revenue opportunities. The concept of *yield management* is best understood as a revenue-maximizing strategy to make full use of service capacity. Advances in microcomputers have created opportunities for innovative point-of-sale devices, and the use of expert systems accessible by laptop computers in the field allows increased customer service.

Yield Management

Through the use of its SABRE reservations system, American Airlines was the first to realize the potential of what is now called yield management. By constantly monitoring the status of both its upcoming flights and competitors' flights on the same route, American makes pricing and allocation decisions on unsold seats. Thus, the number of Supersaver fares allocated to a particular flight can be adjusted to ensure that remaining empty seats have a chance of being sold, but not at the expense of a full-fare seat. This real-time pricing strategy maximizes the revenue for each flight by ensuring that no seat goes empty for want of a bargain-seeking passenger while holding some seats in reserve for late arrivals who are willing to pay full fare.[13]

Thus, yield management is the application of information to improve the revenue that is generated by a time-perishable resource (e.g., airline seats, hotel rooms). The success of yield management for American has not gone unnoticed by other service industries; for example, Marriott Hotels has installed a nationwide yield management system to increase occupancy rates. In addition, American Airlines is capitalizing on its innovation by selling the yield management software to noncompetitive industries such as the French national railroad. The topic of yield management is covered in more detail in Chapter 11.

Point of Sale

Walmart has discovered a new toy for the discount shopper: the VideOcart. As the shopper pushes the VideOcart through the store, information about the department at hand flashes onto the attached video screen. The cart also helps customers find items in the store by listing hundreds of products by department and then displaying a map of the store. The company supplying the cart claims that it has increased sales by $1 per visit in trials at supermarkets.[14] For another example, consider use of the palmsized microcomputer transmitter. With this device, a server in a restaurant can transmit an order directly to the kitchen monitor and the bill to the cashier at the same time. This saves unnecessary steps and allows more time for suggestive selling.

Expert Systems

Otis Elevator Company puts an *expert system* together with laptop computers in the hands of its maintenance staff to speed repairs in the field. Collecting information on the behavior of its elevators over the years has led to a knowledge base that is incorporated into the expert system. Using a laptop computer, a repair person in the field can access the system and receive diagnostic help in identifying the source of a problem. As a result, elevators are placed back in service quickly, and fewer repair people are needed. Some of the earlier applications of expert systems have been in the medical field, and, conceivably, these systems could be accessed by physicians for a fee. As another example, an oil

exploration expert system was able to identify promising drilling sites for a major oil company.

Database Asset

James L. Heskett observed that the database a service firm possesses can be a hidden asset of strategic importance. The expense of assembling and maintaining a large database is itself a barrier to entry by competitors. More important, however, the database can be mined for profiles of customers' buying habits, and these present opportunities for developing new services.[15]

Selling Information

Dun & Bradstreet created a business by selling access to its database of business credit information. American Home Shield, a provider of service contracts for individual home heating, plumbing, and electrical systems, also discovered that it had a valuable asset in its database, accumulated over many years of repair experience; manufacturers now are invited to access this database to evaluate the performance patterns of their products. American Express has detailed information about the spending habits of its cardholders and now offers breakdowns of customer spending patterns to its retail customers.

Developing Services

Club Med, an all-inclusive resort company with locations worldwide, has evolved to reflect the maturing of its membership. Studying the database of member characteristics, Club Med realized that over time its once swinging singles members have become married with children. In order to continue capturing future vacation visits, Club Med modified some of its locations to accommodate families with young children. Now parents can enjoy the beach and water sports while their children are supervised by Club Med counselors at a children's park nearby. More recently, Club Med has added cruise ships to its vacation possibilities to attract the more senior members who are no longer interested in water sports. As this example illustrates, service firms that capture customer data at the time of the initial purchase have the opportunity to establish a lifetime relationship, with the potential for creating new or modified services for future purchase.

Micromarketing

Today, we can see a truly focused service strategy that can target customers at the micro level. Bar coding and checkout scanner technology create a wealth of consumer buying information that can be used to target customers with precision. As Table 3.4 shows, analysis of this database allows marketers to pinpoint their advertising and product distribution. To increase sales, Borden Inc. has used such information to select stores in which to feature its premium pasta sauce. Kraft USA saw its sales of cream cheese increase after targeting its flavors to the tastes of a particular store's shoppers.[16] American Express, by analyzing information about its customers and their changing spending patterns in meticulous detail, can even tell when they get married.

Productivity Enhancement

New developments in the collection and analysis of information have increased our ability to manage multisite service operations. Through use of hand-held computers, retail inventory can be managed on a daily basis to make better use of shelf space by matching displayed products with sales. Information collected on the performance of multisite units can be used to identify the most efficient producers, and productivity is enhanced systemwide when the sources of these successes are shared with other sites. The foundation for a learning organization is then established.

50   Part One *Understanding Services*

TABLE 3.4   Example of Micromarketing Analysis

Source: Michael J. McCarthy, "Marketers Zero in on Their Customers," *The Wall Street Journal,* March 18, 1991, p. B1. Reprinted with permission of *The Wall Street Journal,* © 1991 Dow Jones & Company, Inc. All Rights Reserved Worldwide.

Hitting the Bull's-Eye
Micromarketers can now target a product's best customers and the stores where they're most likely to shop. Here's one company's analysis of three products' best targets in the New York area.

Brand	Heavy User Profile	Lifestyle and Media Profile	Top Three Stores
Peter Pan peanut butter	Households with kids headed by 18–54-year-olds, in suburban and rural areas	• Heavy video renters • Go to theme parks • Below average TV viewers • Above average radio listeners	**Foodtown Super Market** 3350 Hempstead Turnpike Levittown, NY **Pathmark Supermarket** 3635 Hempstead Turnpike Levittown, NY **King Kullen Market** 598 Stewart Ave. Bethpage, NY
Stouffer's Red Box frozen entrees	Households headed by people 55 and older, and upscale suburban households headed by 35–54-year-olds	• Go to gambling casinos • Give parties • Involved in public activities • Travel frequently • Heavy newspaper readers • Above average TV viewers	**Dan's Supreme Super Market** 69-62 88th St. Flushing, NY **Food Emporium** Madison Ave. & 74th St. New York, NY **Waldbaum Super Market** 196-35 Horace Harding Flushing, NY
Coors light beer	Head of household 21–34 years old, middle to upper income, suburban and urban	• Belong to a health club • Buy rock music • Travel by plane • Give parties, cookouts • Rent videos • Heavy TV sports viewers	**Food Emporium** 1498 York Ave. New York, NY **Food Emporium** First Ave. & 72nd St. New York, NY **Gristede's Supermarket** 350 E. 86th St. New York, NY

Inventory Status

Using a hand-held computer, Frito-Lay sales representatives have eliminated paper forms. They download the data collected on their routes each day via the Internet to the Plano, Texas, headquarters, and the company then uses these data to keep track of inventory levels, pricing, product promotions, and stale or returned merchandise. These daily updates on sales, manufacturing, and distribution keep fresh products moving through the system, matching consumer demands. For a perishable product like potato chips, having the right product at the right place and in the proper amount is critical to Frito-Lay's success. One spokesperson said that the company saved more than $40 million in its first year because of reduced paperwork, reduced losses from stale products, and route consolidation.[17]

Data Envelopment Analysis

Data envelopment analysis (DEA) is a linear programming technique developed by A. Charnes, W. W. Cooper, and E. Rhodes to evaluate nonprofit and public sector organizations. Subsequently, it has found applications in for-profit service organizations. DEA compares each service delivery unit with all other service units for a multisite organization, and it computes an efficiency rating that is based on the ratio of resource inputs to outputs. Multiple inputs (e.g., labor-hours, materials) and multiple outputs (e.g., sales, referrals) are possible and desirable in measuring a unit's efficiency. Taking this information, the linear programming model determines the efficiency frontier on the basis of those few units producing at 100 percent efficiency. Areas for improvement can be identified by comparing the operating practices of efficient units with those of less efficient units. Sharing management practices of efficient units with less efficient units provides an opportunity for the latter's improvement and enhancement of total system productivity. Repeated use of DEA can establish a climate of organizational learning that fuels a competitive strategy of cost leadership.

Banker and Morey applied DEA to a 60-unit fast-food restaurant chain and found 33 units to be efficient.[18] In their analysis, three outputs (i.e., food sales for breakfast, lunch, and dinner) and six inputs (i.e., supplies and materials, labor, age of store, advertising expenditures, urban versus rural location, and existence of a drive-in window) were used. It is interesting to note that the inputs included both discretionary and uncontrollable variables (e.g., the demographic variable of urban/rural locations, whether or not the unit had a drive-in window). The topic of data envelopment analysis is covered in more detail as a supplement to Chapter 8 Process Improvement.

The Virtual Value Chain[19]

Today, businesses compete in two worlds: a physical world of people and things called a *marketplace* and a virtual world of information called a *marketspace*. For example, after Barnes and Noble opened a Web site it established a presence in the virtual marketspace created by the Internet, but it also continues its competitive position as the leading bookstore in the marketplace. The nature of the marketspace that requires customer information for order fulfillment also enables the service provider to collect useful information such as customer buying behavior and addresses. The marketspace information can also be used to improve the service delivery process and create customer value.

The process of creating value has long been described as stages linked together to form a *value chain*. The traditional physical value chain, as shown at the top of Figure 3.3, consists of a sequence of stages beginning with manufacturing and ending with sales to a customer. The virtual value chain, as shown at the bottom of Figure 3.3, traditionally has been treated as information supporting physical value-adding elements, but not as a source of value itself. For example, managers use information on inventory levels to monitor the process, but they rarely use information itself to create new value for the customer. This is no longer the case for breakthrough service companies. For example, FedEx now exploits its information database by allowing customers to track packages themselves using the company's Web site on the Internet. Now customers can locate a

FIGURE 3.3
Exploiting the Virtual Value Chain

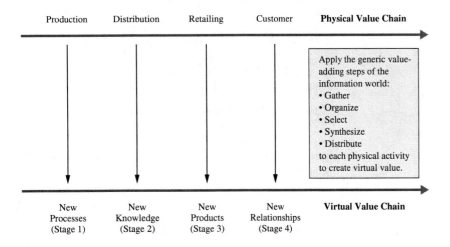

Data on customer usage allows for targeted recommendations.

package in transit by entering the airbill number, and they can even identify the name of the person who signed for it when delivered. Convenient tracking of a package added customer value and initially differentiated FedEx from its competitors.

To create value with information, managers must look to the marketspace. Although the value chain of the marketspace can mirror that of the marketplace, the value-adding process first must gather raw information that is processed and finally distributed. The value-adding steps are virtual in that they are performed through and with information. Creating value in any stage of a virtual value chain involves a sequence of five activities: gathering, organizing, selecting, synthesizing, and distributing information.

The United Services Automobile Association (USAA), which provides financial services to military personnel and their families, has become a world-class competitor by exploiting the virtual value chain. USAA moved from the marketplace to marketspace in a three-stage evolution.

First Stage (New Processes)

The first stage involves seeing the physical operations more effectively with information. USAA became a "paperless operation," as it moved from a manual paper-based filing system to one based on a central computerized database with access via desktop terminals.

Second Stage (New Knowledge)

In the second stage, virtual alternatives substitute for physical activities. At USAA, information systems were installed to automate the core business of insurance sales and underwriting. In the process, USAA captured significant amounts of information about customers who are members of the association. Unlike a typical insurance company, USAA has no traveling sales force and all of its business is conducted by telephone, mail, or Internet. All member-contact employees are trained to evaluate members' needs and provide appropriate products and services. Consequently, USAA has been able to build a database on its members who are accustomed to doing business with relatively little human interaction.

Third Stage (New Products)

In the final stage, member information is analyzed to discover new product needs and methods to deliver value. As the database accumulated, USAA prepared member risk profiles and customized policies. Analyzing the flow of information harvested along the virtual value chain, in particular the aging of its members, USAA instituted products targeted to members' evolving needs, such as property and casualty insurance, banking products and services, life and health insurance, mutual funds, and retirement communities. The "event-oriented service" anticipates individual member needs such as a teenage child requiring auto insurance. Today, members can manage their financial portfolio using the USAA Web site.

Fourth Stage (New Relationships)

In the final stage, opportunities for customer collaboration in the co-creation of value are explored. Retired and active duty members of USAA need financial planning. In response, USAA created Web-based investment planning tools and frequent online interactive seminars dealing with current financial issues.

Limits in the Use of Information

So far only the benefits of using information as a competitive strategy have been addressed. Some of these strategies, however, raise questions of fairness, invasion of privacy, and anticompetitiveness. Also, if these strategies were abused, the result could harm consumers.

Anticompetitive

To create entry barriers, the use of reservation systems and frequent user programs has been identified as potentially anticompetitive. For example, how should a frequent flyer's free-trip award be considered, particularly when the passenger has been traveling on business at corporate expense? The IRS is considering taxing the free trip as income in kind, and corporations believe that the free tickets belong to the company. The long-run implication, however, is the removal of price competition in air travel.

Fairness

Perhaps the easiest way to start a riot is asking airline passengers on a flight how much their tickets cost. Under yield management, ticket prices can change every hour; therefore, price is a moving target and the ticketing process a lottery. At the extreme, is yield management fair and equitable to the public, or has every service price always been negotiable? Are customers only now becoming aware of their buying power?

Invasion of Privacy

The concept of micromarketing has the potential to create the most violent backlash from consumers because of the perceived invasion of privacy. When a record of your every purchase at the local supermarket is shared with eager manufacturers, very manipulative sales practices, such as targeting buyers of a competitor's soft drink with enticements to buy an alternative, could result. Lotus Development Corporation felt the sting of consumer displeasure after announcing the availability of its MarketPlace household database to anyone with a PC and modem. Lotus received more than 30,000 requests from irate persons wanting to be removed from this database. Lotus subsequently withdrew its offer of general availability, but it continues to sell access to the database to large corporations.[20]

Data Security

Allowing information to get into hands of others for inappropriate use is a significant problem for government agencies such as the IRS; however, releasing personal medical records to insurance firms or potential employers without the consent of the patient is far more common—and damaging. Some businesses market lists of people who have filed worker compensation claims or medical malpractice suits, and such databases can be used to blackball prospective employees or patients.

Reliability

Are the data accurate? Data kept on individuals can be corrupted and create havoc in people's lives. For example, a new law ameliorates such dilemmas by requiring credit-report agencies to allow individuals to review their credit records for accuracy.

Using Information to Categorize Customers[21]

Service firms have become sophisticated in the use of information to target those customers who are worth extra pampering because of heavy purchases while ignoring others who are only casual users. The following popular techniques are used to serve customers based on their profitability to the company:

- *Coding* grades customers based on how profitable their business is. Each account is given a code with instructions for service staff on how to handle each category.
- *Routing* is used by call centers to place customers in different queues based on a customer's code. Big spenders are whisked to high-level problem solvers. Others may never speak to a live person at all.
- *Targeting* allows choice customers to have fees waived and get other hidden discounts based on the value of their business. Less valuable customers may never even know the promotions exist.
- *Sharing* corporate data about your transaction history with other firms is a source of revenue. You can be slotted before you even walk in the door, because your buying potential has already been measured.

Stages in Service Firm Competitiveness[22]

If a service firm is to remain competitive, continuous improvement in productivity and quality must be part of its strategy and corporate culture. The framework shown in Table 3.5 was developed by Chase and Hayes to describe the role of operations in the strategic development of service firms. This framework also is useful as an illustration of the many sources of productivity and quality improvement (i.e., new technology is only one source). In addition, the framework provides a way to measure and evaluate a firm's progress in the development of its service delivery system. It organizes service firms into four different stages of development according to their competitiveness in service delivery, and for each stage, the management practices and attitudes of the firm are compared across key operational dimensions.

It should be noted that services need not start at stage 1, but during their life cycle, they could revert to stage 1 out of neglect. For example, one might argue that Federal Express began service as a stage 3 competitor because of its innovative hub-and-spoke network concept, whereby all sorting is accomplished at the single Memphis hub (thus guaranteeing overnight delivery).

Available for Service

Some service firms—and, often, government services in particular—fall into this category because they view operations as a necessary evil to be performed at minimum cost. There is little motivation to seek improvements in quality because the customers often have no alternatives. Workers require direct supervision because of their limited skills and the potential for poor performance that results from minimal investment in training. Investment in new technology is avoided until it is necessary for survival (e.g., consider

TABLE 3.5 **Four Stages of Service Firm Competitiveness**

Source: Reprinted from "Operations' Role in Service Firm Competitiveness," by R. B. Chase and R. H. Hayes, *Sloan Management Review* 33, no. 1 (Fall 1991), p. 17 by permission of publisher. Copyright 1991 by the Sloan Management Review Association. All rights reserved.

	1. Available for Service	2. Journeyman	3. Distinctive Competence Achieved	4. World-Class Service Delivery
Reputation	Customers patronize service firms for reasons other than performance.	Customers neither seek out nor avoid the firm.	Customers seek out the firm on the basis of its sustained reputation for meeting customer expectations.	The company's name is synonymous with service excellence. Its service doesn't just satisfy customers; it *delights* them and thereby expands customer expectations to levels its competitors are unable to fulfill.
Operations	Operations is reactive, at best.	Operations functions in a mediocre, uninspired fashion.	Operations continually excels, reinforced by personnel management and systems that support an intense customer focus.	Operations is a quick learner and fast innovator; it masters every step of the service delivery process and provides capabilities that are superior to competitors.
Service quality	Is subsidiary to cost, highly variable.	Meets some customer expectations; consistent on one or two key dimensions.	Exceeds customer expectations; consistent on multiple dimensions.	Raises customer expectations and seeks challenges; improves continuously.
Back office	Counting room.	Contributes to service, plays an important role in the total service, is given attention, but is still a separate role.	Is equally valued with front office; plays integral role.	Is proactive, develops its own capabilities, and generates opportunities.
Customer	Unspecified, to be satisfied at minimum cost.	A market segment whose basic needs are understood.	A collection of individuals whose variation in needs is understood.	A source of stimulation, ideas, and opportunities.
Introduction of new technology	When necessary for survival under duress.	When justified by cost savings.	When promises to enhance service.	Source of first-mover advantages, creating ability to do things your competitors can't do.
Workforce	Negative constraint.	Efficient resource; disciplined; follows procedures.	Permitted to select among alternative procedures.	Innovative; creates procedures.
First-line management	Controls workers.	Controls the process.	Listens to customers; coaches and facilitates workers.	Is listened to by top management as a source of new ideas. Mentors workers to enhance their career growth.

the long-overdue adoption of Doppler radar by the Federal Aviation Administration for air traffic control). These firms are essentially noncompetitive, and they exist in this stage only until they are challenged by competition.

Journeyman

After maintaining a sheltered existence in stage 1, a service firm may face competition and, thus, may be forced to reevaluate its delivery system. Operations managers then must adopt industry practices to maintain parity with new competitors and avoid a significant loss of market share. For example, if all successful airlines used the same kind of plane, then a fledgling airline just entering the market also might be inclined to use that same aircraft. The contribution of operations in this hypothetical situation becomes competitive-neutral, because all the firms in the industry have adopted similar practices and even look like each other (because they have purchased equipment from the same supplier).

When firms do not compete on operations effectiveness, they often are creative in competing along other dimensions (e.g., breadth of product line, peripheral services, advertising). The workforce is disciplined to follow standard procedures and is not expected to take any initiative when unusual circumstances arise. These firms have not yet recognized the potential contribution of operations to a firm's competitiveness.

Distinctive Competence Achieved

Firms in stage 3 are fortunate to have senior managers with a vision of what creates value for the customer and who understand the role that operations managers must play in delivering the service. For example, Jan Carlzon, CEO of Scandinavian Airlines (SAS), realized that recapturing the business-traveler market, which had been lost to aggressive competition, required improving on-time departure performance. To achieve this goal, he had to provide a leadership role that fostered operations innovations, which then would improve the delivery system.

Operations managers are the typical advocates of continuous improvement (Six Sigma) in their firms and take the lead in instituting service guarantees, worker empowerment, and service-enhancing technologies. Workers in these organizations often are cross-trained and encouraged to take the initiative when necessary to achieve operational goals that are stated clearly (e.g., overnight delivery for Federal Express). Firms in this category implement management strategies to achieve the corporate vision and, thereby, differentiate themselves from their competition.

World-Class Service Delivery

Not satisfied with just meeting customer expectations, world-class firms expand on these expectations to levels that competitors find difficult to meet. Management is proactive in promoting higher standards of performance and identifying new business opportunities by listening to customers. World-class service firms such as Disney, Marriott, and American Airlines define the quality standards by which others are judged.

New technology no longer is viewed only as a means to reduce costs; it is considered to be a competitive advantage that is not easily duplicated. For example, Federal Express developed COSMOS (*C*ustomer *O*perations *S*ervice *M*aster *O*n-line *S*ystem) to provide a system that tracks packages from pickup to delivery. Customers, using the Internet and the FedEx Web site, can receive information on the exact location of their packages. This system also can be used to tell a driver en route to make customer pickups.

Working at a world-class firm is considered to be something special, and employees are encouraged to identify with the firm and its mission. For example, a Disney trash collector is considered to be a "cast member" who helps visitors to enjoy the experience.

Sustaining superior performance throughout the delivery system is a major challenge. Duplicating the service at multiple sites, however, and in particular overseas, is the true test of a world-class competitor.

Service Benchmark

CENTRAL MARKET SHUNS CONVENTIONAL WISDOM AND BIG-NAME PRODUCTS

Central Market's opening in January 1994 prompted some friendly wagering among food-industry heavyweights who were left out in the cold.

The odds favored Frito-Lay's snacks appearing in the store, a specialty and fresh food supermarket, by the end of the summer. Other wagers bet that Coca-Cola and Budweiser trucks would pull up to the market's loading docks within six months. Now all bets are off.

Shunning big-name product lines is one reason why Central Market has caught the attention of the nation's $279.4 billion supermarket industry. The market—which within a year has become a flagship of the 225 Texas stores owned by parent-company H.E.B. Food Stores—has made it a practice to defy many of the standards that the country's 30,000 supermarkets embrace.

Although most supermarkets subscribe to the notion that customers want one-stop shopping, Central Market has proved that food alone sells well.

At Central Market, which carries virtually nothing except food, the average shopper spends $30 at the checkout counter, said Central Market general manager John Campbell. The national industry average, which also includes spending on general merchandise and health and beauty products, is $18.11, according to the Washington, D.C.–based Food Marketing Institute. The lower industry average results from shoppers who dash in for a few items, such as diapers or mascara, and then check out through the 10-items-or-fewer express lanes, Campbell said. "Here, they do serious shopping," he said.

Central Market also looks different from traditional stores. Its layout forces customers to walk through serpentine sections instead of straight aisles. It also houses a cooking school. There are 250 kinds of mustard, dozens of olive oils, and jams from all over the world on its shelves.

While at least half of the nation's 3.2 million supermarket workers are part-time employees, 90 percent of Central Market's 400 workers are full-time employees who receive health benefits, paid vacation time, tuition reimbursements, and profit-sharing. It's an expensive staffing decision that Campbell says pays off by generating greater enthusiasm and product knowledge among workers, two factors that he says are vital to building customer satisfaction.

At Central Market at least 20 percent of the store's sales come from its roomy produce section, which eats up almost a third of the store's 60,000 square feet of sales space. The section, kept at 65 degrees, stocks on any given day as many as 450 kinds of fruits and vegetables.

Seventy-five feet of refrigerator space display fresh fish, while the 68-foot meat counter sells more than 100 types of meat, game, and poultry. The cheese department offers 600 varieties.

In all, about two-thirds of the store's floor space is stocked with perishables. And each day, a truck from a local food bank comes by to take away the items that have failed Central Market's freshness guidelines.

Although the market risks losing money if too many of its meats and fruits aren't sold quickly, those items have higher profit margins than dry groceries. The margins for perishables are larger because those items are priced higher to make up for losses, refrigeration costs, and the increased labor expenses that result from product displays.

"The more sales you can move to perishable, the better, because the amount you can charge for Coke, Pepsi, or Tide is tight," said Kevin Coupe, executive editor of *Progressive Grocer* trade magazine in Stamford, Connecticut.

H.E.B. began discussing the Central Market concept in the mid-1980s when its market studies found that customers were increasingly interested in home cooking, nutrition, and better-tasting foods.

"With Central Market, we were trying to get ahead of what we see as a definite trend and one that we feel like will only continue to grow," Company spokesperson Kristy Ozmun said.

Source: Adapted from Diana Dworin, "Central Market Proves It Can Thrive Even as It Shuns Conventional Wisdom and Big-Name Products," © *Austin American Statesman*, October 2, 1994, p. H1.

Summary

We first looked at the strategic service vision and answered a number of questions before implementing the service. Our discussion then turned to the economic nature of competition in the service sector. The fragmented nature of service industries populated with many small- to medium-sized firms suggests a rich environment for the budding entrepreneur.

The three generic competitive strategies of overall cost leadership, differentiation, and focus were used to outline examples of creative service strategies. Because of the transferability of concepts among service firms, strategies that are successful in one industry may find application in firms seeking a competitive advantage in another service industry.

Next, we looked at several dimensions of service competition and examined the concepts of service winners, qualifiers, and losers as competitive criteria.

The strategic role of information in service strategies is organized into four categories: creation of barriers to entry, revenue generation, database asset, and productivity enhancement. Information-based competitive strategies were illustrated for each category.

The concept of a virtual value chain provides a view of service innovation that creates value by using information gathered while serving customers. The discussion of the limits in the use of information suggests that service managers always must be sensitive to the perceptions of their actions by the public they serve.

The chapter concluded with a discussion of the stages in a service firm's competitiveness based on operational dimensions.

Key Terms and Definitions

Data envelopment analysis a linear programming technique that measures the performance of service units to determine an efficiency frontier for internal benchmarking. *p. 50*

Differentiation a competitive strategy that creates a service that is perceived as being unique. *p. 42*

Expert system a computer program that can make inferences using a knowledge base and decision rules. *p. 48*

Five forces model analysis of an industry structure considers competitive rivalry, new entrants, substitutes, and bargaining power of suppliers and customers. *p. 38*

Focus a competitive strategy built around the concept of serving a particular target market very well by addressing the customers' specific needs. *p. 43*

Overall cost leadership a competitive strategy based on efficient operations, cost control, and innovative technology. *p. 41*

Qualifiers criteria used by a customer to create a subset of service firms meeting minimum performance requirements. *p. 46*

Service losers criteria representing failure to deliver a service at or above the expected level, resulting in a dissatisfied customer who is lost forever. *p. 46*

Service winners criteria used by a customer to make the final purchase decision among competitors that have been previously qualified. *p. 46*

Strategic service vision formulated by addressing questions about the target market, service concept, operating strategy, and delivery system. *p. 38*

Switching cost inconvenience cost for the customer to switch to another provider. *p. 47*

SWOT analysis assesses a firm's strengths, weaknesses, opportunities, and threats. *p. 44*

Virtual value chain stages in the customer relationship where information is gathered, organized, selected, synthesized, and distributed to create a virtual delivery platform. *p. 51*

Yield management an information system that attempts to maximize revenue for services with time-perishable capacity (e.g., airlines, hotels). *p. 48*

Interactive Exercise

The class divides and debates the proposition "Frequent flyer award programs are anticompetitive."

Topics for Discussion

1. Give examples of service firms that use both the strategy of focus and differentiation and the strategy of focus and overall cost leadership.

2. What ethical issues are associated with micromarketing?

3. For each of the three generic strategies (i.e., cost leadership, differentiation, and focus), which of the four competitive uses of information is most powerful?

4. Give an example of a firm that began as world-class and has remained in that category.

5. Could firms in the "world-class service delivery" stage of competitiveness be described as "learning organizations"?

Selected Bibliography

Evans, Philip, and Thomas Wurster. "Strategy and the New Economics of Information." *Harvard Business Review.* September–October 1997, pp. 71–82.

Heskett, James L.; W. Earl Sasser, Jr.; and Leonard A. Schlesinger. *The Service Profit Chain.* New York: Free Press, 1997.

Hill, Terry. *Manufacturing Strategy,* 3rd ed. New York: Irwin/McGraw-Hill, 2000.

Karmarkar, U. S., and R. Pitbladdo. "Service Markets and Competition." *Journal of Operations Management* 12, nos. 3–4 (June 1995), pp. 397–412.

Prokesch, Steven. "Competing on Customer Service." *Harvard Business Review,* November–December 1995, pp. 101–12.

Rayport, Jeffrey F., and John J. Sviokla. "Exploiting the Virtual Value Chain." *Harvard Business Review,* November–December 1995, pp. 78–85.

Roth, Aleda V., and Marjolijn van der Velde. "Operations as Marketing: A Competitive Service Strategy." *Journal of Operations Management* 10, no. 3 (August 1991), pp. 303–28.

Voss, Chris; Aleda V. Roth; and Richard B. Chase. "Experience, Service Operations Strategy, and Services as Destinations: Foundations and Exploratory Investigation" *Production and Operations Management* 17, no. 3 (May–June 2008), pp. 247–66.

Endnotes

1. From Bernie Ward, "Microspace, Maxiprofits," *Sky,* December 1990, pp. 22–31.
2. Adapted from James L. Heskett, "Positioning in Competitive Service Strategies," in *Managing in the Service Economy* (Boston: Harvard Business School Press, 1986).
3. Michael E. Porter, "Generic Competitive Strategies," in *Competitive Strategy* (New York: Free Press, 1980).
4. W. H. Davidow and B. Uttal, "Service Companies: Focus or Falter," *Harvard Business Review,* July–August 1989, pp. 77–85.
5. Michael E. Porter, *Competitive Advantage: Creating and Sustaining Superior Performance,* (New York: The Free Press, 1985).
6. Terry Hill, *Manufacturing Strategy,* (Homewood, Ill: Irwin 1989), pp. 36–46.
7. Adapted from James A. Fitzsimmons, "Strategic Role of Information in Services," in Rakesh V. Sarin (ed.), *Perspectives in Operations Management: Essays in Honor of Elwood S. Buffa* (Norwell, Mass; Kluwer Academic Publishers, 1993).
8. James L. Heskett, "Operating Strategy Barriers to Entry," in *Managing in the Service Economy* (Boston: Harvard Business School Press, 1986).
9. For specific allegations, see "Frontier Airlines, Inc. (A)," Harvard Business School Case no. 9-184-041, HBS Case Services, 1983.
10. R. L. Rose and J. Dahl, "Skies Are Deregulated, but Just Try Starting a Sizable New Airline," *The Wall Street Journal,* July 19, 1989, p. A1.
11. Ibid., p. A8.
12. From Harold S. Bott, "Information for Competitive Advantage," *Operations Management Review,* Fall 1985, p. 35.
13. Barry C. Smith, J. F. Leimkuhler, and R. M. Darrow, "Yield Management at American Airlines," *Interfaces* 22, no. 1 (January–February 1992), pp. 8–31.
14. From Kevin Helliker, "Wal-Mart's Store of the Future Blends Discount Prices, Department-Store Feel," *The Wall Street Journal,* May 17, 1991, p. B1.

64   Part One *Understanding Services*

15. Heskett, op. cit., p. 43.

16. Michael J. McCarthy, "Marketers Zero in on Their Customers," *The Wall Street Journal,* March 18, 1991, p. B1.

17. Peter H. Lewis, "Looking beyond Innovation, an Award for Results," *New York Times,* June 23, 1991, p. 8.

18. R. D. Banker and R. C. Morey, "Efficiency Analysis for Exogenously Fixed Inputs and Outputs," *Operations Research* 34, no. 4 (July–August 1986), pp. 518–19.

19. Adapted from Jeffrey F. Rayport and John J. Sviokla, "Exploiting the Virtual Value Chain," *Harvard Business Review,* November–December 1995, pp. 75–85.

20. "How Did They Get My Name?" *Newsweek,* June 3, 1991, p. 41.

21. Adapted from Diane Brady, "Why Service Stinks," *BusinessWeek,* October 23, 2000, p. 124.

22. Adapted from R. B. Chase and R. H. Hayes, "Operations' Role in Service Firm Competitiveness," *Sloan Management Review* 33, no. 1 (Fall 1991), pp. 15–26.

23. Prepared by Bryan R. Bradford, Will Reale, Brian Barrow, Jason Dillee, and Chris McClung under the supervision of Professor James A. Fitzsimmons

24. Prepared by Robert Ferrell, Greg Miller, Neil Orman, and Trent Reynolds under the supervision of Professor James A. Fitzsimmons.

Chapter

7

Supporting Facility and Process Flows

Learning Objectives

After completing this chapter, you should be able to:

1. Describe the impact of the "servicescape" on the behavior of customers and employees.
2. Identify and discuss the three environmental dimensions of servicescapes.
3. Identify the six critical design features of a service supporting facility.
4. Draw a swim lane flowchart, process flow diagram, and a Gantt chart of a service process.
5. Calculate performance metrics such as throughput time and direct labor utilization.
6. Identify the bottleneck operation in a product layout, and regroup activities to create new jobs that will increase the overall service capacity.
7. Use operations sequence analysis to determine the relative locations of departments in a process layout that minimize total flow-distance.

Subtle differences in facility design are important. Consider the rivalry between the home improvement stores, Home Depot and Lowe's. Home Depot, the senior citizen of the pair, conveys a "roll up your sleeves and let's get at it" message . . . the aisles are narrow and lined with ceiling-high stores of merchandise, lighting is industrial, and lines at the checkout counters usually are long. The newcomer, Lowe's, began by copying its rival, but since then it has taken a different approach. A shopper at today's Lowe's finds wide aisles, bright lighting, and merchandise that is displayed in a way that encourages browsing and inspires many project ideas. Lowe's strategy appears to be working because its recent revenue growth of 18.1 percent has surpassed Home Depot's 11.3 percent growth.[1]

Lowe's has successfully used facility design to differentiate itself from its competitors. Using facility design as part of a differentiation strategy is very common. For example, the A-frame structure and blue roof of IHOP (International House of Pancakes) attract travelers to a pancake breakfast just as the "golden arches" of McDonald's signal a hamburger lunch.

Using a standard, or "formula," facility design is an important feature in the overall cost leadership strategy. Major gasoline retailers have perfected the design of their service stations to facilitate construction (often completed within two weeks) and lower costs, and to create a consistent image awareness that will attract customers.

For theme restaurants and bars (e.g., a western bar, an Irish pub), facility design is central to the focus strategy of targeting a particular market and creating a unique ambiance. In retail banking, however, tradition still reigns, except for an innovative bank with headquarters in Columbus, Ohio, called Banc One. Banc One has designed branches that look more like mini-shopping malls than banks, with glass atriums, "boutiques" offering special services, signs of blue neon, comfortable seating areas, and fresh coffee. With its community focus, Banc One even has branches that are open on Saturdays and Sundays.[2]

Chapter Preview

The chapter begins with the topic of environmental psychology as applied to facility design and layout to avoid customer disorientation and frustration upon entering an unfamiliar structure. The concept of servicescapes is based on the idea that the physical environment influences the behavior and perception of the service for both customers and workers. Facility design issues are addressed with respect to objectives of the service, its space requirements, flexibility, aesthetic factors, and the environment. Facility layout is discussed with attention to traffic flow, space planning, and the need to avoid unnecessary travel. The concept of process flow analysis used by industrial engineers is modified for service operations and illustrated by a mortgage service in which all the process analysis terms are evaluated.

The traditional product and process layouts from manufacturing are shown to have service counterparts and can be studied using the techniques of assembly-line balancing and relative location analysis.

Environmental Psychology and Orientation

Orientation is the first behavioral need of an individual on entering a place. It includes questions of place orientation (e.g., "Where am I?") as well as of function orientation (e.g., "How does this organization work, and what do I do next?"). On entering a physical setting, customers gain control when they can use spatial cues, along with previous experience, to identify where they are, where they should go, and what they need to do. Anxiety and a sense of helplessness can result if spatial cues are not present or previous experience cannot be used to avoid disorientation. Richard E. Wener argues that the causes of disorientation in service settings can be reduced by a facility design that incorporates the following: previous experience, design legibility, and orientation aids.[3]

Using formula facilities, franchised services have effectively removed the anxiety of disorientation so that customers know exactly what to do. Holiday Inn took this concept a step further by advertising that a guest will find no surprises at any of its locations, capitalizing on the need for familiarity to attract repeat customers.

Orientation also can be aided by facility designs that allow customers to see both into and through the space. Layouts for banks and hotels often use an entrance atrium that allows the entire space to be viewed and conceptualized at a glance. In addition, such a layout allows customers to observe the actions of others for behavioral cues.

Orientation aids and signage such as "You Are Here" maps, if properly aligned with the user's perspective (i.e., "up" on the sign equates to straight ahead for the user) and complete with environmental landmarks, can be effective as well. Strategically located plants and artwork can act as points of reference. Color-coded subway routes with corresponding color-coded connecting arrows represent an excellent use of signage to assist visitors and to promote smooth flow of traffic.

Servicescapes[4]

The physical environment or *servicescape* of the supporting service facility influences both customer and employee behavior and should be designed with an image and feel that is congruent with the service concept. A typology of servicescapes shown in Figure 7.1 is organized according to who participates within the service environment and the degree of complexity of the servicescape.

Because of the absence of employees, the servicescape for a self-service operation plays a central role in guiding customer behavior through the use of signage (e.g., direction to the next golf tee) and intuitive design of interfaces (e.g., hot buttons on a Web site). For remote services, employee satisfaction, motivation, and operational efficiency are the primary

FIGURE 7.1

Typology of Servicescapes

Source: Adapted from Mary Jo Bitner, "Servicescapes: The Impact of Physical Surroundings on Customers and Employees," *Journal of Marketing* 56, April 1992, p. 59.

Who Performs within Servicescape	Physical Complexity of the Servicescape	
	Elaborate	Lean
Self-service (customer only)	Golf course Water slide park	Post office kiosk ATM E-commerce Web site
Interpersonal services (both customer and employee)	Luxury hotel Restaurant Disneyland Airline terminal	Budget motel Hot dog stand Roadside snake farm Bus station
Remote service (employee only)	Professional services L. L. Bean	Telemarketing Online technical support

physical design objectives because customers do not visit the site physically. Offices of professional services such as those of lawyers and physicians, however, should project competence and authority. Interpersonal services are the most challenging because social interaction between employees and customers and among customers should be facilitated by the servicescape. For example, the servicescape at Disneyland is famous for creating a fantasy experience for customers and a stage for employees (i.e., cast members).

Consider the photographs of two restaurant servicescapes below. Note how the table settings, furniture, room decor, and even customer attire communicate distinct expectations for customers and employees alike.

Behaviors in Servicescapes

An organization's service facility reflects its values and is instrumental in executing its strategy. Without words, a building communicates a message to both its customers and employees. For example, the building may communicate modernity and progressiveness or other features such as pleasantness, safety, and convenience. Obviously facility design should support the goals of the institution and be deliberate because this is the place where service is delivered.

As shown in Figure 7.2, a mix of environmental dimensions consisting of ambient conditions, space/function, and signs/symbols/artifacts describes the servicescape, which is viewed as a holistic environment by customers and employees.

Restaurants use their servicescapes to create desired expectations and behaviors for employees and customers.
BananaStock/PunchStock; Steve Mason/Getty Images

156 Part Two *Designing the Service Enterprise*

FIGURE 7.2 Servicescape Framework

Source: Adapted from Mary Jo Bitner, "Servicescapes: The Impact of Physical Surroundings on Customers and Employees," *Journal of Marketing,* 56, April 1992, p. 60.

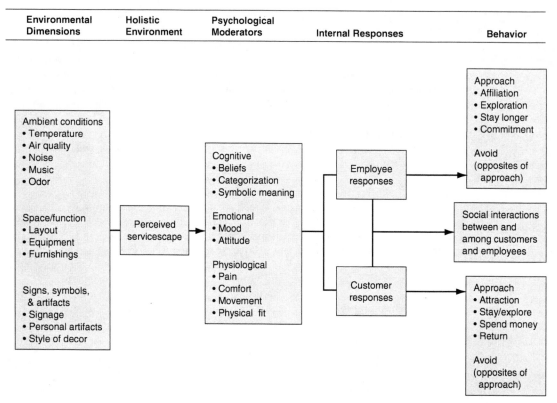

The employee or customer internal response to the servicescape is either approach or avoidance behavior. For example, arousal-seekers enjoy and look for high levels of stimulation (e.g., a bright and loud disco), whereas arousal-avoiders prefer lower levels of stimulation (e.g., a quiet museum). The internal response is modified by personal attributes (e.g., prior experience) and psychological dimensions which are cognitive (e.g., reassurance of signage), emotional (e.g., calming effect of music), and physiological (e.g., discomfort of poor lighting). The servicescape is designed to invoke social interaction between and among customers and employees.

A well-conceived servicescape will encourage an approach behavior for both employees (e.g., commitment and desire to remain with the firm) and customers (e.g., exploration, spending money, and returning).

Because the physical environment elicits an emotional response and influences behavior, the design of the service facility can intentionally mold the behavior of the participants to support the organization's goals. Thus, unpleasant environments that are also high in arousal (lots of stimulation, noise, confusion) are to be avoided.

Environmental Dimensions of Servicescapes

The dimensions of the physical environment surroundings include all the objective factors that can be controlled by the firm to enhance employee and customer actions and perceptions of the service. Although these dimensions will be discussed independently, it is important to realize that people respond to their environment holistically; that is, the total combined effect on all our senses defines our perception of the servicescape.

Ambient Conditions

The background of our environment, such as temperature, lighting, noise, music, and scent, affects all five of our senses. Music tempo, for example, can affect a customer's pace of shopping, length of stay, and amount of money spent. Consider a convenience store that played "elevator music" successfully to drive away teenagers who were loitering and discouraging paying customers from entering the store. A cookie shop in a busy mall can leave its doors open to invite customers with the fragrance of freshly baked cookies. All of these factors, including color of surroundings, also influence employee performance and job satisfaction.

Spatial Layout and Functionality

The arrangement of furnishings and equipment and the relationships among them create a visual and functional landscape for delivery of the service. This landscape can communicate order and efficiency (e.g., formal garden) or chaos and uncertainty for both employees and customers. For self-service activities, the functionality or ease of use of equipment is important to allow customers to perform unattended activities. Fast-food restaurants purposely design the facility to communicate visually the appropriate activities of diners. Menus are posted over the cash registers, self-serve drink machines are positioned between the counter and the tables, and waste containers are located near exits.

Signs, Symbols, and Artifacts

Many items in the physical environment serve as explicit or implicit signals that communicate acceptable norms of behavior. Explicit signs such as "no smoking" communicate rules of behavior, whereas "recycle bins" encourage responsible acts. The quality of the floor covering, artwork, and furnishings can create an overall aesthetic impression for the visitor and a pleasant workplace for the employee. Professional services can use interior decorating to communicate competence and enhance their professional image with the client. Restaurants communicate full service and high prices with signs such as pictures of famous diners, symbols such as tablecloths, and artifacts such as antiques or pottery. Studies of faculty offices indicate that desk placement, selection of wall pictures or posters, and tidiness of the office influence students' beliefs about the person who occupies the office.

Our discussion of servicescapes suggests that the physical environment may assume a variety of strategic roles in support of the service concept. First, the servicescape provides a visual metaphor for an organization's offering. The environmental dimensions of the servicescape create a package, similar to the packaging of a product that conveys an image suggesting relative quality, potential usage, and target market segment. For example, return to the earlier comparison of Home Depot and Lowe's. A visit to Home Depot with its orange colors, bare floors, industrial lighting, and generally cluttered look conveys a masculine image of the construction industry. However, Lowe's with soft blues, tidy aisles, and attractively displayed merchandise projects a more female friendly image for the home improvement customer.

Second, the servicescape can facilitate the delivery of the service by either aiding or hindering the ability of customers and employees to carry out their respective activities. In a physical setting, the floorplan, signage, and equipment (e.g., self-scanning checkout) impact the user friendliness of the facility and the ability to service customers effectively. In the virtual world, for example, consider how the servicescape (i.e., layout, use of color, functionality) of a good Web site facilitates the screen-to-face interaction and creates a rewarding experience.

AIGA, the professional association for design, together with the U.S. Department of Transportation has produced a set of passenger/pedestrian symbols designed and used internationally at the crossroads of modern life (i.e., airports, train stations, Olympic Games). The complete set of 50 symbols can be found at: http://www.aiga.org/content.cfm/symbol-signs.

Third, the servicescape can also encourage social interaction among customers. For example, the layout of a waiting room that has chairs grouped together around tables encourages social interaction and makes time pass more pleasantly.

Finally, the physical environment can serve as a subtle method to focus employee behavior. The design of the Mid-Columbia Medical Center in Columbia River, Oregon, for example, gave much attention to the employee entrance. A special employee-only entrance was designed as an atrium that could grace a five star hotel. Employees were greeted with a breakfast buffet in an environment of overstuffed chairs, potted plants, paintings, and inspiring music. The design was a deliberate attempt to foster a good mood for the day's work and encourage employees to leave personal cares and troubles at the door.

Facility Design

Service operations can be directly affected by the design of the facility. For example, a restaurant with inadequate ventilation for nonsmoking diners may discourage many customers. Alternatively, a physical fitness center with easy wheelchair access may be able to enlarge its services to include a new clientele.

Design and layout represent the supporting facility component of the *service package*. Together, they influence how a service facility is used and, sometimes, if it is even used at all. Consider again Toronto's Shouldice Hospital (discussed in Chapter 3). A good portion of its success in repairing inguinal hernias results from thoughtful facility design and layout. For example, operating rooms are grouped together so that surgeons may consult with each other easily during procedures. Because early ambulation promotes faster healing, the hospital is designed to provide ample pleasant places to walk—and even to climb a few steps. Meals are served only in community dining rooms rather than in patient rooms, which requires more walking and, as an added benefit, allows patients to get together and "compare notes." While functional and comfortable, patient rooms are not equipped with "extras" such as television sets, which might encourage patients to "lie around."

Other factors of design and layout can be "urgent." Consider the generally inadequate supply of rest-room facilities for women in most public buildings, especially during mass entertainment events. During intermission at your next concert or play, observe how long it takes individual females and males to use the rest rooms. Do you see any evidence of "potty parity" being designed into the building? In addition, count the number of rest rooms for men and the number for women in your classroom building. Chances are that equal numbers exist for each gender, but this does not necessarily ensure equality of access.

Clearly, good design and layout enhance the service, from attracting customers to making them feel more comfortable to ensuring their safety (e.g., adequate lighting, fire exits, proper location of dangerous equipment). Facility design also has an impact on the implicit service component of the service package—in particular, on criteria like privacy and security, atmosphere, and sense of well-being.

Several factors influence design: (1) the nature and objectives of the service organization, (2) land availability and space requirements, (3) flexibility, (4) security, (5) aesthetic factors, and (6) the community and environment.

Nature and Objectives of Service Organizations

The nature of the core service should dictate the parameters of its design. For example, a fire station must have a structure that is large enough to house its vehicles, on-duty personnel, and maintenance equipment. A bank must be designed to accommodate some type of vault. Physicians' offices come in many shapes and sizes, but all must be designed to afford patients some degree of privacy.

Beyond such fundamental requirements, however, design can contribute much more to defining the service. It can engender immediate recognition, as in the case of McDonald's arches or IHOP's blue roof. External design also can provide a clue about the nature of the service inside. One would expect to see well-manicured grounds, freshly painted or marble columns, and perhaps a fountain in front of a funeral home. A school, however, might have colorful tiles on its facade and certainly a playground or athletic field nearby.

Appropriateness of design is important as well. A gasoline service station can be constructed of brightly colored, prefabricated sheet metal; however, would you deposit money in a bank that was using a trailer on wheels for a temporary branch?

Land Availability and Space Requirements

The land that is available for a service facility often comes with many constraints, such as costs, zoning requirements, and actual area. Good design must accommodate all these constraints. In an urban setting, where land is at a premium, buildings only can be expanded upward, and organizations often must exhibit great creativity and ingenuity in their designs to use a relatively small space efficiently. For example, in some urban areas (e.g., in Copenhagen), McDonald's has incorporated a second-floor loft to provide eating space.

Suburban and rural areas frequently offer larger, more affordable parcels of land that ameliorate the space constraints of urban facilities. Many sites, however, and especially urban ones, may have strict zoning laws on land usage and ordinances governing the exterior appearance of structures. Space for off-street parking also is a requirement. In any event, space for future expansion always should be considered.

Flexibility

Successful services are dynamic organizations that can adapt to changes in the quantity and nature of demand. How well a service can adapt depends greatly on the flexibility that has been designed into it. Flexibility also might be called "designing for the future." Questions to address during the design phase might be: how can this facility be designed to allow for later expansion of present services, and how can we design this facility to accommodate new and different services in the future? For example, many of the original fast-food restaurants built for walk-in traffic have had to modify their facilities to accommodate customer demands for drive-through window service.

Several airports face facility problems today because designers failed to anticipate either the tremendous growth in the numbers of people flying or the advent of the hub-and-spoke airline network following deregulation. Consequently, passengers often must tote carry-on luggage through a maze of stairways and long passageways to reach the departure gate of their connecting flights. In addition, consider the frustration facing passengers trying to retrieve checked luggage from a baggage-handling operation that was designed for circa 1960s air travelers!

Designing for the future often can translate into financial savings. For example, consider a church that locates in a developing community but does not have the resources to build the sanctuary it would like plus the necessary ancillary facilities it will need. Good design might lead the congregation to build a modest structure that can be used as a temporary sanctuary but later adapted easily and economically to serve as a fellowship hall, a Sunday school, and even a day care facility to meet the needs of a growing community.

In other instances, designing for the future may require additional expenses initially, but it will save financial resources in the long run. In fact, it may provide for growth that might not be possible otherwise. For example, cities often invest in oversized water and wastewater treatment plants in anticipation of future growth.

Security

Anyone who has flown on a commercial airliner since the terrorist attack against the United States on September 11, 2001, has observed modifications in airports. Some of the security technology is obvious to the traveler (e.g., more sophisticated carry-on luggage x-ray scanners, "wipes" or tissues that can detect residue of drugs or explosives on the surfaces of bags, and hand-held magnetic detectors). Other airport security measures are less visible to travelers. Information technology plays a part in providing profiles of potential terrorists, although the use of profiling is problematical. By government mandate, all checked luggage in U.S. airports is screened, either by workers or by some type of automatic scanner. Some airlines are making use of "smart facilities" that recognize magnetic ID cards to control entrance or, recently, scans of eyes to establish identity.

Security in facilities can be enhanced by installing surveillance cameras. Banks and convenience stores, for example, use cameras to discourage would-be robbers or to identify those who aren't discouraged. "Granny cams" allow families to monitor the care that is given to a patient in a nursing home, and "nanny cams" allow parents to see the care their child receives from a babysitter in the home.

Another example of a security system for a facility can be seen at something as ordinary as a neighborhood pool. A high fence surrounds the pool and safety equipment such as a ring buoy and shepherd's hook is readily available at positions around the pool. Other examples of facilities adapted for security are jails and level-four labs, both of which have many levels of modifications to ensure that "bad things" don't get out.

Slightly less obtrusive security measures can be seen at many retail stores. Consider the row of concrete posts or "bollards" outside the entrance to some stores and the scanners and tags affixed to clothing items to discourage shoplifting. Consider, also, that "window shopping" might become a nostalgic pastime as more stores do away with big windows that invite burglaries. Imagine Macy's Department Store without holiday windows because our need for security has exploded.

Aesthetic Factors

Compare two shopping trips to successful, upscale clothing stores. First, we go to an upscale department store such as Nordstrom's. As we enter the women's fine dresses department, we are aware of the carpeting beneath our feet, the ample space between clothing racks, the lack of crowding of dresses on the racks, the complimentary lighting, and most certainly, the very well-groomed salesperson who is ready to serve us immediately. Fitting rooms are located in an area separate from the display area, are roomy and carpeted, and have mirrors on three sides so that you can appreciate every aspect of your appearance. Everything in the department is designed to give a sense of elegance and attention to our needs.

Our second trip takes us to an Eddie Bauer Factory Outlet store. Within just a few steps of the entrance, we are confronted by tables piled high with a vast assortment of clothing. Along the walls and among the tables are racks packed as full as possible with more clothing. Only a maze of narrow pathways is visible around the floor. Salespersons are stationed at cash-register counters and are available to help when you seek them out. Fitting rooms are small "stalls" on the showroom floor and are equipped with only one mirror. (It helps to shop here with a companion, who can give you the advantage of "hindsight.") This is a large warehouse type of store rather than a modest-sized, serene, elegant place to shop; however, the outlet store offers great bargains in exchange for sacrificing plushness and lots of personal attention.

Both stores offer attractive, quality clothing. We feel very different in each one, however, and their respective designs have played an important part in shaping our attitudes. Clearly, the aesthetic aspects of a design have a marked effect on the consumer's perceptions and behaviors, but they also affect the employees and the service they provide. Lack of attention to aesthetic factors during the design phase can lead to surly service rather than to "service with a smile."

The Community and Environment

The design of a service facility may be of greatest importance where it affects the community and its environment. Will the planned church allow enough space for parking, or will neighbors find it impossible to enter or exit their properties during church activities? Can Priscilla Price design a boarding kennel facility that will not "hound" neighboring businesses with undue noise and odor? How can a community design a detention facility that will provide adequately for the inmates' health and welfare yet still ensure the safety of the town's residents? Has the local dry cleaner designed his or her facility to keep hazardous chemicals out of the local environment?

These questions illustrate how crucial facility design can be in gaining community acceptance of a service. Zoning regulations and many public interest groups also can provide guidance in designing service facilities that are compatible with their communities and environment.

Process Analysis

Types of Processes

Students of manufacturing long ago found it useful to categorize processes in order to derive general management principles that would apply across industries sharing the same process. For example, all manufacturing assembly operations be they automobiles or personal computers share characteristics of a "flow" process. Using the traditional manufacturing process types listed in Table 7.1, we show that services also can be categorized by process to identify management challenges. For example, any service that has a "batch" process shares the challenge of managing a perishable asset such as a seat on an airplane, a hotel room, or a cabin on a cruise ship. After identifying the type of process, we then diagram the process as the first step in process analysis.

Flowcharting

The ability to diagram a process, identify the bottleneck operation, and determine the system capacity are fundamental skills in managing service operations and making improvements. An acknowledged axiom is, "If you can't draw it, then you don't really understand it."

Our discussion begins with Figure 7.3, an example of a swim lane flowchart of a typical graduate school admissions process. Swim lane flowcharts diagram organizational activities that cross functional lines (i.e. the swim lanes) highlighting the handoffs between lanes. The hardest task in developing a flowchart is getting everyone to agree on what the process looks like. However, the final diagram is useful for training, helping to coordinate activities between functions, and facilitating creative ideas for improvement. For example, from an applicant's viewpoint, how could the process be improved? Perhaps an online inquiry system would allow the applicant to follow the process and thus reduce the need for the admissions clerk to "contact applicant" when a folder is incomplete.

The standard symbols used in flowcharting are illustrated in Figure 7.3.

Terminator: An *ellipse* represents a start or stop in a process.

Operation: A *rectangle* represents a process or action step.

Decision: A *diamond* represents a question or branch.

Wait: A *triangle* represents a delay or inventory of goods.

Flow: An *arrow* shows movement of customers, goods, or information.

TABLE 7.1   **Service Process Types with Management Challenges**

Process Type	Service Example	Characteristic	Management Challenge
Project	Consulting	One-of-a-kind engagement	Staffing and scheduling
Job Shop	Hospital	Many specialized departments	Balancing utilization and scheduling patients
Batch	Airline	Group of customers treated simultaneously	Pricing of perishable asset (seat inventory)
Flow	Cafeteria	Fixed sequence of operations	Adjust staffing to demand fluctuations
Continuous	Electric Utility	Uninterrupted delivery	Maintenance and capacity planning

FIGURE 7.3   Swim Lane Flowchart of Graduate School Admissions

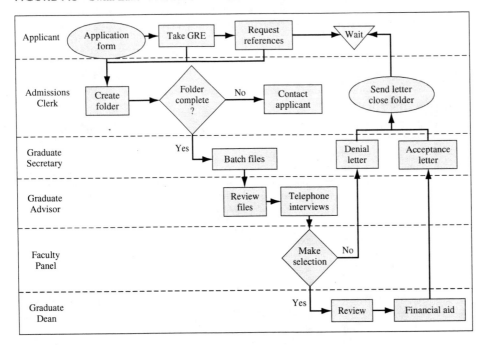

Example 7.1 illustrates a simplified process flow for a mortgage service.

**Example 7.1
Mortgage Service**

The purchase of real estate usually involves taking out a loan or "mortgage" on the property. The lending institution requires an accurate description of the property and proof that the title is clear of any outstanding liens. Furthermore, the creditworthiness of the buyer must be determined. Many independent mortgage service firms offer these services.

Figure 7.4 shows a simplified process flow diagram of the mortgage application process. Because we intend to use this example to illustrate process terminology such as the bottleneck operation and throughput time, we include the cycle time (CT) of each activity (i.e., the average time in minutes to perform the activity) in the diagram.

Gantt Chart

An activity-based schedule of the mortgage service process provides another visual representation for understanding and analysis. In Figure 7.5, we follow the progress of three

FIGURE 7.4   Process Flow Diagram of Mortgage Service

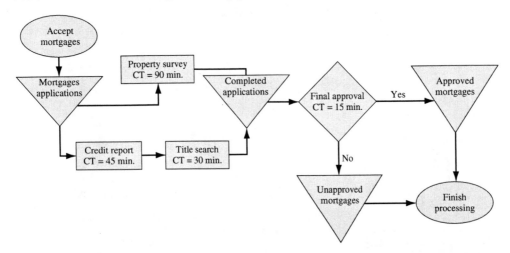

applications through time. We see that "property survey" is an unusual activity because application 1 is immediately followed by application 2 and then by application 3 in unbroken procession. Because the "property survey" activity is never idle it is referred to as the *bottleneck* (an activity that constrains output) and its CT of 90 minutes defines the system output of one mortgage application completed every 90 minutes. Also, it can be observed that "credit report" and "title search" could be combined into one activity taking a total time of 75 minutes (45 min. + 30 min.) at no loss of system productivity because together these activities still have 15 minutes of idle time per each 90 minute cycle. The Gantt chart has many uses and will be seen again in Chapter 15, Managing Service Projects.

Process Terminology

The following process-analysis terms are defined and illustrated using our mortgage service process example, assuming one worker is assigned to each operation and an unlimited supply of mortgage applications.

Cycle Time

Cycle time (CT) is the average time between completions of successive units. For an operation, CT is the average service time to perform the activity. In our example, securing a Credit Report requires 45 minutes on average. Cycle time, however, could also apply to a *work area* in which several servers are performing the same operation. For example, if two surveyors were employed, the CT for Property Survey *work area* would be 90/2 = 45 minutes. Finally the entire system has a cycle time defined as the time between successive customers exiting during a busy period. Before the system cycle time can be determined, however, the bottleneck must be identified.

Bottleneck

A **bottleneck** is the factor that limits production. Usually the bottleneck is the slowest operation (or longest CT), which is the Property Survey with a CT = 90 minutes in our example. Just as the neck of a bottle constricts the flow of liquid, a process bottleneck sets a ceiling on how quickly units can move through the process, and thus determines the CT of the entire system. The bottleneck is a constraint on the output of the system and could arise from several sources in addition to the slowest operation such as labor availability, information, and, most importantly for services, the rate of customer arrivals. Queues or wait areas are intentionally positioned *before* a bottleneck to protect the operation from starvation and thus compromise its output. Keep in mind that an hour lost at the

FIGURE 7.5 **Gantt Chart of Mortgage Service**

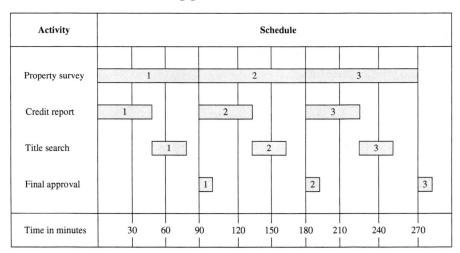

Activity	Schedule								
Property survey		1			2			3	
Credit report	1			2			3		
Title search		1			2			3	
Final approval			1			2			3
Time in minutes	30	60	90	120	150	180	210	240	270

bottleneck is an hour lost in system output. The role of the bottleneck in understanding processes is the central theme of *The Goal*, a novel by Eli Goldratt that is a "must read" for aspiring operations managers.

Capacity

Capacity is a measure of output per unit of time when *fully busy* (e.g., activity is never idle). The unconstrained capacity of any operation is measured as 1/CT. For example, the capacity of the Title Search activity is 2 applications per hour because each application takes 30 minutes to process. The capacity of the entire system is determined by the *bottleneck* capacity. Property Survey is the bottleneck in the mortgage process with the longest CT = 90 minutes. Thus, the system capacity is (60 minutes/hour)(1/90 minutes) = 2/3 applications per hour or 5.33 applications per 8-hour day.

Capacity Utilization

Capacity utilization is a measure of how much output is actually achieved relative to the process capacity when fully busy. If, for a given day, we process 5 mortgages, then the capacity utilization on that day is 5/5.33 = 93.75 percent. Because of the variability in customer arrivals and service times, we will find in Chapter 12, Managing Waiting Lines, that it is impossible to achieve 100 percent capacity utilization for service firms. Be aware that for nonbottleneck operations, striving for full capacity utilization only results in unnecessary work-in-process and not more system output. Capacity utilization, particularly of individual operations, is a *dangerous* management performance metric and should be used only with great caution.

Throughput Time

Throughput time is the time it takes to complete a process from time of arrival to time of exit. Throughput time is the sum of the *critical path* operation times plus the average time spent in all queues. The critical path is defined in Chapter 15, Managing Service Projects, as the longest time path from beginning to end of a process flow diagram. For our mortgage example the critical path begins and ends with the terminator symbols Accept Mortgages and Finish Processing and includes only the Property Survey and Final Approval activities.

$$\begin{aligned} \text{Throughput time} \; = \; & \text{Average time in Mortgage Applications Queue} \\ & + \text{Property Survey (90 min.)} \\ & + \text{Average time in Completed Applications Queue} \\ & + \text{Final Approval (15 min.).} \end{aligned}$$

Note that the operations of Credit Report and Title Search together sum to 75 minutes and thus are not on the critical path that includes the bottleneck operation, Property Survey. The average time in the queues can be estimated using queuing formulas found in Appendix D or by computer simulation, but in any event, are very dependent on the rate of arrivals of mortgage applications.

Rush Order Flow Time

Rush order flow time is the time it takes to go through the system from beginning to end without any time in queue. In our example the rush order flow time following the critical path is 105 minutes, the sum of Property Survey (90 min.) plus Final Approval (15 min.).

Total Direct Labor Content

Total direct labor content is the sum of all the operations times (i.e., touch time) consumed in performing the service. In professional services this often is referred to as "billable" hours. Indirect labor hours and overhead (e.g., maintenance and management) are not included in the calculation. For the mortgage example the total direct labor content is 90 + 45 + 30 + 15 = 180 minutes.

Direct Labor Utilization

Direct labor utilization is a measure of the percentage of time that workers actually contribute value to a fully busy service organization. Direct labor utilization for the mortgage service process is calculated as:

$$\text{Direct labor utilization} = \frac{\text{Total direct labor content}}{(\text{Process cycle time})(\text{Number of workers})}$$

$$= \frac{180}{(90)(4)} = 50 \text{ percent}$$

Facility Layout

In addition to facility design, the layout, or arrangement, of the service delivery system is important for the convenience of the customer as well as the service provider. No customer should be subjected to unnecessary aggravation from a poorly planned facility. Further, a poor layout can be costly in time that is wasted when service workers are engaged in unproductive activity.

Product Layout and the Work Allocation Problem

Some standard services can be divided into an inflexible sequence of steps or operations that all customers must experience. This is an example of a *product layout* most often associated with manufacturing assembly lines, where a product is assembled in a fixed sequence of steps. The most obvious analogy is to a cafeteria, where diners push their trays along as they assemble their meal. Staffing such a service requires allocating tasks among servers to create jobs that require nearly equal time. The job requiring the most time per customer creates a *bottleneck* and defines the capacity of the service line. Any change in the capacity of the service line requires that attention be given to the bottleneck activity. Several options are available: adding another worker to the job, providing some aid to reduce the activity time, or regrouping the tasks to create a new line balance with different activity assignments. A well-balanced line would have all jobs be of nearly equal duration to avoid unnecessary idleness and inequity in work assignments. A service-line approach has the additional advantage of allowing for division of labor and use of dedicated special equipment, as illustrated by Example 7.2.

Example 7.2
Automobile
Driver's License
Office

The state automobile driver's license office is under pressure to increase its productivity to accommodate 120 applicants per hour with the addition of only one clerk to its present staff. The license renewal process currently is designed as a service line, with customers being processed in the fixed sequence listed in Table 7.2. Activity 1 (i.e., review application for correctness) must be performed first, and activity 6 (i.e., issue temporary license) must be the last step and, by state policy, be handled by a uniformed officer. Activity 5 (i.e., photograph applicant) requires an expensive digital camera and color printer.

The process flow diagram for the current arrangement, as shown in Figure 7.6a, identifies the bottleneck activity (i.e., the activity with the slowest flow rate per hour) as activity 3 (i.e., check for violations and restrictions), which limits the current capacity to 60 applicants per hour. By focusing only on the bottleneck, one might think that assigning an additional

TABLE 7.2
License Renewal Process Times

Activity	Description	Cycle Time, Sec.
1	Review application for correctness	15
2	Process and record payment	30
3	Check for violations and restrictions	60
4	Conduct eye test	40
5	Photograph applicant	20
6	Issue temporary license (state trooper)	30

FIGURE 7.6
(*a*) **Present and** (*b*)
Proposed Process Flow
Diagrams

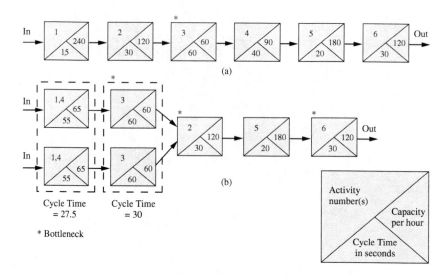

(a)

(b)

Cycle Time = 27.5   Cycle Time = 30

* Bottleneck

Activity number(s) / Capacity per hour / Cycle Time in seconds

clerk to perform activity 3 would double the flow through the bottleneck and achieve the goal of 120 applicants per hour. However, the flow for this system would be limited to 90 applicants per hour, because the bottleneck would shift to activity 4.

The proposed process design, as shown in Figure 7.6*b* with seven clerks, can achieve the desired capacity of 120 applicants per hour, because activities 1 and 4 have been grouped together to create a new job (i.e., review applications for correctness and conduct eye test) that better balances the work load among the staff. How did we know to group these two activities together? First, remember that a flow rate of at least 120 applicants per hour must be achieved at each step in the process. Because activities 2 and 6 already are being performed at this rate, they need not be considered further. An additional clerk is required to perform activity 3, however, because only with two clerks working in parallel can we achieve a combined flow rate of 120 applicants per hour. Next, we must ask if it is possible to combine activities requiring small amounts of time to arrive at a job that can be performed in 60 seconds or less (i.e., achieve a flow rate of at least 60 applicants per hour). By combining activity 1, which requires 15 seconds, with activity 4, which requires 40 seconds, we can achieve a combined job requiring 55 seconds per applicant (or a flow rate of 65 applicants per hour). Note that this solution requires the acquisition of one additional eye-testing machine. Another solution would be to combine activities 4 and 5 to create a job yielding a flow rate of 60 applicants per hour; however, an additional expensive camera would need to be purchased. Can you think of another process design that meets the capacity goal but could be viewed by customers and employees as offering more personalized service?

The example of the driver's license office lends itself to a radical rethinking of the product layout. If money were available to invest in computers, additional eye-testing equipment, and cameras, then the entire process could be reengineered. Consider training each clerk to perform all five activities with a combined time of 165 seconds, or an individual flow rate of approximately 22 customers per hour. Now, an arriving customer would be faced with choosing from among six clerks working in parallel, as shown in Figure 7.7. This system would be appealing to customers, however, because one clerk would handle all the transactions and, thus, customers would not be passed from one clerk to another and be required to wait in between. Further, one would expect that the total time could be shortened because information would not need to be repeated as before. Finally, staffing of the office would now be flexible because only the number of clerks required to meet anticipated demand need be on duty. This savings in labor could justify easily the investment in six work stations.

Process Layout and the Relative Location Problem

A process layout allows the customers to define the sequence of service activities to meet their needs and, thus, affords some degree of customization. The process layout also allows the service to be tailored to the customer's specifications, thereby delivering personalized services. The ability to customize service requires more highly skilled

FIGURE 7.7
Reengineered Driver's
License Office

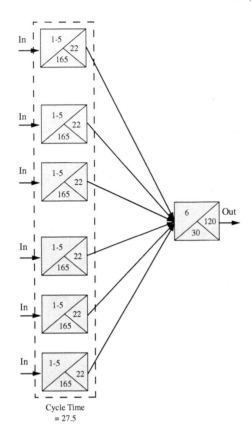

service providers, who have discretion to personalize the service to customers' needs. Professional services such as law, medicine, and consulting, which are organized into specialties, provide examples.

From the service provider's perspective, the flow of customers appears to be intermittent, so there is a need for a waiting area in each department. The variability in demand at each department results when customers choose different sequences of services and place different demands on the service provided. On arriving at a particular department, customers often will find it busy and will need to join a queue, which usually operates on a first-come, first-served basis (FCFS).

A dramatic and physical example of a service process layout is a university campus with buildings dedicated to various disciplines, giving students the flexibility of choosing classes from among them. The relative location problem can be seen in the layout of the campus. For both student and faculty convenience, we would expect selected departments such as engineering and physical sciences to be in close proximity to each other, while perhaps economics and business administration would be located together in another area. The library and administration offices would be located in a central part of the campus. One possible objective for selecting such a layout would be to minimize the total distance traveled by faculty, staff, and students between all pairs of departments. Many different layouts are possible, however. In fact, if we have identified n departments to be assigned to n locations, then n factorial layouts (i.e., 3,628,800 layouts for 10 departments) are possible. Because finding the best layout among these possibilities is beyond complete enumeration, we will use a heuristic approach to finding a good layout in Example 7.3.

Example 7.3
Ocean World
Theme Park

The architect for Ocean World is beginning to formulate plans for the development of property outside New Orleans, Louisana, for a second marine theme park after the success of its Neptune's Realm on the West Coast. Because of the hot and humid gulf weather during the

TABLE 7.3
Daily Flow of Visitors between Attractions, Hundreds*

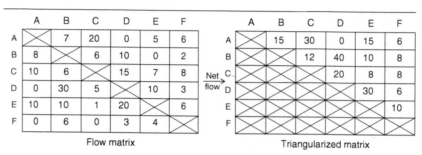

	A	B	C	D	E	F			A	B	C	D	E	F
A		7	20	0	5	6		A		15	30	0	15	6
B	8		6	10	0	2		B			12	40	10	8
C	10	6		15	7	8	Net flow	C				20	8	8
D	0	30	5		10	3		D					30	6
E	10	10	1	20		6		E						10
F	0	6	0	3	4			F						

Flow matrix Triangularized matrix

*Description of attractions: A = killer whale, B = sea lions, C = dolphins, D = water skiing, E = aquarium, F = water rides.

summer months, ways to minimize the visitors' total travel distance between attractions are being considered. Data showing a typical day's flow of visitors between attractions at San Diego are given in Table 7.3 and will be used in the layout planning.

A heuristic called *operations sequence analysis* will be used to identify a good layout for this relative location problem.[5] This method uses as input the matrix of flows between departments and a grid showing the geographic center location for department assignments. In Table 7.3, we have created a triangularized form of the original flow matrix to sum the flows in either direction because we are interested only in the total.

The heuristic begins with an initial layout, shown on the grid in Figure 7.8a. This initial layout is arbitrary but could be based on judgment or past experience. Table 7.3 suggests that attractions with high daily flow between them should be placed adjacent to each other. For example, we cannot see a need to place A adjacent to D, but it would be appropriate to place A close to C.

For nonadjacent attractions, the flow between them is multiplied by the number of grids that separate the attractions. Note we have assumed that diagonal separation is approximately equal to the distance of a grid side instead of using the Pythagorean theorem. These products are summed to arrive at a total flow distance of 124 for this initial layout. Considering the large contribution made to this sum by the separation of attractions A and C, we decide to move C adjacent to A to form the revised layout shown in Figure 7.8b, with a total flow distance of 96. The revised layout shown in Figure 7.8c is the result of exchanging attractions A and C. This exchange has placed attraction C adjacent to attractions D, E, and F, thereby reducing the total flow distance to 70. However, the nonrectangular layout in Figure 7.8c is not acceptable for the real estate in question. Thus, the final layout, in Figure 7.8d, is created by exchanging attractions B and E and by moving attraction F to form a rectangular space; exchanging B and E keeps E and F adjacent as we move F to form a more compact space. By making high-flow attractions adjacent, we have reduced total nonadjacent flow distance to a value of 58 for our final site plan, which when rotated 90° to the right is shown in Figure 7.9.

FIGURE 7.8
Ocean World Site Planning Using Operations Sequence Analysis

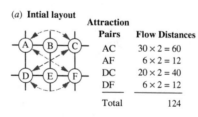

(*a*) **Intial layout**

Attraction Pairs	Flow Distances
AC	$30 \times 2 = 60$
AF	$6 \times 2 = 12$
DC	$20 \times 2 = 40$
DF	$6 \times 2 = 12$
Total	124

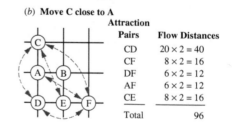

(*b*) **Move C close to A**

Attraction Pairs	Flow Distances
CD	$20 \times 2 = 40$
CF	$8 \times 2 = 16$
DF	$6 \times 2 = 12$
AF	$6 \times 2 = 12$
CE	$8 \times 2 = 16$
Total	96

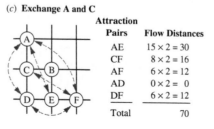

(*c*) **Exchange A and C**

Attraction Pairs	Flow Distances
AE	$15 \times 2 = 30$
CF	$8 \times 2 = 16$
AF	$6 \times 2 = 12$
AD	$0 \times 2 = 0$
DF	$6 \times 2 = 12$
Total	70

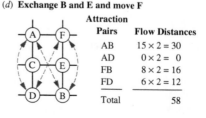

(*d*) **Exchange B and E and move F**

Attraction Pairs	Flow Distances
AB	$15 \times 2 = 30$
AD	$0 \times 2 = 0$
FB	$8 \times 2 = 16$
FD	$6 \times 2 = 12$
Total	58

FIGURE 7.9
Final Site Plan for Ocean World Theme Park

Source: Map by Kate O'Brien, Desert Tale Graphics.

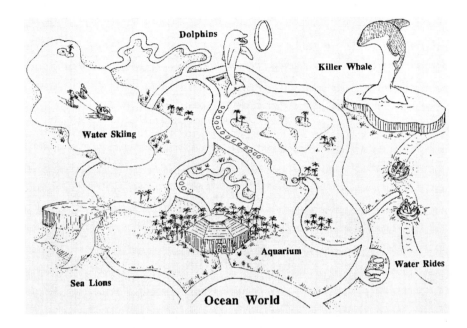

The departmental exchange logic of operations sequence analysis was incorporated into a computer program known as *CRAFT (Computerized Relative Allocation of Facilities Technique).*[6] CRAFT requires the following inputs: an interdepartmental flow matrix, a cost matrix (i.e., cost/unit/unit distance moved), and an initial layout with exact departmental dimensions filling the space available. CRAFT can incorporate some constraints, such as fixing the location of a department. The program logic depicted in Figure 7.10 shows the incremental nature of the heuristic, which selects at each iteration

FIGURE 7.10
Flow Diagram for CRAFT Logic

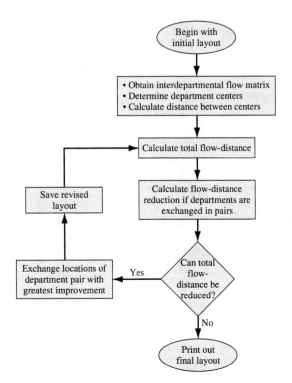

Service Benchmark

WHERE, OH WHERE SHALL WE GO?

Airports are gateways to great adventures for millions of people around the world. Finding these gateways, however, can be adventures themselves.

Wall Street Journal reporter Bridget O'Brian explored the subject of signage outside airports.[*] She cites examples of problems such as a lack of necessary or helpful signs, ambiguous words or phrases, "inconspicuous" signs, and signs that are placed inappropriately. The consequences of poor signage can lead to bad tempers, missed flights, motor vehicle accidents, and deaths.

National standards for airport signage in the United States to cure these ills have been proposed. Such standards, if adopted, would represent an important service breakthrough.

Getting to the airport is only part of the adventure, however. Signage within airports often challenges the traveler. Consider two experienced passengers who are booked on a Delta Air Lines trip from Oakland, California, to Austin, Texas. They arrive at the Oakland International Airport and are told by the Delta agent that their Oakland–Dallas flight has been canceled. The agent gives them a voucher for an American Airlines flight and explains that they are still booked on Delta's Dallas–Austin flight, a 30-minute trip. They proceed to the American check-in counter where they receive their boarding passes. The trip is uneventful until they arrive in the Dallas–Fort Worth International Airport.

The travelers arrive at Gate 22, Concourse C, and quickly discover that the departure/arrival monitors display only American Airlines flights; the posted airport "maps" show Concourses A, B, and C—they do not indicate the existence of any other concourses. Signs for a train to the other two concourses direct the two passengers to a tram station on a lower level. They find that Concourses A and B also have gates—and monitors—for American Airlines flights only. They do not find a single sign for any airline or airport transportation service other than those for American Airlines. They finally ask for directions from an AA gate agent in Concourse A who tells them to leave the concourse opposite Gate 21A, go downstairs, and take the airport train (i.e., not the AA train) to Concourse E. Signs for a way downstairs are lacking and personnel at the concourse exit cannot speak English well enough to be helpful. Eventually they locate an elevator, descend to the lower level, and find that they must exit the building to get to the tram station. The tram station, however, is closed and a sign directs them to the next tram station to the right. They set off in that direction, although they cannot see another station. It is nighttime and the walk is deserted until a security guard comes in sight. He says the next open station is in the other direction. The transfer from an American Airlines gate to a Delta gate can be made in less than 10 minutes, but the complete absence of appropriate signs and knowledgeable personnel extends the transfer time to more than one hour.

[*]Bridget O'Brian, "Signs and Blunders: Airport Travelers Share Graphic Tales," *The Wall Street Journal,* March 28, 1995, p. B1.

the two departments that, if exchanged, will yield the most improvement in flow distance reduction. CRAFT has been used extensively in service layout planning—for example, in insurance offices, hospitals, movie studios, and universities.

An objective other than minimization of travel distance also could be appropriate for designing the layout of a service. For example, if we had a core business with several ancillary businesses, we would want a layout that encouraged customers to browse in these other areas. Consider the layout of a gambling casino. Guests must walk through corridors lined with trendy shops and must always pass through the slot machine area to reach the front door or the restaurant.

Summary

The psychological implications of service facility design and layout were addressed to avoid customer disorientation and to mold behavior. The concept of a servicescape was used to illustrate the behavioral impact on customer and employee of environmental features in a service facility design. Facility design was seen as a package shaping the service experience and included features such as flexibility, security, and aesthetics. Process analysis begins with the construction of a process flow diagram that can be used to identify the system bottleneck and determine the throughput time. Facility layout was divided into product and process categories with graphic tools introduced for analysis.

Key Terms and Definitions

Bottleneck the activity in a product layout that takes the most time to perform and thus defines the maximum flow rate for the entire process. *p. 163*

Capacity a measure of output per unit of time when *fully busy. p. 164*

Capacity utilization a measure of how much output is actually achieved relative to the process capacity when fully busy. *p. 164*

CRAFT (Computerized Relative Allocation of Facilities Technique) a computer program that uses the departmental exchange logic of operations sequence analysis to solve the relative location problem of process layouts. *p. 169*

Cycle time the average time between completions of successive units. *p. 163*

Direct labor utilization a measure of the percentage of time that workers are actually contributing value to the service. *p. 165*

Operations sequence analysis a procedure to improve the flow distance in a process layout by arranging the relative location of departments. *p. 168*

Process layout a service permitting customization because customers determine their own sequence of activities (e.g., an amusement park). *p. 166*

Product layout a standardized service performed in a fixed sequence of steps (e.g., cafeteria). *p. 165*

Rush order flow time the time it takes to go through the system from beginning to end without any wait time in queue. *p. 164*

Servicescape the physical environment of a service facility that influences the behavior and perceptions of the service for both the customers and the workers. *p. 154*

Throughput time the time it takes to get completely through a process from time of arrival to time of exit. *p. 164*

Total direct labor content the sum of all the operations times. *p. 164*

Topics for Discussion

1. Compare the attention to aesthetics in waiting rooms that you have visited. How did the different environments affect your mood?

2. From a customer perspective, give an example of a servicescape that supports the service concept and an example that detracts from the service concept. Explain the success and the failure in terms of the servicescape dimensions.

3. Select a service and discuss how the design and layout of the facility meet the five factors of nature and objectives of the organization, land availability and space requirements, flexibility, aesthetics, and the community and environment.

4. For Example 7.3, the Ocean World theme park, make an argument for not locating popular attractions next to each other.

5. The CRAFT program is an example of a heuristic programming approach to problem solving. Why might CRAFT not find the optimal solution to a layout problem?

Interactive Exercise

The class divides into small groups. One-half of the groups produce examples based on work experience with *supportive* servicescapes in terms of job satisfaction and productivity. The other one-half of the groups provide examples of *poor* servicescapes in terms of job satisfaction and productivity.

Solved Problems

1. Work Allocation for Product Layout

Problem Statement

Arriving at JFK airport in New York from overseas requires a sequence of immigration and customs-clearing activities before a passenger can board a domestic flight for home. The table on the next page lists the activities and their average times. Except for baggage claim, these activities must be performed in the sequence noted. What is the bottleneck activity and maximum number of passengers who can be processed per hour? What would you recommend to improve the balance of this process?

Activity	Average Time, Sec.
1. Deplane	20
2. Immigration	16
3. Baggage claim	40
4. Customs	24
5. Check baggage	18
6. Board domestic flight	15

Solution

First, draw the process flow diagram and identify the bottleneck activity. The slowest activity is "baggage claim," which results in a system capacity of 90 passengers per hour.

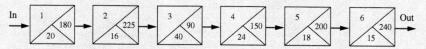

A recommendation for increasing system capacity could include doubling the capacity of the baggage claim area and combining the activities of the immigration and customs areas. This new product layout is shown in the process flow diagram below, with the result of doubling the system capacity to 180 passengers per hour.

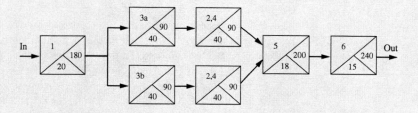

2.   Process Analysis

Problem Statement

Consider the original process flow diagram shown above for overseas arrivals at JFK airport. Calculate the values for system capacity, total direct labor content, rush order flow time, and direct labor utilization.

Solution

The first step in process analysis is the identification of the *bottleneck* activity, which in this case is "baggage claim" with a CT of 40 seconds. The *system capacity* is determined by the bottleneck CT and is calculated as (60 minutes/hour)(60 seconds/minute)(1/40 seconds) = 90 passengers per hour. Assuming no waiting time between activities, the *rush order flow time* is the sum of all the activity times: 20+16+40+24+18+15= 133 seconds. Because there is only one path in the process, *total direct labor content* is also the sum of all the activity times or 133 seconds. Direct labor utilization is total direct labor content divided by system process cycle time (bottleneck CT) multiplied by number of workers.

$$Direct\ labor\ utilization = \frac{133}{(40)(6)}(100) = 50\ percent$$

3. Relative Location for Process Layout

Problem Statement

The architect for the new undergraduate library is interested in a floor plan that would be viewed as convenient by users. Based on survey data from the old library, student movements between different areas in hundreds of trips per month are noted in the flow matrix below. Prepare a good initial rectangular layout that minimizes total flow distance between nonadjacent areas; then use operations sequence analysis to improve the layout.

Library Area	A	B	C	D	E	F
A Reserve Room	—	5	9	3	7	1
B Reference Room	3	—	8	2	6	2
C Copy Room	1	1	—	7	2	3
D Stacks	2	2	10	—	2	5
E Periodical Room	1	2	6	3	—	2
F Computer Room	1	1	1	4	2	—

Solution

First, create a triangularized total flow matrix by summing flows across the diagonal.

Library Area	A	B	C	D	E	F
A Reserve Room	—	8	10	5	8	2
B Reference Room	—	—	9	4	8	3
C Copy Room	—	—	—	17	8	4
D Stacks	—	—	—	—	5	9
E Periodical Room	—	—	—	—	—	4
F Computer Room	—	—	—	—	—	—

Second, locate library areas on the schematic rectangular layout shown below by placing high-flow areas adjacent to each other.

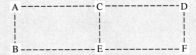

Next, calculate the total flow distance of nonadjacent pairs as shown below:

Nonadjacent Area Pairs	Flow		Distance		Total
AD	5	×	2	=	10
AF	2	×	2	=	4
BD	4	×	2	=	8
BF	3	×	2	=	6
					28

Finally, look for improvement by exchanging a pair of nonadjacent areas. Because no improvement is possible, accept the above layout.

Exercises

7.1. Passengers arriving at an airport departure gate must first wait for their row to be called before proceeding to the gate to have their boarding pass authenticated. If the boarding pass does not match the departing flight, the passenger is directed to the appropriate gate. A passenger attempting to carry on an excessively large bag is directed to check the luggage piece and return. Passengers with the proper boarding pass and appropriate sized carry-on are allowed to enter the jet way and board the plane. Draw a process flow diagram of the departure gate process. How might this process be improved to avoid delays?

7.2. Consider the Mortgage Service Process shown in Figure 7.3, and assume the Title Search cycle time has changed to 60 minutes.

   a. What is the bottleneck operation and corresponding system capacity?

   b. What is the rush order flow time?

   c. What is the system capacity, if the same person performs Credit Report and Title Search?

7.3. Revisit the Automobile Driver's License Office example.

   a. What is the direct labor utilization for the process shown in Figure 7.6*a*?

   b. What is the direct labor utilization for the process shown in Figure 7.6*b*?

   c. What is the direct labor utilization for the process shown in Figure 7.7?

   d. What do you conclude from these calculations?

7.4. Revisit the Automobile Driver's License Office, and assume that some of our previous recommendations for investment have been implemented. For example, "checking for violations and restrictions" will be done on a computer terminal, with that activity now taking 30 instead of 60 seconds. However, no additional eye-test machines or cameras were purchased.

   a. Assuming that one worker is assigned to each activity, what is the bottleneck activity and the maximum number of applicants who can be seen per hour?

   b. Suggest a reallocation of activities among the six workers that would result in a service capacity of 120 applicants per hour. What investment would be required to implement your layout recommendation?

7.5. Getting a physical examination at a physician's office involves a series of steps. The table below lists these activities and their average times. The activities can occur in any order, but the doctor's consultation must be the last. Three nurses are assigned to perform activities 1, 2, and 4.

Activity	Average Time, Min.
1. Blood pressure, wt., temp.	6
2. Medical history	20
3. Doctor's checkup	18
4. Lab work	10
5. Doctor's consultation	12

   a. What are the bottleneck activity and the maximum number of patients who can be seen per hour?

   b. Suggest a reallocation of nursing and/or doctor activities that would result in increased service capacity, and draw a product flow diagram. What is the capacity of your improved system?

7.6. A school cafeteria is operated by five persons performing the activities listed below in the average times shown.

Activity	Average Time, Sec.
1. Serve salad and dessert	10
2. Pour drinks	30
3. Serve entree	60
4. Serve vegetables	20
5. Tally and collect payment	40

a. What are the bottleneck activity and the maximum service capacity per hour?

b. Suggest a reallocation of activities that would increase capacity and use only four employees, and draw a product flow diagram. What is the capacity of your improved system?

c. Recommend a way to maintain the serving capacity found in part b using only three employees.

7.7. Every fall, volunteers administer flu vaccine shots at a local supermarket. The process involves the following four steps:

Activity	Average Time, Sec.
1. Reception	30
2. Drug allergy consultation	60
3. Fill out form and sign waiver	45
4. Administer vaccination	90

a. What are the bottleneck activity and maximum number of people who can be processed per hour?

b. If a fifth volunteer is assigned to help administer vaccinations, what activity now becomes the bottleneck? How has this arrangement influenced the capacity of the system?

c. Using five volunteers, suggest a reallocation of activities that would result in increased service capacity, and draw a product flow diagram. What is the capacity of your improved system?

7.8. Revisit the Ocean World Theme Park, and use the daily flow of visitors between attractions found in Example 7.3 for a different analysis.

a. Recommend a layout that would *maximize* the total travel distance between attractions.

b. What benefit would such a layout have for the owners of Ocean World Theme Park?

c. What reservations do you have about using the data from Table 7.3 for this new approach to the Ocean World Theme Park layout?

7.9. The Second Best Discount Store is considering rearranging its stockroom to improve customer service. Currently, stock pickers are given customer orders to fill from six warehouse areas. Movement between these areas is noted in the flow matrix below:

	A	B	C	D	E	F
A	—	1	4	2	0	3
B	0	—	2	0	2	1
C	2	2	—	4	5	2
D	3	0	2	—	0	2
E	1	4	3	1	—	4
F	4	3	1	2	0	—

82 Business Process - Management

176 Part Two *Designing the Service Enterprise*

Using the initial layout below, perform an operations sequence analysis to determine a layout that minimizes total flow between nonadjacent departments. Calculate your flow improvement.

7.10. A convenience store is considering changing its layout to encourage impulse buying. The triangular flow matrix below gives the measure of association between different product groups (e.g., beer, milk, magazines). A plus sign (+) indicates a high association, such as between beer and peanuts; a minus sign (−) indicates a repulsion, such as between beer and milk; and a zero (0) indicates no association.

	A	B	C	D	E	F
A		+	+	0	0	−
B			+	0	−	−
C				+	+	0
D					+	+
E						0
F						

Using the initial layout below, perform an operations sequence analysis to determine a layout that will encourage impulse buying by placing high-association product groups close to one another.

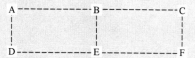

7.11. A community college that recently acquired a parcel of land is now preparing site plans. There is interest in locating academic departments in each of six buildings along a mall with three buildings on each side. Based on registration patterns, the daily flow of students between these six departments in hundreds is shown below.

	A	B	C	D	E	F
A. Psychology	—	6	4	8	7	1
B. English	6	—	2	3	9	5
C. Mathematics	6	1	—	12	2	4
D. Economics	3	2	10	—	3	5
E. History	7	11	2	1	—	6
F. Biology	6	2	8	10	3	—

Using the initial layout below, perform an operations sequence analysis to determine a site plan for the community college that will minimize the distance that students need to walk between classes.

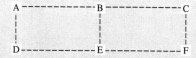

Selected Bibliography

Aubert-Gamet, Veronique. "Twisting Servicescapes: Diversion of the Physical Environment in a Re-appropriation Process." *International Journal of Service Industry Management* 8, no. 1 (1997), pp. 26–41.

Bitner, Mary Jo. "Evaluating Service Encounters: The Effects of Physical Surroundings and Employee Responses." *Journal of Marketing* 54 (April 1990), pp. 69–82.

Blackstone, John H., Jr. "Theory of Constraints—A Status Report." *International Journal of Production Research* 39, no. 6 (2001), pp. 1053–80.

Goldratt, Eliyahu M., and J. Cox. *The Goal.* New York: North River Press, 2004.

Morrin, Maureen, and Jean-Charles Chebat. "The Interactive Effects of Shopper Style and Mall Atmospherics on Consumer Expenditures." *Journal of Service Research* 8, no. 2 (November 2005), pp. 181–91.

Nasar, J. L., ed. *Environmental Aesthetics: Theory, Research, and Applications.* Cambridge: Cambridge University Press, 1988.

Parish, Janet Turner; Leonard L. Berry; and Shun YinLam. "The Effects of the Servicescape on Service Workers." *Journal of Service Research* 10, no. 3 (February 2008), pp. 220–38.

Strati, A. *Organization and Aesthetics.* London: Sage Publications, 1999.

Vilnai-Yavetz, Iris, and Anat Rafaeli. "Aesthetics and Professionalism of Virtual Servicescapes." *Journal of Service Research* 8, no. 3 (February 2006), pp. 245–59.

Wener, Richard E. "The Environmental Psychology of Service Encounters." In *The Service Encounter,* eds. J. A. Czepiel, M. R. Solomon, and C. F. Surprenant. Lexington, Mass on Books, 1985, pp. 101–13.

Endnotes

1. Peg Tyre, "Retailing: Trading Spaces, and Jabs," *Newsweek,* April 5, 2004, p. 46.
2. Steve Lohr, "The Best Little Bank in America," *New York Times,* July 7, 1991, sec. 3, p. 1.
3. Richard E. Wener, "The Environmental Psychology of Service Encounters," in J. A. Czepiel, M. R. Solomon, and C. F. Surprenant (eds.), *The Service Encounter,* Lexington, Mass.: Lexington Books, 1985, pp. 101–13.
4. Mary Jo Bitner, "Servicescapes: The Impact of Physical Surroundings on Customers and Employees," *Journal of Marketing* 56 (April 1992), pp. 57–71.
5. Elwood S. Buffa, "Sequence Analysis for Functional Layouts," *Journal of Industrial Engineering* 6, no. 2 (March–April 1955), pp. 12–13.
6. E. S. Buffa, G. C. Armour, and T. E. Vollmann, "Allocating Facilities with CRAFT," *Harvard Business Review* 42, no. 2 (March–April 1964), pp. 136–59.
7. Prepared by Charles Morris, Allison Pinto, Jameson Smith, and Jules Woolf under the supervision of Professor James A. Fitzsimmons.

Chapter 1

Enterprise Resource Planning Systems

Enterprise resource planning (ERP) systems have become very important in modern business operations. One study found more than 60 percent of Fortune 500 companies had adopted of ERP systems.[1] These systems have been credited with reducing inventories, shortening cycle times, lowering costs, and improving supply-chain management practices. ERP systems are designed to integrate all of an organization's information system computing. ERP has been credited with increasing the speed with which information flows through a company.[2]

ERP has also been credited with creating value through integrating activities across a firm, implementing best practices for each business process, standardizing processes within organizations, creating one-source data that results in less confusion and error, and providing on-line access to information.[3] All of these features facilitate better organizational planning, communication, and collaboration. Applied Robotics increased on-time deliveries 40 percent after implementing ERP, and Delta Electronics reduced production control labor requirements by 65 percent.[4]

ERP merits study for a number of reasons. From a *technical* perspective, the idea of integrating all aspects of an organization's computing is attractive because it fosters consistency across the system through use of single-source files and efficiency through making single data entry possible for all of the organization's applications. ERP has *financial* attraction, promising economic savings through integrating all applications into one big system. ERP also is attractive from an *organizational* perspective, as all

[1] G. Stewart, M. Milford, T. Jewels, T. Hunter, and B. Hunter, "Organizational readiness for ERP implementation," *Proceedings of the Americas Conference on Information Systems* (August 2000), pp. 966–971.

[2] T. H. Davenport, "Putting the Enterprise into the Enterprise System," *Harvard Business Review,* July–August 1998, pp. 121–31.

[3] D. E. O'Leary, *Enterprise Resource Planning Systems: Systems, Life Cycle, Electronic Commerce, and Risk* (Cambridge: Cambridge University Press, 2000). For business process reengineering, see M. Hammer and S. Stanton, "How Process Enterprises *Really* Work" *Harvard Business Review,* November–December 1999, pp. 108–18.

[4] M. Weil, "Managing to Win," *Manufacturing Systems* 17, no. 11 (November 1999), p. 14.

members of the organization learn to use the same system, thus enhancing intraorganizational communication.

While there are problems between the conception of an ERP system and the delivery, ERP is an attractive idea. ERP can provide lower costs of doing business, making it a competitive tool in many industries. Often business partners within supply chains require use of ERP. The concept of ERP has revolutionized the information system/information technology (IS/IT) field.

This chapter:

- Provides an initial description of ERP.
- Reviews development of ERP.
- Briefly looks at the current state of the market.
- Discusses advantages and disadvantages of ERP.
- Presents an example of a real ERP implementation failure as well as a subsequent success.
- Outlines where we are going with the rest of the book.

The Market for ERP

ERP has become a major software product line. An idea started by SAP in the early 1970s has evolved into a major information system software product line, which has revolutionized how large organizations approach business computing. Initial arguments were for integrated systems, yet vendors usually made sales in the form of modules, covering only limited functions of a business's computing needs. Because of the high price tags involved, companies apparently wanted to minimize their risks by trying only part of the ERP system. ERP vendor sales peaked in the late 1990s, driven in part by concerns about Y2K problems. This induced many large organizations to adopt ERP as a way to kill two birds with one stone—cleaning up and integrating their organizational computing services at the same time that they assured themselves they would be Y2K compliant. After that pre-Y2K rush, sales dropped. Vendors then shifted gears, seeking to fill in missing modules in large company systems and developing products more attractive to small to midsize firms. Additionally, vendors have made great strides in reducing some of the trauma of implementing ERP, making it possible to implement systems much faster (a matter of months rather than years) and offering more sophisticated functionality, such as customer relationship management and e-business system support. Furthermore, ERP is being marketed heavily in both government and educational sectors.

The prosperity of ERP vendors is a matter of dispute. The market for this product does not appear to have recovered its pre-Y2K boom levels, but there still appears to be a viable market. Vendor survival seems to depend on the ability to adapt to new market realities, which will continue to evolve.

There are currently more than 100 vendors of ERP products, although this field is dominated by the firms shown in Table 1.1. These firms are often referred to by the acronym BOPSE, using the initial letters of the five vendors.

SAP began ERP product development in Germany in the early 1970s. Former IBM employees designed their new product with the intent of implementing the **best practices**

TABLE 1.1
Major ERP
Vendors

Source: T. H.
Davenport, "Putting
the Enterprise into the
Enterprise System."
*Harvard Business
Review,* July–
August 1998.

Vendor	Origin	Salient Features
BAAN	Holland	An early ERP vendor
Oracle	United States	A relative newcomer, but quickly gaining share
PeopleSoft	United States	Originally focused on human resources management
SAP	Germany	The pioneer and the largest firm
JDEdwards	United States	Internet emphasis

for a firm's information system processes. The idea of best practices is fundamental to an ERP system. SAP devotes significant resources to identify the best way to deal with common business functions and then incorporates those practices within its systems. However, these best practices are not best for each particular firm.[5] The business world is dynamic, and a rigid approach has drawbacks. Additionally, some firms develop a core competency, something that they do better than their competitors. The idea of a best practice implies that everyone ought to do things the same way. Yet, if a firm develops a core competency, it would be foolish to sacrifice that competitive advantage to utilize the ERP system to its fullest extent.

ERP systems were designed to integrate all information processing support for a business. Table 1.2 presents some business functions supported by ERP.

In the early 1970s, information systems were supported by mainframe architectures. SAP marketed R/2, a mainframe-supported software product in 1974. In the early 1990s, **client/server** architectures became popular, with an organization's computation supported by one or more servers linked to allow distribution of computing and storage. Client/server architectures are more flexible than mainframe systems, and thus are capable of better supporting dynamic ERP environments. In the mid-1990s, SAP developed a client/server version of its ERP product, which was named R/3. About this time, the field for ERP took off, with SAP holding the dominant portion of the market worldwide. Typically, an organization uses one server for application software, another for database software, and yet another server for user interface. Associated servers can also be used for additional support, such as dialog management and gateway services. Currently R/3 is the most popular ERP product on the market in terms of dollar volume. As noted, the market for ERP peaked in early 1999, when many firms were concerned with potential Y2K problems. Since ERP products are for the most part large-scale systems (typically involving multiple years for installation), the demand dropped off after mid-1999, when it was too late to implement a system in time for the feared calendar turnover. However, SAP and Oracle business continued to be brisk, primarily by expanding sales to existing clients and to midsize firms. The general business malaise for technology firms has been a notable factor in reducing sales growth in the latter portion of 2000 through the time of writing this book.

Chapter 2 discusses ERP modules. Other major business functions supported by ERP are customer relationship management (Chapter 8) and Web-based systems (Chapter 9).

---

[5] Davenport, "Putting the Enterprise into the Enterprise System."

4   Chapter 1   Enterprise Resource Planning Systems

TABLE 1.2
Business Functions Potentially Supported by ERP

Source: T. H. Davenport, "Putting the Enterprise into the Enterprise System." *Harvard Business Review*, July–August 1998.

Financial	Human Resources	Operations and Logistics	Sales and Marketing
Accounts receivable and payable	Time accounting	Inventory management	Order management
Asset accounting	Payroll	Materials Requirement Planning (MRP)	Pricing
Cash forecasting	Personnel planning	Plant maintenance	Sales management
Cost accounting	Travel expenses	Production planning	Sales planning
Executive information systems		Project management	
Financial consolidation		Purchasing	
General ledger		Quality management	
Profitability analysis		Shipping	
Standard costing		Vendor evaluation	

ERP Advantages and Disadvantages

There are many reasons to adopt ERP. It offers an integrated system shared by all users rather than a diverse set of computer applications, which rarely can communicate with each other and which each possess its own set of data and files. ERP provides a means to coordinate information system assets and information flows across the organization. The main benefit is the elimination of suborganizational silos that focus on their own problems rather than serving the interests of the overall organization. On the downside, ERP systems impose one procedure for the entire organization, which requires everyone to conform to the new system. But the benefits of integration are usually much greater than the costs of conformity.

Data can be entered once, at the most accurate source, so that all users share the same data (**data integration**). This can be very beneficial. As the shared data are used more and by more people, it becomes more complete and accurate. As errors are encountered, users demand correction. Procedures are needed to ensure that changes do not introduce new errors. This makes it harder to correct data, but again, this added inconvenience is usually well worth the gains of data integration.

ERP systems also can provide better ways of doing things. This idea is the essence of best practices, a key SAP system component. The downsides to best practices are that identifying the best way to proceed with specific business functions takes great effort, and such practices can involve significant change in how organizational members do their work. Further, as with any theory, what is considered best by one is often not considered best by all.

TABLE 1.3
ERP Pros
and Cons

Factor	Pro	Con
System integration	Improved understanding across users	Less flexibility
Data integration	Greater accuracy	Harder to make corrections
Best practices	More efficient methods	Imposition of how people do their work
		Less freedom and creativity
Cost of computing	More efficient system planned	Changing needs
		Underbudgeted training expense
		Hidden costs of implementation

ERP systems are usually adopted with the expectation that they will yield lower computing costs in the long run. Ideally, adopting one common way of doing things is simpler and involves less effort to provide computing support to an organization. In practice, savings are often not realized, due to failure to anticipate all of the detailed nuances of user needs, as well as the inevitable changes in the business environment that call for different best practices and computer system relationships. As we will discuss in Chapter 7, training needs are typically underbudgeted in ERP projects. Furthermore, these training budgets don't usually include the hidden costs of lost productivity as employees cope with complex new systems. Table 1.3 recaps these pros and cons of ERP systems.

The key rationales for implementing ERP systems are:

- Technology—more powerful, integrated computer systems.
  - Greater flexibility.
  - Lower IT cost.
- Business practices—better ways of accomplishing tasks.
  - Better operational quality.
  - Greater productivity.
- Strategic—cost advantages gained through more efficient systems.
  - Improve decision making.
  - Support business growth.
  - Build external linkages.
- Competitive—Keep up with competitors adopting ERP. Greater cost efficiencies.
  - Better customer service.

We conclude this chapter with a case based on one of the most popularly discussed implementations of ERP. The SAP implementation has been claimed as a technical success. However, the overall impact was a spectacular failure, leading to bankruptcy of the adopting firm. The ultimate cause of this failure is subject to debate (in the court system).

Real Application: How Not to Implement ERP

Probably the most famous implementation of ERP was by FoxMeyer Drug, a holding company in the health care services industry specializing in wholesale distribution of drugs and beauty aids. Its customers were drugstores, chains, hospitals, and care facilities. FoxMeyer had 23 distribution centers across the United States. Due to an aging population and growth in health care in the United States, FoxMeyer anticipated high growth in the industry; but extreme price competition in the industry threatened FoxMeyer's margins. FoxMeyer adopted long-term strategies of efficiently managing inventory, seeking low operating expenses, building stronger sales and marketing efforts, and expanding services.[6]

Before adoption of SAP's ERP, FoxMeyer had three linked data processing centers. Its old system involved customers filling out electronic orders, which were sent to one of three data processing centers. Orders were filled manually and packaged within 24 hours. The company had recently completed a national distribution center with multiple carousels and automated picking, with the capability of tracking inventory to secondary locations.

The new distribution system was adopted to capitalize on growth. FoxMeyer anticipated large volumes to enable it to lower unit costs, and thus undercut competitors on price. The company hoped to save $40 million in annual operating costs. The new ERP would need to handle hundreds of thousands of transactions, and meet Drug Enforcement Administration (DEA) and Food and Drug Administration (FDA) regulations. SAP's R/3 system was selected, and Andersen Consulting was hired to integrate the $65 million system. At the same time, FoxMeyer adopted an $18 million project with another firm to install a warehouse automation system.

The major fundamental error FoxMeyer seems to have committed was to anticipate full savings from its ERP and warehouse systems based upon timely project completion within 18 months. To take full advantage of these anticipated savings, the company signed large new contracts, underbidding competitors based upon new expected lower costs. However, there were coordination problems across systems, as might reasonably have been anticipated. The new contracts that FoxMeyer signed also forced changes in system requirements. Unfortunately, these changes needed to be made after testing and development were under way. Because the ERP project was running late, FoxMeyer revised its schedule arbitrarily, telling project management to complete it 90 days earlier than project management thought reasonable.

At the same time, the warehouse system consistently failed, suffering from late orders, incorrect and lost shipments, and operating losses of more than $15 million. In August 1996, FoxMeyer filed for bankruptcy. Subsequently, the firm's assets were purchased by McKesson.[7]

While it is impossible to know exactly why the project went amiss, some issues seem relatively clear. SAP takes the position that its system was successfully installed and functioned appropriately. The apparent factor of concern was an unmerited confidence in the project keeping on schedule, and working as planned. Historically, IS/IT projects tend not to do that. It is only prudent to allow for some slippage in time and budget, and to not count on full project functionality until after testing and installation are complete.

[6] Most information on FoxMeyer Drug was gathered by Jason Donalson, Julie Seibold, Matthew Welch, and Sok Woo Yoon, graduate students at Texas A&M University, as part of the requirements of a semester project.

[7] T. Ehrhart, "Tech Lawsuits, Insurance Costs Escalate–as Does Cost of Doing Nothing," *National Underwriter* 10, no. 46 (November 12, 2001), pp. 17–20.

Case
Questions

1. Risk analysis: FoxMeyer's project management failed to consider the possibility of project delays. Unfortunately, information systems projects are notorious for time overruns (Gartner Group often cites figures in the 70 percent range). The magnitude of FoxMeyer's ERP project, and its importance to operations, made delays very damaging. There are two broad approaches to developing an information system project—do it all at once (referred to as the "big-bang" approach in ERP literature) or develop the project in phases. Would FoxMeyer have benefited from a more conservative project development approach?

2. Change management: Another risk-related factor was reliance upon key customers. FoxMeyer suffered the loss of a key customer in the midst of its ERP development. It reacted by aggressively seeking replacement business by assuming the system was going to work as planned, and cost no more than planned. Using these optimistic costs, FoxMeyer bid low on new work. Costs did not turn out to be as low as expected. Should FoxMeyer have anticipated this? What would have been a better approach to solve its problem of lost business?

3. Human issues: FoxMeyer included a warehouse automation project in its strategic plans. Employees at the warehouse saw the writing on the wall and apparently did not cooperate to the fullest. One primary reason information systems projects are adopted is to reduce cost by getting more done with fewer people, which means fewer employees if there is not significant increase in volume of work. The employees accurately perceived the impact of the automated system on their futures. What could FoxMeyer have done to avoid this problem?

After FoxMeyer's bankruptcy filing, the major drug firm McKesson purchased FoxMeyer's assets and reported some success with ERP. But before that, McKesson had adopted SAP's R/3 for an initial implementation in the mid-1990s. This project was cancelled in 1996 after spending $15 million. It had included **business process reengineering** but the new processes didn't mesh well with R/3. In 1997, McKesson acquired FoxMeyer Corporation. Based upon its past experiences, McKesson carefully designed a new R/3 implementation project.[8]

The new project was scaled back by dropping a number of modules, and it was implemented one module at a time to ensure proper functionality. The project management team developed a cautious rollout schedule and rigorously held to that schedule. A separate group was formed to test the ERP system to avoid developer bias. This approach proved successful. The final phase of the $50 million system neared on-time completion within budget and without business disruptions.

The system imposed tremendous changes in end-user jobs. The implementation included careful analysis of these changes, with surveys, focus groups, demonstrations, and computer-based training adopted before formal training classes. Over 3,000 end users were expected to work on the system by completion of project implementation.

This example demonstrates that it is possible to bring an ERP implementation project in on time, within budget, and with full functionality. However, as demonstrated by

[8] C. Wilder and S. Davis, "False starts strong finishes," *Information Week* 711 (November 30, 1998), pp. 41–46; C. Stedman, "Flash! ERP works if you're careful," *Computerworld* 33, no. 11 (December 13, 1999), pp. 1, 14.

McKesson's experience, such success comes at the cost of a great deal of planning and project management effort.

The Rest of the Book

Chapter 2 will review the historical development of ERP from the aspect of manufacturing applications. The next two chapters will look at ERP from the perspective of the projects needed for its implementation. Chapter 3 will discuss techniques available for analysis of ERP adoption proposals. Methods will be demonstrated with examples, and factors in selecting from these techniques will be discussed. Chapter 4 will examine alternative configurations of ERP, to include consultant support and outsourcing and will look at the concept of reengineering and its relationship to ERP. Reengineering is directly related to the concept of best practices, which SAP includes as a key element of its system. Chapter 5 will discuss ERP implementation and its risks. Chapter 6 will present basic project management tools that can be used to support ERP implementation. Chapter 7 is concerned with ERP system maintenance and the need to train organizational members in the use of ERP to gain maximum benefit from the system. Chapter 8 presents supplemental tools that are often used to extend ERP into areas of customer relationship management and other data mining forms. Chapter 9 concerns Web and e-business aspects of ERP. Chapter 10 discusses some advanced features of ERP, including bolt-ons that expand ERP outside of its client organization into supply-chain and Web environments. Chapter 10 also addresses the related topic of ERP security.

This introductory look at ERP reveals a number of issues. First, ERP can be adopted in a variety of forms. Vendors would prefer to sell complete systems, but are happy to start organizations with modules of parts of their systems. Organizations could also develop their own ERP system, although this is usually much more expensive and slower. A number of options are available, calling for careful analysis of expected costs and benefits.

Another major element of an ERP system is the opportunity to reengineer how organizations accomplish the business they do. SAP uses the idea of "best practices" as a key component of its product. SAP has spent a great deal of research identifying how particular common activities should be done. These best practices are incorporated within SAP's products. Implementing such best practices, however, often involves dramatic changes in how people do their work. This leads to difficulty in the initial year or so of ERP implementation, as organizations get used to the new ways of doing things. While best practices are often adopted, a lot of people get lost along the way, and best practice for one organization has not always proven best for all organizations.

Implementing an ERP is a massive project. Information technology projects are time-consuming, costly activities, with high levels of risk. Adopting a vendor product completely is usually less time consuming than redesigning the system from scratch. Sound IS project management approaches will be needed to successfully implement ERP. A major element of this implementation process involves human subjects. If a new ERP system is expected to succeed, either current employees must buy in to the system, or new employees must be found. In either case, extensive training is needed.

The basic idea of ERP systems has proven beneficial, but the market continues to change, and vendors have found it necessary to keep up with new demands. Two of the more interesting new features offered within ERP systems are customer relationship management and e-business. Customer relationship management involves the use of large sets of data (obtainable from ERP systems, for instance) to better identify the value and needs of specific customers. E-business has been a very important new development (although the past few years have shown that any new opportunity needs to have sound business uses behind it). Incorporation of e-business within ERP has been a matter of interest to organizations and vendors. This need in part is driven by the growth of supply-chain operations, linking organization ERP systems. While a great deal of efficiency can be gained, a number of problems are created as well, especially in the area of security.

Summary

ERP is a software system that has had a tremendous impact on organizational computing. It offers technological, process efficient, financial, strategic, and organizational benefits over disparate and diverse computing systems. This chapter gave a brief review of the evolution of the ERP market, as well as a brief overview of the current state of this market. ERP has a number of advantages, primarily in centralized efficiency. But it also has disadvantages. ERP is usually very expensive, involving millions of dollars in vendor purchase price, as well as additional millions for consultant expertise and in-house development. Costs of ERP often do not fully reflect the negative impact of changing how an organization does business. This involves massive impact on personnel, who often have to relearn their jobs and need to spend many hours in training. Sound management requires careful consideration of benefits and costs of proposed ERP systems.

Humans learn best from failure. An ERP system can be very helpful to organizations. Any vendor will swamp you with success stories from its website. You are encouraged to look at these. However, keep in mind the motivations of the source. ERP vendors do not make money publicizing problems. It is good to review such failures as the FoxMeyer case from the perspective of gaining better understanding of problems to be overcome through planning.

Key Terms

Best practices Application of business processes in a manner deemed the best way.

Business process reengineering (BPR) Analysis of a business process (typical task the organization needs done) to accomplish it in a better way.

Client/Server Architecture Computer system where users (clients) are linked to one or more servers so computing and storage can be distributed.

Data integration Information system designed so that data are ideally entered only once and accurately, and is easily accessible by all organizational users.

Enterprise resource planning system (ERP) Integrated system engineered to apply best practices to organizational computing.

Questions

1. At the library and/or on the Web, review current sales claims by the five BOPSE vendors over the past year. Identify any trends. Are other vendors making progress to break into the top tier of this market?

2. What is the principle behind the idea of best practices?

3. What is the difference between a client/server system and alternative computer platforms?

4. What is the alternative to ERP?

5. If the idea behind ERP is centralization and uniformity, why is it often sold in modules?

6. What advantage is there to an organization in purchasing only a few modules of an ERP vendor product?

7. Why would an ERP system developed by an organization be expected to be more expensive and take longer to implement than a vendor system?

8. Discuss the pros and cons of computer system integration within an organization.

9. What is attractive about data integration? What does ERP have to do with data integration?

10. Visit ERP vendor websites, and compile a list of advantages they claim for ERP systems. Are all vendors relatively consistent?

11. Research the library and/or Web for updated information about FoxMeyer.

2

ERP Modules and Historical Development

Enterprise resource planning systems arose from a variety of origins. SAP developed its product around supporting the function of manufacturing, integrating that with financial and accounting functions. Other vendors developed products from other sources. For instance, PeopleSoft began by developing a respected human resources software product, which it expanded to include a slate of other modules. Before entry into the ERP market directly, Oracle was the leading database software vendor.

This chapter:

- Reviews development of ERP.
- Presents the concept of ERP modules.
- Views relative use and modification of modules.
- Discusses issues of customization versus adoption of vendor software as is.

Development of ERP

In the early 1970s, business computing relied upon centralized mainframe computer systems. These systems proved their value by providing a systematic way to measure what businesses did financially. The reports these systems delivered could be used for analysis of budgets and plans, and the systems served as a place to archive business data. Computing provided a way to keep records much more accurately and on a massively larger scale than was possible through manual means.

Business computing systems were initially applied to those functions that were easiest to automate and that called for the greatest levels of consistency and accuracy. Payroll and accounting functions were an obvious initial application. Computers can be programmed to generate accurate paychecks, considering tax and overtime regulations of any degree of complexity. They also can implement accounting systems for tax, cost, and other purposes. Because these functional applications tend to have precise rules that cover almost every case, computers can be entrusted to automatically and rapidly take care of everything related to these functions.

12 Chapter 2   ERP Modules and Historical Development

ERP Modules

ERP systems in concept cover all computing for an organization. The idea is to centralize data and computation, so that data can be entered once in a clean form, and then be used by everyone in the organization (and even by supply-chain partners outside the organization) with confidence that the information is correct. However, in practice, ERP vendors sell their software in **modules**. Table 2.1 lists SAP modules and parallel sets of modules offered by other vendors.

One of the more popular computer systems supporting manufacturing before ERP was **materials requirement planning (MRP)**. SAP'S module MM covers the functions of MRP. MRP began as an inventory reordering tool in operations involving dependent demand (the demand for materials depends upon the demand for end items in which the materials are used). The capability of MRP systems evolved to support planning of all company resources, and currently can support business planning, production planning, purchasing, inventory control, shop-floor control, cost management, capacity planning, and logistics management. The use of MRP resulted in better inventory and raw materials control, reduced need for clerical support, and reduced lead times in obtaining materials. Improved communication and better integration of planning were also gained.

MRP II (manufacturing resource planning) is a method to plan all resources for a manufacturer. A variety of business functions are tied into MRP II systems, including order processing as in MRP, business planning, sales and operations planning, production planning, master production scheduling, capacity requirements planning, and capacity planning. MRP II systems are integrated with accounting and finance subsystems to produce reports including business plans, shipping budgets, inventory projections, and purchase plans. There is a tendency within the operations management field to consider ERP as a natural extension of MRP II. Manetti gave the American Production Inventory Control Society (APICS) definition for ERP as a method for effective planning and control of all resources needed to take, make, ship, and account for customer orders.[1] There is at least some truth to this view, but ERP systems fit more than manufacturing operations. ERP systems are found in practically all types of large organizations, including chemical facilities and universities. MRP II functions are covered by SAP's PP module as well as other modules.

Another interesting aspect of the ERP vendor market is industry-specific product lines. BAAN has similar modules to those in Table 2.1, but focuses its marketing on industry-specific product variations. This demonstrates the specialization that all ERP vendors have adopted since 2000. Table 2.2 shows some industry-specific product variations.

PeopleSoft also lists product lines of Customer Relationship Management, an add-on function offered by most vendors, and Portal Solutions, a Web access service also provided by most vendors.

An interesting development is Microsoft's entry into the ERP market. Its website includes a catalog for Microsoft Great Plains Business Solutions (and eight other products related to ERP), which seem very similar to ERP vendor functionality, offering

---

[1] J. Manetti, "How Technology Is Transforming Manufacturing," *Production and Inventory Management Journal* (first quarter, 2001), pp. 54–64.

TABLE 2.1   Modules Offered by Leading Vendors

Functional Description	SAP	Oracle	PeopleSoft	JDEdwards
Records sales orders and scheduled deliveries, customer information	**SD** (Sales and Distribution)	Marketing Sales Supply Chain	Supply chain management	Order management
Purchasing and raw materials inventory, work-in-process, finished goods	**MM** (Materials Management)	Procurement	Supplier Relationship Management	Inventory Management Procurement
Production planning and scheduling, actual production	**PP** (Production Planning)	Manufacturing		Manufacturing Management
Product inspections, material certifications, quality control	**QM** (Quality Management)		Enterprise Performance Management	Technical Foundation
Preventive maintenance, resource management	**PM** (Plant Maintenance)	Service	Enterprise Service Automation	
Recruiting, hiring, training, payroll, benefits	**HR** (Human Resources)	Human Resources	Human Capital Management	Workforce Management
General ledger account transaction, generates financial statements	**FI** (Financial Accounting)	Financials	Financial Management Solutions	Financial Management
Internal management, cost analysis by cost center	**CO** (Controlling)			Time and Expense Management
Fixed-asset purchase and depreciation	**AM** (Asset Management)	Asset Management		Enterprise Asset Management
R&D, construction, marketing projects	**PS** (Project System)	Projects		Project Management
		Contracts		Subcontract Management
				Real Estate Management
Automate system, task-flow analysis, prompt actions	**WF** (Workflow)			
Best practices	**IS** (Industry Solutions)			

Source: Vendor websites and J. A. Brady, E. F. Monk, and B. J. Wagner, *Concepts in Enterprise Resource Planning* (Boston: Course Technology, 2001).

14   Chapter 2   ERP Modules and Historical Development

TABLE 2.2   Industry-Specific Variants

Vendor	BAAN	BAAN	PeopleSoft	PeopleSoft
Product	Discrete Manufacturing	Process Manufacturing	Industry Solutions	Nonprofit
Industries served	Aerospace and defense	Chemicals	Communications	Federal government
	Automobile	Food and beverage	Financial services	Higher education
	Industrial machinery and equipment	Pharmaceuticals	High technology	Public sector
	Electronics	Cable and wire	Professional services	Human resources and payroll
	Telecommunications	Pulp and paper	Utilities	Manufacturing
	Construction	Metals	Consumer products	Project accounting
	Logistics		Health care	
			Industrial products	
			Staffing	
			Wholesale distribution	

Sources: www.baan.com, www.peoplesoft.com.

solutions for accounting and finance, customer relationship management, e-business, human resources and payroll, manufacturing, project accounting, and supply-chain management.

Relative Module Use

The degree of module use was reported by Mabert et al., and replicated by Olhager and Selldin.[2] Mabert et al. surveyed 479 ERP users from the American Inventory and Inventory Control Society in the Midwest. Olhager and Selldin patterned their study after Mabert et al., using 190 Swedish manufacturing firms. Table 2.3 and Figure 2.1 present information extracted from that study.

The most popular module in the United States was financial and accounting, which is the most obvious application needed by an organization. The Swedish study indicated that materials management, production planning, order entry, and purchasing modules were very popular. Other modules, listed in Table 2.3 with adoption rates or less than 50 percent, are either not considered as critical or involve less specificity in best practices. These are similar for both studies, although human resources modules were more popular in Sweden.

There have been noted differences in the ease with which modules are implemented. All financial modules tend to be relatively easy to implement. Those modules relating to manufacturing and human resources also have been implemented with noted success. But modules supporting less structured activities, such as sales and marketing, have encountered notable implementation difficulty.

[2] V. M. Mabert, A. Soni, and M. A. Venkataramanan, "Enterprise Resource Planning Survey of Manufacturing Firms," *Production and Inventory Management Journal* 41, no. 20 (2000), pp. 52–58 and J. Olhager and E. Selldin, "Enterprise Resource Planning Survey of Swedish Manufacturing Firms," *European Journal of Operational Research* 146 (2003), pp. 365–73.

TABLE 2.3
Relative ERP
Module Use

Sources: V. M. Mabert,
A. Soni, and
M. A. Venkataramanan,
"Enterprise Resource
Planning Survey of
Manufacturing Firms,"
*Production and
Inventory Management
Journal* 41, no. 20
(2000), and J. Olhager
and E. Selldin,
"Enterprise Resource
Planning Survey of
Swedish Manufacturing
Firms," *European
Journal of Operational
Research* 146 (2003).

Module	Midwestern ERP Users	Swedish ERP Users
Financial and Accounting	91.5%	87.3%
Materials management	89.2	91.8
Production planning	88.5	90.5
Order entry	87.7	92.4
Purchasing	86.9	93.0
Financial control	81.5	82.3
Distribution/logistics	75.4	84.8
Asset management	57.7	63.3
Quality management	44.6	47.5
Personnel/human resources	44.6	57.6
Maintenance	40.8	44.3
R&D management	30.8	34.2

FIGURE 2.1

**Display of
Relative ERP
Module Use**

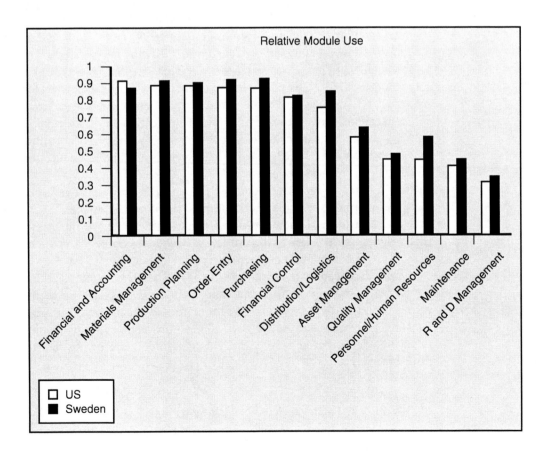

One reason to implement ERP in modules is to obtain specific functionality. Another (and probably the compelling) reason is cost. Full ERP systems cost a reported $5 million for very small versions to more than $100 million for very large implementations. The fewer modules implemented, the lower the cost. Additionally, it sometimes makes sense to implement the system in bits (phased implementation) rather than try to bring the entire massive system on-line at one time (big-bang implementation). Thus, rolling out an ERP by module sometimes makes sense.

Often firms will apply the concept of **best-of-breed,** mixing modules from different vendors. The Mabert et al. study found that a single ERP package was utilized as the vendor designed by only 40 percent of the more than 400 survey respondents. The most common strategic approach in the United States, used by 50 percent of respondents, was to supplement a single ERP package. The idea of best-of-breed was applied in only 4 percent of cases. As might be expected by the enormity of the undertaking, less than 1 percent of the surveyed implementations were entirely constructed in-house.

The idea of best-of-breed approaches is to utilize what is perceived as a specific vendor relative advantage in particular areas of application. One vendor's human resource module might be used in conjunction with another vendor's financial and accounting system, and yet a third vendor's materials management module. Stevens reported one instance of best-of-breed integration triggered by merger.[3] In 1999, Honeywell and AlliedSignal were merged, and the best approaches of each firm's existing ERP systems were examined, with those components judged to be superior retained in the merged firm. Often third-party software designed to integrate software applications from several vendors (**middleware;** see Chapter 10) is needed.[4] Middleware products enable cross-platform operating system communications. This means that software applications such as e-commerce, data warehouses, customer relationship management, supply-chain software, and other enhancements can be added to ERP systems. Middleware also allows connection of best-of-breed modules to the ERP backbone.

If a firm utilizes its own methods within an ERP, Davenport gave choices of rewriting the code internally or using the existing system with interfaces.[5] Both approaches add time and cost to implementation, and thus would dilute the integration benefits of the ERP. The more **customization** of an ERP, the less ability to communicate seamlessly within system components and across supplier and customer systems.

A related concept is the idea of **federalization**. Davenport used this term to describe the process of rolling out different versions of an ERP system in each regional unit, tailoring each location's system to accommodate local operating practices.[6] Hewlett-Packard, Monsanto, and Nestlé have all used this approach, establishing a common core of ERP modules shared by all units, but allowing other modules to be operated and controlled locally.

[3] T. Stevens, "All's Fair in Integration," *Industry Week,* April 16, 2001, pp. 24–29.

[4] P. Bingi, M. K. Sharma, and J. K. Godla, "Critical Issues Affecting an ERP Implementation," *Information Systems Management,* Summer 1999, pp. 7–14.

[5] T. H. Davenport, "Putting the Enterprise into the Enterprise System," *Harvard Business Review,* July–August 1998, pp. 121–131.

[6] Ibid.

Customization Issues

Organizations adopting ERP systems face the dilemma of deciding what degree of customization to adopt. The best fit with organizational needs would involve intensive reengineering and development of ERP software by internal staff. But this method is extremely slow and expensive. It is much faster and less troublesome to adopt a vendor's software directly. However, in practice, almost every organization adopting an ERP system must modify vendor software to some degree. The following applications report modifications of ERP systems adopted by two organizations (referred to here as Firm A and Firm B).[7] These experiences demonstrate typical modifications required when vendor ERP software is implemented.

Firm A's experiences emphasize the extra effort involved in almost any ERP implementation . If the system is obtained from a vendor, as it was here, modifications will be requested. The organization has choices—it can modify the vendor software, as in items 1, 2, 5, and 6 below; it can create new tools to cope with problems, as in items 3 and 4 above, or it can deny requests, as Firm A did. In some cases, the vendor would argue that if the system's procedures were adopted, the users would do their work better in the long run. Information technology personnel are focused on getting the system up and running quickly and within budget, which are the performance indicators by which they are usually evaluated. They also are interested in making the system relatively painless to operate. Users would usually prefer more modifications, and information technology staff would usually prefer fewer modifications. The first year of operation of an ERP tends to be quite traumatic, with users learning to do their work differently, and information technology staff struggling to run the system, often leading to conflict. Usually this extra work was unanticipated, sometimes leading to much longer implementation times, as in item 1. Often decisions must be made with respect to getting the system functioning now at the risk of future problems (items 2 and 5) or developing solutions now at the cost of extra work (items 3 and 4). Future impact was also a major consideration in the decision not to change labels and terminology.

There is inherently a divergence of interest between users and information technology staff members. Users are interested in getting the information they need. Making the system more responsive to users would lead to fewer changes in how they do their work, but would also require more modifications of the vendor system. Early in the implementation of the ERP system, a number of requests for changes in labels and terminology were received. *These requests were denied*, seeking to retain systematic terminology across all users. Another reason for denying requests was the implication on future maintenance that such customizations would have generated.

Again, the modification of vendor ERP software involved many compromises. In items 1 and 3, this burden was entirely placed on internal IT resources, taxing the budget. Items 2, 4, 5, 6, and 7 emphasize the impact of modifications on future operations.

---

[7] B. Light, "The Maintenance Implications of the Customization of ERP Software," *Journal of Software Maintenance and Evolution: Research and Practice* 13, no. 5 (2001), pp. 415–29.

Real Application: ERP Customization

Firm A was an international firm producing and distributing copper cable. The organization had evolved primarily through acquisition, and thus had a variety of computer systems. In the late 1990s, there were 10 manufacturing systems, 13 sales systems, 15 purchasing systems, 5 planning systems, 18 finance systems, and 18 personnel systems. This resulted in a variety of data views that often conflicted and in systems using incompatible platforms. The options that every ERP adopter has are represented by the extremes of:

- An all-internal system—revising how the software works to fit the organization
- An all-vendor system—revising how the organization works to fit the software
- Practical compromise—varying degrees available between the two extremes.

The Firm A ERP implementation was intended to be as close to the vendor design as possible. However, instances cited here show where customization was required.

1. In the MRP system, cable lengths needed by the corporation did not fit the vendor setup. A customization was specified by Firm A. The ERP vendor built a customization into the ERP system, which provided Firm A with a working solution. However, this customization *delayed system delivery by five months*, emphasizing the impact of modifications to vendor ERP systems.

2. Copper prices vary daily. Firm A coped with this risk through inventory stocks of copper, valued at the purchaser price. Therefore, details of purchase time, price, and contractual information had to be retained. This functionality was incorporated into the ERP software by the vendor. However, this *led to requirements for recustomization in future software upgrades*.

3. The ERP system reporting screens for shop-floor control were complex and cluttered. Test trials found a data entry error rate of 17 percent. Implementation of a software applications programming *interface tool* (automation of a process) solved this problem.

4. Every sales order required dispatch notes. The original ERP setup involved about 16 user operations to generate the required notes. Another *software applications programming interface* developed one screen that the user could mark to accomplish all needed work. The average time to accomplish the business process was thus reduced from 20 minutes to 5 minutes.

5. A number of documents associated with each sales order were standardized to include addition of a company logo. These changes were not affected by upgrades. However, *subsequent acquisitions led to the need to revise documents*, a typical adaptive maintenance activity.

6. The inventory reports generated by the ERP system did not provide all needed management information. The development team had to devote considerable *effort to create new reports*. In the meantime, users created their own reports through SQL queries. Firm A's IT staff sought to curb such activity and generate needed reports within the system.

Firm B provided a second example of a real ERP implementation, confirming the results experienced by Firm A. Firm B was a British retailer with 20 outlets. This organization's legacy systems were very fragmented. ERP was adopted to integrate systems, avoid data entry duplication, and replace a number of manual systems. Maintenance issues in this case included the following:

1. Pricing was based in part on travel distance to deliver the product. Thus, there were millions of prices in the system. Customization to support this was extensive. Maintenance issues involved were that this *customization was not supported by the service agreement*, and that only one IT person at Firm B fully understood the customization.

2. Because costs were a function of delivery distance, addresses had to be accurate and easy to find. The ERP software allowed free format. Firm B required a predefined list of addresses from post office address files. Some delivery sites were to streets that did not yet physically exist. Regular updates were not easy to apply. The scope of addresses in the system was expected to cause *future problems in any ERP software upgrades*.

3. Firm B utilized a number of shipping firms, which traditionally used self-billing, a *function not supported by the ERP software*. A customization was implemented producing shipper statements each month with details, as well as the amount Firm B intended to pay each shipper. Queries were collected and adjustments made the following month. This extensive customization was found to be very expensive.

4. Dispatch procedures embedded in the ERP system led to entry of the same data a number of times. Keystroke emulation software was used to automate this data entry. Future *upgrades would likely require heavy redevelopment*.

5. Corporate document sets were modified and standardized, and the company logo was added. Future upgrades were expected, realizing that such *upgrades would require additional changes* in the document set.

6. Many ERP software screens were modified, removing unused fields. Many Sales module screens were changed, while only four Purchasing module screens required change. These *changes had to be carefully documented* to reduce problems in future upgrades (which would wipe out changes).

7. A large number of control reports were developed, designed to highlight exceptions. Business users developed 908 control reports. The resources needed to *revise in the future as required* presented maintenance implications.

Both cases demonstrate the importance of considering future ERP system maintenance. Future modifications to ERP systems will arise from organizational changes (mergers and acquisitions, significant organizational growth or contraction, radically changing markets, etc.) or from vendor changes (ERP vendors systematically improve their software, and upgrades rarely will accommodate using organization modifications).

Key performance indicators are essential in ERP systems. Both Firm A and Firm B examples involved identification of key performance indicators. For Firm A, these were:

- Production cycle time.
- Daily cost of production receipts.

- Monthly production volume analysis.
- Daily cost of sales dispatches.
- Goods in the warehouse longer than a specified maximum number of days.

This information was captured by ERP reports, but led to increased maintenance activity. For Firm B, most key performance indicator reports were obtained from the organization's data warehouse rather than from the ERP. However, some key performance indicator reports were obtained directly from the ERP. IT staff had to devote resources to create and revise these reports.

Summary

The core idea of ERP is complete integration of an organization's computing system. Almost none of ERP implementations involve installing a vendor's entire suit of modules.[8] It is very common for organizations to select modules, which makes great sense because not every organization needs every module vendors develop. In fact, vendors seem to recognize this through their recent emphasis on products tailored to a specific industry.

There are also other very important reasons for implementing ERP products different from the vendor's design. A very important one is that full system implementation is very expensive. By selecting particular modules, organizations can cut initial implementation costs significantly. While vendors might argue that in the long run this might be less effective than full implementation now, in practice information systems projects rarely go as planned, nor do they tend to stay within originally planned budgets. Thus, organizations reduce their risks by trying particular modules first, often seeing how the new system is digested by the organization before going ahead with additional modules.

There also is a difference in the difficulty of implementing different modules. Financial and accounting modules are typically installed first, as they involve the most structured application. This makes it easier to implement, and easier for the organization to digest. Other modules such as materials management and planning also tend to work well. Conversely, support to less structured environments, such as sales and marketing, tends to be more problematic.

Related to the idea of implementing ERP in modules are the concepts of best-of-breed, middleware, customization, and federalization. Best-of-breed implementation is idealistic, seeking the best module across vendors and combining whatever mix is viewed as best for the particular organization. This approach is not widely adopted, probably because it involves obvious coordination risks. It also tends to be more expensive. Middleware is an important type of software making it possible to add on specialty software products. Customization is an approach to implement a vendor's ERP system tailored to organizational needs. Customization is done internally, as opposed to middleware, which is usually accomplished from third-party vendor software. Federalization allows different parts of the organization to utilize different modules, or possibly different levels of customization.

[8]Mabert et al., "Enterprise resource planning survey of manufacturing firms."

Key Terms

Best-of-breed Concept of mixing ERP modules from different vendors.

Customization Modification of vendor software to meet specific organizational requirements.

Federalization Tailoring ERP systems differently for each regional unit of an organization.

Key performance indicators Measures of organizational performance in areas deemed critical to success.

Manufacturing resource planning (MRP II) Computer system created to add planning support to MRP.

Material requirements planning (MRP) Computer system created to organize the materials purchasing of an assembly operation.

Middleware Third-party software created to integrate software applications from multiple sources.

Module Vendor software capable of independent operation that provides ERP support for a specific function.

Questions

1. What is the relationship between MRP and ERP?
2. What is the most commonly used ERP module, and why?
3. Have manufacturing-related modules been the basis of all ERPs?
4. Quality is an important emphasis in manufacturing. What has been the relative use of quality modules in ERP?
5. What is the relative importance of manufacturing-related modules in ERP?
6. What is the best-of-breed concept?
7. Describe the concept of federalization.
8. Research the library and/or Web and identify current modules offered by the BOPSE firms.
9. Research the library and/or Web and identify Microsoft's ERP system success.

Chapter 4

Business Process Reengineering and Best Practices

Once an organization decides what form of ERP system it wants to adopt, it will next need to specify how the ERP system will be designed. In conventional IS/IT projects, requirements analysis involves much effort to identify what users need. ERP projects vary highly in the amount of effort needed to identify system requirements. In vendor ERP projects, the functionality is given, based on vendor research into best practices. (SAP in particular has devoted significant effort to identification of best practices.) In ERP implementations developed with in-house assets, an integrated system serving all of the organization's information system needs must be developed through extensive **business process reengineering** (BPR).[1] BPR is an effort to identify the best way to do each business task supported by the system.

This chapter:

- Describes business processes.
- Demonstrates business process reengineering and why it is needed.
- Reviews best practices and related concepts.
- Compares clean slate and technology-enabled business process reengineering.
- Presents a discussion of how BPR was used in a real case.

Business Processes

A **process** is a logical set of related activities taking inputs, adding value through doing things, and creating an output.[2] In business, there are many different ways to get work done. Information systems play a key role in providing a means to collect data, store it efficiently,

---

[1] An article on BPR by its most vocal academic proponent is M. Hammer and S. Stanton, "How Process Enterprises Really Work," *Harvard Business Review,* November–December 1999, pp. 108–18.

[2] H. J. Harrington, E. K. C. Essing, and H. van Nimwegen, *Business Process Improvement Workbook: Documentation, Analysis, Design, and Management of Business Process Improvement.* (New York: McGraw-Hill, 1997), p. 1.

generate reports to let management know what the organization is doing, and archive data for future reference as needed. Tables 4.1 and 4.2 provide a generic view of two kinds of processes—operational and infrastructure. Operational processes help accomplish typical business functions, including product development, order management, and customer support. Infrastructure processes are more administrative, such as establishing and implementing strategy, and managing many aspects of the organization, including human resources, physical assets, and information systems. Each of these processes involves sets of tasks needed to accomplish work. For example, in the operational process of order management, it is necessary to forecast the volume of demand expected for the products produced by an organization. Forecasting can be accomplished in many ways:

- Using last month's demand as a prediction for this month.
- Using the monthly demand from a year ago as the prediction for this month.
- Applying a spreadsheet algorithm such as exponential smoothing over available monthly data.
- Incorporating seasonality indices into such a spreadsheet algorithm.
- Taking known orders and adjusting forecasts based on past demand records.
- Relying upon managerial judgment.
- Using a Ouija board (throwing darts; rolling dice; guessing).

Business process reengineering involves identifying the best way to design the flow and processing of information to obtain forecasts that yield the organization the greatest profit. That requires avoiding the most damaging kinds of forecast error and giving the organization the greatest flexibility to respond to risk.

Business Process Reengineering

BPR analyzes the way an organization accomplishes each business task with the intent of identifying the best way of doing things. BPR is closely tied to ERP, because for ERP to benefit the organization, at least some of the ways in which that organization does business must change.

Hammer and Stanton note that reengineering has sometimes been a euphemism for mindless downsizing but they provide an example of how reengineering should work.[3] In the early 1990s, Texas Instruments faced long cycle times and declining sales. BPR was applied to calculator development, which was to be accomplished by cross-disciplinary teams from engineering, marketing, and other departments. These teams were to be in control of every aspect of product development, from design through marketing. The first pilot teams failed, sabotaged by the existing organization, which felt threatened. Functional departments were unwilling to give up good people, space, or responsibility. Power continued to lie in the old functional departments. Texas Instruments responded by changing the way it was organized. Development teams became the primary organizational units. Functional departments focused on redefined missions supporting the product teams. Budget was accomplished by process instead of by department. Office space

---

[3] Hammer and Stanton, "How Process Enterprises Really Work."

TABLE 4.1
Typical Operational Business Processes

Function	Process
Develop new products/services	Plan and manage the development process
	Research and analyze need
	Define customer requirements
	Develop and design new product/service concepts
	Refine existing product/service concepts
	Conduct prototype and market tests
	Plan, release, and roll out new products/services
	Plan, release, and roll out changes to existing products/services
Market and sell products/services	Develop and execute market plans
	Conduct market and consumer research
	Develop competitor intelligence
	Manage product/service pricing
	Identify and qualify target customers
	Develop/maintain customer relationships
	Define customer's buying requirements
	Develop and propose a solution to the customer
	Estimate solution cost and price
	Influence customer buying process
	Negotiate and close the sale
Order management	Forecast order volumes
	Enter and process orders
	Manage customer credit exposure
	Plan production/service delivery
	Bill and collect revenue
Manufacture products and/or provide services	Manage overall production/service requirements and capacity
	Plan production/service delivery
	Design and engineer customer solution
	Produce products and/or provide service
	Manage change orders
	Plan and manage subcontract services
	Control production/service schedule
Manage logistics	Define logistics strategy
	Establish and maintain supplier relationships
	Measure and certify supplier performance
	Procure materials/services
	Manage inventory storage and movement
	Manage packing and packaging
	Manage outbound logistics
Provide customer support	Provide customer training
	Provide customer interface to the organization
	Receive and respond to customer inquiries
	Receive and respond to internal inquiries
	Dispatch and provide field service/support
	Manage return/warranty activities

50   Chapter 4   Business Process Reengineering and Best Practices

	Function	Process
TABLE 4.2 **Typical** **Infrastructure** **Business** **Processes**	Plan and manage performance	Formulate business strategy and vision
		Establish and prioritize goals and objectives
		Develop financial/operational performance
		Measure and monitor financial/operational performance
		Manage business performance
		Plan and manage quality and service levels
		Design and improve business processes
		Design and improve organizational structures and job roles
		Manage change
		Establish policies and procedures
	Manage finances and accounting	Manage accounts receivable
		Manage accounts payable
		Manage payroll
		Manage the general ledger
		Plan and manage taxes
		Plan and manage cash
		Plan and manage budgets
		Plan and manage capital expenditures
		Plan and manage risk to corporate assets
		Plan and manage loans and equity
		Report financial performance
		Perform financial analysis and cost accounting
		Maintain financial records
		Ensure financial control
	Manage human resources	Define human resource needs and skill requirements
		Manage the acquisition and termination of human resources
		Educate, train, and develop employees
		Ensure employee communication
		Establish reward and recognition systems
		Manage compensation and benefits
		Provide employee services
	Manage information resources	Define and plan for information resource needs
		Develop and enhance data architecture
		Develop and enhance communications infrastructure
		Develop and enhance software applications
		Manage information systems operations
		Provide information user support
		Archive and dispose of information
	Manage physical assets	Acquire production/service equipment and technology
		Maintain production/service equipment and technology
		Acquire facilities
		Manage and maintain facilities
		Manage other fixed assets
	Manage support services	Manage public/external relations
		Perform the legal function
		Manage administrative services
		Plan and manage environmental programs

was reallocated. After the new system became established, time to new product launch was cut by as much as half, and profitability was enhanced, with return on investment multiplied fourfold.

A business process is what the organization does to get its work done. For instance, if you go into a drugstore to purchase prescription medicine, the process is for the drugstore to sell merchandise to a customer and collect money. There are a number of actions in this process. Before computer automation, this manual business process went like this:

Customer gives pharmacist prescription.

Pharmacist recognizes face, checks doctor's signature.

If both OK, pharmacist checks controlled substance list.

If OK, pharmacist fills prescription.

Pharmacist gives bill to customer.

Customer pays by cash or check (if pharmacist finds that acceptable).

A number of elements in this process involve risk. First, there is a need to control some substances that drugstores deal in. While in the above process, the expertise of the pharmacist might catch most problems, computer support would be more reliable, especially if the pharmacist faces a large population of customers and cannot possibly know all of them. Second, many drugs involve the risk of reactions. It is the pharmacist's business to understand some of these risks, but as the number of drugs on the market has grown dramatically, computer automation can help track these risks and to add a step in the process where the pharmacist reads the warnings to the customer and obtains some assurance of customer understanding. There also is a more complex set of payment possibilities, much of which can be supported by Internet connection to insurance providers and to credit providers. Therefore, a new automated business process might be:

Customer gives clerk prescription.

Clerk checks doctor's authorization via an electronic authorization system.

If authorization OK, clerk gives prescription to pharmacist.

Pharmacist checks computer file for controlled substances.

System connects to insurance carrier and confirms how much insurance will cover.

If both OK, pharmacist fills prescription.

System automatically computes bill to customer and prints out receipt.

System prints out dosage instructions and warnings for clerk to read to customer.

Clerk collects payment from customer.

   If cash, records in cash register.

   If check, checks file for bad check writers, and if OK, records in cash register.

   If credit or debit card, connects to credit source for approval, and if OK, obtains signature; records in cash register.

This is only one of many ways to perform this business process. Business process reengineering would analyze how a particular operation is performed and seek better ways to do it, either through more automation or by adding people to do specific tasks to relieve bottlenecks in the process. For instance, if a particular pharmacy averages 100 customers per hour, extra personnel performing specific specialty activities can be included to relieve the pharmacists from collecting payment or other administrative tasks not calling for their higher-paid expertise. Additionally, other professional specialists might be introduced into the system to take care of drug inventories and security activities.

Business process reengineering predates the popular phase of ERP. Most reengineering efforts in the 1980s, which sought more efficient ways to do business, degenerated into wholesale layoffs.[4] The bad ways of doing business sometimes remained, but with fewer people to do them. Reengineering's primary impact has been massive reductions in workforce and other short-term cost savings, with less impact on diffusing computer-based automation. ERP software has been credited with rescuing the idea of BPR, forcing companies to redefine and redesign work flows to fit the new software.

Deregulation and competition are drivers for the creation of new business models (BPR) in many fields, such as telecommunications. ERP systems provide a higher level of flexibility in meeting growing customer demands, while demanding higher levels of automation and integration in almost all business processes.[5]

The change implicit in BPR has many risks. Even advocates of BPR cite failure rates of 50 to 70 percent.[6] Sutcliffe reviewed reasons for the difficulty of implementing BPR:[7]

- Employee resistance to change.
- Inadequate attention to employee concerns.
- Inadequate and inappropriate staffing.
- Inadequate developer and user tools.
- Mismatch of strategies used and goals.
- Lack of oversight.
- Failure in leadership commitment.

Blanket adoption of an ERP product could discard processes in which the organization has developed a competitive advantage.[8] Instead of changing those processes, the ERP system should be modified. Other activities might be better done following the ERP system's best practices. Even here, a transition period can be expected when employees have to radically change what they do. Productivity will decline while users adapt to the new system. In the long run, the new system is usually better. Those who refuse to adapt to it usually have to learn new skills with their next employer.

The following example demonstrates business process reengineering in an ERP system applied to an academic institution.[9] Babson College implemented a three-year project to

---

[4] M. Hammer, "Reengineering Redux," *CIO* 13, no. 10 (March 1, 2000), pp. 143–56.

[5] S. Levine, "The ABCs of ERP," *America's Network* 103, no. 13 (September 1, 1999), pp. 54–58.

[6] G. Hall, J. Rosenthal, and J. Wade, "How to Make Reengineering Work," *Harvard Business Review,* November–December (1993), pp. 119–31.

[7] N. Sutcliffe, "Leadership Behavior and Business Process Reengineering (BPR) Outcomes: An Empirical Analysis of 30 BPR Projects," *Information & Management* 36, no. 5 (1999), pp. 273–86.

[8] J. D. Schultz, "Hunt for Best Practices," *Traffic World,* September 25, 2000, pp. 41–42.

[9] R. M. Kesner, "Building an Internet Commerce Capability: A Case Study," *Information Strategy,* Winter 1998, pp. 27–36.

transform its business processes. The primary objective was to improve the quality of service delivery to students for admission, records, registration, advising, financial aid, career services, and field-based learning. The college also sought to reduce administrative costs so as to redirect these funds to teaching and academic support. Change management teams were formed to reengineer each of the operational areas supported by the system. Critical performance measures were established for each application. The focus was on easy-to-use and effective information systems that students could access themselves. The existing system was a mainframe system with dial-up network and text-based applications. The new system was a multitiered client/server infrastructure with 6,000 nodes, over 50 servers, and 1,500 workstations. Data warehousing was used. The system reduced operating costs about 20 percent after the system was implemented, half of the planned 40 percent, because some vendor systems were late. One problem faced by the information technology team was how to organize system access for customers or service providers. Initially, it was decided that a graphical electronic-mail system front end would be used, with applications written as executables within mail system file folders. But end users rejected this design because the mail system was not robust or fast enough for the transaction volume experienced. The Internet proved to be a solution. The Internet provided widespread access, and while the platform was not as reliable as it needed to be, it was expected to improve with time.

In another example of how best practices in BPR can be implemented, Nestlé obtained a very large mySAP.com system from SAP for over $200 million in 2000.[10] This system affected the way in which all 230,000 Nestlé employees in 80 countries did their work. Each Nestlé employee has a customized browser-based start page relating to his or her job function to guide the employee to the selected best practice.

Yet another example is Sunoco Products Co., which implemented e-procurement software allowing the company to reduce purchasing costs for operating resources.[11] The software aided the company in monitoring and enforcing business process changes as part of the ERP implementation. Sunoco was able to reduce its supplier base by 5 percent to 10 percent. It had a goal of a 10 percent reduction in spending on operating resources, which if attained would more than pay back the investment.

On the negative side, lack of up-front business process changes has been blamed for installation problems at Farmland Industries Inc.[12] Without BPR, finance and order-entry operations were unable to get the savings anticipated. This forced the company having to redo BPR and revise system implementation.

Within the manufacturing arena, a concept related to BPR is **lean manufacturing.** We will look more at lean manufacturing in Chapter 9. Lean manufacturing is an effort to cut waste by avoiding activities that don't add value. Throughout a supply chain, manufacturing can often involve continuous flows of material without bottlenecks, producing only what the customer has ordered. This reflects a system of demand pull rather than supply push. In the personal computer market, for instance, Dell has a demand-pull system. Some of its competitors had a supply-push system, where product was made in the

---

[10] S. Konicki, "Nestlé Taps SAP for e-Business," *Informationweek* 792 (June 26, 2000), p. 185.

[11] M. Shaw, "ERP and e-Procurement Software Assist Strategic Purchasing Focus at Sunoco," *Pulp & Paper* 74, no. 2, (February 2000) pp. 45–51.

[12] C. Stedman, "ERP Flops Point to Users' Plans," *Computerworld* 33, no. 46 (November 15, 1999), pp. 273–86.

most efficient way from the perspective of manufacturing. Finished goods are inventoried in a supply-push system. It appears that Dell's demand-pull approach is outperforming the supply-push approach.

Best Practices in ERP

One primary feature of the SAP ERP product has been **best practices.** A best practice is a method that has been judged to be superior to other methods. This implies the most efficient way to perform a task. Business process reengineering is designed to identify a best practice. Once a best practice that would seem applicable to most organizations is identified, it can be incorporated into an ERP system. SAP devotes considerable research to identifying the best way of doing conventional ERP tasks. Between 800 and 1,000 best practices are included in SAP's R/3 software.[13] Consultants often develop further specialized expertise that firms can purchase.

A related concept is **benchmarking.** Benchmarking compares an organization's methods with peer groups, with the purpose of identifying the best practices that lead to superior performance. Best practices are usually identified through the benchmarking phase of a business process reengineering activity. Best practices often change the organizational climate and attempt to bring about dramatic improvements in performance.

Vendors attempt to be comprehensive and to be all things to all people. Yet Scott and Kaindle state that at least 20 percent of the functionality needed by ERP users is missing from vendor packages.[14] There are also many reports of missed deadlines, excessive costs, and employee frustrations in ERP implementation. A more participative design approach could help in implementing ERP. If a client implements the entire suite of SAP modules, as well as the tools for system implementation, SAP can ensure timely implementation within budget. However, this approach disregards the human factors of the client business culture.

While business process reengineering was designed to consider human values and business purposes, Taylor states that these factors are clearly neglected in ERP application, and he outlines a process emphasizing human factors in ERP implementation.[15] The human factor costs of training and obtaining cooperative participation are key to the successful implementation of ERP.

Reengineering Options

O'Leary gives two basic ways to implement reengineering: clean slate versus technology-enabled BPR.[16] While these are not the only choices (they are the extremes of a spectrum

---

[13] J. E. Scott and L. Kaindle, "Enhancing Functionality in an Enterprise Software Package," *Information & Management* 37, no. 2 (2000), pp. 111–22, and C. Dean, "ERP Best Practices Checklist," www.deansystem.com, (2002).

[14] Scott and Kaindle (2000), "Enhancing Functionality."

[15] J. C. Taylor, "Participative design: Linking BPR and SAP with an STS approach," *Journal of Organizational Change Management* 11, no. 3 (1998), pp. 233–45.

[16] D. E. O'Leary, *Enterprise Resource Planning Systems: Systems, Life Cycle, Electronic Commerce, and Risk* (Cambridge: Cambridge University Press, 2000).

of reengineering implementation possibilities), they are good concepts to explain the choices available in accomplishing reengineering.

Clean Slate Reengineering

In **clean slate reengineering,** everything is designed from scratch. In essence, clean slate engineering involves reengineering, followed by selection of that software best supporting the new system design. Processes are reengineered based on identified needs and requirements of the organization. As its name implies, clean slate reengineering has no predefined constraints. This theoretically enables design of the optimal system for the organization. This approach is more expensive than technology-enabled reengineering, but clean slate reengineering is more responsive to organizational needs.

Clean slate reengineering is slower and harder to apply than the technology-enabled approach to implementation. However, clean slate reengineering offers a way to retain competitive advantages that the organization has developed. Ideally, this approach can develop the optimal system for the organization. Clean slate reengineering can also involve significant changes in the way the organization does business. However, the adjustment in how organization members do their business often retains the features that were found to work well in the past. Thus, while training is required, the impact is probably less than in the technology-enabled approach.

Technology-Enabled Reengineering

In **technology-enabled reengineering,** first the system is selected and then reengineering is conducted. O'Leary refers to this approach as constrained reengineering. The reengineering process is thus constrained by the selected system. This approach is faster and cheaper than clean slate reengineering, because the software does not have to be changed (it is the basis of the design). Cap Gemini refers to technology-enabled reengineering as **concurrent transformation.**

The technology-enabled approach designs the organizational system around the abilities of the vendor software. SAP's best practices, for instance, are designed to do things right in the first place. If SAP's research came up with better methods for everything a company does, this would be the best option. Technology-enabled reengineering is the easiest to implement, is usually much faster to implement, and thus costs less to implement. On the negative side, it also usually involves the most change in organizational practice, and thus the most complications for training. In practice, therefore, while the ERP installation project looks great from time, budget, and functionality perspectives, the actual benefits to the organization are often disappointing.

O'Leary calls the technology-enabled approach the most dominant in practice. He cited a survey of SAP R/3 implementers that found only 16 percent had planned reengineering before they obtained SAP. Of this set of implementers, 33 percent felt that no BPR was needed before implementation, although only 10 percent felt that way after implementation. The most common approach was to undertake BPR simultaneously with implementation of R/3. After the fact, 35 percent thought that reengineering should have come first (the clean slate approach). Table 4.3 compares advantages and disadvantages of both extremes.

56 Chapter 4 Business Process Reengineering and Best Practices

TABLE 4.3 Comparison of Clean Slate and Technology-Enabled Reengineering

Clean Slate Advantages	Technology-Enabled Advantages
Not constrained by tool limitations	Focus on ERP best practices
Not limited by completeness of best practice database	Tools help structure and focus reengineering
Company may have unique features where vendor best practices aren't appropriate	Process bounded and thus easier
Not subject to vendor software changes	Know that design is feasible
May be only way to embed processes such as Web and bar coding into new technology	Experience of others ensures design will work
Maintain competitive advantage	Greater likelihood of cost, time achievement
	Software available (already developed)
Clean Slate Disadvantages	**Technology-Enabled Disadvantages**
No preexisting structure to design	Reengineering limited by tool
Greater likelihood of infeasibility	System evolution possibly limited by technology
May involve more consultants	System evolution may be limited by technology
May be more costly, slower	No relative advantage (others can purchase same system)
May not work with selected ERP	All best practices may not be available

Source: D. E. O'Leary, *Enterprise Resource Planning Systems: Systems, Life Cycle, Electronic Commerce, and Risk* (Cambridge: Cambridge University Press, 2000).

O'Leary's advice is that clean slate reengineering should be used by large firms with ample reserve funds. Such firms would have the needed resources and would be more likely to use processes as a basis of strategic advantage. Technology-enabled reengineering should be used by firms that are constrained by budgets or with urgent time requirements. The more standard processes used by an organization, the more attractive technology-enabled reengineering is. Whichever approach is used, business process reengineering is considered a necessity for firms adopting ERP.

The technology-enabled strategy dominated the survey cited by O'Leary. Firms were surveyed before and after their ERP implementation. Before their experience, only 16 percent of those firms surveyed thought BPR should be applied before installation of the SAP system. This statistic jumped to 35 percent after the experience. Before implementation, 33 percent of those surveyed thought that BPR was unnecessary. After their experience, only 10 percent felt the same. Thus, even if the technology-enabled strategy is adopted, it seems clear that BPR is needed.

There are other implementation issues in ERP installation. Many organizations focus on one vendor's products. As discussed in Chapter 2, the best-of-breed approach involves mixing modules from multiple vendor sources.

Many organizations have difficulty switching from old legacy systems to ERP. These legacy systems included distribution, financial, and customer service systems developed in-house over the years. A case in point is Russ Berrie and Co., which makes teddy bears. It selected J. D. Edwards & Co.'s OneWorld ERP for customer relationship management and financial applications. The ERP installation project was

Real Application: McDonnell Douglas's Integrated Manufacturing Control System [17]

In the early 1990s, the St. Louis McDonnell Aircraft & Missile Systems factory (a Boeing subsidiary) was one of the world's largest manufacturing plants. But its IS/IT systems were not very up-to-date. They consisted of an antiquated material control system, with inadequate resource planning and no MRP. The St. Louis factory was one of the few aircraft producers without MRPII. It had just tried to update a mainframe system, and while the pilot test was successful, it was not scalable, in that it was unable to cope with the full volume of plant information. In 1994 a task force was formed to recommend methods to reduce costs in light of declining defense budgets and to refocus the information system to return on net assets.

The task force recommended implementation of a Western Data Systems ERP (which McDonnell Douglas named IMACS, the first use of commercial, off-the-shelf, client/server ERP in military aircraft).[18] The system was built around Hewlett-Packard hardware and an Oracle relational database. The task force felt that a large, expensive, vendor-supplied ERP was not needed. The functional goals of the IMACS system were to reduce inventory levels by several hundreds of millions of dollars, reduce support costs by hundreds of people, make it easier to move work between Boeing sites and suppliers, institutionalize improvements, and improve return on investment.

The first activity undertaken after adoption of the project was business process reengineering. BPR was conducted from 1994 through 1996. Customers were involved in this BPR study. The starting point of BPR was with business processes rather than systems. Thus, a clean slate approach was adopted. Efforts were made to modify selected software as little as possible. The BPR process yielded best practices.

Extensive employee training was applied. Eight courses were developed and delivered on CD-ROMs for 18 positions. This training media was estimated to save McDonnell Douglas more than $250,000 over alternative means of delivering training.

The IMACS integrated 38 systems. The ERP project team consisted of 150 Boeing employees, supplemented by vendor team members from Western Data Systems, Hewlett-Packard, and Oracle. The system was tested in 1995 and modified in 1997. In 1999, all products were converted to the system. The IMACS measured inventory, cycle time, cost, delivery performance, and product quality. Work in process was much easier to identify. Lead times were reduced, and there were fewer materials shortages. Product costs were lowered through the use of the IMACS as well.

---

[17] The information for this section was generated by Ratnesh Dubey, Sharon King, Laurie Lewandowski, Lucia Rodriguez, and Geoffrey Woodbury, graduate students at Texas A&M University, as part of the requirements of a class on information systems project management.

[18] T. Womeldorf, "Aerospace Defense Turns to Enterprise Apps," *Manufacturing Systems* 16, no. 8 (August 1998), pp. 56–66.

scheduled in phases over 18 months.[19] The system was adopted in an effort to more than quadruple sales revenue by accessing Customer Relationship Management (CRM) and Internet links.

Other organizations are supported by multiple ERP systems, sometimes a different system for each region. This would tend to be more attractive for larger firms. An example is Mobil, which is so large and spread out in global operations that it has operated with SAP, BAAN, and Oracle. Mobil was reported to be applying SAP's R/3 in the United States.[20] Mobil's Asia Pacific operations had smaller volume and different needs than the U.S. division and selected J. D. Edwards' software. Best practices have been applied throughout Mobil's operations, yielding standardized processes. Before use of this model, an ERP product took 18 months and cost $2.5 million to install. Using the standardized approach, a later installation at another affiliate took only six months and cost only $600,000. Mobil's approach discouraged local customization. In yet another regional ERP installation, it required six months to remove local customizations to the IT system before beginning installation of the new ERP system.

Summary

Business process reengineering is often a major component of an ERP installation. This implies massive changes in the way in which organizations conduct business. BPR has great potential payoff, but also implies a great deal of change in people's work lives, which requires a lot of attention to demonstrate benefits, as well as a great deal of retraining.

Requirements analysis is important in identifying what a proposed system is to do. In ERP projects, requirements analysis takes the form of business process reengineering to identify the best way (best practice) for each business process supported by the system. There are two extremes in the many ways in which business process reengineering can be accomplished. Clean slate reengineering starts from scratch. Technology-enabled reengineering begins with the software selected. This is faster and less expensive, as many of the processes are selected from the system. In practice, neither extreme is necessarily best.

BPR has enabled companies to operate faster and more efficiently, and to use information technology more productively. Employees often obtain more authority and a better understanding of the role their work plays for the organization as a whole. Customers get higher-quality products and more responsive service. Shareholders obtain larger dividends and higher stock value because BPR reduces cost and increases revenues. Executives no longer see their organizations as separate entities, but instead see them as related elements in larger systems linked through information flows across the business, reaching customers and suppliers.

---

[19] M. L. Songini, "Teddy Bear Maker Prepares for Second Attempt at ERP Rollout," *Computerworld*, February 11, 2002, www.computerworld.com.

[20] B. Zerega, "Mobil Model Simplifies ERP Overseas," *InfoWorld* 20, no. 25 (June 22, 1998), p. 76.

Key Terms

Benchmarking Comparison of organizational procedures with those of peer organizations.

Best practices The set of best ways to accomplish business processes.

Business process reengineering (BPR) Analysis of the set of tasks making up a business process with the intent of identifying the best way of accomplishing it.

Clean slate reengineering BPR conducted from scratch.

Concurrent transformation Synonym for technology-enabled reengineering.

Lean manufacturing BPR applied to cut waste in supply chains by eliminating non-value-adding activities.

Process Logical set of related activities taking inputs, adding value through doing things, and creating an output.

Technology-enabled reengineering BPR conducted after system is adopted, so that BPR is constrained by system features.

Questions

1. Describe business processes.
2. Define business process reengineering.
3. Search the library and/or Internet for business process reengineering practice.
4. Identify risks involved in adopting BPR.
5. Identify a specific business process, and analyze it with the intent of improvement through the use of information technology.
6. Describe the concept of best practices.
7. Search the library and/or Internet for best practices in ERP.
8. Describe benchmarking and its relationship to ERP.
9. Search the library and/or Internet for benchmarking practice in ERP.
10. Compare clean slate reengineering with technology-enabled reengineering.
11. Search the library and/or Internet for use of business process reengineering, especially associated with ERP.

Chapter 6

Service Quality

Learning Objectives

After completing this chapter, you should be able to:

1. Describe and illustrate the five dimensions of service quality.
2. Use the service quality gap model to diagnose quality problems.
3. Illustrate how poka-yoke methods are applied to quality design in services.
4. Construct a "house of quality" as part of a quality function deployment project.
5. Construct a statistical process control chart for a service operation.
6. Describe the features of an unconditional service guarantee and its managerial benefits.
7. Discuss the concept of service recovery.
8. Perform a walk-through audit (WtA).
9. Explain what service recovery is and why it's important.

Service "with a smile" used to be enough to satisfy most customers. Today, however, some service firms differentiate themselves in the marketplace by offering a "service guarantee." Unlike a product warranty, which promises to repair or replace the faulty item, service guarantees typically offer the dissatisfied customer a refund, discount, or free service. Take, for example, the First Interstate Bank of California. After interviewing its customers, the bank management discovered that they were annoyed by a number of recurring problems, such as inaccurate statements and broken automatic teller machines (ATMs). Account retention improved after the bank began to pay customers $5 for reporting each such service failure. What is surprising, however, is that the service guarantee also had a motivating effect on the employees. When an ATM failed at a branch, the employees, out of pride, decided to keep the branch open until the machine was repaired at 8:30 PM.

Another hidden benefit of a guarantee is customer feedback. Now customers have a reason and motivation to talk to the company instead of just to their friends.

In addition to advertising the firm's commitment to quality, a service guarantee focuses employees by defining performance standards explicitly and, more important, builds a loyal customer base. The experience of Hampton Inns, an early adopter of a "100 percent satisfaction guarantee," illustrates that superior quality is a competitive advantage. In a survey of 300 guests who invoked the guarantee, more than 100 already had stayed again at a Hampton Inn. The hotel chain figures that it has received $8 in revenue for every $1 paid to a disgruntled guest.[1]

Chapter Preview

Service quality is a complex topic, as shown by the need for a definition that includes five dimensions: reliability, responsiveness, assurance, empathy, and tangibles. We use these dimensions to introduce the concept of a service quality gap. This gap is based on the difference between a customer's expectations of a service and the perceptions of the service that is delivered. A survey instrument that measures service quality, called SERVQUAL, is based on implementing the service quality gap concept.

Quality begins with the design of the service delivery system. Thus, concepts borrowed from product design such as Taguchi methods, poka-yoke, and quality function deployment are applied to the design of service delivery systems. Statistical process control is used to monitor variation in service performance metrics and signal when intervention is necessary. A customer satisfaction survey instrument, called a *walk-through audit* (WtA), is built on the premise that each customer is a participant in the service process.

However, service failures do occur and the use of an unconditional service guarantee may be offered as the equivalent of a product warranty. Because the customer is present during service delivery, service recovery strategies can be planned in anticipation of a service failure.

Defining Service Quality

For services, the assessment of quality is made during the service delivery process. Each customer contact is referred to as a moment of truth, an opportunity to satisfy or dissatisfy the customer. Customer satisfaction with a service can be defined by comparing perceptions of service received with expectations of service desired. When expectations are exceeded, service is perceived to be of exceptional quality—and also to be a pleasant surprise. When expectations are not met, however, service quality is deemed unacceptable. When expectations are confirmed by perceived service, quality is satisfactory. As shown in Figure 6.1, these expectations are based on several sources, including word of mouth, personal needs, and past experience.

Dimensions of Service Quality

The dimensions of service quality as shown in Figure 6.1 were identified by marketing researchers studying several different service categories: appliance repair, retail banking, long-distance telephone service, securities brokerage, and credit card companies. They identified five principal dimensions that customers use to judge service quality—reliability, responsiveness, assurance, empathy, and tangibles, which are listed in order of declining relative importance to customers.[2]

> *Reliability.* The ability to perform the promised service both dependably and accurately. Reliable service performance is a customer expectation and means that the service is accomplished on time, in the same manner, and without errors every time. For example, receiving mail at approximately the same time each day is important to most people. Reliability also extends into the back office, where accuracy in billing and record keeping is expected.
>
> *Responsiveness.* The willingness to help customers and to provide prompt service. Keeping customers waiting, particularly for no apparent reason, creates unnecessary

FIGURE 6.1
Perceived Service Quality

Source: Reprinted with permission of the American Marketing Association: adapted from A. Parasuraman, V. A. Zeithaml, and L. L. Berry, "A Conceptual Model of Service Quality and Its Implications for Future Research," *Journal of Marketing* 49, Fall 1985, p. 48.

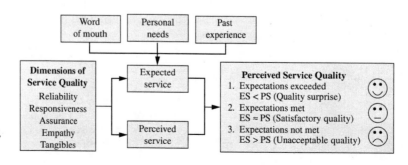

negative perceptions of quality. If a service failure occurs, the ability to recover quickly and with professionalism can create very positive perceptions of quality. For example, serving complimentary drinks on a delayed flight can turn a potentially poor customer experience into one that is remembered favorably.

Assurance. The knowledge and courtesy of employees as well as their ability to convey trust and confidence. The assurance dimension includes the following features: competence to perform the service, politeness and respect for the customer, effective communication with the customer, and the general attitude that the server has the customer's best interests at heart.

Empathy. The provision of caring, individualized attention to customers. Empathy includes the following features: approachability, sensitivity, and effort to understand the customer's needs. One example of empathy is the ability of an airline gate attendant to make a customer's missed connection the attendant's own problem and to find a solution.

Tangibles. The appearance of physical facilities, equipment, personnel, and communication materials. The condition of the physical surroundings (e.g., cleanliness) is tangible evidence of the care and attention to detail that are exhibited by the service provider. This assessment dimension also can extend to the conduct of other customers in the service (e.g., a noisy guest in the next room at a hotel).

Customers use these five dimensions to form their judgments of service quality, which are based on a comparison between expected and perceived service. The gap between expected and perceived service is a measure of service quality; satisfaction is either negative or positive.

Gaps in Service Quality

Measuring the gap between expected service and perceived service is a routine customer feedback process that is practiced by leading service companies. For example, Club Med, an international hotel chain operating resort villages worldwide, uses the questionnaire shown in Figure 6.2. This questionnaire is mailed to all guests immediately after their departure from a Club Med vacation to assess the quality of their experience. Note that the first question explicitly asks the guest to evaluate the gap between his or her expectations and the actual Club Med experience.

In Figure 6.3, the gap between customer expectations and perceptions is defined as GAP 5. Customer satisfaction is dependent on minimizing gaps 1 through 4 that are associated with delivery of the service.

The market research gap is the discrepancy between customer expectations and management perceptions of these expectations. GAP 1 arises from management's lack of full understanding about how customers formulate their expectations on the basis of a number of sources: advertising, past experience with the firm and its competitors, personal needs, and communications with friends. Strategies for closing this gap include improving market research, fostering better communication between management and its contact employees, and reducing the number of levels of management.

The service design gap results from management's inability to formulate target levels of service quality to meet perceptions of customer expectations and translate these into workable specifications. GAP 2 may result from a lack of management commitment to service quality or a perception of the unfeasibility of meeting customers' expectations; however, setting goals and standardizing service delivery tasks can close this gap.

The conformance gap occurs because actual delivery of the service does not meet the specifications set by management. GAP 3 can arise for a number of reasons, including lack of teamwork, poor employee selection, inadequate training, and inappropriate job design.

Customer expectations of the service are formed by media advertising and other communications from the firm. GAP 4 is the discrepancy between service delivery and external communications in the form of exaggerated promises and lack of information provided to contact personnel.

FIGURE 6.2   Customer Satisfaction Questionnaire

Source: After Club Med, 40 West 57th Street, New York, NY 10019.

G.M. Questionnaire

Club Med Village: _____

Dates of your stay: From: _____ Month/Day/Year _____ to: _____ Month/Day/Year

Name: _____ Member # _____

Address: _____

City: _____ State: _____ Zip: _____

	OVERALL IMPRESSION	ORGANIZATION	TEAM OF G.O.s	FOOD	BAR	SPORTS	DAYTIME AMBIANCE	EVENING ENTERTAINMENT	MUSIC AND DANCE	MINI CLUB	EXCURSIONS	ACCOMMODATIONS	CLUB FLIGHTS AND TRANSFERS	CLEANLINESS
EXCELLENT	6	6	6	6	6	6	6	6	6	6	6	6	6	6
VERY GOOD	5	5	5	5	5	5	5	5	5	5	5	5	5	5
GOOD	4	4	4	4	4	4	4	4	4	4	4	4	4	4
FAIR	3	3	3	3	3	3	3	3	3	3	3	3	3	3
POOR	2	2	2	2	2	2	2	2	2	2	2	2	2	2
VERY POOR	1	1	1	1	1	1	1	1	1	1	1	1	1	1

Your Comments: _____
_____

1. Did Club Med meet your expectations?
   □ Far below expectations   □ Surpassed expectations
   □ Fell short of expectations   □ Far surpassed expectations
   □ Met expectations

2. If this was not your first Club Med, how many other times have you been to a Club Med village? _____

3. How did you make your Club Med reservations?
   □ Through a travel agent   □ Through Club Med Reservations

4. Quality of your reservations handling (pre-travel information):
   □ Very poor   □ Poor   □ Fair   □ Good   □ Excellent

5. Which one factor was most important in your choosing Club Med for your vacation?
   □ Previous stay with us   □ Advertisement   □ Editorial Article
   □ Travel Agent Recommendation   □ Friend/Relative Recommendation

6. Kindly indicate your age bracket:
   □ Under 25   □ 25-34   □ 35-44   □ 45-54   □ 55 or over

7. Kindly indicate your marital status: □ Married   □ Single

8. Would you vacation with Club Med again?   □ Yes   □ No

9. If you answered yes to question 8, where would you like to go on your next Club Med vacation?
   □ U.S.A.   □ Mexico   □ French West Indies   □ Caribbean   □ Europe
   □ Other: _____

FIGURE 6.3
Service Quality Gap Model

Source: Reprinted with permission of Professor Uttarayan Bagchi, University of Texas at Austin.

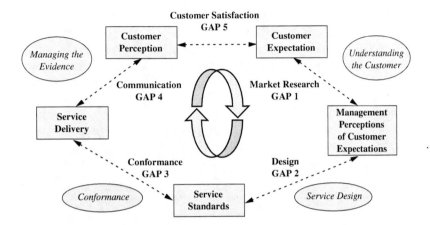

The numbering of the gaps from 1 to 5 represents the sequence of steps (i.e., market research, design, conformance, communication, and customer satisfaction) that should be followed in new service process design. The remainder of this chapter will address ways of closing these gaps in service quality. We begin by considering approaches to measuring service quality.

Measuring Service Quality

Measuring service quality is a challenge because customer satisfaction is determined by many intangible factors. Unlike a product with physical features that can be objectively measured (e.g., the fit and finish of a car), service quality contains many psychological features (e.g., the ambiance of a restaurant). In addition, service quality often extends beyond the immediate encounter because, as in the case of health care, it has an impact on a person's future quality of life. The multiple dimensions of service quality are captured in the SERVQUAL instrument, which is an effective tool for surveying customer satisfaction that is based on the service quality gap model.

SERVQUAL[3]

The authors of the service quality gap model shown in Figure 6.3 developed a multi-item scale called *SERVQUAL* for measuring the five dimensions of service quality (i.e., reliability, responsiveness, assurance, empathy, and tangibles). This two-part instrument, which can be found in the Student CD-ROM, pairs an *expectation* statement with a corresponding *perception* statement. Customers are asked to record their level of agreement or disagreement with the statements using a seven point Likert scale. The 22 statements in the survey describe all aspects of the five dimensions of service quality.

A score for the quality of service is calculated by computing the differences between the ratings that customers assign to paired expectation and perception statements. This score is referred to as GAP 5, as was shown in Figure 6.3. Scores for the other four gaps also can be calculated in a similar manner.

This instrument has been designed and validated for use in a variety of service encounters. The authors have suggested many applications for SERVQUAL, but its most important function is tracking service quality trends through periodic customer surveys. For multisite services, SERVQUAL could be used by management to determine if any unit has poor service quality (indicated by a low score); if so, management can direct attention to correcting the source of customers' poor perceptions. SERVQUAL could be used in marketing studies to compare a service with a competitor's and again identify the dimensions of superior or inadequate service quality.

Quality Service by Design

Quality can neither be inspected into a product nor somehow added on, and this same observation applies to services. A concern for quality begins with the design of the service delivery system. How can quality be designed into a service? One approach is to focus on the four dimensions of the service package that we explored in Chapter 2, The Nature of Services.

Incorporation of Quality in the Service Package

Consider the example of a budget hotel competing on overall cost leadership:

1. *Supporting facility.* Architecturally, the building is designed to be constructed of materials that are maintenance-free, such as concrete blocks. The grounds are watered by an automated underground sprinkler system. The air-conditioning and heating system is decentralized by using individual room units to confine any failure to just one room.
2. *Facilitating goods.* Room furnishings are durable and easy to clean (e.g., bedside tables are supported from the wall to facilitate carpet cleaning). Disposable plastic cups are used instead of glass, which is more expensive, requires cleaning, and, thus, would detract from the budget image.
3. *Information.* An online computer tracks guest billing, reservations, and registration processing. Keeping a record of customer's prior stay speeds future check-in, avoids billing errors, and anticipates needs (e.g., non-smoking room). This system allows guests to check out quickly and automatically notifies the cleaning staff when a room is free to be made up. Noting time of check-out allows for scheduling early maid service and inventorying available rooms for early arrivals.
4. *Explicit services.* Maids are trained to clean and make up rooms in a standard manner. Every room has the same appearance, including such "trivial" matters as the opening of the drapes.
5. *Implicit services.* Individuals with a pleasant appearance and good interpersonal skills are recruited as desk clerks. Training in standard operating procedures (SOPs) ensures uniform and predictable treatment for all guests.

Table 6.1 illustrates how the budget hotel has taken these design features and implemented a quality system to maintain conformance to the design requirements. The approach is based on the definition of quality as "conformance to requirements." This example illustrates the need to define explicitly, in measurable terms, what constitutes conformance to requirements. Quality is seen as an action-oriented activity requiring corrective measures when nonconformance occurs.

Taguchi Methods

The budget hotel example illustrates the application of *Taguchi methods,* which are named after Genichi Taguchi, who advocated "robust design" of products to ensure their proper functioning under adverse conditions.[4] The idea is that for a customer, proof of a product's quality is in its performance when abused. For example, a telephone is designed to be far more durable than necessary because more than once it will be pulled off a desk and dropped on the floor. In our budget hotel example, the building is constructed of concrete blocks and furnished with durable furniture.

Taguchi also applied the concept of robustness to the manufacturing process. For example, the recipe for caramel candy was reformulated to make plasticity, or chewiness, less sensitive to the cooking temperature. Similarly, our budget hotel uses an online computer to notify the cleaning staff automatically when a room has been vacated. Keeping the maids posted on which rooms are available for cleaning allows this task to be spread throughout the day, thus avoiding a rush in the late afternoon that could result in quality degradation.

TABLE 6.1   **Quality Requirements for Budget Hotel**

Service Package Feature	Attribute or Requirement	Measurement	Nonconformance Corrective Action
Supporting facility	Appearance of building	No flaking paint	Repaint
	Grounds	Green grass	Water grass
	Air-conditioning and heating	Temperature maintained at 68° ± 2°	Repair or replace
Facilitating goods	TV operation	Reception clear in daylight	Repair or replace
	Soap supply	Two bars per bed	Restock
	Ice	One full bucket per room	Restock from ice machine
Information	Guest preferences	Complete	Update
Explicit services	Room cleanliness	Stain-free carpet	Shampoo
	Swimming-pool water purity	Marker at bottom of deep end visible	Change filter and check chemicals
	Room appearance	Drapes drawn to width of 3 ft	Instruct maid
Implicit services	Security	All perimeter lights working	Replace defective bulbs
	Pleasant atmosphere	Telling departing guests "Have a nice day"	Instruct desk clerk
	Lobby congestion	No customer having to wait for a room	Review room cleaning schedule

Taguchi believed that product quality was achieved by consistently meeting design specifications. He measured the cost of poor quality by the square of the deviation from the target, as shown in Figure 6.4. Once again, note the attention to standard operating procedures (SOPs) used by the budget hotel to promote uniform treatment of guests and consistent preparation of the rooms.

Poka-Yoke (Failsafing)

Shigeo Shingo believed that low-cost, in-process, quality-control mechanisms and routines used by employees in their work could achieve high quality without costly inspection. He observed that errors occurred, not because employees were incompetent, but because of interruptions in routine or lapses in attention. He advocated the adoption of *poka-yoke* methods, which can be translated roughly as "foolproof" devices. The poka-yoke methods use checklists or manual devices that do not let the employee make a

FIGURE 6.4
Taguchi Quality Loss Function

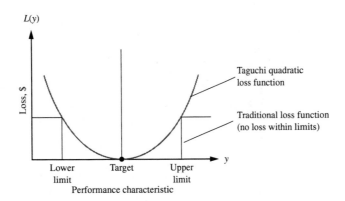

122   Part Two *Designing the Service Enterprise*

TABLE 6.2
Classification of
Service Failures

Server Errors	Customer Errors
Task:	*Preparation:*
• Doing work incorrectly	• Failure to bring necessary materials
• Doing work not required	• Failure to understand role in transaction
• Doing work in the wrong order	• Failure to engage the correct service
• Doing work too slowly	
Treatment:	*Encounter:*
• Failure to acknowledge the customer	• Failure to remember steps in process
• Failure to listen to the customer	• Failure to follow system flow
• Failure to react appropriately	• Failure to specify desires sufficiently
Tangible:	• Failure to follow instructions
• Failure to clean facilities	*Resolution:*
• Failure to provide clean uniforms	• Failure to signal service failure
• Failure to control environmental factors	• Failure to learn from experience
• Failure to proofread documents	• Failure to adjust expectations
	• Failure to execute post-encounter action

mistake.[5] As noted by Chase and Stewart and summarized in Table 6.2, service errors can originate from both the server and the customer. Poka-yoke methods therefore should address both sources.[6]

Service provider errors fall into three categories: tasks, treatments, and tangibles. The use of a french fry scoop at McDonald's to measure out a consistent serving of potatoes is an example of a *task* poka-yoke device that also enhances cleanliness and, hence, the aesthetic quality of the service as well. A novel *treatment* poka-yoke devised by a bank for tellers to ensure customer eye contact requires them to enter the customer's eye color on a checklist at the start of the transaction. An example of a *tangible* poka-yoke is the placement of mirrors in employee break rooms to promote appropriate appearance upon returning to the customer area. The automatic spell check feature of Microsoft Outlook assures that an e-mail is not sent until it has been proofed for errors.

Because customers play an active role in the delivery of services, they also need help to avoid errors. These errors fall into three categories: preparation, encounter, and resolution. Shouldice Hospital located in Toronto, Canada, performs only inguinal hernia operations. All potential patients are required to fill out a comprehensive medical survey, that is, a *preparation* poka-yoke, to ensure that the medical condition is appropriate for treatment at Shouldice. Many *encounter* poka-yokes are unobtrusive, such as the use of height bars at amusement rides to ensure that riders exceed size limitations or frames at airport check-in counters to gauge allowable size of carry-on luggage. *Resolution* poka-yokes help mold the behavior of customers as they exit the service. Fast-food restaurants strategically locate tray-return stands and trash bins at the exits.

Airlines use this poka-yoke device to alert passengers to the size limits of carry-on luggage. Myrleen Ferguson Cate/PhotoEdit

Using physical design to control employee and customer discretion is an important preemptive strategy to avoid mistakes. Because it is difficult for management to intervene in the service process and impose a quality appraisal system (i.e., inspection and testing), limiting discretion and incorporating poka-yoke methods facilitate mistake-free service. It is interesting to note how these unobtrusive design features channel service behavior without a suggestion of coercion, such as a "beep" from our word processor to warn us that an invalid keystroke has been made.

Quality Function Deployment

To provide customer input at the product design stage, a process called *quality function deployment* (QFD) was developed in Japan and used extensively by Toyota and its suppliers. The process results in a matrix, referred to as a "house of quality," for a particular product that relates customer attributes to engineering characteristics. The central idea of QFD is the belief that products should be designed to reflect the customers' desires and tastes; thus, the functions of marketing, design engineering, and manufacturing must be coordinated. The "house of quality" provides a framework for translating customer satisfaction into identifiable and measurable conformance specifications for product or service design.[7]

Although QFD was developed for use in product planning, its application to the design of service delivery systems is very appropriate, as shown by the following example.

Example 6.1
Quality Function
Deployment for
Village Volvo

Recall the Village Volvo case from Chapter 2. Village Volvo is an independent auto service garage that specializes in Volvo auto maintenance and competes with Volvo dealers for customers. Village Volvo has decided to assess its service delivery system in comparison with that of the Volvo dealer to determine areas for improving its competitive position. The steps in conducting the QFD project and constructing a "house of quality" follow:

1. *Establish the aim of the project.* In this case, the objective of the project is to assess Village Volvo's competitive position. QFD also could be used when a new service delivery system is being considered for the first time.

2. *Determine customer expectations.* Based on the aim of this project, identify the customer group to be satisfied and determine their expectations. For Village Volvo, the target customer group is Volvo owners with nonroutine repairs (i.e., exclude routine maintenance for this study). Customer expectations could be solicited by interviews, focus groups, or questionnaires. In this example, we will use the five dimensions of service quality to describe customer expectations. As shown in Figure 6.5, these are the *rows* of the house of quality. In a more sophisticated QFD project, customer expectations are broken down into primary, secondary, and tertiary levels of detail; for example, the primary expectation of "reliability" could be further specified with "accuracy" at the secondary level and "correct problem diagnosed" as the tertiary level of detail.

3. *Describe the elements of the service.* The *columns* of the house of quality matrix contain the service elements that management can manipulate to satisfy customer expectations. For Village Volvo, we have selected training, attitudes, capacity, information, and equipment.

FIGURE 6.5
"House of Quality"
for Village Volvo

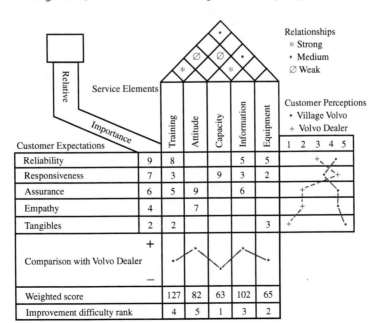

4. *Note the strength of relationship between the service elements.* The *roof* of the house of quality provides an opportunity to note the strength of correlation between pairs of service elements. We have noted three levels of strength of relationship: * = strong, • = medium, and Ø = weak. As you might expect, we note a strong relationship between training and attitudes. Noting these relationships between elements may provide useful points of leverage to improve service quality.

5. *Note the association between customer expectations and service elements.* The *body* of the matrix contains numbers between 0 and 9 (9 indicating a very strong link) to indicate the strength of the link between a service element and a corresponding customer expectation. These numbers would follow a discussion by the project team about how various service elements affect the firm's capacity to satisfy the different customer expectations.

6. *Weighting the service elements.* This step is taken to measure the importance of a customer's assessment of the service element. The *chimney* of the house of quality contains a listing of the relative importance of each customer expectation. These weights on a scale of 1 to 9 indicate the importance that customers place on each of their expectations and could be determined by a customer survey. The relative importance will be multiplied by the strength of the link number in the body of the matrix under each service element to arrive at a weighted score for that element. For example, the training element would have a weighted score calculated as

$$(9)(8) + (7)(3) + (6)(5) + (4)(0) + (2)(2) = 127$$

The weighted scores are entered in the *basement* of the house of quality and represent a measure of each service element's importance to satisfying customer needs. These weighted results should be treated with caution and common sense, however, because they depend on uncertain estimates of relative importance and relationship scores.

7. *Service element improvement difficulty rank.* In the basement of the house is a ranking for the difficulty of improving each service element, with a rank of 1 being the most difficult. Capacity and equipment have a high rank because of their capital requirements. This exercise demonstrates that even though customers may give a service element a high rank, the firm might be unable to deliver it.

8. *Assessment of competition.* A study of the Volvo dealer is made to assess customers' perceptions of service at the dealer compared with that at Village Volvo. The result of a customer survey (using customers who have experienced both providers) using a five-point scale is plotted to the *right* of the matrix. Based on knowledge of the dealer (perhaps from mechanics), a relative comparison of the level (plus or minus) of each service element is plotted at the *bottom* of the matrix. This information will be used to assess the competitive strengths and weaknesses of Village Volvo.

9. *Strategic assessment and goal setting.* Looking at the completed house of quality, Village Volvo can see some strengths and weaknesses in its strategic position relative to the Volvo dealer. Except for responsiveness, it is viewed favorably by its customers. This result must be viewed with caution, however, because these data were obtained from a survey of Village Volvo customers and, thus, were not unexpected. The comparison of service elements with the Volvo dealer and weighted scores yields some possible directions for improvement in service. In the area of attitudes and information, Village Volvo is in a superior position, but there appears to be a problem with capacity, training, and equipment. The high weighted score given to training suggests that a first-priority goal of an investment in training might be in order. In addition, leverage would be achieved because training has relationships, from strong to weak, with attitudes, capacity, and equipment. Finally, the improvement difficulty rank for training is fourth out of five.

Walk-Through Audit

Delivery of a service should conform to customers' expectations from the beginning to the end of the experience. Because the customer is a participant in the service process, his or her impressions of the service quality are influenced by many observations. An environmental audit can be a proactive management tool for the systematic evaluation of a customer's view of the service provided. A walk-through audit (WtA) is a customer-focused survey to uncover areas for improvement.

Fitzsimmons and Maurer developed such a walk-through audit for full-service sit-down restaurants.[8] The audit consisted of 42 questions spanning the restaurant dining experience. The questions begin with approaching the restaurant from the parking area, then walking into the restaurant and being greeted, waiting for a table, being seated, ordering and receiving food and drinks, and finally receiving the check and paying the bill. The questions include nine categories of variables: (1) maintenance items, (2) person-to-person service, (3) waiting, (4) table and place settings, (5) ambiance, (6) food presentation, (7) check presentation, (8) promotion and suggestive selling, and (9) tipping. Thus, the entire customer experience is traced from beginning to end. Unlike the brief and overall customer satisfaction survey as shown in Figure 6.6, the WtA is focused on the details of the service delivery process in an effort to uncover actionable items for improvement.

The walk-through audit is an opportunity to evaluate the service experience from a customer's perspective, because customers often become aware of cues the employees and managers might overlook. There is no inherently superior service design. There are, instead, designs that are consistent and that provide a signal to customers about the service they can expect. Providing tangibility in a service involves giving the customer verbal, environmental, and sensory cues that create a pleasant experience and encourage repeat visits. Table 6.3 compares the features of a customer satisfaction survey with those of a walk-through audit.

Designing a Walk-Through Audit

The first step in designing a WtA is the preparation of a flowchart of customer interactions with the service system. A WtA for the Helsinki Museum of Art and Design is shown in Figure 6.7. Observe that the questionnaire is divided into five major service delivery process sections (i.e., ticketing, information, experience, facilities, and satisfaction). Within each section a number of statements are made concerning observations that a customer would make (e.g., signs give clear information about exhibits' locations). The statements must be phrased as declarative sentences rather than questions. A five-point Likert scale is used to gauge customer perceptions (i.e., 1 = strongly disagree to 5 = strongly agree). As this WtA illustrates, other questions of interest to management are included such as "Where did you hear about the event" to gauge the effectiveness

FIGURE 6.6
Restaurant Satisfaction Survey

As Your Guest, I Would Like to Tell You . . .

	Great	Good	Fair	Poor
Food quality				
Service speed				
Service attentiveness				
Cleanliness				
Atmosphere				

Name_____
Address _____
City _____ State _____ Zip _____
Phone _____ Date _____

126   Part Two *Designing the Service Enterprise*

TABLE 6.3   **Comparison of Customer Satisfaction Survey with Walk-through-Audit**

Source: Elsa Lai-Ping Leong Koljonen and Richard A. Reid, "Walk-through Audit Provides Focus for Service Improvements for Hong Kong Law Firm," *Managing Service Quality*, 10(1), 2000, pg. 35.

	Customer Satisfaction Survey	Walk-through Audit
Purpose	Determine overall satisfaction associated with the current level of service quality.	Conduct a systematic assessment of the entire customer service experience from beginning to end.
Focus	Measure customer attitudes toward, opinions about, and perceptions of service quality.	Measure customer perceptions of the effectiveness of each stage of the service delivery process.
Process	1. Identify important customer service requirements or quality dimensions. 2. Design, test, and administer questionnaire to a sample of customers. 3. Summarize and analyze questionnaire results with emphasis on low ratings and changes relative to prior survey administrations. 4. Determine areas needing improvements and implement change designed to correct deficiencies. 5. Repeat for continuous quality improvement.	1. Flowchart the service delivery process from the customer's perspective. 2. Design, test, and administer questionnaire to a sample of customers, management personnel, and/or customers at benchmark organizations. 3. Summarize and analyze survey results with emphasis on low rating relative to benchmark firms and gaps between management and customers. 4. Determine deficiencies and implement improvements. 5. Repeat for ongoing improvement.
Features	1. Survey may be completed by customers at any time after receiving service. 2. Management, with some customer input, designs/structures the survey around common service dimensions (e.g., *availability, timeliness, responsiveness, convenience*). 3. Often performed by marketing personnel. 4. Primary emphasis is placed on assessing the determinants of the customer's overall impression of the service.	1. Questionnaire is completed by customers during or immediately after receiving service. 2. A comprehensive audit of the customer's total service experience of all five dimensions of the service package (i.e., *supporting facility, facilitating goods, information, explicit service, implicit service*). 3. Usually conducted by operations personnel. 4. Emphasis is placed on the customer's evaluation of each stage of the service delivery process and his/her overall impression of the organization's performance.

FIGURE 6.7   **Walk-Through Audit for Helsinki Museum of Art and Design**

Source: Prepared by Eivor Biese, Lauren Dwyre, Mikes Koulianos, and Tina Hyvonen under the supervision of Professor James A. Fitzsimmons.

Hello, we are from the Helsinki School of Economics and Business Administration and we are conducting a survey to find out, what do people think about the service experience when visiting this museum. Please answer the following questions.

All information in this questionnaire is strictly confidential!

1. Was it easy getting to the Museum?   ❑ Yes   ❑ No
2. Are the Museum's opening hours acceptable?   ❑ Yes   ❑ No
3. Did you arrive alone or with others?   ❑ Alone   ❑ Others   Number in Party: _____
4. Where did you hear about this event: [Check all that apply]

    ❑ Newspaper   ❑ Internet
    ❑ Magazine   ❑ Friends or relatives
    ❑ Tourist/City guide   ❑ Passing by
    ❑ Radio   ❑ Other: (Specify) _____

5. Did you come here to see

    ❑ Brooching It Diplomacy
    ❑ Wine—Nectar of Gods
    ❑ The Holy Cross
    ❑ The permanent exhibition
    ❑ All exhibitions

(continued)

FIGURE 6.7   (*concluded*)

6. **Which of the following facilities did you visit?**   ❏ Cafeteria   ❏ Gift shop   ❏ Restrooms

7. **How many hours did you spend in the museum?** _____ hours

8. **Ticketing**	Strongly Disagree	Disagree	Not Sure	Agree	Strongly Agree
a. It is easy to find information about ticket prices.	1	2	3	4	5
b. The ticket price is a good value for the money.	1	2	3	4	5
c. You did not spend too much time by waiting in the ticket line.	1	2	3	4	5
d. You would like to purchase tickets ahead of time, via phone or Internet.	1	2	3	4	5

9. **Information**	Strongly Disagree	Disagree	Not Sure	Agree	Strongly Agree
a. Signs gave clear information about exhibits' locations.	1	2	3	4	5
b. After arriving at the exhibition, you found adequate information about the exhibition(s).	1	2	3	4	5
c. The information provided was in your language.	1	2	3	4	5
d. Guide services were available.	1	2	3	4	5
e. There was enough information about the objects.	1	2	3	4	5
f. The explanations provided on the objects were clear.	1	2	3	4	5
g. You would like to see a variety of media (video, etc.) providing explanations.	1	2	3	4	5
h. You would like to have access to self-guided material such as a cassette player.	1	2	3	4	5
i. You would like to have more information about the process for creating the objects.	1	2	3	4	5
j. You would like to learn more when visiting exhibits.	1	2	3	4	5
k. It was easy to get additional information from the staff.	1	2	3	4	5
l. The staff helping you was friendly.	1	2	3	4	5

10. **The experience**	Strongly Disagree	Disagree	Not Sure	Agree	Strongly Agree
a. There was a clear path in which you were guided through the exhibition.	1	2	3	4	5
b. There was enough room to move around the exhibits.	1	2	3	4	5
c. Lighting was adequate.	1	2	3	4	5
d. There was pleasant background music.	1	2	3	4	5
e. The background sounds were pleasant.	1	2	3	4	5
f. The objects on display were adequately spaced apart.	1	2	3	4	5
g. There is enough opportunity for interaction with the displayed objects.	1	2	3	4	5
h. Touching, smelling, and hearing make the experience memorable.	1	2	3	4	5
i. You would also like to touch the material.	1	2	3	4	5

11. **Facilities**	Strongly Disagree	Disagree	Not Sure	Agree	Strongly Agree
a. There were clear signs giving information about the facilities.	1	2	3	4	5
b. The toilettes were easily accessible.	1	2	3	4	5
c. The toilettes were clean.	1	2	3	4	5
d. The food was of good quality.	1	2	3	4	5
e. There was enough variety of food and beverages.	1	2	3	4	5
f. The food was of good value for the money.	1	2	3	4	5
g. Smoking should be allowed in the restaurant.	1	2	3	4	5
h. The selection of gifts (including books) met your needs.	1	2	3	4	5
i. The gifts were of good value for the money.	1	2	3	4	5

12. **Satisfaction**	Strongly Disagree	Disagree	Not Sure	Agree	Strongly Agree
a. The services met my needs.	1	2	3	4	5
b. I found the overall service outstanding.	1	2	3	4	5
c. I am likely to use this service again.	1	2	3	4	5
d. I would recommend this museum to my friend.	1	2	3	4	5
e. Could we improve the service to better meet your expectations?	1	2	3	4	5

13. **Comments**

_____

_____

_____

_____

of advertising. It is also useful to leave a final section for "comments" that may provide customer insights not anticipated in the questions asked. To avoid overwhelming the customer, the WtA should be limited to two pages printed back-to-back.

The WtA can be administered in several ways (e.g., mail, telephone interview, in person) but the most effective method is in person immediately following the service experience. Rewarding the customer with a gift certificate or money off on a return visit has significantly increased participation. Survey design issues such as sample size and stratifying the sample to poll all customer segments should be considered.

The Walk-Through Audit as a Diagnostic Instrument

The walk-through audit can be a useful diagnostic instrument for management to evaluate the gaps in perception between customers and managers of the service delivery system. Customers visit a site less frequently than do managers and, thus, are more sensitive to subtle changes (e.g., peeling paint or worn rugs) than are managers who see the facility every day and who are likely to overlook gradual deterioration of the supporting facility. The quality of customer service also can deteriorate and be less noticeable to employees as well as managers.

To test this use of a WtA, the same Helsinki Museum of Art and Design audit that was given to customers was also given to the managers and employees. The responses for each item on the audit were averaged for the three groups and are shown in Figure 6.8. This figure highlights the gaps in service perceptions among management, employees, and customers. Some of the gaps are not surprising, such as "There was enough information about the objects," because the employees are quite familiar with the exhibits. Other gaps suggest some improvements are in order; for example, "It was easy to get additional information from the staff " and "The staff helping you are friendly." It is interesting to note where management and employee perceptions deviated, such as "The explanations provided on the objects were clear" and "There is enough opportunity for interaction with the displayed objects." In both cases, employees were more in agreement with the statements than customers were and management agreed least.

FIGURE 6.8   **Helsinki Museum of Art and Design Service Audit Gaps**

Source: Prepared by Eivor Biese, Lauren Dwyre, Mikes Koulianos, and Tina Hyvonen under the supervision of Professor James A. Fitzsimmons.

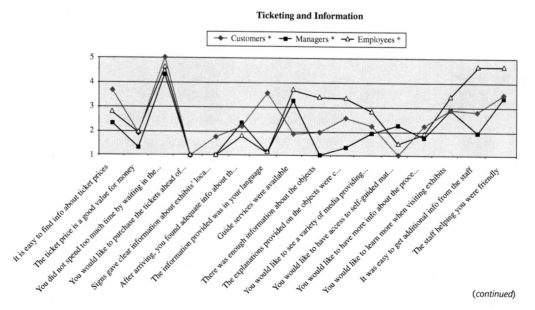

Ticketing and Information

(continued)

FIGURE 6.8   *(concluded)*

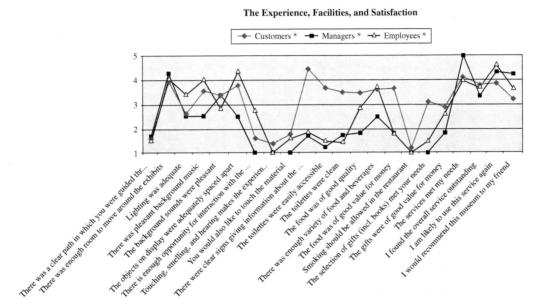

The Experience, Facilities, and Satisfaction

Achieving Service Quality

Services are difficult for customers to evaluate before the fact. As we have already noted, they are intangible and consumed simultaneously with production. This presents a challenge to the service manager because quality-inspection intervention between the customer and the contact employee is not an option as in manufacturing (e.g., no slip of paper can be placed in the box by Inspector Number 12).

Cost of Quality

Caveat emptor—"let the buyer beware"—has become obsolete. As American businesses discovered in the late 1980s and early 1990s, impersonal service, faulty products, and broken promises all carry a price. A very visible example of this reality today is the prominent part that liability concerns and insurance play in almost every service imaginable. Poor quality can lead to bankruptcy. A gourmet soup company, for example, was forced out of business when its vichyssoise was found to contain poison-producing botulism organisms. Announcements of automobile recalls for correcting defects are commonplace as well.

Products can be returned, exchanged, or fixed, but what recourse does the customer of a faulty service have? Legal recourse! Medical malpractice lawsuits have been notorious for their large settlements, and although some cases of abuse by the legal system surely have occurred, the possibility of malpractice litigation does promote a physician's sense of responsibility to the patient. The threat of a negligence suit might induce a responsible doctor to take more time in an examination, seek more training, or avoid performing a procedure for which he or she is not competent. Unfortunately, as evidenced by the frequent claims of physicians that extra testing is necessary to defend against potential malpractice claims, the cost of care might increase without any improvement in quality.

No service has immunity from prosecution. For example, a Las Vegas hotel was sued for failing to provide proper security when a guest was assaulted in her room. An income tax preparer can be fined up to $500 per return if a taxpayer's liability is understated because of the preparer's negligence or disregard of Internal Revenue Service rules and regulations.

A noted quality expert, Joseph M. Juran, has advocated a cost-of-quality accounting system to convince top management of the need to address quality issues.[9] He identified four categories of costs: internal failure costs (from defects discovered before shipment), external failure costs (from defects discovered after shipment), detection costs (for inspection of purchased materials and during manufacture), and prevention costs (for keeping defects from occurring in the first place). Juran found that in most manufacturing companies, external and internal failure costs together accounted for 50 to 80 percent of the total cost of quality. Thus, to minimize this total cost, he advocated that more attention be paid to prevention. Suggestions have been made that $1 invested in prevention is worth $100 in detection costs and $10,000 in failure costs.

In Table 6.4, we have adapted Juran's cost-of-quality system for use by service firms with a banking example. In the prevention row, recruitment and selection of service personnel are viewed as ways to avoid poor quality. Identifying people with appropriate attitudes and interpersonal skills can result in hiring contact persons with the natural instincts that are needed to serve customers well.

Inspection is included in the detection row, but generally it is impractical except in the back-office operations of a service.

Because service is an experience for the customer, any failure becomes a story for that customer to tell others. Service managers must recognize that dissatisfied customers not only will take their future business elsewhere but also will tell others about the unhappy experience, thus resulting in a significant loss of future business.

Statistical Process Control

The performance of a service often is judged by key indicators. For example, the educational performance of a high school is measured by the Scholastic Aptitude Test (SAT) scores of its students. The effectiveness of a police department's crime-prevention program is judged by the crime rate, and a bank teller's performance is judged by the accuracy of his or her end-of-day balances.

What happens if the service process is not performing as expected? Generally, an investigation is conducted to identify the cause of the problem and to suggest corrective action; however, performance variations may result from random occurrences and not have a specific cause. The decision maker wants to detect true degradation in service performance and avoid the failure costs that are associated with poor service. On the other hand, making an unnecessary change in a system that is performing correctly should be avoided. Thus, two types of risks are involved in controlling quality, as shown in Table 6.5. These risks have been given names to identify the injured party. If a process is deemed to be out of control when it in fact is performing correctly, a Type I error has occurred, which is the producer's risk. If a process is deemed to be functioning properly when it in fact is out of control, a Type II error has occurred, which is the consumer's risk.

TABLE 6.4
Costs of Quality for Services

Source: Adapted from C. A. Aubry and D. A. Zimbler, "The Banking Industry: Quality Costs and Improvement," *Quality Progress,* December 1983, pp. 16–20.

Cost Category	Definition	Bank Example
Prevention	Costs associated with operations or activities that keep failure from happening and minimize detection costs	Quality planning Recruitment and selection Training programs Quality improvement projects
Detection	Costs incurred to ascertain the condition of a service to determine whether it conforms to safety standards	Periodic inspection Process control Checking, balancing, verifying Collecting quality data
Internal failure	Costs incurred to correct nonconforming work prior to delivery to the customer	Scrapped forms and reports Rework Machine downtime
External failure	Costs incurred to correct nonconforming work after delivery to the customer or to correct work that did not satisfy a customer's special needs	Payment of interest penalties Investigation time Legal judgments Negative word-of-mouth Loss of future business

TABLE 6.5
Risks in Quality-Control Decisions

	Quality-Control Decision	
True State of Service	**Take Corrective Action**	**Do Nothing**
Process in control	Type I error (producer's risk)	Correct decision
Process out of control	Correct decision	Type II error (consumer's risk)

A visual display called a *control chart* is used to plot average values of a measure of performance (e.g., ambulance response time) over time to determine if the process remains in control (i.e., the performance mean and variance have not changed). Figure 6.9 shows an $\overline{X}$-chart that is used to monitor emergency ambulance response time. This chart is a daily plot of mean response time that permits monitoring performance for unusual deviations from the norm. When a measurement falls outside the control limits – that is, above the upper control limit (UCL) or below the lower control limit (LCL) – the process is considered out of control; consequently, the system is in need of attention. For our ambulance example, the first seven days represent the expected variation about the mean of all observations within the control limits. However, in day 10 our observation exceeds the UCL, a very unusual occurrence, signaling a need for root-cause analysis.

Constructing a control chart is similar to determining a confidence interval for the mean of a sample. Recall from statistics that sample means tend to be distributed normally according to the central-limit theorem (i.e., although the underlying statistic may be distributed in any manner, mean values drawn from this statistic have a normal distribution). We know from standard normal tables that 99.7 percent of the normal distribution falls within 3 standard deviations of the mean. Using representative historical data, both the mean and the standard deviation for some system performance measure are determined. These parameters then are used to construct a 99.7 percent confidence interval for the mean of the performance measure. We expect future sample means that are collected at random to fall within this confidence interval; if they do not, then we conclude that the process has changed and the true mean has shifted.

The steps in constructing and using a quality-control chart can be summarized as:

1. Decide on some measure of service system performance.
2. Collect representative historical data from which estimates of the population mean and variance for the system performance measure can be made.
3. Decide on a sample size, and using the estimates of population mean and variance, calculate (by convention) ± 3 standard deviation control limits.
4. Graph the control chart as a function of sample mean values versus time.
5. Plot sample means collected at random on the chart, and interpret the results as follows:
   i. Process in control (i.e., sample mean falls within control limits).
   ii. Process out of control (i.e., sample mean falls outside control limits, or a run of seven means falling either above or below the average). In this case:
      a. Evaluate the situation.

FIGURE 6.9
$\overline{X}$-chart for Ambulance Response

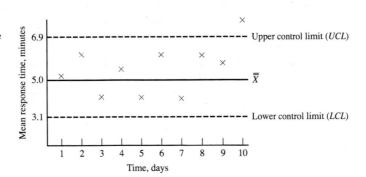

132   Part Two *Designing the Service Enterprise*

   b. Take corrective action.

   c. Check results of action.

6. Update the control chart on a periodic basis, and incorporate recent data.

Control charts for means fall into two categories based on the type of perform-ance measure. Variable control charts ($\bar{X}$-chart) and (R-chart) record measurements that permit fractional values, such as length, weight, or time. An attribute control chart (p-chart) records discrete data, such as the number of defects or errors as a percentage.

Example 6.2 **Control Chart for** **Variables** **(X-chart and** **R-chart)**	The purpose of the $\bar{X}$-chart is to detect changes in the process mean of a continuous vari-able (e.g., ambulance response time). The R-chart for the continuous variable measures the process dispersion. Table 6.6 contains data on response time for an emergency ambulance collected over a historically representative seven days. Four response calls were picked at random each day, one each during the morning, afternoon, evening, and night shifts. For each day the average response (based on the sample of four observations) and range (i.e., the difference between the highest and lowest values) are calculated and noted in the last two rows.

The estimate of population mean response and range are calculated as

$$\bar{\bar{X}} = \frac{5.1 + 6.2 + 3.9 + 5.7 + 4.1 + 6.1 + 4.3}{7} = 5.0$$

$$\bar{R} = \frac{2.9 + 2.7 + 1.8 + 3.2 + 3.1 + 2.0 + 2.8}{7} = 2.6$$

The R-chart is frequently constructed prior to determining the $\bar{X}$-chart in order to ensure that the process variability is under control. The control chart for the range is constructed using the following formulas:

$$\text{Upper Control Limit (UCL)} = D_4 \bar{R} \tag{1}$$

$$\text{Lower Control Limit (LCL)} = D_3 \bar{R} \tag{2}$$

Where $\bar{R}$ = estimate of population range

   D_4 = UCL value from Table 6.7 for sample size n

   D_3 = LCL value from Table 6.7 for sample size n

For our ambulance case, the range control limits are calculated using the control chart con-stants in Table 6.7 for a daily sample size of four:

$$\text{(UCL)} = D_4 \bar{R} = (2.282)(2.6) = 6.0$$

$$\text{(LCL)} = D_3 \bar{R} = (0)(2.6) = 0$$

Because all the range values in the last column of Table 6.6 fall within the UCL and LCL of R-chart for the seven day period the process variability is in control and thus we can proceed to the construction of the $\bar{X}$-chart.

TABLE 6.6 **Ambulance Response** **Times, minutes**	**Day**	**1**	**2**	**3**	**4**	**5**	**6**	**7**

Day	**1**	**2**	**3**	**4**	**5**	**6**	**7**
Morning	3.6	4.5	2.9	7.1	4.3	6.7	2.8
Afternoon	5.2	6.3	4.7	6.2	2.8	5.8	5.6
Evening	6.5	7.2	3.8	3.9	5.9	6.9	3.8
Night	4.9	6.9	4.3	5.6	3.2	4.9	4.9
$\bar{X}$	5.1	6.2	3.9	5.7	4.1	6.1	4.3
Range	2.9	2.7	1.8	3.2	3.1	2.0	2.8

TABLE 6.7
Variable Control
Chart Constants

Source: Adapted from Table 27 of *ASTM Manual on Presentation of Data and Control Chart Analysis,* copyright 1976, Philadelphia; American Society for Testing and Materials.

Sample Size	($\bar{X}$-chart)	R-chart	
n	A_2	D_3	D_4
2	1.880	0	3.267
3	1.023	0	2.574
4	0.729	0	2.282
5	0.577	0	2.114
6	0.483	0	2.004
7	0.419	0.076	1.924
8	0.373	0.136	1.864
9	0.337	0.184	1.816
10	0.308	0.223	1.777
12	0.266	0.283	1.717
14	0.235	0.328	1.672
16	0.212	0.363	1.637
18	0.194	0.391	1.608
20	0.180	0.415	1.585
22	0.167	0.434	1.566
24	0.157	0.451	1.548

Appropriate formulas for calculating the control limits for an $\bar{X}$-chart use A_2 found in Table 6.7 and $\bar{R}$ as a measure of process dispersion.

$$UCL = \bar{\bar{X}} + A_2 \bar{R} \tag{3}$$

$$LCL = \bar{\bar{X}} - A_2 \bar{R} \tag{4}$$

The control limits for our sample size of four are calculated as follows:

$$UCL = \bar{\bar{X}} + A_2 \bar{R} = 5.0 + (0.729)(2.6) = 6.9$$

$$LCL = \bar{\bar{X}} - A_2 \bar{R} = 5.0 - (0.729)(2.6) = 3.1$$

Figure 6.9 shows the $\bar{X}$-chart for ambulance response with the mean $\bar{\bar{X}} = 5.0$, UCL = 6.9, and LCL = 3.1. The sample means $\bar{X}$ for the first seven days from Table 6.6 are plotted on the chart to describe visually the week's performance to ascertain that the process is in control before placing the control chart in use. As seen for the first seven days all observations fall between the UCL and LCL and thus the process is in control. However, on day 10 the sample average exceeds the UCL; consequently, the system is in need of attention. Assume our ambulance example represents data from the city of Fort Lauderdale, Florida, and spring break began on day eight. The longer response times, therefore, could be explained by extended trips to the beaches. Prepositioning an ambulance on the beach during spring break might improve performance.

Example 6.3
Control Chart
for Attributes
(*p*-chart)

In some cases, system performance is classified as either "good" or "bad." Of primary concern is the percentage of bad performance. For example, consider the operator of a mechanized sorting machine in a post office. The operator must read the ZIP code on a parcel and, knowing its location in the city, divert the package by conveyor to the proper route truck. From past records, the error rate for skilled operators is about 5 percent, or a fraction defective of 0.05. Management wants to develop a control chart to monitor new operators to ensure that personnel who are unsuited for the job can be identified. Equations (5) and (6) below are used to construct a percentage or *p*-chart. These formulas should be familiar because they represent the ± 3 standard deviation confidence interval for a percentage.

134   Part Two *Designing the Service Enterprise*

$$UCL = \bar{p} + 3\sqrt{\frac{\bar{p}(1 - \bar{p})}{n}} \tag{5}$$

$$LCL = \bar{p} - 3\sqrt{\frac{\bar{p}(1 - \bar{p})}{n}} \tag{6}$$

where

$\sqrt{\dfrac{\bar{p}(1 - \bar{p})}{n}}$ = standard error of percentage

$\bar{p}$ = estimate of population percentage

n = sample size

The *p*-chart control limits for the sorting operation are calculated using equations (5) and (6) and random samples of 100 parcels drawn from the route trucks. Note that if the calculation of an *LCL* results in a negative number, then *LCL* is set equal to zero.

$$UCL = 0.05 + 3\sqrt{\frac{(0.05)(0.95)}{100}} = 0.05 + 3(0.0218) = 0.1154 \approx 0.11$$

$$LCL = 0.05 - 3\sqrt{\frac{(0.05)(0.95)}{100}} = 0.05 - 3(0.0218) = -0.0154 \; [\text{set} = 0.0]$$

The *p*-chart for this operation is shown in Figure 6.10. Given this 9-day probationary experience for the new employee, would you conclude that the person is suitable for the sorting position?

Unconditional Service Guarantee[10]

Whenever you buy a product, a warranty to guarantee its performance is expected—but to guarantee a service? Impossible! Not so, according to Christopher Hart, who writes that service guarantees such as the example shown in Figure 6.11 have five important features:

1. *Unconditional.* Customer satisfaction is unconditional, without exceptions. For example, L. L. Bean, a Maine mail-order house, accepts all returns without question and provides a replacement, refund, or credit.

2. *Easy to understand and communicate.* Customers should know precisely what to expect from a guarantee in measurable terms. For example, Bennigan's promises that if a lunch is not served within 15 minutes, the diner receives a free meal.

3. *Meaningful.* The guarantee should be important to the customer in financial as well as in service terms. Domino's Pizza guarantees that if an order is not delivered within 30 minutes, the customer gets $3 off rather than a free pizza, because its customers consider a rebate to be more reasonable.

FIGURE 6.10
p-chart for ZIP Code
Sorting Operator

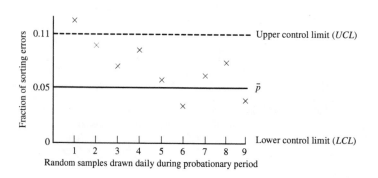

FIGURE 6.11

The Hampton Inn Unconditional Service Guarantee

Hampton Inn

**100%
SATISFACTION
GUARANTEE**

We guarantee high quality accommodations, friendly and efficient service, and clean, comfortable surroundings.

If you're not completely satisfied, we don't expect you to pay.

4. *Easy to invoke.* A dissatisfied customer should not be hassled with filling out forms or writing letters to invoke a guarantee. Cititravel, a service of Citibank, guarantees the lowest airfares or a refund of the difference; a toll-free call to an agent is all that is necessary to confirm a lower fare and get a refund.

5. *Easy to collect.* The best guarantees are resolved on the spot, as illustrated by Domino's Pizza and Bennigan's.

A service guarantee has obvious marketing appeal. More important, however, the service guarantee can redefine the meaning of service for an industry by setting quality standards. For example, Federal Express defined small-parcel delivery with its overnight delivery guarantee. A service guarantee promotes organizational effectiveness in several ways:

1. *Focuses on customers.* A guarantee forces a company to identify its customers' expectations. In a survey of its passengers, British Airways found that they judged its service on four dimensions: care and concern, initiative, problem solving, and—to the airline's surprise—recovery when things go wrong.

2. *Sets clear standards.* A specific, unambiguous guarantee for the customer also sets clear standards for the organization. The Federal Express guarantee of delivery "absolutely positively by 10:30 AM" defines the responsibilities of all its employees.

3. *Guarantees feedback.* Customers invoking a guarantee provide valuable information for quality assessment. Dissatisfied customers now have an incentive to complain and to get management's attention. Manpower Inc., a temporary-worker agency, takes a proactive approach by calling the client after the first day to get feedback on customer satisfaction.

4. *Promotes an understanding of the service delivery system.* Before a guarantee is made, managers must identify the possible failure points in their system and the limits to which these can be controlled. Burger Bug Killers, Inc., a Florida exterminator, will not guarantee or accept a job unless the client adheres to recommended facility improvements such as sealing doors and windows from insect penetration. Federal Express adopted a hub-and-spoke network to ensure that all packages would be brought to Memphis in the evening for sorting and flown out that very night for delivery by 10:30 the next morning.

5. *Builds customer loyalty.* A guarantee reduces the customer's risk, makes expectations explicit, and builds market share by retaining dissatisfied customers who otherwise would leave for the competition.

Service Recovery

Table 6.8 contains some statistics on the behavior of dissatisfied customers that suggests a quick resolution to service failure is an important way to create loyal customers. Because customers participate in the service delivery process, an alert employee trained in service recovery techniques can turn a potential disaster into a loyal customer.

A service failure can be turned into a service delight by empowering frontline employees with the discretion to "make things right." For example, when an airplane full of anxious passengers is delayed for some minor mechanical problem, it's time to break out complimentary drinks. More heroic efforts become legends, such as the story of a Federal Express employee who hired a helicopter to repair a downed telephone line during a snowstorm. Expenses incurred to accomplish a recovery are "pennies on the dollar" compared with the possible adverse "word-of-mouth" stories that are now turned into good stories of how an employee went the extra mile to accommodate a customer. Training employees in approaches to service recovery should be the first line of defense against defections and "poor word-of-mouth."

The service recovery framework shown in Figure 6.12 is illustrated by the example of Club Med, an all inclusive resort for guests who want to worry about nothing except relaxing and enjoying themselves. In the *pre-recovery phase,* expectations are set high by past experience or word-of-mouth. However, weather is an uncontrollable variable for Club Med and storms have the potential of ruining expectations of sunbathing on the beach. The *immediate recovery phase* requires initiative by the staff to guarantee a pleasant experience for the guests despite poor weather. Stories abound about the creative responses to poor weather, such as organizing group games and putting on stage shows. This ability of the staff to create a memorable experience for guests is called "the Club Med magic." In the *follow-up phase,* guests receive photographs and trinkets of the vacation and in severe cases a discounted invitation to return the following year.

Approaches to Service Recovery[11]

There are four basic approaches to service recovery: the case-by-case, the systematic-response, the early intervention, and the substitute service recovery approaches.

1. *The case-by-case approach* addresses each customer's complaint individually. This inexpensive approach is easy to implement, but it can be haphazard. The most persistent or aggressive complainers, for example, often receive satisfactory responses while more "reasonable" complainers do not. The haphazardness of this approach can generate perceptions of unfairness.

2. *The systematic-response approach* uses a protocol to handle customer complaints. It is more reliable than the case-by-case approach because it is a planned response based on identification of critical failure points and prior determination of appropriate recovery criteria. As long as the response guidelines are continuously updated, this approach can be very beneficial because it offers a consistent and timely response.

TABLE 6.8
Customer Feedback and Word of Mouth

- The average business only hears from 4 percent of its customers who are dissatisfied with the products or services. Of the 96 percent who do not bother to complain, 25 percent of them have serious problems.
- The 4 percent who complain are more likely to stay with the supplier than are the 96 percent who do not complain.
- About 60 percent of the complainers would stay as customers if their problem were resolved and 95 percent would stay if the problem were resolved quickly.
- A dissatisfied customer will tell from 10 to 20 other people about his or her problem.
- A customer who has had a problem resolved by a company will tell approximately 5 people about her or his situation.

FIGURE 6.12 **Service Recovery Framework**

Source: Reprinted with permission of Elsevier: Janis L. Miller, Christopher W. Craighead, and Kirk R. Karwan, "Service Recovery: A Framework and Empirical Investigation," *Journal of Operations Management* 18, 2000, p. 388.

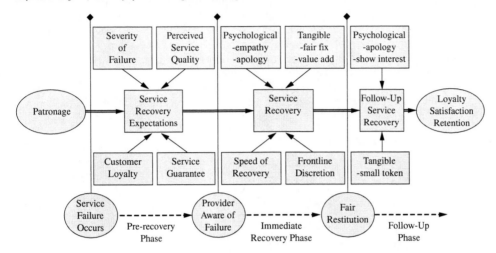

3. *An early intervention approach* adds another component to the systematic-response approach by attempting to intervene and fix service-process problems before they affect the customer. A shipper who realizes that a shipment is being held up by a truck breakdown, for example, can choose to notify the customer immediately so the customer can develop alternative plans if necessary.

4. An alternate approach capitalizes on the failure of a rival to win the competitor's customer by providing a *substitute service recovery*. At times the rival firm may support this approach. A desk person at an overbooked hotel, for example, may send a customer to a rival hotel. The rival hotel may be able to capitalize on such an opportunity if it can provide a timely and quality service. This approach is difficult to implement because information about a competitor's service failures is usually closely guarded.

Complaint Handling Policy[12]

A customer complaint should be treated as a gift. A complaining customer is volunteering her time to make the firm aware of an error because she cares. This opportunity should be seized upon not just to satisfy the customer but also to create a relationship with someone who will become an advocate for the firm. A complaint-handling policy should be incorporated into the training of all customer-contact employees. An example policy might include the following features:

- Every complaint is treated as a gift.
- We welcome complaints.
- We encourage customers to complain.
- We make it easy to complain.
- We handle complaints fast.
- We treat complaints in a fair manner.
- We empower our employees to handle complaints.
- We have customer- and employee-friendly systems to handle complaints.
- We reward employees who handle complaints well.
- We keep records of complaints and learn from them.

Stages in Quality Development

In this chapter we looked at the most important issues of incorporating quality into the delivery of services. Some aspects of quality assurance in a service organization may occur simultaneously, but it is useful to look at the development in a systematic way.

The service quality ladder shown in Figure 6.13 summarizes the progressive steps in quality development. Inspection is shown as the first rung because organizations usually begin here with their first attempts to address quality problems (e.g., checking hotel rooms after cleaning). Quality function deployment is shown as the top rung because quality must finally be recognized as a basic customer requirement that must be incorporated in the design of the service delivery process.

FIGURE 6.13
The Service Quality Ladder

QUALITY FUNCTION
DEPLOYMENT

Define voice of the
customer in operational terms

QUALITY SERVICE BY DESIGN

Design service process for
robustness and foolproof operation

UNCONDITIONAL SERVICE
GUARANTEE

Focus operations and marketing
on a service performance measure

COST OF QUALITY

Quantifying the cost of poor quality

QUALITY TRAINING PROGRAMS

Employee empowerment and
responsibility for quality

STATISTICAL PROCESS CONTROL

Quality assurance during service delivery

INSPECTION

Quality checked after service delivered

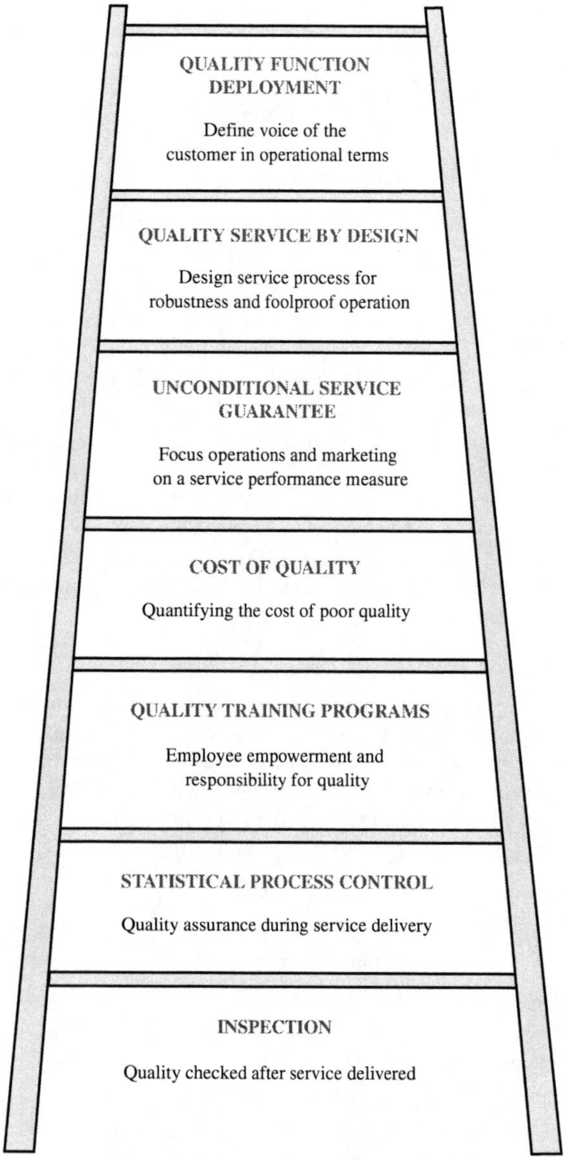

Service Benchmark

BRONSON METHODIST HOSPITAL

Bronson Methodist Hospital (BMH), a regional hospital that serves southwest Michigan, is a cut above most such institutions ... the Malcolm Baldrige National Quality Program says so; the U.S. Department of Health and Human Services (HHS) says so; HealthGrades, the nation's leading health care ratings company, says so; the American Hospital Association says so; *Fortune* magazine says so; and, most important, its patients say so.

This innovative hospital combines its vision of providing excellent health care, its philosophy of nursing, and its three corporate strategies (clinical excellence, corporate effectiveness, and customer and service excellence) to be a national leader in health care delivery. Bronson is consistently named as a "best practice" health care organization in different measures of quality care. For example, the hospital received a nationwide 5-star ranking, the highest possible, for its heart attack and hip replacement practices.

A Gallup poll reports that patient satisfaction ranks in the 97th percentile or better for inpatients, outpatient surgery, and outpatient testing. This remarkable achievement is the result of several efforts to focus on patient needs: patient surveys, post-discharge telephone calls, focus groups, community surveys, hospital "rounds" conducted by BMH leaders and patient-relations staff members, and a significant commitment to employee support.

BMH maintains a program for Customer Service Standards and Expectations that outlines each staff member's personal responsibility to provide excellent care for each patient. Employees are regarded as valuable resources—for example, the hospital has a formal plan to develop and retain its workforce and includes strategies such as supporting continuing education for the employee and awarding higher-education scholarships to children of employees. Employees also receive reimbursable wellness benefits in the form of personal trainers, massage therapy, smoking cessation, and weight-loss programs. The hospital's employee-supportive culture has resulted in significantly low employee turnover rates—for example, in one recent reporting period the rate of vacant positions for registered nurses was less than one-half of a national best practices comparison.

In addition to being a national leader in providing excellent health care, Bronson also leads in its commitment to its environment and community. Hospital staff volunteer an extraordinary number of hours to community health-related needs, and the hospital has received an environmental leadership award for reducing waste and pollution.

Source: http://www.quality.nist.gov/PDF_files/Bronson_Profile.pdf

Summary

We began our study of quality issues in services by noting that customers are the ultimate judges of a service's value. Market researchers have identified five principal dimensions that customers use to judge service quality. Customers use those dimensions to make their assessments, which are based primarily on a comparison of their expectations for the service desired with their perceptions of the service delivered. We then looked at the different types of gaps that can occur when customers' expectations do not meet their perceptions of the service.

Next we turned to the problem of measuring service quality. The walk-through audit and SERVQUAL are two useful approaches that can be used to measure quality in a variety of services.

We noted the necessity of "designing in" quality and examined the Taguchi concept of robustness, poka-yoke fail-safe strategies, and quality function deployment methods of incorporating customer requirements in design for quality.

The costs of quality are categorized as failure costs, detection costs, and prevention costs. We illustrated the application of statistical process control to avoid high failure costs in service operations.

Finally, because service failures do occur, we examined the concept of service recovery and unconditional guarantee programs.

Key Terms and Definitions

Control chart a chart with an upper control limit and a lower control limit on which sample means are plotted periodically to show visually when a process is out of control. *p. 131*

Poka-yoke a "foolproof" device or checklist to assist employees in avoiding a mistake. *p. 121*

Quality function deployment a process in which a "house of quality" is constructed to incorporate customer needs into the design of a service process. *p. 123*

Service recovery converting a previously dissatisfied customer into a loyal customer. *p. 136*

SERVQUAL a customer survey instrument used to measure service quality gaps. *p. 119*

Statistical process control the use of a control chart to monitor a process performance measure that signals when intervention is needed. *p. 130*

Taguchi methods approaches to service process design that ensure

"robustness" or an ability to function under adverse conditions. *p. 120*

Unconditional service guarantee a service warranty that provides a customer focus for the firm. *p. 134*

Walk-through audit a process-oriented survey given to customers and managers to evaluate the perception of the customer service experience. *p. 124*

Topics for Discussion

1. How do the five dimensions of service quality differ from those of product quality?
2. Why is measuring service quality so difficult?
3. Illustrate the four components in the cost of quality for a service of your choice.
4. Why do service firms hesitate to offer a service guarantee?
5. How can recovery from a service failure be a blessing in disguise?

Interactive Exercise

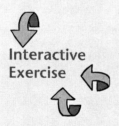

The class breaks into small groups. Each group identifies the *worst* service experience and the *best* service experience that any member has had. Return to class and discuss what has been learned about service quality.

Solved Problems

1. Control Chart for Variables ($\overline{X}$-chart and R-chart)

Problem Statement

To become productive, Resort International is interested in setting standards for the time that telephone reservation clerks spend with vacationers making tour arrangements. Collecting data on the amount of time the reservation clerks spend with customers has been proposed to determine the mean time and average range as well as to establish a process control chart for this operation. The table below records the time in minutes that reservation clerks spent answering calls as found by observing one call at random each day during a typical week. The fifth row contains the $\overline{X}$ values for each day. The last row contains the Range (i.e., high—low) values for each day (e.g., the high for Monday was 14 and the low was 5, yielding a range of 9).

Clerk	Mon.	Tue.	Wed.	Thru.	Fri.
Alice	5	11	12	13	10
Bill	6	5	12	10	13
Janice	14	13	10	9	9
Mike	8	6	9	12	14
$\overline{X}$	8.25	8.75	10.75	11.0	11.5
Range	9	8	3	4	5

Solution

First, we establish the population mean and range using the sample results from the five days shown above:

$$\overline{\overline{X}} = \frac{8.25 + 8.75 + 10.75 + 11.0 + 11.5}{5} = 10.05$$

$$\overline{R} = \frac{9 + 8 + 3 + 4 + 5}{5} = 5.8$$

Second, we establish limits for the range of call times for these samples of four calls each by constructing an *R*-chart using equations (1) and (2).

$$UCL = D_4 \overline{R} = (2.282)(5.8) = 13.2$$

$$LCL = D_3 \overline{R} = (0)(5.8) = 0$$

Third, we establish the control limits for an $\overline{X}$-chart using equations (3) and (4) when sampling four random calls each day for each clerk. The sample size of 4 was selected for convenience.

$$UCL = \overline{\overline{X}} + A_2 \overline{R} = 10.05 + (0.729)(5.8) = 14.28$$

$$LCL = \overline{\overline{X}} - A_2 \overline{R} = 10.5 - (0.729)(5.8) = 5.82$$

Plotting the average call time, which is based on a random sample of four calls for each clerk for each day, provides a record of performance for each clerk. If the average call time for any clerk falls outside the control limits, then an explanation is in order. If the average is above the UCL, too much time is being spent taking reservations, which results in lost productivity. If the average falls below the LCL, the clerk might be too curt, resulting in a customer perception of unresponsiveness.

2. Control Chart for Attributes (*p*-chart)

Problem Statement

A regional airline is concerned about its record of on-time performance. The Memphis hub experiences 20 flight operations each day of the week, with the following record of on-time departures for the previous 10 days: 17, 16, 18, 19, 16, 15, 20, 17, 18, and 16. Prepare a *p*-chart with a sample size consisting of 1 week's average on-time departure percentage.

Solution

First, we calculate the expected population fraction of on-time departures, which is the sum of the 10-day experience divided by a total of 200 flights:

$$\overline{p} = \frac{17 + 16 + 18 + 19 + 16 + 15 + 20 + 17 + 18 + 16}{(10)(20)} = 0.86$$

Then, the control limits are determined using equations (5) and (6) with a sample size of 7:

$$UCL = \overline{p} + 3\sqrt{\frac{\overline{p}(1 - \overline{p})}{n}} = 0.86 + 3\sqrt{\frac{0.86(1 - 0.86)}{7}}$$

$$= 0.86 + 3(0.13) = 1.25 \,[\text{set} = 1.00]$$

$$LCL = \overline{p} - 3\sqrt{\frac{\overline{p}(1 - \overline{p})}{n}} = 0.86 - 3(0.13) = 0.47$$

As often is the case for *p*-charts, one limit is set equal to the extreme value (i.e., UCL = 1.00 or LCL = 0.0). In this case, an average percentage of on-time departures for the week would be calculated, and only if this is found to be less than 47 percent (or 9 out of 20 departures late) would action be taken to investigate the abnormal occurrence for cause.

Exercises

6.1. In Example 6.1, Village Volvo wants to test the results of the QFD exercise for sensitivity to changes in the relative importance of customer expectations. Recalculate the weighted scores for the QFD exercise when customer expectations are given equal relative importance (e.g., five). Has this changed the previous recommendation to focus on training?

6.2. In Example 6.2, the ambulance supervisor now has decided to double the response time sample size to 8 calls per day. Calculate the new UCL and LCL for a revised $\overline{X}$-chart. For the next week, you record the following sample of daily mean response times: 5.2, 6.4, 6.2, 5.8, 5.7, 6.3, and 5.6. Would you be concerned?

6.3. The time to make beds at a motel should fall into an agreed-on range of times. A sample of four maids was selected, and the time needed to make a bed was observed on three different occasions:

Maid	Service Time, Sec.		
	Sample 1	Sample 2	Sample 3
Ann	120	90	150
Linda	130	110	140
Marie	200	180	175
Michael	165	155	140

a. Determine the upper and lower control limits for an $\overline{X}$-chart and an R-chart with a sample size of four.

b. After the control chart was established, a sample of four observations had the following times in seconds: 185, 150, 192, and 178. Is corrective action needed?

6.4. The management of the Diners Delight franchised restaurant chain is in the process of establishing quality-control charts for the time that its service people give to each customer. Management thinks the length of time that each customer is given should remain within certain limits to enhance service quality.

A sample of six service people was selected, and the customer service they provided was observed four times. The activities that the service people were performing were identified, and the time to service one customer was recorded as noted below:

Service Person	Service Time, Sec.			
	Sample 1	Sample 2	Sample 3	Sample 4
1	200	150	175	90
2	120	85	105	75
3	83	93	130	150
4	68	150	145	175
5	110	90	75	105
6	115	65	115	125

a. Determine the upper and lower control limits for an $\overline{X}$-chart and an R-chart with a sample size of 6.

b. After the control chart was established, a sample of six service personnel was observed, and the following customer service times in seconds were recorded: 180, 125, 110, 98, 156, and 190. Is corrective action called for?

6.5. After becoming familiar with their jobs, the sorting machine operators of Example 6.3 now average only two address errors per 100 parcels sorted. Prepare a *p*-chart for experienced sorting operators.

6.6. Several complaints recently have been sent to the Gotham City police department regarding the increasing incidence of congestion on the city's streets. The complaints attribute the cause of these traffic tie-ups to a lack of synchronization of the traffic lights. The lights are controlled by a main computer system, and adjusting this program is costly. Therefore, the controllers are reluctant to change the situation unless a clear need is shown.

During the past year, the police department has collected data at 1,000 intersections. The data were compiled on a monthly basis as shown below:

Month	Congestion Incidence
January	14
February	18
March	14
April	12
May	16
June	8
July	19
August	12
September	14
October	7
November	10
December	18

a. Construct a *p*-chart based on the above data.

b. Should the system be modified if, during the next 3 months, reports of congestion at these 1,000 intersections indicate the following:

Month	Congestion Incidence
January	15
February	9
March	11

6.7. The Speedway Clinical Laboratory is a scientific blood-testing facility that receives samples from local hospitals and clinics. The blood samples are passed through several automated tests, and the results are printed through a central computer that reads and stores the information about each sample that is tested.

Management is concerned about the quality of the service it provides and wants to establish quality-control limits as a measure for the quality of its tests. Such managerial practice is viewed as significant, because incorrect analysis of a sample can lead to a wrong diagnosis by the physician, which in turn might cost the life of a patient. For this reason, 100 blood samples were collected at random each day after they had gone through testing. After retesting was performed manually on this sample, the results were:

Day	Incorrect Analysis	Day	Incorrect Analysis
1	8	11	4
2	3	12	6
3	1	13	5
4	0	14	10
5	4	15	2
6	2	16	1
7	9	17	0
8	6	18	6
9	3	19	3
10	1	20	2

a. Construct a *p*-chart to be used in assessing the quality of the service described above.

b. On average, what is the expected number of incorrect tests per 100 samples?

c. Later, another sample of 100 was taken. After the accuracy of the tests was established, 10 samples were found to have been analyzed incorrectly. What is your conclusion about the quality of this service?

6.8. The Long Life Insurance Company receives applications to buy insurance from its salespeople, who are specially trained in selling insurance to new customers. After the applications are received, they are processed through a computer. The computer is programmed so that it prints messages whenever it runs across an item that is not consistent with company policies. The company is concerned with the accuracy of the training that its salespeople receive, and it contemplates recalling them for more training if the quality of their performance is below certain limits. Five samples of 20 applications received from specific market areas were collected and inspected with the following results:

Sample	No. of Applications with Errors
1	2
2	2
3	1
4	3
5	2

a. Determine the upper and lower control limits for a *p*-chart using a sample size of 20.

b. After the control limits were established, a sample was taken and four applications were found to have mistakes. What can we conclude from this?

Selected Bibliography

Andreassen, Tor Wallin. "What Drives Customer Loyalty with Complaint Resolution?" *Journal of Service Research* 1, no. 4 (May 1999), pp. 324–32.

Bell, Simon J., and James A. Luddington. "Coping with Customer Complaints." *Journal of Service Research* 8, no. 3 (February 2006), pp. 221–33.

Boshoff, Christo. "RECOVSAT: An Instrument to Measure Satisfaction with Transaction-Specific Service Recovery." *Journal of Service Research* 1, no. 3 (February 1999), pp. 236–49.

——, and Jason Leong. "Empowerment, Attribution, and Apologising as Dimensions of Service Recovery: An Experimental Study." *International Journal of Service Industry Management* 9, no. 1 (1998), pp. 24–47.

Bowen, David E., and Robert Johnston. "Internal Service Recovery: Developing a New Construct." *International Journal of Service Industry Management* 10, no. 2 (1999), pp. 118–31.

Carr, L. P. "Applying Cost of Quality to a Service Business." *Sloan Management Review,* Summer 1992, pp. 72–77.

Chebat, Jean-Charles; Moshe Davidow; and Isabelle Codjovi. "Silent Voices: Why Some Dissatisfied Consumers Fail to Complain." *Journal of Service Research* 7, no. 4 (May 2005), pp. 328–43.

Collier, Joel E., and Carol C. Bienstock. "Measuring Service Quality in E-Retailing." *Journal of Service Research* 8, no. 3 (February 2006), pp. 260–75.

Cronin, J. J., and S. A. Taylor. "SERVPERF versus SERVQUAL: Reconciling Performance-Based and Perceptions-Minus-Expectations Measurement of Service Quality." *Journal of Marketing* 58 (January 1994), pp. 125–31.

Dagger, Tracey S., and Jillian C. Sweeney. "Service Quality Attribute Weights: How Do Novice and Longer-Term Customers Construct Service Quality Perceptions?" *Journal of Service Research* 10, no. 1 (August 2007), pp. 22–42.

——, —— and, Lester W. Johnson. "A Hierarchical Model of Health Service Quality: Scale Development and Investigation of an Integrated Model." *Journal of Service Research* 10, no. 2 (November 2007), pp. 123–142.

de Matos, Celso Augusto; Jorge Luiz Henrique; and Carlos Ablerto Vargas Rossi. "Service Quality Paradox: A Meta-Analysis." *Journal of Service Research* 10, no. 1 (August 2007), pp. 60–77.

DeWitt, Tom, and Michael K. Brady. "Rethinking Service Recovery Strategies: The Effect of Rapport on Consumer Responses to Service Failure." *Journal of Service Research* 6, no. 2 (November 2003), pp. 193–206.

_____; Doan T. Nguyen; and Roger Marshall. "Exploring Customer Loyalty Following Recovery: The Mediating Effects of Trust and Emotions." *Journal of Service Research* 10, no. 3 (February 2008), pp. 269–87.

Dubé, Laurette; Michael D. Johnson; and Leo Mark Renaghan. "Adapting the QFD Approach to Extended Service Transactions." *Production and Operations Management* 8, no. 3 (Fall 1999), pp. 301–17.

Duffy, Jo Ann. "Service Recovery." In *New Service Development*, J. A. Fitzsimmons and M. J. Fitzsimmons (eds.), Thousand Oaks, Calif.: Sage Publications, 2000, pp. 277–90.

Eisingerich, Andreas B., and Simon J. Bell. "Perceived Service Quality and Customer Trust: Does Enhancing Customers' Service Knowledge Matter?" *Journal of Service Research* 10, no. 3 (February 2008), pp. 256–68.

Estelami, Hooman. "Competitive and Procedural Determinates of Delight and Disappointment in Consumer Complaint Outcomes." *Journal of Service Research* 2, no. 3 (February 2000), pp. 285–99.

Fassnacht, Martin, and Ibrahim Koese. "Quality of Electronic Services: Conceptualizing and Testing a Hierarchical Model." *Journal of Service Research* 9, no. 1 (August 2006), pp. 19–37.

Gupta, Praveen, and Cary W. Adams. *Six-Sigma Deployment*. Boston: Elsevier Science, 2003.

Harvey, Jean. "Service Quality: A Tutorial." *Journal of Operations Management* 16, no. 1 (February 1998), pp. 583–97.

Hays, Julie M., and Arthur V. Hill. "The Market Share Impact of Service Failures." *Production and Operations Management* 8, no. 3 (Fall 1999), pp. 208–20.

————, ————."An Extended Longitudinal Study of the Effects of a Service Guarantee." *Production and Operations Management.* 15, no. 1 (Spring 2006), pp. 117–31.

————, ————, and Susan E. Geurs. "The Impact of Service Guarantees on Service Quality at Radisson Hotels Worldwide." In *New Service Development*, J. A. Fitzsimmons and M. J. Fitzsimmons (eds.), Thousand Oaks, Calif.: Sage Publications, 2000, pp. 264–76.

Hill, Arthur V.; Julie M. Hays; and Eitan Naveh. "A Model for Optimal Delivery Time Guarantees." *Journal of Service Research* 2, no. 3 (February 2000), pp. 254–64.

Hogreve, Jens, and Dwayne D. Gremler. "Twenty Years of Service Guarantee Research: A Synthesis." *Journal of Service Research* 11, no. 4 (May 2009), pp. 322–43.

Holloway, Betsy B., and Sharon E. Beatty. "Service Failure in Online Retailing: A Recovery Opportunity." *Journal of Service Research* 6, no. 1 (August 2003), pp. 92–105.

Iglesias, Victor. "Preconceptions about Service: How Much Do They Influence Quality Evaluations?" *Journal of Service Research* 7, no. 1 (August 2004), pp. 90–103.

Johnston, Robert. "The Zone of Tolerance: Exploring the Relationship between Service Transactions and Satisfaction with the Overall Service." *International Journal of Service Industry Management* 6, no. 2 (1995), pp. 46–61.

————, and Sandy Mehra. "Best-Practice Complaint Management." *Academy of Management Executive* 16, no. 4 (2002), pp. 145–54.

Jones, Thomas O., and W. Earl Sasser, Jr. "Why Satisfied Customers Defect." *Harvard Business Review,* November–December 1995, pp. 89–99.

Karande, Kiran; Vincent P. Magnini and Leona Tam. "Recovery Voice and Satisfaction After Service Failure: An Experimental Investigation of Mediating and Moderating Factors," *Journal of Service Research* 10, no. 2 (November 2007), pp. 187–203.

Mattila, Ana S., and Paul G. Patterson. "Service Recovery and Fairness Perceptions in Collectivist and Individualist Contexts." *Journal of Service Research* 6, no. 4 (May 2004), pp. 336–46.

Miller, Janis, L.; Christopher W. Craighead; and Kirk R. Karwan. "Service Recovery: A Framework and Empirical Investigation." *Journal of Operations Management* 18 (2000), pp. 387–400.

Parasuraman, A.; Valarie A. Zeithmal; and Arvind Malhotra. "E-S-QUAL: A Multiple-Item Scale for Assessing Electronic Service Quality." *Journal of Service Research* 7, no. 3 (February 2005), pp. 213–33.

Posselt, Thorsten; Eitan Gerstner; and Dubravko Radic. "Rating E-Tailers' Money Back Guarantees." *Journal of Service Research* 10, no. 3 (February 2008), pp. 207–19.

Raajpoot, Nusser. "Reconceptualizing Service Encounter Quality in a Non-Western Context." *Journal of Service Research* 7, no. 2 (November 2004), pp. 181–99.

Rafaeli, Anat; Lital Ziklik; and Lorna Doucet. "The Impact of Call-Center Employees' Customer Orientation Behaviors in Service Quality." *Journal of Service Research* 10, no. 3 (February 2008), pp. 239–55.

Reimann, Martin; Ulrich F. Lunemann; and Richard B. Chase. "Uncertainty Avoidance as a Moderator of the Relationship between Perceived Service Quality and Customer Satisfaction." *Journal of Service Research* 11, no. 1 (August 2008), pp. 63–73.

Reynoso, Javier, and Brian Moores. "Towards the Measurement of Internal Service Quality." *International Journal of Service Industry Management* 6, no. 3 (1995), pp. 64–83.

Schoefer, Klaus, and Adamantios Diamantopoulos. "The Role of Emotions in Translating Perceptions of (In)Justice into Postcomplaint Behavioral Responses." *Journal of Service Research* 11, no. 1 (August 2008), pp. 91–103.

Simons, Jacob V., Jr., and Mark Kraus. "An Analytical Approach for Allocating Service Recovery Efforts to Reduce Internal Failures." *Journal of Service Research* 7, no. 3 (February 2005), pp. 277–89.

Smith, Amy K., and Ruth N. Bolton. "An Experimental Investigation of Customer Reactions to Service Failure and Recovery Encounters: Paradox or Peril?" *Journal of Service Research* 1, no. 1 (August 1998), pp. 65–81.

Soteriou, Andreas C., and George C. Hadjinicola. "Resource Allocation to Improve Service Quality Perceptions in Multistage Service Systems." *Production and Operations Management* 8, no. 3 (Fall 1999), pp. 221–39.

Sousa, Rui, and Christopher A. Voss. "Service Quality in Multichannel Services Employing Virtual Channels." *Journal of Service Research* 8, no. 4 (May 2006), pp. 356–71.

Stauss, Bernd, and Christian Friege. "Regaining Service Customers: Costs and Benefits of Regain Management." *Journal of Service Research* 1, no. 4 (May 1999), pp. 347–61.

Stewart, Douglas M. "Piecing Together Service Quality: A Framework for Robust Service." *Production and Operations Management* 12, no. 2 (Summer 2003), pp. 246–65.

———, and Richard B. Chase. "The Impact of Human Error on Delivering Service Quality." *Production and Operations Management* 8, no. 3 (Fall 1999), pp. 240–63.

Teas, R. Kenneth, and Thomas E. DeCarlo. "An Examination and Extension of the Zone-of-Tolerance Model: A Comparison to Performance-Based Models of Perceived Quality." *Journal of Service Research* 6, no. 3 (February 2004), pp. 272–86.

Voss, Christopher A.; Aleda V. Roth; Eve D. Rosenzweig; Kate Blackmon; and Richard B. Chase. "A Tale of Two Countries' Conservatism, Service Quality, and

Feedback on Customer Satisfaction." *Journal of Service Research* 6, no. 3 (February 2004), pp. 212–30.

Wangenheim, Florian V. "Postswitching Negative Word of Mouth." *Journal of Service Research* 8, no. 1 (August 2005), pp. 67–78.

Wood, Michael. "Statistical Methods for Monitoring Service Processes." *International Journal of Service Industry Management* 5, no. 4 (1994), pp. 53–68.

Yeung, Andy C. L.; T. C. Edwin Cheng; and Kee-hung Lai. "An Operational and Institutional Perspective on Total Quality Management." *Production and Operations Management* 15, no. 1 (Spring 2006), pp. 156–70.

Youngdahl, W. E., and D. L. Kellogg. "The Relationship between Service Customers' Quality Assurance Behaviors, Satisfaction, and Effort: A Cost of Quality Perspective." *Journal of Operations Management* 15, no. 1 (February 1997), pp. 13–32.

Endnotes

1. Daniel Pearl, "More Firms Pledge Guaranteed Service," *The Wall Street Journal,* July 17, 1991, p. B1.

2. A. Parasuraman, V. A. Zeithaml, and L. L. Berry, "SERVQUAL: A Multiple-Item Scale for Measuring Consumer Perceptions of Service Quality," *Journal of Retailing* 64, no. 1 (Spring 1988), pp. 12–40.

3. Ibid.

4. G. Taguchi and D. Clausing, "Robust Quality," *Harvard Business Review,* January–February 1990, pp. 65–75.

5. Shigeo Shingo, *Zero Quality Control: Source Inspection and the Poka-Yoke System* (Stanford, Conn.: Productivity Press, 1986).

6. R. B. Chase and D. M. Stewart, "Make Your Service Fail-Safe," *Sloan Management Review,* Spring 1994, pp. 35–44.

7. J. R. Hauser and D. Clausing, "The House of Quality," *Harvard Business Review,* May–June 1988, pp. 63–73.

8. J. A. Fitzsimmons and G. B. Maurer, "Walk-Through Audit to Improve Restaurant Performance," *Cornell HRA Quarterly,* February 1991, pp. 95–99.

9. J. M. Juran and F. M. Gryna, Jr., *Quality Planning and Analysis,* (New York: McGraw-Hill, 1980).

10. From Christopher W. L. Hart, "The Power of Unconditional Service Guarantees," *Harvard Business Review,* July–August 1988, pp. 54–62.

11. T. C. Johnston and M. A. Hewa, "Fixing Service Failures," *Industrial Marketing Management* 26, 1997, pp. 467–77.

12. Private communication from Ms. Jeanne Zilmer, lecturer at Copenhagen Business School, Denmark.

13. Prepared by Eivor Biese, Lauren Dwyre, Mikes Koulianos, and Tina Hyvonen under the supervision of Professor James A. Fitzsimmons.

Chapter

8

Process Improvement

Learning Objectives

After completing this chapter, you should be able to:

1. Use quality tools for process analysis and problem solving.
2. Describe and contrast corporate quality improvement programs.
3. Lead a team in a process improvement initiative.
4. Measure the capability of a process.
5. Describe the philosophy of lean service.
6. Conduct a data envelopment analysis (DEA).

Changing demographics and the anticipated future labor shortage will force services to become more productivity conscious. Consider the labor-saving ideas that have been incorporated by the new Sleep Inn chain to reduce the labor costs of operating a hotel unit. For example, clothes washers and dryers are located behind the front desk, so the night clerk can load and unload laundry while on duty. To help reduce housekeeping chores, nightstands are bolted to the wall so that maids need not vacuum around legs, and the shower stall is round to prevent dirt from collecting in corners. In addition, the computerized electronic security system has eliminated room keys: guests use their own credit cards to enter their rooms. Also, to reduce energy costs, heat or air-conditioning is turned on or off automatically when the guest checks in or out. In addition, the computer records the time that maids spend cleaning each room. Thus, creative facility design, effective use of labor, and innovative use of computers can have a major impact on increasing service productivity.[1]

Chapter Preview

The focus of this chapter is on continuous improvement in service organizations using productivity and quality initiatives. World-class service firms are noted by their commitment to ongoing improvement in customer service, thus raising the bar of excellence for the industry. Continuous improvement is a way of thinking that needs to be incorporated into a firm's culture.

The philosophy of continuous improvement is captured in the plan-do-check-act (PDCA) cycle proposed by Deming. Quality tools for analysis and problem solving are described and illustrated using an example in the airline industry. At the corporate level, organizations embrace continuous improvement through personnel development programs, the Baldrige National Quality Award, adopting process quality captured in ISO 9000 standards and more comprehensive programs such as Six Sigma and Lean Service.

Finally, a linear programming model referred to as data envelopment analysis (DEA) is found in the chapter supplement. DEA is an empirical method of measuring the efficiency of service delivery units by comparing one unit against all others. This comparative analysis of unit performance provides an opportunity to promote continuous improvement through shared learning.

182   Part Two *Designing the Service Enterprise*

Quality and Productivity Improvement Process

Foundations of Continuous Improvement

Continuous improvement is based on the teachings and philosophy of W. Edwards Deming. Deming is credited with helping Japanese industry recover from WWII and pursue a strategy of exporting goods of high quality at affordable prices. This combination of quality and low cost was thought impossible because people took for granted that quality was only achieved at high cost. The foundations of Deming's teachings consisted of three principles:

1. *Customer satisfaction.* Focusing on satisfying customers' needs should be paramount in workers' minds. This requires an attitude of putting the customer first and a belief that this principle is the object of one's work.

2. *Management by facts.* To encourage scientific thinking, objective data must be collected and presented to management for decision making. This approach requires formal data gathering and statistical analysis of the data by the quality improvement teams.

3. *Respect for people.* A companywide quality-improvement program assumes that all employees have a capacity for self-motivation and for creative thought. Employees are given support, and their ideas are solicited in an environment of mutual respect.

Plan-Do-Check-Act (PDCA) Cycle[2]

Deming's approach to quality recognizes that checking or inspecting for quality is too late and instead one should focus on the process. Deming's approach, represented by a wheel, consists of four steps: *plan,* select and analyze the problem; *do,* implement the solution; *check* the results of the change; and *act* to standardize the solution and reflect on the learning. As shown in Figure 8.1, the Deming wheel is a repetitive cycle with quality improvements resulting from continuous incremental turns of the wheel.

Plan. Planning begins with the selection of the problem. Problems will appear as changes to important customer indicators, such as rate of defections or complaints. Narrow the project focus and describe the improvement opportunity. The current process is documented, perhaps with a flowchart, and data are collected.

The possible causes are brainstormed and, using data, agreement is reached on the root cause(s). Develop an action plan that includes a workable solution, measures of success, and the implementation targets agreed upon.

Do. Implement the solution or process change perhaps on a trial basis. Monitor the implementation plan by collecting data on performance measures and noting progress against milestones.

Check. Review and evaluate the result of the change. Check that the solution is having the intended effect and note any unforeseen consequences.

Act. Reflect and act on learning from the experience. If successful, the process changes are standardized and communicated to all involved workers with training in

FIGURE 8.1
Deming's Quality-Improvement Wheel

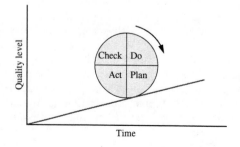

the new methods as needed. In some cases this could include external participants such as customers and suppliers. Celebrate the success and repeat the PDCA cycle on another problem.

Problem Solving

A systematic approach to solving problems is central to a worker-empowered program of continuous improvement in quality and productivity. The principal objective of continuous improvement is eliminating the cause of problems so they do not recur. A problem-solving approach based on Deming's PDCA cycle is described in Table 8.1.

TABLE 8.1   **Problem-Solving Steps in the PDCA Cycle**

Source: From D. C. S. Summers, *Quality,* 2nd ed., Upper Saddle River, N.J.: Prentice Hall, 2000, pp. 64–109.

Step 1	**Recognizing the Problem and Establishing Priorities**
	During the recognition stage, the problem is outlined by management in very general terms based on information from many sources.
Step 2	**Forming Quality Improvement Teams**
	An interdisciplinary team of individuals close to the problem is created and given a mandate to address the problem. Management involvement sets the team focus and shows buy-in on finding a solution that will be implemented.
Step 3	**Defining the Problem**
	The team first must define the problem and its scope clearly. Pareto analysis often can point to significant areas to investigate.
Step 4	**Developing Performance Measures**
	The effect of changes on the process can be verified only by taking before- and after-measures of performance.
Step 5	**Analyzing the Problem/Process**
	Flowcharting the process is often the first step at this stage to get a full understanding of all the intricacies involved. Information gathered at this stage will help determine potential solutions.
Step 6	**Determining Possible Causes**
	The cause-and-effect diagram is particularly helpful in identifying possible causes of the problem. The team can use the diagram to brainstorm ideas for the root cause. In a brainstorming session the team members are encouraged to throw out ideas without comment from the other members. Absolutely no arguing, criticism, or evaluation of ideas is allowed during this session, which is devoted to generating possible causes. After the possible causes are identified, data are organized using check sheets, scatter diagrams, histograms, and run charts to discover the root cause.
Step 7	**Selecting and Implementing the Solution**
	This is the most exciting stage, but temptation to propose solutions immediately must be curtailed. The criteria for selecting a solution include focus on the root cause, prevention of problem recurrence, cost-effectiveness, and timeliness.
Step 8	**Evaluating the Solution: The Follow-Up**
	Once the solution has been implemented and time has passed, the process is checked to verify that the problem has been solved. Run charts are useful for comparing prior data with current performance.
Step 9	**Ensuring Permanence**
	New methods need to be established and workers must be trained. Control charts can be used to monitor the process to ensure that the process remains stable.
Step 10	**Continuous Improvement**
	As the Deming wheel in Figure 8.1 suggests, quality and productivity are ramped up only with repetitions of the PDCA cycle. Once a problem is solved, another opportunity is identified for a new round of improvement analysis.

184 Part Two *Designing the Service Enterprise*

Quality Tools for Analysis and Problem Solving[3]

Quality improvement teams use many tools in the PDCA process. The tools aid in data analysis and provide a foundation for decision making. In the following section, eight tools are described with an example application to a problem that Midway Airlines faced. Midway Airlines, a regional carrier, served business travelers from a hub at the Midway Airport in Chicago until taken over by Southwest Airlines in 1991. The hub-and-spoke network required on-time departures to avoid delays that would compromise the efficient transfer of passengers during their multileg journeys. Midway monitored departure delays and found its systemwide on-time performance had deteriorated, causing irritation among its business passengers. The quality tools are presented next in the sequence in which they would be used in the problem-solving process.

Check Sheet

A check sheet is a historical record of observations and represents the source of data to begin the analysis and problem identification. Originally a check sheet was simply a sheet of paper listing potential problems, and each day workers would place check marks in the appropriate column to tally the frequency of occurrence. Today, data on problem frequency are entered online in an Excel spreadsheet to facilitate data interpretation. Figure 8.2 is an Excel spreadsheet record of problems faced by Midway during the prior year.

Run Chart

A run chart tracks change in an important process variable over time to detect trends, shifts, or cycles in performance. Run charts are easy to interpret and useful in predicting trends. Teams can use run charts to compare a performance measure before and after implementation of a solution. As shown in Figure 8.3, Midway experienced a steady increase in the number of departure delays.

Histogram

A histogram presents data collected over a period of time as a frequency distribution in bar-chart form. Using the chart command in Excel, data from the check sheet can be presented visually to obtain a sense of the distribution. Unusual features become obvious,

FIGURE 8.2
Excel Check Sheet

Month			Problem Area		
	Lost Luggage	Departure Delay	Mechanical	Overbooked	Other
January	1	2	3	3	1
February	3	3	0	1	0
March	2	5	3	2	3
April	5	4	4	0	2
May	4	7	2	3	0
June	3	8	1	1	1
July	6	6	3	0	2
August	7	9	0	3	0
September	4	7	3	0	2
October	3	11	2	3	0
November	2	10	1	0	0
December	4	12	2	0	1
Total	44	84	24	16	12

FIGURE 8.3
Run Chart of Departure Delays

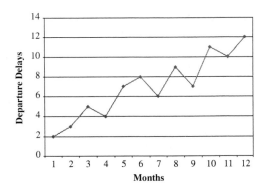

such as lack of symmetry, or skewness. A distribution with two peaks, or bimodal, suggests that two distributions with different means underlie the data. For airlines, a bimodal distribution of departure delays could be explained by a seasonality effect based upon weather conditions. In Figure 8.4 we selected "lost luggage" for our histogram. Note that the distribution is not symmetrical but skewed toward the fewer occurrences.

Pareto Chart

A *Pareto chart* orders problems by their relative frequency in a descending bar graph to focus efforts on the problem that offers the greatest potential improvement. Vilfredo Pareto, a 19th-century Italian economist, observed that relatively few factors usually account for a large percentage of the total cases (e.g., 80 percent of a country's wealth resides with 20 percent of its citizens). This principle, known as the *80/20 rule,* has been observed in many situations. For example, 80 percent of a retailer's sales are generated by 20 percent of the customers. Figure 8.5 presents the total number of problem occurrences for the year as a Pareto chart to identify "departure delay" as the most serious customer-related problem to address.

Flowchart

Flowcharts are a visual representation of the process and help team members identify points where problems might occur or intervention points for solution. Flowcharting conventions use diamonds to represent decision points, rectangles for activities, and ovals for beginning and ending points. All symbols are connected with arrows to represent the

FIGURE 8.4 **Histogram of Lost Luggage**

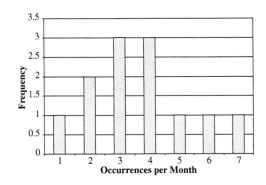

FIGURE 8.5 **Pareto Chart**

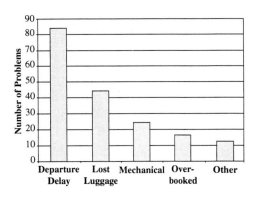

FIGURE 8.6
Flowchart at Departure Gate

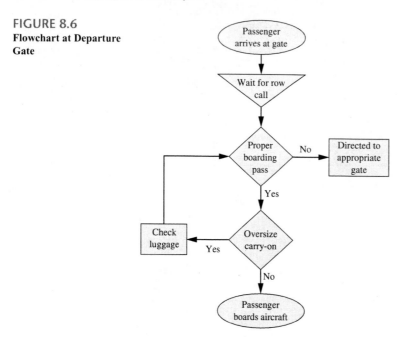

sequence of activities. In Figure 8.6 we provide a flowchart of the process at the departure gate to capture possible sources of delay, such as customers attempting to board with oversized luggage.

Cause-and-Effect Diagram

Cause-and-effect analysis offers a structured approach for a team to identify, explore, and display graphically, in increasing detail, all of the possible causes related to a problem in order to discover the root cause. The cause-and-effect diagram is also known as a

FIGURE 8.7   Cause-and-Effect Diagram for Delayed Flight Departures

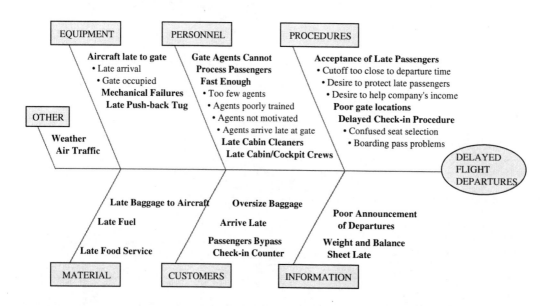

fishbone chart, owing to its skeletal shape, or an Ishikawa chart, named after its origina-tor. Figure 8.7 contains a cause-and-effect diagram for departure delays. The construction of the chart begins with the problem at the head and traces the major categories of causes back along the spine. For services, categories such as information, customers, material, procedures, personnel, and equipment are typical. Using the brainstorming technique, the detailed causes are filled in under each category and subcategory. Often causes are uncov-ered by asking the *who, what, where, when, why,* and *how* questions. The fishbone chart now can be used to eliminate the causes of delayed departure through a process of discus-sion and consensus; the remaining possibilities are targeted for additional data gathering.

Table 8.2, for example, shows a Pareto chart of the possible causes. Note that approxi-mately 88 percent of the departure delays are accounted for by four root causes. Finally, fishbone charts become records of cause-and-effect relationships and often are posted in work areas for consultation.

Scatter Diagram

A scatter diagram visually shows the relationship between two variables. Plotting possible-cause variables against the problem can identify where a strong correlation exists (i.e., scatter points form a tight trend line). As shown in Figure 8.8, the scatter diagram of late passengers versus departure delays confirms the identification of a root cause.

Acceptance of late passengers, thus, was shown to be the major root cause of depar-ture delays. Because gate agents were anxious to avoid antagonizing latecomers, they delayed flight departures, and, consequently, inconvenienced punctual passengers. As a solution, Midway established and advertised a policy of on-time departures that would be implemented by refusing late passengers to board even if the plane is still at the gate. After passengers realized that Midway was serious, the incidence of late arrivals declined significantly. Other causes of delay (e.g., waiting for pushback or fueling) were then addressed.

Control Chart

Control charts are used to monitor a process. As shown in Figure 8.9, a control chart shows when a process is out of control (i.e., the plot did not remain within the boundaries

TABLE 8.2
Pareto Analysis of Flight Departure Delay Causes

Cause	Percentage of Incidents	Cumulative Percentage
Late passengers	53.3	53.3
Waiting for pushback	15.0	68.3
Waiting for fuel	11.3	79.6
Late weight and balance sheet	8.7	88.3

FIGURE 8.8 Scatter Diagram

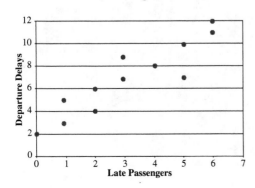

FIGURE 8.9 Control Chart of Midway Departure Delays

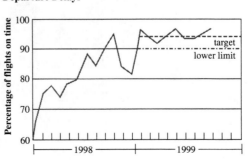

during the prior year). After the problem solution is implemented, the control chart is a check that the process is under control (e.g., percentage of on-time departures remains above 90 percent with a target of 95 percent). For the current year, the process is in control and the solution appears permanent.

Benchmarking

The measure of the quality of a firm's performance can be made by comparison with the performance of other companies known for being "best in class," which is a process known as *benchmarking*. For example, Singapore Airlines has a reputation for outstanding cabin service, Federal Express for consistent overnight delivery, Hampton Inns for clean rooms, and Nordstrom's department store for attentive salespersons. For every performance dimension, some firm has earned the reputation for being "best in class" and, thus, is a benchmark for comparison. Benchmarking, however, involves more than comparing statistics. It also includes visiting the leading firm to learn firsthand how management has achieved such outstanding performance. For obvious proprietary reasons, this often requires going outside one's own field. Some manufacturers, for example, have visited the pit stops at automobile races to learn methods of reducing the time for production-line changeovers. Others have visited Domino's Pizza to understand how it delivers customized products within 30 minutes.

The benchmarking process involves five steps: (1) select a critical process that needs improvement, (2) identify an organization that excels in the process, (3) contact the benchmark firm, make a visit, and study the process, (4) analyze the findings, and (5) improve your process accordingly.

For a typical example, consider an electronics company seeking to improve its purchasing function. This company formed a study team that visited Ford to learn how it reduced the number of its suppliers, talked with Toyota about vendor relationships, and observed the buying process at Reliance Electric. The team returned with quantifiable measures that benchmarked the superior performance of these leading firms and with knowledge of how these gains were accomplished.

Airlines have learned to reduce turnaround time at the gate by observing the teamwork at automobile racetracks.
U.S. Air Force photo by Senior Airman Mike Meares

Improvement Programs

Service quality begins with people. All our measurements to detect nonconformance do not produce a quality service; instead, quality begins with the development of positive attitudes among all people in the organization. How is this accomplished? Positive attitudes can be fostered through a coordinated program that begins with employee selection and progresses through training, initial job assignments, and other aspects of career advancements. To avoid complacency, an ongoing quality-improvement program is required. These programs emphasize preventing poor quality, taking personal responsibility for quality, and building an attitude that quality can be made certain.

Personnel Programs for Quality Assurance

Multisite service firms face special problems of maintaining consistent service across all units. For example, customers expect the same service from a hotel unit in Chicago that they found previously in a New Orleans unit of the same chain. In fact, the idea of "finding no surprises" is used as a marketing feature.

G. M. Hostage[4] believes the success of Marriott Corporation results in part from personnel programs that stress training, standards of performance, career development, and rewards. He finds that service quality is enhanced by the attitude a company takes toward its employees. The following eight programs have been the most effective:

1. *Individual development.* Using programmed instruction manuals, new management trainees acquire the skills and technical knowledge that are needed for the entry-level position of assistant manager. For a geographically dispersed organization, these manuals ensure that job skills are taught in a consistent manner.

2. *Management training.* Management personnel through the middle levels attend one management development session each year. A variety of professional management topics are addressed in 2- and 3-day seminars that are attended by lower-level managers from various operating divisions.

3. *Human resources planning.* The kinds of people who will be needed to fill key company positions in the coming years are identified, and an inventory of good prospects is created for future promotion. A key element of the plan is periodic performance review of all management personnel.

4. *Standards of performance.* A set of booklets was developed to instruct employees in how to conduct themselves when dealing with guests and, in some cases, even in how to speak. The *Marriott Bellman* stresses how to make a guest feel welcome and special. The *Switchboard Operator* tells in detail how to speak with a guest and handle a variety of specific situations. The *Housekeeper* tells precisely how a room is to be made up, right down to the detail of placing the wrapped soap bar on the proper corner of the washbasin with the label upright. In many cases, booklets are accompanied by a DVD to demonstrate proper procedures. Adherence to these standards is checked by random visits from a flying squad of inspectors.

5. *Career progression.* A job-advancement program with a ladder of positions of increasing skill and responsibility gives employees the opportunity to grow with the company.

6. *Opinion surveys.* An annual rank-and-file opinion survey is conducted by trained personnel at each unit. Subsequently, the results are discussed at a meeting. This survey has acted as an early warning system to head off the build-up of unfavorable attitudes.

7. *Fair treatment.* Employees are provided with a handbook of company expectations and obligations to its personnel. The formal grievance procedure includes access to an ombudsperson to help resolve difficulties.

8. *Profit sharing.* A profit-sharing plan recognizes that employees are responsible for much of the company's success and that they deserve more than just a paycheck for their efforts.

Deming's 14-Point Program

W. Edwards Deming generally is credited with initiating the highly successful Japanese quality revolution. In Deming's view, management was responsible for 85 percent of all quality problems and, therefore, had to provide the leadership in changing the systems and processes that created them. Management needed to refocus attention on meeting customer needs and on continuous improvement to stay ahead of the competition. His philosophy is captured in a 14-point program:[5]

1. *Create constancy of purpose for improvements of product and service.* Management must stop its preoccupation solely with the next quarter and build for the future. Innovation in all areas of business should be expected.

2. *Adopt the new philosophy.* Refuse to allow commonly accepted poor levels of work, delays, and lax service.

3. *Cease dependence on mass inspection.* Inspection comes too late and is costly. Instead, focus on improving the process itself.

4. *End the practice of awarding business on price tag alone.* The purchasing department should buy on the basis of statistical evidence of quality, not on the basis of price. Reduce the number of vendors, and reward high-quality suppliers with long-term contracts.

5. *Constantly and forever improve the system of production and service.* Search continually for problems in the system, and seek ways of improvement. Waste must be reduced and quality improved in every business activity, both front office and back office.

6. *Institute modern methods of training on the job.* Restructure training to define acceptable levels of work. Use statistical methods to evaluate training.

7. *Institute modern methods of supervising.* Focus supervision on helping workers to do a better job. Provide the tools and techniques to promote pride in one's work.

8. *Drive out fear.* Eliminate fear by encouraging the communication of problems and expression of ideas.

9. *Break down barriers between departments.* Encourage problem solving through teamwork and use of quality-control circles.

10. *Eliminate numerical goals for the workforce.* Goals, slogans, and posters cajoling workers to increase productivity should be eliminated. Such exhortations cause worker resentment, because most of the necessary changes are outside their control.

11. *Eliminate work standards and numerical quotas.* Production quotas focus on quantity, and they guarantee poor quality in their attainment. Quality goals such as an acceptable percentage of defective items do not motivate workers toward improvement. Use statistical methods for continuing improvement of quality and productivity.

12. *Remove barriers that hinder hourly workers.* Workers need feedback on the quality of their work. All barriers to pride in one's work must be removed.

13. *Institute a vigorous program of education and training.* Because of changes in technology and turnover of personnel, all employees need continual training and retraining. All training must include basic statistical techniques.

14. *Create a structure in top management that will push every day on the above 13 points.* Clearly define management's permanent commitment to continuous improvement in both quality and productivity.

Baldrige National Quality Award

The Baldrige National Quality Award (BNQA) was created by Congress on August 20, 1987. The award is named for Malcolm Baldrige, who served as Secretary of Commerce from 1981 until his death in a rodeo accident in 1987. The award is given annually to recognize U.S. companies that excel in quality achievement and management. There are five eligibility categories for the award: manufacturing companies, service companies, health care, education, and small businesses.

Each company participating in the award process submits an application, which includes an Award Examination; sample examination items and point values are listed in Figure 8.10. Note the heavy emphasis on "results." The Award Examination is designed not only to serve as a reliable basis for making awards but also to permit a diagnosis of the applicant's overall quality management. All applicants receive feedback prepared by teams of U.S. quality experts. Because of this quality-audit aspect of the award, Motorola requires all its vendors to apply for the award.

FIGURE 8.10   **Baldrige National Quality Award Criteria**

2010 Categories and Items	Point Values
1 Leadership	**120**
1.1 Senior Leadership..70	
1.2 Governance and Social Responsibilities...................................50	
2 Strategic Planning	**85**
2.1 Strategy Development...40	
2.2 Strategy Deployment...45	
3 Customer and Market Focus	**85**
3.1 Customer and Market Knowledge 40	
3.2 Customer Relationships and Satisfaction...............................45	
4 Measurement, Analysis, and Knowledge Management	**90**
4.1 Measurement, Analysis, and Improvement of Organizational Performance..45	
4.2 Management of Information, Information Technology, and Knowledge..45	
5 Workforce Focus	**85**
5.1 Workforce Engagement 45	
5.2 Workforce Environment 40	
6 Process Management	**85**
6.1 Work Systems Design...35	
6.2 Work Process Management and Improvement 50	
7 Results	**450**
7.1 Product and Service Outcomes......................................100	
7.2 Customer-Focused Outcomes..70	
7.3 Financial and Market Outcomes......................................70	
7.4 Workforce-Focused Outcomes.......................................70	
7.5 Process Effectiveness Outcomes.....................................70	
7.6 Leadership Outcomes..70	
TOTAL POINTS	**1,000**

ISO 9000

The ISO 9000 series of quality management system standards is fast becoming a de facto requirement for doing business in many industries, despite the fact that it is a voluntary standard. ISO (derived from Greek for "same") is a series of quality standards defined by the International Organization for Standardization, which is a consortium of the world's industrialized nations. The sheer extent of its global adoption makes it a critical business standard and it assumes the status of a "qualifier." Firms therefore seek certification regardless of whether they expect to achieve or believe in the need for improvements in quality.

Certification to an ISO 9000 standard signals that the firm has a quality management system in place that ensures consistency of output quality. The system is embedded in procedures, hence the common paraphrasing of the ISO 9000 requirements as "say what you do, and do what you say." ISO 9000 has several important characteristics. First, it does not prescribe specific practices. Second, it does not say anything directly about the quality of the product or service itself. Third, certification is provided by a highly decentralized system of auditors and accreditation bodies. ISO itself is only involved in design and updating of the standards, not in certification.

Documentation of processes and consistent performance are the key features of ISO standards. ISO 9000 seeks to achieve this by requiring that businesses implement a three-component cycle:

1. *Planning.* Activities affecting quality must be planned to ensure that goals, authority, and responsibility are both defined and understood.
2. *Control.* Activities affecting quality must be controlled to ensure that specified requirements at all levels are met, problems are anticipated and averted, and corrective actions are planned and carried out.
3. *Documentation.* Activities affecting quality must be documented to ensure an understanding of quality objectives and methods, smooth interaction within the organization, feedback for the planning cycle, and to serve as objective evidence of quality system performance.

The motivation for considering ISO 9000 arises from the fact that the European Economic Community has adopted this certification as a requirement for doing business in the member countries. Many companies follow and implement the ISO 9000 quality standards for reasons other than compulsory requirements, however. Companies have found that the very process of implementing the standard and the benefits from quality improvement are significant enough to justify this effort.

Six Sigma

In the mid 1980s, Motorola engineers wanted to highlight quality problems to drive process improvement and decided to report quality levels in defects per million of output. Motorola adopted this new standard and implemented a methodology called Six Sigma that, with top level management leadership, created a culture change within the organization. As a result of these efforts, Motorola documented $16 billion in savings that fell directly to the bottom-line, unlike an equal increase in revenues from which cost of goods must be subtracted. This financial performance did not go unnoticed; hundreds of firms around the world have adopted Six Sigma as a way of doing business. For example, rumor has it that Larry Bossidy of Allied Signal (now Honeywell) and Jack Welch of General Electric were playing golf one day and Jack bet Larry that he could implement Six Sigma faster and with greater results at GE than Larry could at Allied Signal. The financial results for GE far exceeded expectations, and Six Sigma became the cornerstone of the Jack Welch legend. Six Sigma has evolved over time to become more than just a quality system, but a way of doing business that can be seen as a vision, a philosophy, a symbol, a metric, a goal, and a methodology.[6]

Variation is part of any process—just look at an airline's on-time arrivals in Figure 8.11. Organizations typically describe their efforts in terms of "averages" such as average wait

FIGURE 8.11
Distribution of On-Time Arrivals

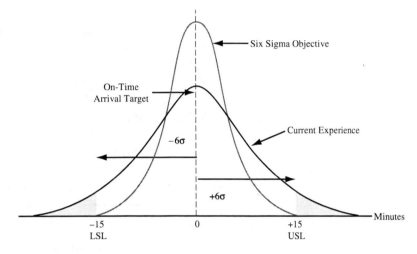

time that can hide problems by ignoring variation. The objective of Six Sigma is to reduce or narrow variation in performance to such a degree that six standard deviations can be squeezed within the limits defined by the customer's expectations. These limits are defined as an upper specification limit (USL) and a lower specification limit (LSL). Figure 8.11 shows that the current variation far exceeds the customer expectation of a plus or minus 15-minute deviation from scheduled departure or arrival. A Six Sigma objective is achieved when sufficient variation is removed from the process such that the plus or minus 15-minute range would span plus or minus 6 standard deviations (σ) of the on-time arrival target.

The effort to reduce the variability requires a measure of progress in reaching the specification objective. A *process capability index* is a statistical measure of how much the process variability has been reduced in achieving the goal. When the mean is centered between the specification limits the, C_p process capability index is used:

$$C_p = \frac{USL - LSL}{6\sigma} \qquad \qquad 8.1$$

The value of $C_p \geq 2.0$ is considered the acceptable level of process capability for Six Sigma standards. For our example on-time arrival distribution illustrated in Figure 8.11, we see that a $\sigma = 15/6 = 2.5$ is required to meet the minimum level of variation for the Six Sigma objective.

$$C_p = \frac{USL - LSL}{6\sigma} = \frac{+15 -(-15)}{6(2.5)} = 2.0$$

When the mean is not centered between the specification limits, the C_{pk} process capability index is used:

$$C_{pk} = \min\left[\frac{USL - \mu}{3\sigma}, \frac{\mu - LSL}{3\sigma}\right] \qquad \qquad 8.2$$

Returning to our Figure 8.11 let us assume the on-time mean has shifted from $\mu = 0$ to $\mu = +1$ and the standard deviation σ has remained at 2.5.

$$C_{pk} = \min\left[\frac{USL - \mu}{3\sigma}, \frac{\mu - LSL}{3\sigma}\right] = \min\left[\frac{15 - 1}{3(2.5)}, \frac{1 - (-15)}{3(2.5)}\right] = \min[1.87, 2.13] = 1.87$$

194 Part Two *Designing the Service Enterprise*

FIGURE 8.12
Six Sigma Organization Roles and Responsibilities

Source: Paul Fox, "Six Sigma Deployment," presented at session Driving Improvement through Six Sigma, National Quality Conference of the European Society for Quality in Healthcare, Dublin, Ireland, November 8, 2001.

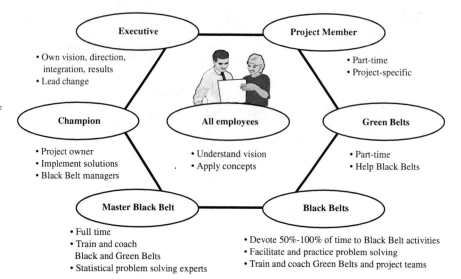

We no longer have a process that meets the Six Sigma expectation of $C_{pk} \geq 2.0$ unless we increase the value for USL to 16 to reflect the new mean.

Six Sigma is a rigorous and disciplined methodology that uses data and statistical analysis to measure and improve a company's operational performance by identifying and eliminating defects to enhance customer satisfaction. Six Sigma requires that an organization adopt a culture whereby everyone at all levels embrace a passion for continuous improvement with the ultimate aim of achieving virtual perfection equal to 3.4 errors per million customer encounters. In statistical terms, if one assumes process variation has a normal distribution, then six standard deviations (6σ) define a probability of 0.0000034 in the tail of the distribution. The focus of Six Sigma is on reporting errors, which is more motivating than stating performance in terms of percent success. For example, an overnight package delivery firm, such as FedEx, could take pride in delivering 99.9 percent of packages correctly. However, if it processes approximately one million packages per day, the result is 1,000 errors per day! Interestingly one-half of these errors could be customer-induced and, thus, the process will never reach a Six Sigma objective unless customer input is improved—a typical problem with service quality.

Six Sigma is project oriented with emphasis on top-down support and leadership that identifies targets of opportunity to maximize financial benefits. The objective of a Six Sigma project could be the reduction of defects (service failures), costs, or process variability, the increase of productivity, or the improvement of customer satisfaction. Six Sigma project responsibilities are structured by the use of a hierarchy for training and assignment of responsibilities. Figure 8.12 shows the roles and assigned responsibilities that in hierarchical order consist of executive, champion, master black belt, black belt, green belt, and project member. Skill development is encouraged, for example, a project member can advance with training to become a green belt, and then later to higher levels of responsibility in the organization's Six Sigma program. As shown in Table 8.3,

TABLE 8.3
Six Sigma DMAIC Process Steps

Step	Definition
Define	Define project objectives, internal and external customers.
Measure	Measure current level of performance.
Analyze	Determine causes of current problems.
Improve	Identify how the process can be improved to eliminate the problems.
Control	Develop mechanisms for controlling the improved process.

TABLE 8.4 **Comparison of ISO 9000, Baldrige National Quality Award, and Six Sigma**

Source: Lavanya Ravi, "Six Sigma in Service Organizations," Master of Science in Engineering Report, The University of Texas at Austin, December 2003, p. 23.

ISO 9000	Baldrige Award	Six Sigma
A framework for creating "Quality Thinking."	A framework for creating "Performance Thinking."	A framework for linking improvement to profitability.
Facilitates process management through documentation and compliance.	Facilitates benchmarking to improve performance levels to best-in-class levels.	Facilitates dramatic improvement to achieve performance excellence.
Specifies all business functions except accounting.	Specifies key aspects of business.	Specifies a methodology for improvement, irrespective of functionality.
Promotes management responsibility through communication and management review.	Promotes exceptional leadership behaviors as a way of life in society.	Requires leadership to aim at highest performance with high profitability.
Main aspect is compliance to documented practices and improving effectiveness.	Main aspect is to achieve total customer satisfaction through superior practices and performance.	Main aspect is to achieve and maintain a high improvement rate for business aspects that affect profitability.
About 50,000 companies have implemented it worldwide.	About 4 to 8 companies annually win at the national level; similar number at state level and in other countries.	Has been adopted by several companies to achieve dramatic improvement and profitability.
Savings are difficult to quantify.	Performance of publicly traded companies has shown advantage over others by 3 or 4 times.	Companies have reported huge savings in production and service areas.
Mass application of the standards.	Limited to a few companies.	Selectively used by companies committing to be best in class.
It is a third-party certification.	It is recognition for excellence.	It is a methodology to optimize performance and maximize profitability.
Is on decline due to diversification in series.	Stabilized due to limited recognition. Has expanded into health care and education.	Growing rapidly as an attractive means to realize superior financial results.

Six Sigma uses a DMAIC (Define, Measure, Analyze, Improve, Control) cycle to structure the improvement efforts for existing processes that are not performing as well as desired. A comparison of Six Sigma with ISO 9000 and the Baldrige National Quality Award is found in Table 8.4.

Lean Service

Lean service is an extension of lean principles pioneered by the Toyota Production System (TPS) with a focus on waste elimination, continuous flow, and customer demand pull, and is referred to in manufacturing as Just-in-Time production. The objective of a lean service process is a continuous rapid flow of value adding activities to satisfy customer needs. The lean philosophy has three guiding principles:

1. Satisfy the needs of the customer by performing only those activities that add value in the eyes of the customer.
2. Define the "value stream" by flowcharting the process to identify both value added and nonvalue added activities.
3. Eliminate waste. Waste in the value stream is any activity that the customer is not willing to pay for.

Lean service is an approach to achieving the perfect process with three goals: the right purpose (value); the best method (process); and the highest sense of accomplishment (people). The right purpose is driven by a focus on customer valued activities that are capable (e.g., Six Sigma), available (e.g., staffing level), adequate (e.g., trained staff), and flexible (e.g., employee discretion). The best process has a flow capable of low volume with high variety and is responsive to customer demand pull. The process is satisfying for workers because they have a sense of providing a valuable service and personal fulfillment.

The following steps provide a guide to achieving a lean service:[7]

1. Identify the key processes in your organization.
   * Which are primary?
   * Which are support?
   * Which are most important to the customer?
   * Which are most important to the success of the organization?
   * Which are most troubling to your people?

2. Select the most important processes and order by importance.
   * Form a team of people involved in the process including customers.
   * Create a "current state" value stream map of the process.

3. Analyze how the process can be changed to move toward perfection.
   * Create a "future state" value stream map of the improved process.

4. Ask what changes will be needed to sustain the "future state" process.
   * Establish a new process manager position?
   * Rearrange existing departments and functions?
   * Introduce new metrics to align department and function performance?

5. Implement the necessary changes to create the "future state" process.
   * Measure the performance compared with the "current state."
   * Introduce necessary changes to adjust the process.
   * Determine whether the adjusted process is stable and sustainable. .

6. Once the "future state" process has been proven
   * Determine what you will do with excess people and assets.

7. Once all processes have been improved
   * Start the cycle again.
   * Consider downstream and upstream processes shared with other organizations.

Summary

The foundation of continuous process improvement rests upon Deming's incremental approach to problem solving captured in the PDCA cycle. The improvement process uses the seven quality tools: check sheet, run chart, histogram, Pareto chart, flowchart, scatter diagram, and fishbone chart. These tools can be used by anyone in the organization to make a contribution to process improvement. However, senior management needs to provide leadership by promoting quality improvement programs. Of many programs, such as ISO 9000 and the Baldrige National Quality Award, the most recent is Six Sigma that is credited with significant results at firms such as Motorola, Allied Signal, and General Electric.

Service Benchmark

SERVICE, EDUCATION, AND HEALTH CARE WINNERS OF THE BALDRIGE NATIONAL QUALITY AWARD

Year	Service	Health Care	Education
1990	Federal Express		
1992	AT&T Universal Card Services The Ritz-Carlton Hotel		
1994	AT&T Consumer Communications Services GTE Directories		
1996	Dana Commercial Credit		
1997	Merrill Lynch Credit Xerox Business Services		
1999	The Ritz-Carlton Hotel BI		
2000	Operations Management International		
2001			Chugach School District Pearl River School District University of Wisconsin-Stout
2002		SSM Health Care	
2003	Boeing Aerospace Support Caterpillar Financial Services Corporation	Baptist Hospital, Inc. Saint Luke's Hospital of Kansas City	Community Consolidated School District 15
2004		Robert Wood Johnson University Hospital Hamilton	Kenneth W Monfort College of Business
2005	DynMcDermott Petroleum Operations	Bronson Methodist Hospital	Jenks Public Schools Richland College
2006	Premier, Inc.	North Mississippi Medical Center	
2007		Mercy Health System Sharp HealthCare	
2008		Poudre Valley Health System	Iredell-Statesville Schools
2009		AtlantiCare Heartland Health	

Source: http://baldrige.nist.gov/

198   Part Two *Designing the Service Enterprise*

Key Terms and Definitions

Baldrige National Quality Award (BNQA) an annual award for quality excellence earned by firms in manufacturing, services, healthcare, and education. *p.191*

Benchmarking the practice of comparing one's performance with that of other firms that are known as "best in class." *p.188*

Cause-and-effect analysis a process using a chart shaped like a fishbone to discover the root cause of a service quality problem. *p.186*

ISO 9000 an international program that certifies a firm as having a quality management system to ensure consistent output quality. *p.192*

Lean service a process improvement philosophy based on eliminating nonvalue added activities. *p.195*

Pareto chart presents problems in a bar graph by their relative frequency in descending order. *p.185*

PDCA Cycle a process of continuous improvement consisting of four steps: plan, do, check, and act. *p.182*

Process capability index measures the ability of a process to meet specifications. *p.193*

Six Sigma a rigorous and disciplined methodology to improve a firm's operational performance by eliminating process defects. *p.192*

Topics for Discussion

1. Discuss why Deming's 14-point program was rejected by U.S. firms but embraced by the Japanese following World War II.
2. Explain how the application of the PDCA cycle can support a competitive strategy of low cost leadership.
3. What are the limitations of "benchmarking"?
4. Explain why the introduction of Six Sigma at 3M was blamed for stifling creativity.

Interactive Exercise

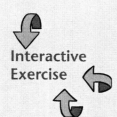

Have the class prepare a process flow chart (value stream map) of a familiar service and identify the non-value added activities. Make suggestions for elimination of waste.

Selected Bibliography

Banker, Rajiv D.; A. Charnes; and W. W. Cooper. "Some Models for Estimating Technical and Scale Inefficiencies in Data Envelopment Analysis." *Management Science* 30, no. 9 (September 1984), pp. 1078–92. (The "BCC" Model)

Charnes, A.; W. W. Cooper; and E. Rhodes. "Measuring the Efficiency of Decision Making Units." *European Journal of Operations Research* 2, no. 6 (November 1978), pp. 429–44. (The "CCR" Model)

Cooper, W. W.; L. M. Seiford; and K. Tone. *Introduction to Data Envelopment Analysis with DEA-Solver Code and References.* New York: Springer Science and Economics Publisher, 2006.

Corbett, Charles, and David A. Kirsch. "International Diffusion of ISO 14000 Certification." *Production and Operations Management* 10, no. 3 (Fall 2001), pp. 327–42.

Dessler, Gary, and D. L. Farrow. "Implementing a Successful Quality Improvement Programme in a Service Company: Winning the Deming Prize." *International Journal of Service Industry Management* 1, no. 2 (1990), pp. 45–53.

Frei, Francis X., and Patrick T. Harker. "Measuring the Efficiency of Service Delivery Processes: An Application to Retail Banking." *Journal of Service Research* 1 no. 4 (May 1999), pp. 300–12.

Gupta, Praveen, and Cary W. Adams. *Six-Sigma Deployment.* Boston: Elsevier Science, 2003.

George, Michael L.; David Rowlands; and Bill Kastle. *What is Lean Six Sigma.* New York: McGraw-Hill, 2003.

Iacobucci, Dawn. "The Quality Improvement Customers Didn't Want." *Harvard Business Review,* January–February 1996, pp. 20–36.

Johnson, Perry L. *ISO 9000: Meeting the New International Standards.* New York: McGraw-Hill, 1993.

Metters, Richard D.; Frances X. Frei; and Vicente A. Vargas. "Measurement of Multiple Sites in Service Firms with Data Envelopment Analysis." *Production and Operations Management* 8, no. 3 (Fall 1999), pp. 264–81.

Endnotes

1. From David Wessel, "With Labor Scarce, Service Firms Strive to Raise Productivity," *The Wall Street Journal,* June 1, 1989, p. 1.

2. From Michael Brassard and Diane Ritter, *The Memory Jogger II* (Methuen, Mass.: GOAL/QPC 1994), pp. 115–31.

3. From D. Daryl Wyckoff, "New Tools for Achieving Service Quality," *Cornell HRA Quarterly* 25, no. 3 (November 1984), pp. 78–91.

4. G. M. Hostage, "Quality Control in a Service Business," *Harvard Business Review* 53, no. 4 (July–August 1975), pp. 98–106.

5. W. Edwards Deming, *Quality, Productivity, and Competitive Position* (Cambridge, Mass.: MIT Center for Advanced Engineering Study, 1982).

6. http://www.isixsigma.com

7. From James P. Womack, "An Action Plan for Lean Services," presentation at Lean Service Summit—Amsterdam, June 23, 2004.

8. Reprinted and selectively adapted with permission from M. Gaudard, R. Coates, and L. Freeman, "Accelerating Improvement," *Quality Progress* 24, no. 10 (October 1991), pp. 81–88.

Chapter 11

Managing Capacity and Demand

Learning Objectives

After completing this chapter, you should be able to:

1. Describe the strategies for matching capacity and demand for services.
2. Determine the overbooking strategy for a service that minimizes expected loss.
3. Use a linear programming model to prepare a weekly workshift schedule with two consecutive days off for each employee.
4. Prepare a work schedule for part-time employees.
5. Explain what yield management is, when its use is appropriate, and how it can be accomplished using the critical fractile criterion.

After fixed capacity investment decisions have been made (e.g., number of hotel rooms to be built or aircraft to be purchased), the hotel beds must be filled or the airline seats sold to make the daily operations profitable. The subject of this chapter is the challenge that is faced by managers of matching service capacity with customer demand on a daily basis in a dynamic environment.

Service capacity is a perishable commodity. For example, a plane flying with empty seats has lost forever the revenue opportunity of carrying those additional passengers. American Airlines was the first in its industry to address this problem and to realize the potential of using what now is called *yield management,* which was discussed briefly in Chapter 3 and will be addressed in more detail here. Use of information technology to support yield management was not lost on Mr. Donald Burr, CEO of People Express, whose failing airline was bought by Texas Air in 1986. He is quoted as saying, "I'm the world's leading example of a guy killed by a computer chip."[1]

Unlike products that are stored in warehouses for future consumption, a service is an intangible personal experience that cannot be transferred from one person to another. Instead, a service is produced and consumed simultaneously. Whenever demand for a service falls short of the capacity to serve, the results are idle servers and facilities. Further, the variability in service demand is quite pronounced, and, in fact, our culture and habits contribute to these fluctuations. For example, most of us eat our meals at the same hours and take our vacations in July and August, and studies of hospitals indicate low utilization in the summer and fall months. These natural variations in service demand create periods of idle service at some times and of consumer waiting at others.

Chapter Preview

We begin with a discussion of two generic strategies, level capacity and chase demand. For the level capacity strategy, we introduce marketing-oriented strategies such as price incentives that can smooth customer demand to utilize better the fixed capacity. For the chase demand strategy, we consider operations-oriented strategies such as workshift scheduling to vary capacity to match the changing levels of customer demand. In conclusion, a hybrid strategy called yield management is explored that uses sophisticated real-time information systems to maximize revenue.

Generic Strategies of Level Capacity or Chase Demand

There are two generic strategies for capacity management, level capacity and chase demand. Table 11.1 illustrates the trade-offs between these two strategies. Utilities practice a pure form of *level capacity* because power stations are expensive, they involve large increments, and customers expect uninterrupted service. The pure form of *chase demand* is best illustrated by call centers that schedule the number of telephone agents according to expected variations in demand. Most services, however, are able to accommodate a hybrid strategy. For example, facility capacity in hotel beds is fixed but staffing can vary according to seasonal demand. The next two sections address the strategies shown in Figure 11.1 for demand management when a level capacity is being maintained and strategies for capacity management when a chase demand is being pursued.

TABLE 11.1
Level Capacity and Chase Demand Trade-offs

Strategic Dimension	Level Capacity	Chase Demand
Customer waiting	Generally low	Moderate
Employee utilization	Moderate	High
Labor-skill level	High	Low
Labor turnover	Low	High
Training required per employee	High	Low
Working conditions	Pleasant	Hectic
Supervision required	Low	High
Forecasting	Long-run	Short-run

Strategies for Managing Demand

Customer-Induced Variability[2]

The variability in customer arrival rates is a well-known challenge for service managers attempting to match capacity with demand. However, Frances Frei describes five sources of customer-induced variability in service operations. The common *arrival variability* results in either idle servers or waiting customers because independent decisions of customers seeking service are not evenly spaced in time. The level of customer knowledge, physical ability, and skill creates *capability variability* because some customers can perform tasks easily while others require hand-holding. *Request variability* results from the unique demands of customers that create uneven service times, for example, a bank customer who wants to purchase a CD and another customer who wants to cash a check. When customers are expected to perform a role in a service interaction (e.g., return a shopping cart to its corral), the level of commitment results in *effort variability*. Finally, the expectation of what it means to be treated well varies among customers and results in *subjective preference variability*. For example, one diner might appreciate the warmth of a waiter's first name introduction while another resents the presumption of intimacy. Personal preferences introduce an unpredictability that makes it difficult to serve a broad base of customers uniformly.

Strategies for managing customer-induced variability fall into two categories: accommodation and reduction. The accommodation strategy favors customer experience over operational efficiency. The reduction strategy favors operational simplicity over service experience. Creative hybrid strategies that give customers a choice could accomplish

FIGURE 11.1
Strategies for Matching Capacity of and Demand for Services

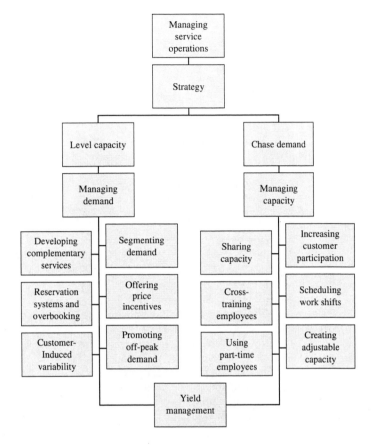

operational simplicity without compromising service experience (e.g., airlines can offer self-service check-in and an option of curbside check-in). Example strategies to manage customer-induced variability are outlined in Table 11.2.

Segmenting Demand

Demand for a service seldom derives from a homogeneous source. For example, airlines differentiate between weekday business travelers and weekend pleasure travelers. Demand often is grouped into random arrivals and planned arrivals. For example, a drive-in bank can expect visits from its commercial account holders on a regular, daily basis and at approximately the same time; it also can expect visits from its personal account holders on a random basis.

An analysis of health clinic demand by E. J. Rising, R. Baron, and B. Averill showed that the greatest number of walk-in patients arrived on Monday and fewer during the remaining weekdays.[3] While walk-in demand is not controllable, appointments are.

TABLE 11.2
Strategies for Managing Customer-Induced Variability

Type of Variability	Accommodation	Reduction
Arrival	Provide generous staffing	Require reservations
Capability	Adapt to customer skill levels	Target customers based on capability
Request	Cross-train employees	Limit service breadth
Effort	Do work for customers	Reward increased effort
Subjective Preference	Diagnose expectations and adapt	Persuade customers to adjust expectations

FIGURE 11.2

Effect of Smoothing Physician Visits

Source: E. J. Rising, R. Baron, and B. Averill, "A Systems Analysis of a University Health-Service Outpatient Clinic." Reprinted with permission from *Operations Research* 21, no. 5, September–October 1973, p. 1035, Operations Research Society of America. No further reproduction permitted without the consent of the copyright owner.

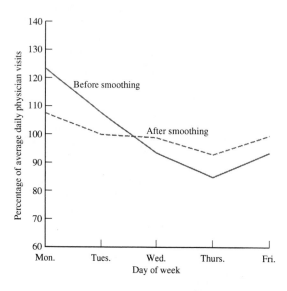

Therefore, why not make appointments in the latter part of the week to level demand? Using data for the same week in the previous year, these researchers noted the number of walk-in patients for each weekday. Subtracting these walk-in patients from daily physician capacity gives the number of appointment patients who are needed each day to smooth demand. For the sample week shown in Figure 11.2, this procedure yielded the number of appointment periods per day shown in Table 11.3.

The daily smoothing of demand was refined further by scheduling appointments at appropriate times during the day. After a two-month shakedown period, smoothing demand yielded the following benefits:

1. The number of patients seen increased by 13.4 percent.
2. This increase in patient demand was met, even though 5.1 percent fewer physician hours were scheduled.
3. The overall time physicians spent with patients increased 5.0 percent because of the increased number of appointments.
4. The average waiting time for patients remained the same.
5. A team of sociologists concluded that physician morale increased.

Offering Price Incentives

There are many examples of differential pricing. Consider the following:

1. Weekend and night rates for long-distance telephone calls.
2. Matinee or reduced prices before 6 PM at movie theaters.
3. Off-season hotel rates at resort locations.
4. Peak-load pricing by utility companies.

TABLE 11.3

Smoothing Demand by Appointment Scheduling

Day	Appointments
Monday	84
Tuesday	89
Wednesday	124
Thursday	129
Friday	114

TABLE 11.4
Suggested Discriminatory Fee Schedule

Experience Type	Days and Weeks of Camping Season	Number of Days	Daily Fee
1	Saturdays and Sundays of weeks 10 to 15, plus Dominion Day and civic holidays	14	$6.00
2	Saturdays and Sundays of weeks 3 to 9 and 15 to 19, plus Victoria Day	23	2.50
3	Fridays of weeks 3 to 15, plus all other days of weeks 9 to 15 that are not in experience type 1 or 2	43	0.50
4	Rest of camping season	78	Free

Differential pricing has been suggested for federal campsites to encourage better use of this scarce resource. For example, J. C. Nautiyal and R. L. Chowdhary developed a discriminatory pricing system to ensure that camping fees accurately reflect the marginal benefit of the last campsite on any given day.[4]

They identified four different camping experiences on the basis of days and weeks of the camping season. Table 11.4 contains a schedule of daily fees by experience type.

These experience groupings were made on the basis of total daily occupancy in the park under the assumption that occupancy is directly affected by available leisure time and climate. Campers in each experience group were interviewed to determine their travel costs. The marginal visitor was assumed to be the camper who incurred the highest cost in coming to the recreation site. This information was used to develop a demand curve for each experience type, and given the available number of campsites, the campsite fee was determined by means of these demand curves. Table 11.5 compares revenues generated under the existing system with those estimated when using discriminatory fees. Note that under the proposal, more campers are attracted, but with a corresponding reduction in total revenue. During the 78 days of free camping, however, a savings in labor cost is possible, because no ranger is needed to collect fees at the campsite. Even so, for the arrangement to work effectively in altering demand, it must be well advertised and include an advance booking system for campsites.

Note the projected increase in demand for experience type 3 because of the substantially reduced fee. The result of off-peak pricing is to tap a latent demand for campsites instead of redistributing peak demand to off-peak times. Thus, discriminatory pricing fills in the valleys (i.e., periods of low demand) instead of leveling off the peaks. The result is better overall utilization of a scarce resource and, for a private-sector firm, the potential for increased profit (assuming that fees cover variable costs). Private firms, however, also would want to avoid directing high-paying customers to low-rate schedules. For example, airlines exclude the business traveler from discount fares through restrictions such as requiring passengers to remain at their destination over a weekend.

Promoting Off-Peak Demand

Creative use of off-peak capacity results from seeking different sources of demand. One example is use of a resort hotel during the off-season as a retreat location for business

TABLE 11.5
Comparison of Existing Revenue and Projected Revenue from Discriminatory Pricing

Experience Type	Existing Fee of $2.50 Campsites Occupied	Existing Fee of $2.50 Revenue	Discriminatory Fee Campsites Occupied (est.)	Discriminatory Fee Revenue
1	5,891	$14,727	5,000	$30,000
2	8,978	22,445	8,500	21,250
3	6,129	15,322	15,500	7,750
4	4,979	12,447	—	—
Total	25,977	$64,941	29,000	$59,000

or professional groups. Another is a mountain ski resort that becomes a staging area for backpacking during the summer. Telephone companies offer unlimited calling on weekends, when the network is underutilized.

The strategy of promoting off-peak demand can be used to discourage overtaxing the facility at other times. A department store's appeal to "shop early and avoid the Christmas rush" as well as a supermarket's offer of double coupons on Wednesdays are examples.

Developing Complementary Services

Restaurants have discovered the benefits of complementary services by adding a bar. Diverting waiting customers into the lounge during busy periods can be profitable for the restaurant as well as soothing to anxious consumers. Movie theaters traditionally have sold popcorn and soft drinks, but now they also include video games in their lobbies. These examples illustrate complementary services being offered to occupy waiting consumers.

Convenience stores have expanded their services to include self-service gas pumps and fast-food meals. The concept of holistic medicine, which combines traditional medical attention with nutritional and psychiatric care, is a further example. Developing complementary services is a natural way to expand one's market, and it is particularly attractive if the new demands for service are contracyclical and result in a more uniform aggregate demand (i.e., when the new service demand is high, the original service demand is low). This explains why nearly all heating contractors also perform air-conditioning services.

Reservation Systems and Overbooking

Taking reservations presells the potential service. As reservations are made, additional demand is deflected to other time slots at the same facility or to other facilities within the same organization. Hotel chains with national reservation systems regularly book customers in nearby hotels owned by their chain when the customer's first choice is not available.

Reservations also benefit consumers by reducing waiting and guaranteeing service availability. Problems do arise, however, when customers fail to honor their reservations. (These customers are referred to as *no-shows*.) Usually, customers are not held financially liable for their unkept reservations. This can lead to undesirable behavior, such as when passengers make several flight reservations to cover contingencies. This was a common practice of business passengers who did not know exactly when they would be able to depart; with multiple reservations, they would be assured of a flight out as soon as they were able to leave. All unused reservations result in empty seats, however, unless the airline is notified of the cancellations in advance. To control no-shows among discount flyers, airlines now issue nonrefundable tickets and hotels require cancellation before 6 PM of the day of arrival or a one night stay is charged to their credit card.

Faced with flying empty seats because of the no-shows, airlines adopted a strategy of *overbooking*. By accepting reservations for more than the available seats, airlines hedge against significant numbers of no-shows; however, the airlines risk turning away passengers with reservations if they overbook too many seats. Because of overbooking abuses, the U.S. Federal Aviation Administration instituted regulations requiring airlines to reimburse overbooked passengers and to find them space on the next available flight. Similarly, many hotels place their overbooked guests in a nearby hotel of equal quality at no expense to the guests. A good overbooking strategy should minimize the expected opportunity cost of idle service capacity as well as the expected cost of turning away reservations. Thus, adopting an overbooking strategy requires training frontline personnel (e.g., front-desk clerks at a hotel) to handle graciously guests whose reservations cannot be honored. At a minimum, a courtesy van should be available to transport the customer to a competitor's hotel after making arrangements for an equivalent room.

Example 11.1 Surfside Hotel

During the past tourist season, Surfside Hotel did not achieve very high occupancy despite a reservation system that was designed to keep the hotel fully booked. Apparently, prospective guests were making reservations that, for one reason or another, they failed to honor. A review of front-desk records during the current peak period, when the hotel was fully booked, revealed the record of no-shows given in Table 11.6.

TABLE 11.6
Surfside Hotel No-Show Experience

No-shows *d*	Probability *P(d)*	Reservations Overbooked *x*	Cumulative Probability *P(d < x)*
0	.07	0	0
1	.19	1	.07
2	.22	2	.26
3	.16	3	.48
4	.12	4	.64
5	.10	5	.76
6	.07	6	.86
7	.04	7	.93
8	.02	8	.97
9	.01	9	.99

A room that remains vacant because of a no-show results in an opportunity loss of the $40 room contribution. The expected number of no-shows is calculated from Table 11.6 as

$$0(.07) + 1(.19) + 2(.22) + \cdots + 8(.02) + 9(.01) = 3.04$$

This yields an expected opportunity loss of 3.04 × $40, or $121.60, per night. To avoid some of this loss, management is considering an overbooking policy; however, if a guest holding a reservation is turned away owing to overbooking, then other costs are incurred. Surfside has made arrangements with a nearby hotel to pay for the rooms of guests whom it cannot accommodate. Further, a penalty is associated with the loss of customer goodwill and the impact this has on future business. Management estimates this total loss to be approximately $100 per guest "walked" (a term used by the hotel industry). A good overbooking strategy should strike a balance between the opportunity cost of a vacant room and the cost of not honoring a reservation; the best overbooking strategy should minimize the expected cost in the long run.

Table 11.7 displays the loss that is associated with each possible overbooking alternative. Note that no costs are incurred along the diagonal of the table, because in each case, the number of reservations that were overbooked exactly matched the no-shows for that day (e.g., if 4 reservations were overbooked and 4 guests failed to arrive, then every guest who did arrive would be accommodated and, further, the hotel is fully occupied, which is a win-win situation). The values above the diagonal are determined by moving across each row and increasing the cost by a multiple of $100 for each reservation that could not be honored,

TABLE 11.7 Overbooking Loss Table

No-shows	Probability	Reservations Overbooked									
		0	1	2	3	4	5	6	7	8	9
0	.07	0	100	200	300	400	500	600	700	800	900
1	.19	40	0	100	200	300	400	500	600	700	800
2	.22	80	40	0	100	200	300	400	500	600	700
3	.16	120	80	40	0	100	200	300	400	500	600
4	.12	160	120	80	40	0	100	200	300	400	500
5	.10	200	160	120	80	40	0	100	200	300	400
6	.07	240	200	160	120	80	40	0	100	200	300
7	.04	280	240	200	160	120	80	40	0	100	200
8	.02	320	280	240	200	160	120	80	40	0	100
9	.01	360	320	280	240	200	160	120	80	40	0
Expected loss($)	—	121.60	91.40	87.80	115.00	164.60	231.00	311.40	401.60	497.40	560.00

because fewer no-shows occurred than anticipated. For example, consider the first row, which is associated with zero no-shows occurring, and note that a $100 loss is associated with over-booking by one reservation. The values below the diagonal are shown as increasing by multiples of $40 as we move down each column, because more no-shows occurred than expected, which resulted in vacant rooms for the night. For example, consider the first column that is associated with not implementing an overbooking strategy, and note the increasing cost implications of trusting guests to honor their reservations.

For each overbooking reservation strategy, the expected loss is calculated by multiplying the loss for each no-show possibility by its probability of occurrence and then adding the products. For example, the expected loss of overbooking by two reservations is calculated by multiplying the probabilities in column 2 (i.e., Probability) by the losses in column 5 (i.e., 2 Reservations Overbooked) as follows:

$$.07(\$200) + .19(\$100) + .22(\$0) + .16(\$40) + .12(\$80) + .10(\$120)$$
$$+ .07(\$160) + .04(\$200) + .02(\$240) + .01(\$280) = \$87.80$$

Table 11.5 indicates that a policy of overbooking by two rooms will minimize the expected loss in the long run. If this policy is adopted, we can realize an average gain of $33.80 per night from overbooking. That is the difference in the expected loss between not overbooking of $121.60 and the expected loss from overbooking by two rooms of $87.80. This substantial amount explains why overbooking is a popular strategy for capacity-constrained service firms such as airlines and hotels.

In the "Managing Service Inventory," chapter the *critical fractile* criterion is derived for perishable goods, which we apply to our inventory of rooms:

$$P(d < x) \leq \frac{C_u}{C_u + C_o} \tag{1}$$

where

C_u = the $40 room contribution that is lost when a reservation is not honored (i.e., the number of no-shows is *under*estimated)

C_o = the $100 opportunity loss associated with not having a room available for an over-booked guest (i.e., the number of no-shows is *over*estimated)

d = the number of no-shows based on past experience

x = the number of rooms overbooked

This critical probability, which is based on marginal analysis, also can be used to identify the best overbooking strategy. Thus, the number of rooms overbooked should just cover the cumulative probability of no-shows and no more, as calculated below:

$$P(d < x) \leq \frac{\$40}{\$40 + \$100} \leq 0.286$$

From Table 11.5, a strategy of overbooking by two rooms satisfies the critical fractile criterion, because the cumulative probability $P(d < x) = 0.26$ and, thus, confirms the earlier decision based on minimizing the expected overbooking loss.

Strategies for Managing Capacity

Defining Service Capacity

Service capacity is defined in terms of an achievable level of output per unit time (e.g., transactions per day for a *busy* bank teller). Notice that for service providers our measure of capacity is based on a busy employee and *not* on observed output that must always be less than capacity as discussed in the Managing Waiting Lines chapter. However, service capacity also can be defined in terms of the supporting facility, such as number of hotel beds or

FIGURE 11.3
Daily Demand for Telephone Operators

Source: E. S. Buffa, M. J. Cosgrove, and B. J. Luce, "An Integrated Work Shift Scheduling System," *Decision Sciences* 7, no. 4, October 1976, p. 622. Reprinted with permission from Decision Sciences Institute, Georgia State University.

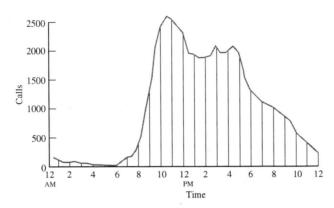

available seat miles at the system level for airlines. Looking at the airline example, we see that capacity can be limited by several factors such as available labor by skill classification (pilots, cabin crew, ground crew, and maintenance personnel), equipment (number and type of aircraft), and availability of gates. The airline example also illustrates a common service operations challenge of deploying capacity to different locations appropriately.

For many services, demand cannot be smoothed very effectively. Consider, for example, demand at a call center as shown in Figure 11.3. These data are the half-hourly call rates during a typical 24-hour day. We see that the peak volume (2,500 calls) occurs at 10:30 AM and the minimum volume (20 calls) occurs at 5:30 AM. The peak-to-valley variation is 125 to 1. No inducements are likely to change this demand pattern substantially; therefore, control must come from adjusting service capacity to match demand. Several strategies can be used to achieve this goal.

Daily Workshift Scheduling

By scheduling workshifts carefully during the day, the profile of service capacity can be made to approximate demand. Workshift scheduling is an important staffing problem for many service organizations that face cyclical demand, such as telephone companies, hospitals, banks, and police departments.

The general approach begins with a forecast of demand by hour, which is converted to hourly service staffing requirements. The time interval could be less than an hour; for example, 15-minute intervals are used by fast-food restaurants to schedule work during meal periods. Next, a schedule of tours, or shifts, is developed to match the staffing requirements profile as closely as possible. Finally, specific service personnel are assigned to tours, or shifts. The telephone-operator staffing problem will be used to demonstrate the analysis required for each step; however, the approach can be generalized to any service organization.

Forecast Demand

Daily demand is forecast in half-hour intervals, as shown in Figure 11.3, and must account for both weekday and weekend variations as well as seasonal adjustments. The Saturday and Sunday call load was found to be approximately 55 percent of the typical weekday load. Summer months were found to be generally lower in demand. Special high-demand days, such as Mother's Day and Christmas, were taken into account.

Convert to Operator Requirements

A profile of half-hour operator requirements is developed on the basis of the forecast daily demand and call distribution. The agreed service level requires that 89 percent of the time, an incoming call must be answered within 10 seconds. The half-hour operator requirements are determined using a conventional queuing model (found in Chapter 16) to ensure that the service level is achieved for each half hour.[5] The result is a topline profile of operators required by the half hour, as shown in Figure 11.4.

274 Part Three *Managing Service Operations*

FIGURE 11.4

Profile of Operator Requirements and Tour Assignments

Source: E. S. Buffa, M. J. Cosgrove, and B. J. Luce, "An Integrated Work Shift Scheduling System," *Decision Sciences* 7, no. 4, October 1976, p. 626. Reprinted with permission from Decision Sciences Institute, Georgia State University.

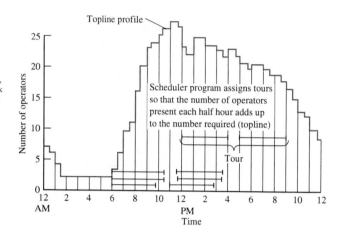

Schedule Shifts

Tours, representing various start and end times of work, need to be assigned so that they aggregate to the topline profile, shown in Figure 11.4. Each tour consists of two working sessions separated by a rest pause or meal period (e.g., 9 AM–1 PM, lunch break, 2 PM–6 PM). The set of possible tours is defined by state and federal laws, union agreements, and company policy. A heuristic computer program prepared especially for this problem chooses tours from the permissible set such that the absolute difference between operator requirements and operators assigned is minimized when summed over all "n" half-hour periods. If R_i is the number of operators required in period i and W_i is the number of operators assigned in period i, then the objective can be stated as follows:

$$\text{Minimize} \qquad \sum_{i=1}^{n} |R_i - W_i| \qquad (2)$$

The schedule-building process is shown schematically in Figure 11.5. At each iteration, one tour at a time is selected from all possible tours. The tour selected at each step is the one that best meets the criterion stated in equation (2). Because this procedure favors shorter tours, the different shift lengths are weighted in the calculation to avoid this bias. The result is a list of tours required to meet the forecast demand, as well as a schedule of lunch and rest periods during those tours.

FIGURE 11.5

The Schedule-Building Process

Source: E. S. Buffa, M. J. Cosgrove, and B. J. Luce, "An Integrated Work Shift Scheduling System," *Decision Sciences* 7, no. 4, October 1976, p. 622. Reprinted with permission from Decision Sciences Institute, Georgia State University.

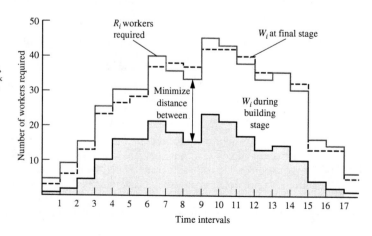

Assign Operators to Shifts

Given the set of tours required, the assignment of operators to these tours is complicated because of the 24-hour, 7-days-per-week operation. Questions of equity arise regarding the timing of days off and the assignment of overtime work, which involves extra pay. Furthermore, when work schedules repeatedly conflict with other priorities such as child care and medical appointments, the result can be poor morale, absenteeism, and attrition. A popular approach to this challenge is the use of a Web-based shift bidding system. It empowers operators to bid directly on the specific tour they desire through online auctions using bonus points, seniority, and rank. Bonus points can be awarded based upon criteria such as operator's performance, completion of previous undesirable tours, or failure to obtain requested tours in the past year. The use of clearly defined criteria results in perceptions of fairness and satisfaction from engaging in the scheduling process.

Weekly Workshift Scheduling with Days-Off Constraint

As noted, developing tours to match the profile of daily demand is only part of the problem. Many public services such as police, fire protection, and emergency hospital care must be available 24 hours a day, every day of the week. For these organizations, a typical employee works 5 days a week with 2 consecutive days off each week, but not necessarily Saturday and Sunday. Management is interested in developing work schedules and meeting the varying employee requirements for weekdays and weekends with the smallest number of staff members possible.

This problem can be formulated as an integer linear programming (ILP) model. To begin, the desired staffing levels are determined for each day in the week. The problem then becomes one of determining the minimum number of employees required for assignment to each of seven possible tours. Each tour consists of 5 days on and 2 consecutive days off; each will begin on a different day of the week and last for 5 consecutive working days. Consider the following general formulation of this problem as an ILP model.

Variable definitions:

x_i = number of employees assigned to tour i, where day i begins 2 consecutive days off (e.g., employees assigned to tour 1 have Sunday and Monday off)

b_j = desired staffing level for day j

Objective function:

Minimize $x_1 + x_2 + x_3 + x_4 + x_5 + x_6 + x_7$

Constraints:

| Sunday | | $x_2 + x_3 + x_4 + x_5 + x_6$ | $\geq b_1$ |

Sunday $\qquad\qquad x_2 + x_3 + x_4 + x_5 + x_6 \qquad\quad \geq b_1$

Monday $\qquad\qquad\quad x_3 + x_4 + x_5 + x_6 + x_7 \geq b_2$

Tuesday $\quad x_1 \qquad\qquad + x_4 + x_5 + x_6 + x_7 \geq b_3$

Wednesday $\ x_1 + x_2 \qquad\qquad + x_5 + x_6 + x_7 \geq b_4$

Thursday $\ x_1 + x_2 + x_3 \qquad\qquad + x_6 + x_7 \geq b_5$

Friday $\qquad x_1 + x_2 + x_3 + x_4 \qquad\qquad + x_7 \geq b_6$

Saturday $\quad x_1 + x_2 + x_3 + x_4 + x_5 \qquad\qquad \geq b_7$

$\qquad\qquad x_i \geq 0$ and integer

**Example 11.2
Hospital
Emergency Room**

The emergency room is operated on a 24-hour, 7-days-per-week schedule. The day is divided into three eight-hour shifts. The total number of nurses required during the day shift is:

Day	Su	M	Tu	W	Th	F	Sa
Nurses	3	6	5	6	5	5	5

TABLE 11.8
Weekly Nurse Staffing Schedule, x = Workday

Nurse	Su	M	Tu	W	Th	F	Sa
A	...	...	x	x	x	x	x
B	x	...	...	x	x	x	x
C	x	x	...	...	x	x	x
D	x	x	...	...	x	x	x
E	x	x	x	x	...	...	x
F	x	x	x	x	...	...	x
G	x	x	x	x	...	...	x
H	...	x	x	x	x	x	...
Total	6	6	5	6	5	5	7
Required	3	6	5	6	5	5	5
Excess	3	0	0	0	0	0	2

The emergency room director is interested in developing a workforce schedule that will minimize the number of nurses required to staff the facility. Nurses work 5 days a week and are entitled to 2 consecutive days off each week.

The ILP model above is formulated with the appropriate right-hand-side constraint values (i.e., $b_1 = 3$, $b_2 = 6$, ..., $b_6 = 5$, $b_7 = 5$), and the solution yields the following results: $x_1 = 1$, $x_2 = 1$, $x_3 = 2$, $x_4 = 0$, $x_5 = 3$, $x_6 = 0$, $x_7 = 1$. This means we have one tour with Sunday and Monday off, one tour with Monday and Tuesday off, two tours with Tuesday and Wednesday off, three tours with Thursday and Friday off, and one tour with Saturday and Sunday off. The corresponding staffing schedule is shown in Table 11.8 with excess staff occurring only on Sunday and Saturday.

These scheduling problems typically result in multiple optimal solutions. For example, in this case, the solution $x_1 = 1$, $x_2 = 1$, $x_3 = 1$, $x_4 = 1$, $x_5 = 1$, $x_6 = 1$, $x_7 = 2$ is feasible and also requires eight nurses. Why might this second solution be preferred to the schedule shown in Table 11.8?

Increasing Customer Participation

The strategy of increasing customer participation is illustrated best by the fast-food restaurants that have eliminated personnel who serve food and clear tables. The customer (now a coproducer) not only places the order directly from a limited menu but also clears the table after the meal. Naturally, the customer expects faster service and less-expensive meals to compensate for this help; however, the service provider benefits in many subtle ways. Of course, there are fewer personnel to supervise and to pay, but more important, the customer as a coproducer provides labor just at the moment it is required. Thus, capacity to serve varies more directly with demand rather than being fixed.

Some drawbacks to self-service do exist, because the quality of labor is not completely under the service manager's control. A self-service gas customer may fail to check the tire pressure and oil level regularly, which eventually can lead to problems. Self-service of "bulk" foods (e.g., cereals, grains, honey, peanut butter) in markets can lead both to contamination of the product in the bulk container and to waste because of spillage.

Creating Adjustable Capacity

Through design, a portion of capacity can be made variable. Airlines routinely move the partition between first class and coach to meet the changing mix of passengers. An innovative restaurant, Benihana of Tokyo, arranged its floor plan to accommodate eating areas serving two tables of eight diners each. Chefs are assigned to each area, and they prepare the meal at the table in a theatrical manner, with flashing knives and animated movements. Thus, the restaurant can adjust its capacity effectively by having only the number of chefs on duty that is needed.

Capacity at peak periods can be expanded by the effective use of slack times. Performing supportive tasks during slower periods of demand allows employees to concentrate on essential tasks during rush periods. This strategy requires some cross-training of employees to allow performance of noncustomer-contact tasks during slow-demand periods. For example, servers at a restaurant can wrap silverware in napkins or clean the premises when demand is low; thus, they are free of these tasks during the rush period.

Sharing Capacity

A service delivery system often requires a large investment in equipment and facilities. During periods of underutilization, it may be possible to find other uses for this capacity. Airlines have cooperated in this manner for years. At small airports, airlines share the same gates, ramps, baggage-handling equipment, and ground personnel. It also is common for some airlines to lease their aircraft to others during the off-season; the lease agreement includes painting on the appropriate insignia and refurbishing the interior.

Cross-Training Employees

Some service systems are made up of several operations. When one operation is busy, another operation sometimes may be idle. Cross-training employees to perform tasks in several operations creates flexible capacity to meet localized peaks in demand.

The gains from cross-training employees can be seen at supermarkets. When queues develop at the cash registers, the manager calls on stockers to operate registers until the surge is over. Likewise, during slow periods, some of the cashiers are busy stocking shelves. This approach also can help to build an esprit de corps and give employees relief from monotony. In fast-food restaurants, cross-trained employees create capacity flexibility, because tasks can be reassigned to fewer employees during slow periods (temporarily enlarging the job) and become more specialized during busy periods (division of labor).

Using Part-Time Employees

When peaks of activity are persistent and predictable, such as at mealtimes in restaurants or paydays in banks, part-time help can supplement regular employees. If the required skills and training are minimal, then a ready part-time labor pool is available from high school and college students as well as others who are interested in supplementing their primary source of income.

Another source of part-time help is off-duty personnel who are placed on standby. Airlines and hospitals often pay their personnel some nominal fee to restrict their activities and be ready for work if they are needed.

Scheduling Part-Time Tellers at a Drive-In Bank[6]

Drive-in banks experience predictable variations in activity on different days of the week. Figure 11.6 shows the teller requirements for a typical week based on customer demand variations. This bank usually employed enough tellers to meet peak demands on Friday; however, the policy created considerable idle teller time on the low-demand days, particularly Tuesday and Thursday. To reduce teller costs, management decided to employ part-time tellers and to reduce the full-time staff to a level that just meets the demand for

FIGURE 11.6
Teller Requirements

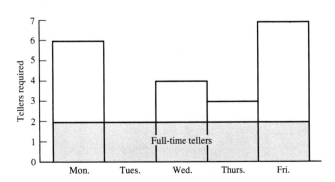

278   Part Three *Managing Service Operations*

Tuesday. Further, to provide equity in hours worked, it was decided that a part-time teller should work at least 2, but no more than 3, days in a week.

A primary objective of scheduling part-time workers is to meet the requirements with the minimum number of teller-days. A secondary objective is to have a minimum number of part-time tellers. This approach is illustrated here using bank tellers, but the same procedure can be used for scheduling part-time employees in many other services.

Determine the Minimum Number of Part-Time Tellers Needed

Figure 11.6 shows that with two full-time tellers, 12 teller-days remain to be covered during the week. Using 3-day schedules, we see that five tellers on Friday determines the feasible minimum in this case.

Develop a Decreasing-Demand Histogram

From Figure 11.6, note the daily part-time teller requirements. Resequence the days in order of decreasing demand, as shown in Figure 11.7.

Assign Tellers to the Histogram

Starting with the first part-time teller, assign that individual in Figure 11.7 to the first block on Friday, the second teller to block two, and so forth. Repeat the sequence with Monday, and carry over the remaining tellers into Wednesday. Table 11.9 summarizes the resulting daily part-time work schedule, which consists of two three-day work assignments for Tellers 1 and 2 and three two-day work assignments for Tellers 3, 4, and 5.

Yield Management[7]

Since deregulation permitted airlines to set their own prices, a new approach to revenue maximization—called *yield management*—has emerged. Yield management is a comprehensive system that incorporates many of the strategies discussed earlier in this chapter (e.g., using reservation systems, overbooking, and segmenting demand).

Because of the perishable nature of airline seats (i.e., once a flight has departed, the potential revenue from an empty seat is lost forever), offering a discount on fares to fill the aircraft became attractive. Selling all seats at a discount, however, would preclude the possibility of selling some at full price. Yield management attempts to allocate the fixed capacity of seats on a flight to match the potential demand in various market segments (e.g., coach, tourist, and supersaver) in the most profitable manner. Although airlines were the first to develop yield management, other capacity-constrained service industries (e.g., hotels, rental-car firms, and cruise lines) also are adopting this practice.

The economic motivation behind yield management is captured in Figure 11.8, an illustration of pricing a coach seat on a cross-country flight. Figure 11.8a illustrates the traditional fixed price relationship between a downward sloping demand curve and quantity sold. Provided Q is less than or equal to the seats available, the total revenue for the flight is P (price) $\times$ Q (quantity of seats sold) = PQ. The typical result is empty seats and a large consumer surplus (many passengers willing to spend considerably more for the flight than the fixed price).

Figure 11.8b shows the same demand curve with different prices for three segmented markets: P_1 for full coach, P_2 for advanced purchase, and P_3 for Internet special. A small number of passengers are willing to pay a premium for "full coach" because the ticket

FIGURE 11.7
Histogram of Decreasing Part-Time Teller Demand

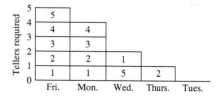

TABLE 11.9
Daily Part-Time Work
Schedule, x = **Workday**

Teller	Mon.	Tues.	Wed.	Thurs.	Fri.
1	x	...	x	...	x
2	x	...	...	x	x
3, 4	x	...	...	...	x
5	...	...	x	...	x

can be purchased at anytime and is fully refundable. Advanced purchase tickets must be purchased 14 days in advance and are not refundable. Internet special is a nonrefundable e-ticket available on the airline Web site whenever the flight is not expected to be fully booked (i.e., an opportunity to sell excess seats at a discount). For yield management the total revenue is the sum of (price) $\times$ (quantity) for passengers in each segment: $P_1Q_1 + (Q_2-Q_1)P_2 + (Q_3-Q_2)P_3$. The result explains why passengers find few empty seats in today's market. Furthermore, consumer surplus has been significantly reduced yielding higher total revenue for the airlines.

Yield management is most appropriate for service firms that exhibit the following characteristics:

Relatively fixed capacity. Service firms with a substantial investment in facilities (e.g., hotels and airlines) can be considered as being capacity-constrained. Once all the seats on a flight are sold, further demand can be met only by booking passengers

FIGURE 11.8
Airline Pricing for a
Coach Seat on a Cross-
Country Flight

a. Traditional Fixed Price

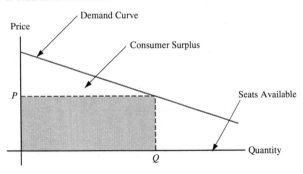

Total Revenue = PQ

b. Multiple Pricing Using Yield Management

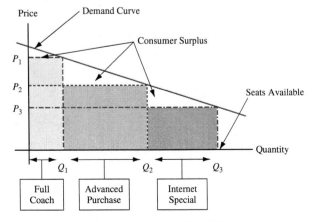

Total Revenue = $P_1Q_1 + (Q_2 - Q_1)\,P_2 + (Q_3 - Q_2)P_3$

280   Part Three *Managing Service Operations*

FIGURE 11.9

Seasonal Allocation of Rooms by Service Class for a Resort Hotel

Source: Adapted from Christopher H. Lovelock, "Strategies for Managing Demand in Capacity-Constrained Service Organizations," *Service Industries Journal* 4, no. 3, November 1984, p. 23.

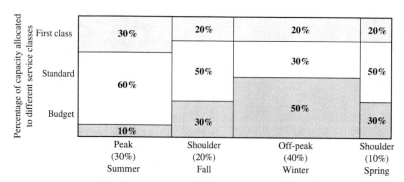

Percentage of capacity allocated to different seasons

on a later flight. Motel chains with multiple inns in the same city, however, have some capacity flexibility, because guests attempting to find room at one site can be diverted to another location within the same company.

Ability to segment markets. For yield management to be effective, the service firm must be able to segment its market into different customer classes. By requiring a Saturday-night stay for a discounted fare, airlines can discriminate between a time-sensitive business traveler and a price-sensitive customer. Developing various price-sensitive classes of service is a major marketing challenge for a firm using yield management. Figure 11.9 shows how a resort hotel might segment its market into three customer classes and adjust the allocation of available rooms to each class on the basis of the seasons of the year.

Perishable inventory. For capacity-constrained service firms, each room or seat is referred to as a *unit* of inventory to be sold (actually, to be rented). As noted for the airlines, revenue from an unsold seat is lost forever. Airlines attempt to minimize this spoiled inventory by encouraging standby passengers. Given this time-perishable nature of an airline seat, what is the cost to the airline when a passenger is awarded a free frequent flyer ticket on a flight that has at least one empty seat?

Product sold in advance. Reservation systems are adopted by service firms to sell capacity in advance of use; however, managers are faced with the uncertainty of whether to accept an early reservation at a discount price or to wait and hope to sell the inventory unit to a higher-paying customer. In Figure 11.10, a demand control

FIGURE 11.10

Demand Control Chart for a Hotel

Source: Adapted from Sheryl E. Kimes, "Yield Management: A Tool for Capacity-Constrained Service Firms," *Journal of Operations Management* 8, no. 4, October 1989, p. 359. Reprinted with permission, The American Production and Inventory Society.

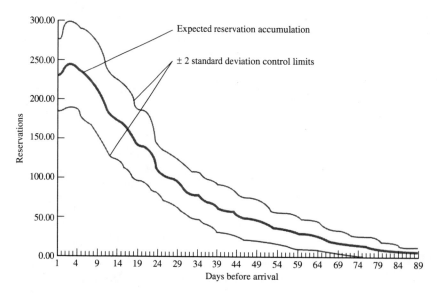

chart (recall quality-control charts from Chapter 6) is drawn for a hotel on the basis of past bookings for a particular day of the week and season of the year. Because some variation in demand is expected, an acceptable range (in this case, ± 2 standard deviations) is drawn around the expected reservation accumulation curve. If demand is higher than expected, budget-rate classes are closed and only reservations at standard rates accepted. If the accumulation of reservations falls below the acceptable range, then reservations for rooms at budget rates are accepted.

Fluctuating demand. Using demand forecasting, yield management allows managers to increase utilization during periods of slow demand and to increase revenue during periods of high demand. By controlling the availability of budget rates, managers can maximize total revenue for the constrained service. Yield management is implemented in real time by opening and/or closing reserved sections—even on an hourly basis if desired.

Low marginal sales costs and high marginal capacity change costs. The cost of selling an additional unit of inventory must be low, such as the negligible cost of a snack for an airline passenger. The marginal cost of capacity additions is large, however, because of the necessary lumpy facility investment (i.e., a hotel addition must be at least an increment of 100 rooms).

Example 11.3 **Blackjack Airline**	During the recent economic slump, Blackjack Airline discovered that airplanes on its Los Angeles–to–Las Vegas route have been flying with more empty seats than usual. To stimulate demand, it has decided to offer a special, nonrefundable, 14-day advance-purchase "gamblers' fare" for only $49 one way based on a round-trip ticket. The regular full-fare coach ticket costs $69 one way. The Boeing 737 used by Blackjack, as shown in Figure 11.11, has a capacity of 95 passengers in coach, and management wants to limit the number of seats that are sold at the discount fare in order to sell full-fare tickets to passengers who have not made advance travel plans. Considering recent experience, the demand for full-fare tickets appears to have a normal distribution, with a mean of 60 and a standard deviation of 15.

The yield management problem can be analyzed with the critical fractile model used earlier in the chapter [equation (1)] for analyzing the overbooking problem.

$$P(d < x) \le \frac{C_u}{C_u + C_o}$$

where

x = seats reserved for full-fare passengers

d = demand for full-fare tickets

C_u = lost revenue associated with reserving too few seats at full fare (underestimated demand). The lost opportunity is the difference between the fares ($69 − $49 = $20) because we assume that the nonshopper passenger, willing to pay full fare, purchased a seat at the discount price.

C_o = cost of reserving one too many seats for sale at full fare (overestimated demand). We assume that the empty full-fare seat could have been sold at the discount price of $49.

The critical fractile value $P(d < x) = \$20/(\$20 + \$49) = 0.29$ (see Figure 11.12). From Appendix A, "Areas of a Standard Normal Distribution," the z value for a cumulative probability of 0.29 is -0.55. Thus, the number of full-fare seats to reserve is found as follows:

$$\text{Reserved full-fare seats} = \mu + z\sigma$$
$$= 60 + (-0.55)(15)$$
$$= 51$$

Philip E. Pfeifer observed that the critical fractile model could be modified to account for the percentage of shoppers (i.e., customers looking for a discount).[8] The value for C_o would

282   Part Three *Managing Service Operations*

FIGURE 11.11
The Boeing 737 Cabin

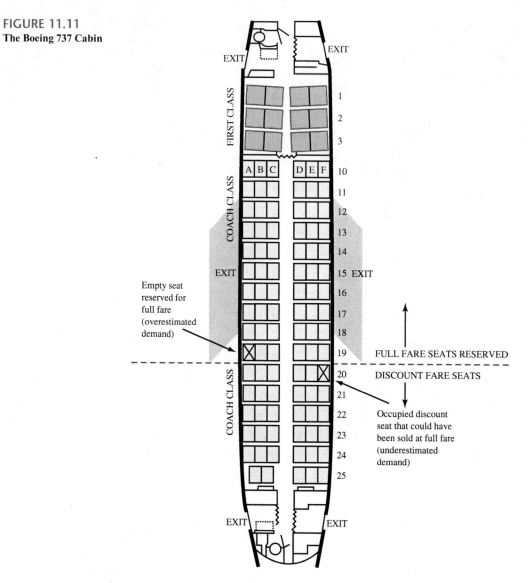

FIGURE 11.12
Critical Fractile for Blackjack Airline

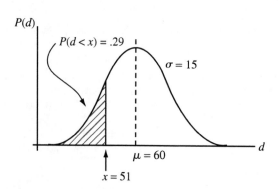

now take on two values depending on the buying behavior of the passenger who would have purchased the seat if not reserved for full fare. In our example,

$$C_o = \begin{cases} \$49 & \text{if passenger is a shopper} \\ -(\$69 - \$49) & \text{if passenger is a nonshopper} \end{cases}$$

For the nonshopper case, the cost is reduced by the difference between the fares, because the airline profits from the nonshopper, who did not make the purchase, paying the full rather than the discount fare. To establish an expected value for C_o, however, we need the proportion p of passengers who are shoppers. In this case, market research determined that approximately 90 percent of passengers are discount seekers; thus, the expected value for the cost of overage becomes

$$C_o = (0.9)(\$49) - (1 - 0.9)(\$69 - \$49) = \$42.10$$

The critical fractile value $P(d < x) = \$20/(\$20 + \$42.10) = 0.32$. From Appendix A, "Areas of a Standard Normal Distribution," the z value for a cumulative probability of 0.32 is -0.47. Thus, the number of full-fare seats to reserve is found as follows:

$$
\begin{aligned}
\text{Reserved full-fare seats} &= \mu + z\sigma \\
&= 60 + (-0.47)(15) \\
&= 53
\end{aligned}
$$

Substituting symbols for the values used in the example above, we can derive a simple expression for determining the number of full-fare seats to reserve.

$$P(d < x) \le \frac{(F - D)}{p \cdot F} \tag{3}$$

where

x = seats reserved for full-fare passengers

d = demand for full-fare tickets

F = price of full fare

D = price of discount fare

p = probability that a passenger is a shopper

Note that having information on the percentage of shoppers has allowed us to reserve more full-fare seats.

Yield Management Applications

The following discussion provides a sampling of how yield management is used by other companies that face high fixed costs/low variable costs, spoilage, and temporary demand imbalances to accomplish the same goals that airline pricing and yield management systems achieve.

Holiday Inn Reservation Optimization (HIRO)[9]

The hotel industry is similar to the airline industry, because hotels have extremely high costs invested in real estate and maintenance, temporary capacity, and demand imbalances. Imbalances such as varying peak and low seasons, spoilage, and rooms not rented out for a night all represent lost revenue opportunities. Holiday Inn has recognized these classic management problems and uses both demand and capacity management to maximize revenues.

To achieve Holiday Inn's corporate objectives of ensuring that maximum occupancy and revenue are realized in each hotel and that guests, franchises, and internal staff are experiencing the highest level of customer satisfaction, Holiday Inn installed HIRO. The goal of maximizing occupancy and revenue means renting as many rooms as possible for the best price that the market will bear. With more than 500,000 rooms in the equation, a yield management optimization system could increase revenue tremendously.

HIRO, which is similar to American Airlines' SABRE, uses historical and current booking behavior to analyze room requests for each hotel. The yield management optimization equation includes seasonal occupancy patterns, local events, weekly cycles, and current trends to develop a hurdle price (i.e., the lowest point at which rooms should be booked at that particular hotel). The system predicts full occupancy at hotels and "filters out" discounted requests. HIRO even uses overbooking to account for cancellations and no-shows. As with any yield management system in the service industry, HIRO helps the hotel manager balance the ability to charge full price for a room and still maintain satisfaction from Holiday Inn's loyal customer base.

Ryder's RyderFirst[10]

Ryder must manage the same logistical problems that are faced by any transportation company, and the shipping and trucking industry can use yield management to maximize revenue very effectively. Again, we see the classic business problem of high fixed costs/ low variable costs with an expansive fleet of trucks, temporary capacity, and demand imbalances resulting from the seasonality of shipping (i.e., holidays and other peak inventory stocking periods), the threat of spoilage, and valuable unused capacity.

With the help of the American Airlines Decision Technology Group (AADT), Ryder implemented a yield management, pricing, and logistics system that helps it react quickly to competition and take advantage of the price elasticities of its different customer segments. The yield management system allows Ryder to move its truck capacity from areas of surplus to areas of demand by modeling the historical utilization patterns in each market.

Restaurant Catering Software[11]

Yield management techniques are being incorporated into software for use in the restaurant catering industry to ensure efficient utilization of expensive kitchens. Yield management software alerts operators to the potential for increased off-premise or catering bookings during anticipated low in-store demand days, thus enhancing overall profitability. Computer modeling also includes the manipulation of prices based on demand fluctuations. For example, a restaurant may reduce its menu item prices to increase customer count and overall revenue. Similarly, in peak demand periods, item prices may be raised to increase the average check revenue. Yield management helps to smooth the fluctuating demand patterns in the catering industry by anticipating when temporary demand and capacity imbalances will occur.

Amtrak[12]

As far back as 1988, Amtrak introduced a pricing and yield management system identical to that of airlines. This yield management system utilizes a tiered-fare structure, overbooking, discount allocation, and traffic management to maximize yields and capacity utilization. Like the airlines, Amtrak uses the yield management market information to decide what routes to enter and how much capacity is necessary to satisfy demand. Amtrak's flexible capacity allows it to make last-minute capacity adjustments much more easily than in the airline industry by attaching and detaching different classes of rail cars.

Summary

The inherent variability of demand creates a challenge for managers trying to make the best use of service capacity. The problem can be approached from two generic strategies, level capacity and chase demand.

With level capacity strategy the focus is on smoothing demand to permit fuller utilization of a fixed service capacity. Various alternatives for managing demand are available, such as segmenting demand, offering price incentives, promoting off-peak use, and developing complementary services and reservation systems.

With a chase demand strategy the focus is on opportunities to adjust capacity to match changes in demand levels. Many alternatives have been proposed to adjust service capacity including workshift scheduling, using part-time employees, cross-training employees, increasing customer coproduction, and sharing capacity with other firms.

A mixed, or hybrid, strategy is best illustrated by the use of yield management that maximizes revenue through price discrimination and capacity allocation in real-time.

Service Benchmark

PAY UP FRONT AND TAKE YOUR CHANCES

Looking for some adventure in your life? Try shopping an opaque Web site such as Priceline. com or Hotwire.com where you can book reservations for a dream holiday at a resort or a flight to an exotic location for a bargain rate. The keyword here is *opaque*, which translates into "make a nonrefundable payment up front and take what you get sight unseen." Of course, you do have an opportunity to set some parameters for your adventure, such as an ultimate destination, a quality rating for accommodations, and sometimes a particular area of a city, before you commit your hard-earned $$$, but you don't know what you actually get until it's too late.

If a hotel, an airline, or an auto rental company have unsold rooms, seats, or vehicles, they lose money. Opaque Internet sites represent an opportunity for such businesses to get some return from those available resources (*or* on their excess capacity) without incurring the wrath of customers who pay the customary rates.

Key Terms and Definitions

Critical fractile the cumulative probability of demand formed by the ratio of the cost of *under*estimating demand divided by the sum of the costs of *under*estimating demand and *over*estimating demand. *p. 272*

Chase demand a strategy of adjusting capacity to match demand fluctuations. *p. 266*

Level capacity a strategy of holding capacity fixed allowing for underutilization and some customer waiting. *p. 266*

Overbooking taking reservations in excess of available capacity in anticipation of customer no-shows. *p. 270*

Yield management a comprehensive system to maximize revenue for capacity-constrained services using reservation systems, overbooking, and partitioning demand. *p. 278*

Topics for Discussion

1. What organizational problems can arise from the use of part-time employees?
2. How can computer-based reservation systems increase service capacity utilization?
3. Illustrate how a particular service has implemented successful strategies for managing both demand and capacity.
4. What possible dangers are associated with developing complementary services?
5. Will the widespread use of yield management eventually erode the concept of fixed prices for any service?
6. Go to http://en.wikipedia.org/wiki/Yield_management/ and discuss the ethical issues associated with yield management.

Interactive Exercise

Watch the PowerPoint presentation concerning the overbooking experience at the Doubletree Hotel in Houston, Texas. How could this situation have been handled differently?

Solved Problems

1. Overbooking Problem

Problem Statement

A family-run inn is considering the use of overbooking, because the frequency of no-shows listed below has left many rooms vacant during the past summer season.

An empty room represents an opportunity cost of $69, which is the average room rate. Accommodating an overbooked guest is expensive, however, because the nearby resort rooms average $119 and the inn must pay the difference. What would be the expected gain per night from overbooking?

No-shows	0	1	2	3
Frequency	4	3	2	1

Solution

First, create an overbooking loss table using $69 as the cost of an empty room and $119 − $69 = $50 as the cost of "walking" a guest.

| No-shows | Probability | Reservations Overbooked | | | |
		0	1	2	3
0	.4	0	50	100	150
1	.3	69	0	50	100
2	.2	138	69	0	50
3	.1	207	138	69	0
Expected loss		$69.00	$47.60	$61.90	$100.00

Second, calculate the expected loss by multiplying each overbooking column by the corresponding probability of no-shows and then adding each term. For 0 reservations overbooked, this yields

$$(0)(.4) + (69)(.3) + (138)(.2) + (207)(.1) = 69$$

Looking across the expected-loss row, we find that overbooking by one reservation will minimize the expected loss and result in an expected nightly gain from overbooking of $69.00 − $47.60 = $21.40.

2. Weekly Workshift Scheduling

Problem Statement

The telephone reservation department for a major car-rental firm has the daily shift requirements for operators below:

Day	Su	M	Tu	W	Th	F	Sa
Operators	4	8	8	7	7	6	5

Prepare a weekly workshift schedule with two consecutive days off.

Solution

Formulate the problem as an integer linear programming model, and solve using Excel Solver.

Objective function:

Minimize $x_1 + x_2 + x_3 + x_4 + x_5 + x_6 + x_7$

Constraints:

Sunday $\quad x_2 + x_3 + x_4 + x_5 + x_6 \geq 4$

Monday $\quad x_3 + x_4 + x_5 + x_6 + x_7 \geq 8$

Tuesday	x_1	$+ x_4 + x_5 + x_6 + x_7 \geq 8$
Wednesday	$x_1 + x_2$	$+ x_5 + x_6 + x_7 \geq 7$
Thursday	$x_1 + x_2 + x_3$	$+ x_6 + x_7 \geq 7$
Friday	$x_1 + x_2 + x_3 + x_4$	$+ x_7 \geq 6$
Saturday	$x_1 + x_2 + x_3 + x_4 + x_5$	≥ 5
	$x_i \geq 0$ and integer	

Using Excel Solver yields the following: $x_1 = 2, x_2 = 0, x_3 = 0, x_4 = 0, x_5 = 3,$
$x_6 = 1, x_7 = 4.$

The corresponding weekly workshift schedule is

	Schedule Matrix, x = Workday						
Operator	Su	M	Tu	W	Th	F	Sa
A	...	...	x	x	x	x	x
B	...	...	x	x	x	x	x
C	x	x	x	x	...	...	x
D	x	x	x	x	...	...	x
E	x	x	x	x	...	...	x
F	x	x	x	x	x	...	...
G	...	x	x	x	x	x	...
H	...	x	x	x	x	x	...
I	...	x	x	x	x	x	...
J	...	x	x	x	x	x	...
Total	4	8	10	10	7	6	5
Required	4	8	8	7	7	6	5
Excess	0	0	2	3	0	0	0

3. Yield Management

Problem Statement

A ski resort is planning a year-end promotion by offering a weekend special for $159 per person based on double occupancy. The high season rate for these rooms, which includes lift tickets, normally is $299. Management wants to hold some rooms for late arrivals who are willing to pay the season rate. If the proportion of skiers who are willing to pay full rate is approximately 20 percent and their average weekend demand has a normal distribution with a mean of 50 and a standard deviation of 10, how many rooms should be set aside for full-paying skiers?

Solution

Using equation (3), we can determine the critical fractile as follows:

$$P(d < x) \leq \frac{(F - D)}{p \cdot F} = \frac{(299 - 159)}{(0.8)(299)} \leq 0.58$$

Turning to areas of a standard normal distribution in Appendix A, the z value for a cumulative probability of 0.58 is 0.02. Thus, the number of rooms to protect for full-paying skiers is

$$\mu + z\sigma = 50 + (0.02)(10)$$
$$= 52 \text{ rooms}$$

Exercises

11.1. An outpatient clinic has kept a record of walk-in patients during the past year. The table below shows the expected number of walk-ins by day of the week:

Day	Mon.	Tues.	Wed.	Thurs.	Fri.
Walk-ins	50	30	40	35	40

The clinic has a staff of five physicians, and each can examine 15 patients a day on average.

a. What is the maximum number of appointments that should be scheduled for each day if it is desirable to smooth out the demand for the week?

b. Why would you recommend against scheduling appointments at their maximum level?

c. If most walk-ins arrive in the morning, when should the appointments be made to avoid excessive waiting?

11.2. Reconsider Example 11.1 (Surfside Hotel), because rising costs now have resulted in a $100 opportunity loss from a no-show. Assume that the no-show experience has not significantly changed and that the resulting loss when a guest is overbooked still is $100. Should Surfside revise its no-show policy?

11.3. A commuter airline overbooks all its flights by one passenger (i.e., the ticket agent will take seven reservations for an airplane that only has six seats). The no-show experience for the past 20 days is shown below:

No-shows	0	1	2	3	4
Frequency	6	5	4	3	2

Using the critical fractile $P(d < x) \leq C_u/(C_u + C_o)$, find the maximum implied overbooking opportunity loss C_o if the revenue C_u from a passenger is $20.

11.4. Crazy Joe operates a canoe rental service on the Guadalupe River. He currently leases 15 canoes from a dealer in a nearby city at a cost of $10 per day. On weekends, when the water is high, he picks up the canoes and drives to a launching point on the river, where he rents canoes to white-water enthusiasts for $30 per day. Lately, canoeists have complained about the unavailability of canoes, so Crazy Joe has recorded the demand for canoes and found the experience below for the past 20 days:

Daily demand	10	11	12	13	14	15	16	17	18	19	20
Frequency	1	1	2	2	2	3	3	2	2	1	1

Recommend an appropriate number of canoes to lease.

11.5. An airline serving Denver's International Airport and Steamboat Springs, Colorado, is considering overbooking its flights to avoid flying with empty seats. For example, the ticket agent is thinking of taking seven reservations for an airplane that has only six seats. During the past month, the no-show experience has been

No-shows	0	1	2	3	4
Percentage	30	25	20	15	10

The operating costs associated with each flight are pilot, $150; first officer, $100; fuel, $30; and landing fee, $20.

What would be your recommendation for overbooking if a one-way ticket sells for $80 and the cost of not honoring a reservation is a free lift ticket worth $50 plus a seat on the next flight? What is the expected profit per flight for your overbooking choice?

11.6. Reconsider Example 11.2 (Hospital Emergency Room) to determine if additional nurses will be required to staff the revised daily shift requirements shown below:

Day	Sun.	Mon.	Tues.	Wed.	Thurs.	Fri.	Sat.
Nurses	3	6	5	6	6	6	5

Develop a weekly workshift schedule providing 2 consecutive days off per week for each nurse. Formulate the problem as an integer linear programming model to minimize the number of nurses needed, and solve using Excel Solver. If more nurses are required than the existing staff of eight, suggest an alternative to hiring full-time nurses.

11.7. The sheriff has been asked by the county commissioners to increase weekend patrols in the lake region during the summer months. The sheriff has proposed the following weekly schedule, shifting deputies from weekday assignments to weekends:

Day	Sun.	Mon.	Tues.	Wed.	Thurs.	Fri.	Sat.
Assignments	6	4	4	4	5	5	6

Develop a weekly workshift schedule of duty tours, providing 2 consecutive days off per week for each officer. Formulate the problem as an integer linear programming model to minimize the number of officers needed, and solve using Excel Solver.

11.8. Reconsider Example 11.3 (Blackjack Airline). After initial success with the Los Angeles–to–Las Vegas route, Blackjack Airline's demand for full-fare tickets has increased to an average of 75, with the standard deviation remaining at 15. This early experience has allowed Blackjack to make a better estimate of the percentage of discount-seeking passengers, which appears to be 80 percent. Consequently, Blackjack has decided to raise all ticket prices by $10. Under these new conditions, how many full-fare seats should Blackjack reserve?

11.9. Town and Country has experienced a substantial increase in business volume because of recent fare wars between the major air carriers. Town and Country operates a single office at a major international airport, with a fleet of 60 compact and 30 midsize cars. Recent developments have prompted management to rethink the company's reservation policy. The table below contains data on the rental experience of Town and Country:

Car	Rental Rate	Discount Rate	Discount Seekers, %	Daily Demand	Standard Deviation
Compact	$30	$20	80	50	15
Midsize	$40	$30	60	30	10

The daily demand appears to follow a normal distribution; however, it has been observed that midsize-car customers do not choose to rent a compact when no midsize car is available. The discount rate is available to persons who are willing to reserve a car at least 14 days in advance and agree to pick up that car within 2 hours after their flight arrives. Otherwise, a nonrefundable deposit against their credit card will be forfeited. The current reservation policy is that 40 compact cars are held for customers who are willing to pay the full rate and 25 midsize cars are held for full rate–paying customers.

a. Using yield management, determine the optimal number of compact and midsize cars to be held for customers paying the full rate.

b. Given your optimal reservation policy determined here, would you consider a fleet expansion?

Selected Bibliography

Aksin, Zeynep; Mor Armony; and Vijay Mehrotra. "The Modern Call Center: A Multi-Disciplinary Perspective on Operations Management Research." *Production and Operations Management* 16, no. 6 (November–December 2007), pp. 665–88.

Antle, D. W., and R. A. Reid. "Managing Service Capacity in an Ambulatory Care Clinic." *Hospital & Health Services Administration* 33, no. 2 (Summer 1988), pp. 201–11.

Baker, Timothy K., and David A. Collier. "The Benefits of Optimizing Prices to Manage Demand in Hotel Revenue Management Systems." *Production and Operations Management* 12, no. 4 (Winter 2003), pp. 502–18.

Belobaba, Peter P. "Application of a Probabilistic Decision Model to Airline Seat Inventory Control." *Operations Research* 37, no. 2 (March–April 1989), pp. 183–97.

Bitran, G. R., and S. V. Mondschein. "An Application of Yield Mangement to the Hotel Industry Considering Multiple Day Stays." *Operations Research* 43, no. 3 (May–June 1995), pp. 427–43.

Carroll, William J., and Richard C. Grimes. "Evolutionary Change in Product Management: Experiences in the Car Rental Industry." *Interfaces* 25, no. 5 (September–October 1995), pp. 84–104.

Chevalier, Philippe, and Jean-Christophe Van den Schrieck. "Optimizing the Staffing and Routing of Small-Size Hierarchical Call Centers." *Production and Operations Management* 17, no. 3 (May–June 2008), pp. 306–19.

Crandall, Richard E., and Robert E. Markland. "Demand Management—Today's Challenge for Service Industries." *Production and Operations Management* 5, no. 2 (Summer 1996), pp. 106–20.

Dana, James D. Jr. "New Directions in Revenue Management Research." *Production and Operations Management* 17, no. 4 (July–August 2008), pp. 399–401.

Dietrich, Brenda; Giuseppe A. Paleologo and Laura Wynter. "Revenue Management in Business Services." *Production and Operations Management* 14, no. 4 (July–August 2005), pp. 475–80.

Easton, Fred F.; Donald F. Rossin; and William S. Borders. "Analysis of Alternative Scheduling Policies for Hospital Nurses." *Production and Operations Management* 1, no. 2 (Spring 1992), pp. 159–74.

Goodale, John C., and Enar Tunc. "Tour Scheduling with Dynamic Service Rates." *International Journal of Service Industry Management* 9, no. 3 (1998), pp. 226–47.

———; Rohit Verma; and Madeleine E. Pullman. "A Market Utility-Based Model for Capacity Scheduling in Mass Service." *Production and Operations Management* 12, no. 2 (Summer 2003), pp. 164–85.

Kimes, Sheryl E. "Yield Management: A Tool for Capacity-Constrained Service Firms." *Journal of Operations Management* 8, no. 4 (October 1989), pp. 348–63.

———. "The Basics of Yield Management." *Cornell HRA Quarterly,* November 1989, pp. 14–19.

———. "The Relationship between Product Quality and Revenue per Available Room at Holiday Inn." *Journal of Service Research* 2, no. 2 (November 1999), pp. 138–44.

———, and Richard B. Chase. "The Strategic Levers of Yield Management." *Journal of Service Research* 1, no. 2 (November 1998), pp. 156–66.

———, and Jochen Wirtz. "Has Revenue Management Become Acceptable? Findings From an International Study on the Perceived Fairness of Rate Fences." *Journal of Service Research* 6, no. 2 (November 2003), pp. 125–35.

Mabert, Vincent A., and Michael J. Showalter. "Measuring the Impact of Part-Time Workers in Service Organizations." *Journal of Operations Management* 9, no. 2 (April 1990), pp. 209–29.

Malhotra, Manoj K., and Larry P. Ritzman. "Scheduling Flexibility in the Service Sector: A Postal Case Study." *Production and Operations Management* 3, no. 2 (Spring 1994), pp. 100–17.

Metters, Richard, and Vicente Vargas. "Yield Management for the Nonprofit Sector." *Journal of Service Research* 1, no. 3 (February 1999), pp. 215–26.

Mookherjee, Reetabrata and Terry L. Friesz. "Pricing, Allocation, and Overbooking in Dynamic Service Network Competition When Demand Is Uncertain" *Production and Operations Management* 14, no. 4 (July–August 2005), pp. 455–74.

Ng, Irene C. I.; Jochen Wirtz; and Khai Sheang Lee. "The Strategic Role of Unused Service Capacity." *International Journal of Service Industry Management* 10, no. 2 (1999), pp. 211–38.

Queenan, Carrie Crystal; Mark Ferguson; Jon Higbie; and Rohit Kapoor. "A Comparison of Unconstraining Methods to Improve Revenue Management Systems." *Production and Operations Management* 16, no. 6 (November–December 2007), pp. 729–46.

Radas, Sonja, and Steven M. Shugan. "Managing Service Demand: Shifting and Bundling." *Journal of Service Research* 1, no. 1 (August 1998), pp. 47–64.

Relihan, Walter J., III. "The Yield-Management Approach to Hotel-Room Pricing." *Cornell HRA Quarterly,* May 1989, pp. 40–45.

Sampson, Scott E. "Optimization of Volunteer Labor Assignments." *Journal of Operations Management* 24, no.4 (June 2006), pp. 363–77.

Shemwell, D. J., and J. J. Cronin. "Services Marketing Strategies for Coping with Demand/Supply Imbalances." *Journal of Services Marketing* 8, no. 4 (1994), pp. 14–24.

Shen, Zuo-Jun Max, and Xuanming Su. "Customer Behavior Modeling in Revenue Management and Auctions: A Review and New Research Opportunities." *Production and Operations Management* 16, no. 6 (November–December 2007), pp. 713–28.

Smith, Barry C.; John F. Leimkuhler; and Ross M. Darrow. "Yield Management at American Airlines." *Interfaces* 22, no. 1 (January–February 1992), pp. 8–31.

Thompson, Gary M. "Labor Scheduling, Part 1: Forecasting Demand." *Cornell Hotel and Restaurant Administration Quarterly,* October 1998, pp. 22–31.

———. "Labor Scheduling, Part 2: Knowing How Many On-Duty Employees to Schedule." *Cornell Hotel and Restaurant Administration Quarterly,* December 1998, pp. 26–37.

———. "Labor Scheduling, Part 3: Developing a Workforce Schedule." *Cornell Hotel and Restaurant Administration Quarterly,* February 1999, pp. 86–96.

———. "Labor Scheduling, Part 4: Controlling Workforce Schedules in Real-Time." *Cornell Hotel and Restaurant Administration Quarterly,* June 1999, pp. 86–96.

———, and Robert J. Kwortnik Jr. "Pooling Restaurant Reservations to Increase Service Efficiency." *Journal of Service Research* 10, no. 4 (May 2008), pp. 335–46.

Whitt, Ward. "Staffing a Call Center with Uncertain Arrival Rate and Absenteeism," *Production and Operations Management* 15, no. 1 (Spring 2006), pp. 88–102.

Wirtz, Jochen, and Sheryl E. Kimes. "The Moderating Role of Familiarity in Fairness Perceptions of Revenue Management Pricing," *Journal of Service Research,* 9, no. 3 (February 2007), pp. 229–40.

Xia, Cathy H. and Parijat Dube. "Dynamic Pricing in e-Services under Demand Uncertainty." *Production and Operations Management* 16, no. 6 (November–December 2007), pp. 701–12.

Endnotes

1. R. L. Rose and J. Dahl, "Skies Are Deregulated, but Just Try Starting a Sizable New Airline," *The Wall Street Journal,* July 19, 1989, p. 1.
2. Frances X. Frei, "Breaking the Trade-Off Between Efficiency and Service," *Harvard Business Review* 84, no. 11 (November 2006), pp. 92–101.
3. E. J. Rising, R. Baron, and B. Averill, "A Systems Analysis of a University Health-Service Outpatient Clinic," *Operations Research* 21, no. 5 (September 1973), pp. 1030–47.
4. J. C. Nautiyal and R. L. Chowdhary, "A Suggested Basis for Pricing Campsites: Demand Estimation in an Ontario Park," *Journal of Leisure Research* 7, no. 2 (1975), pp. 95–107.
5. The *M/M/c* queuing model as described in Chapter 16 is used. This model permits the calculation of probabilities for having a telephone caller wait for different numbers of operators.
6. From V. A. Mabert and A. R. Raedels, "The Detail Scheduling of a Part-Time Work Force: A Case Study of Teller Staffing," *Decision Sciences* 8, no. 1 (January 1977), pp. 109–20.
7. From Sheryl E. Kimes, "Yield Management: A Tool for Capacity-Constrained Service Firms," *Journal of Operations Management* 8, no. 4 (October 1989), pp. 348–63.
8. Phillip E. Pfeifer, "The Airline Discount Fare Allocation Problem," *Decision Sciences* 20, Winter 1989, p. 155.
9. Lenny Leibmann, "Holiday Inn Maximizes Profitability with a Complex Network Infrastructure," *LAN Magazine,* 10, no. 6 (June 1995), p.123.
10. "On the Road to Rebound," *Information Week,* September 3, 1991, p. 32.
11. Michael Kasavana, "Catering Software: Problems for Off-Premise Bookings Can Greatly Increase Operational Efficiency," *Restaurant Business* 90, no. 13 (September 1, 1991), p. 90.
12. "Travel Advisory: Amtrak Adopts Fare System of Airlines," *New York Times,* December 4, 1989, Section 3, p. 3.
13. Prepared by James H. Vance under the supervision of Professor James A. Fitzsimmons.
14. Adapted with permission from Kevin Baker and Robert B. Freund, "The Yield Management Analyst," University of Texas at Austin, 1994.
15. Quoted from Barbara Amster, former vice president of the American Airlines Pricing and Yield Management department.

Chapter

12

Managing Waiting Lines

Learning Objectives

After completing this chapter, you should be able to:

1. Describe the economics of waiting lines using examples.
2. Describe how queues form.
3. Apply Maister's two "laws of service."
4. Describe the psychology of waiting components, and suggest strategies to deal with each.
5. Describe the four principles of waiting line management with examples.
6. Describe the essential features of a queuing system.
7. Describe the relationship between a negative exponential distribution of time between arrivals and a Poisson distribution of arrival rates.

On June 14, 1972, the United States of America Bank (of Chicago) launched an anniversary sale. The commodity on sale was money, and each of the first 35 persons could "buy" a $100 bill for $80 in cash. Those farther down the queue could each obtain similar but declining bonuses: the next 50 could gain $10 each; 75, $4 each; 100, $2 each; and the following 100, $1 each. Each of the next 100 persons could get a $2 bill for $1.60 and, finally, 800 (subsequently, it seems, expanded to 1,800) persons could gain $0.50 each. The expected waiting time in such an unusual event was unpredictable; on the other hand, it was easy to assess the money value of the commodity being distributed.

First in line were four brothers aged 16, 17, 19, and 24. Because the smallest was 6'2'', their priority was assured. "I figured," said Carl, the youngest brother, "that we spent 17 hours to make a $20 profit. That's about $1.29 an hour."

"You can make better than that washing dishes," added another of the brothers. Had they been better informed they could have waited less time. The 35th person to join the line arrived around midnight, had to wait just 9 hours, and was the last to earn $20—$2.22 per hour. To confirm her right, she made a list of all those ahead of her in the line.

"Why am I here?" she asked. "Well, that $20 is the same as a day's pay to me. And I don't even have to declare it on my income tax. It's a gift, isn't it?"[1]

The experience described above demonstrates that those in line considered their waiting time as the cost of securing a "free" good. While waiting can have a number of economic interpretations, its true cost is always difficult to determine. For this reason, the trade-off between the cost of waiting and the cost of providing service seldom is made explicit, yet service providers must consider the physical, behavioral, and economic aspects of the consumer waiting experience in their decision making.

Chapter Preview

Our understanding of waiting lines begins with a discussion of the economic considerations from both a provider and customer perspective followed by a discussion of how queues form. We shall discover that the perception of waiting often is more important to the customer than the actual time spent waiting, suggesting that innovative ways should be found to reduce the negative aspects of waiting. Finally, the essential features of a queuing system are described and queuing terminology is defined.

The Economics of Waiting

The economic cost of waiting can be viewed from two perspectives. For a firm, the cost of keeping an employee (i.e., an internal customer) waiting may be measured by unproductive wages. For external customers, the cost of waiting is the forgone alternative use of that time. Added to this are the costs of boredom, anxiety, and other psychological distresses.

In a competitive market, excessive waiting—or even the expectation of long waits—can lead to lost sales. How often have you driven by a filling station, observed many cars lined up at the pumps, and then decided not to stop? One strategy to avoid lost sales is to conceal the queue from arriving customers. In the case of restaurants, this often is achieved by diverting people into the bar, a tactic that frequently results in increased sales. Amusement parks such as Disneyland require people to pay for their tickets outside the park, where they are unable to observe the waiting lines inside. Casinos "snake" the waiting line for nightclub acts through the slot-machine area both to hide its true length and to foster impulsive gambling.

The consumer can be considered a resource with the potential to participate in the service process. For example, a patient who is waiting for a doctor can be asked to complete a medical history record and thereby save valuable physician time (i.e., service capacity). The waiting period also can be used to educate the person about good health habits, which can be achieved by making health publications or filmstrips available. As another example, restaurants are quite innovative in their approaches to engaging the customer directly in providing the service. After giving your order to a waiter in many restaurants, you are asked to go to the salad bar and prepare your own salad, which you eat while the cook prepares your meal.

Consumer waiting may be viewed as a contribution to productivity by permitting greater utilization of limited capacity. The situation of customers waiting in line for a service is analogous to the work-in-process inventory for a manufacturing firm. The service firm actually is inventorying customers to increase the overall efficiency of the process. In service systems, higher utilization of facilities is purchased at the price of customer waiting. Prominent examples can be found in public services such as post offices, medical clinics, and welfare offices, where high utilization is achieved with long queues.

Queuing Systems

A *queue* is a line of waiting customers who require service from one or more servers. The queue need not be a physical line of individuals in front of a server, however. It might be students sitting at computer terminals that are scattered around a college campus, or a person being placed on "hold" by a telephone operator. Servers typically are considered to be individual stations where customers receive service. The stereotypical queue—people waiting in a formal line for service—is seen at the check-out counters of a supermarket and the teller windows in a bank, yet queuing systems occur in a variety of forms. Consider the following variations:

1. Servers need not be limited to serving one customer at a time. Transportation systems such as buses, airplanes, and elevators are bulk services.

What is the economic cost to society of airport screening? Getty Images/Digital Vision

2. The consumer need not always travel to the service facility; in some systems, the server actually comes to the consumer. This approach is illustrated by urban services such as fire and police protection as well as by ambulance service.

3. The service may consist of stages of queues in a series or of a more complex network of queues. For example, consider the haunted-house attraction at amusement parks like Disneyland, where queues are staged in sequence so that visitors can be processed in batches and entertained during the waiting periods (e.g., first outside on the walk, then in the vestibule, and finally on the ride itself).

In any service system, a queue forms whenever current demand exceeds the existing capacity to serve. This occurs when servers are so busy that arriving consumers cannot receive immediate service. Such a situation is bound to occur in any·system for which arrivals occur at varying times and service times also vary.

Waiting is part of everyone's life, and it can involve an incredible amount of time. For example, a typical day might include waiting at several stoplights, waiting for someone to answer the telephone, waiting for your meal to be served, waiting for the elevator, waiting to be checked out at the supermarket—the list goes on and on.

The Psychology of Waiting[2]

If waiting is such an integral and ordinary part of our lives, why does it cause us so much grief? David H. Maister offers some interesting perspectives on this subject.

He suggests two "Laws of Service." The first deals with the customer's expectations versus his or her perceptions. If a customer receives better service than he or she expects, then the customer departs a happy, satisfied person, and the service may benefit from a trickle-down effect (i.e., the happy customer will tell friends about the good service). Note, however, that the trickle-down effect can work both ways: a service can earn a bad reputation in the same manner (and create more interesting stories for the customer to pass along).

Maister's second law states that it is hard to play "catch-up ball." By this, he means that first impressions can influence the rest of the service experience; thus, a service that requires its customers to wait would be advised to make that period a pleasant experience. To do the "impossible"—to make waiting at least tolerable and, at best, pleasant and productive—a creative and competitive service management must consider the following aspects of the psychology of waiting.

That Old Empty Feeling

Just as "nature abhors a vacuum," people dislike "empty time." Empty, or unoccupied, time feels awful. It keeps us from other productive activities; frequently is physically uncomfortable; makes us feel powerless and at the mercy of servers, whom we may perceive as uncaring about us; and, perhaps worst of all, seems to last forever. The challenge to the service organization is obvious: fill this time in a positive way. It may require no more than comfortable chairs and a fresh coat of paint to cheer up the environment. Furnishings in a waiting area can affect indirectly the perception of waiting. The fixed, benchlike seating in bus and rail terminals discourages conversation. The light, movable table-and-chair arrangement of a European sidewalk café brings people together and provides opportunities for socializing. In another situation, a music recording may be enough to occupy a telephone caller who is on hold and, at the same time, reassure the caller that he or she has not been disconnected.

Perhaps the strategy most widely noted in the literature is that of installing mirrors near elevators. Hotels, for example, record fewer complaints about excessive waits for elevators that are surrounded by mirrors. The mirrors allow people to occupy their time by checking their grooming and surreptitiously observing others who are waiting.

Services often can make waiting times productive as well as pleasurable. Instead of treating the telephone caller mentioned above to the strains of Mozart or Madonna, the service can air some commercials. Such a practice involves risk, however, because some people resent being subjected to this tactic when they are being held captive. At one time in the Olive Garden restaurants, diners who were waiting for tables could spend their time in the bar, which benefits the restaurant with added sales, or they could wait in the lobby and watch a chef prepare fresh pastas, which certainly stimulated appetites. No need to play "catch-up ball" here. Each diner reached the table happily anticipating an agreeable experience rather than sourly grumbling, "It's about time!"

Services that consist of several stages, such as one might find at a diagnostic clinic, can conceal waiting by asking people to walk between successive stages. There are innumerable other ways to fill time: reading matter, television monitors, live entertainment, posters, artwork, toys to occupy children, and cookies and pots of coffee. The diversions are limited only by management's imagination and desire to serve the customer effectively.

A Foot in the Door

As noted above, some diversions merely fill time so that waiting doesn't seem so long, and others also can provide the service organization with some ancillary benefits. Happy customers are more likely than unhappy customers to be profitable customers. Another aspect of diversions is important, however.

Maister points out that "service-related" diversions themselves, such as handing out menus to waiting diners or medical history forms (and paper cups) to waiting patients, "convey a sense that service has started." One's level of anxiety subsides considerably once service has started. In fact, people generally can tolerate longer waits, within reason, if they feel service has begun better than they can tolerate such waits if service has not even started. Another view is that customers become dissatisfied more quickly with an initial wait than with subsequent waits after the service has begun.

The Light at the End of the Tunnel

There are many anxieties at work before service begins. Have I been forgotten? Did you get my order? This line doesn't seem to be moving; will I ever get served? If I run to the rest room, will I lose my turn? When will the plumber get here? Will the plumber get here at all? Whether rational or not, anxieties may be the single biggest factor influencing the waiting customer.

Managers must recognize these anxieties and develop strategies to alleviate them. In some cases, this may be a simple matter of having an employee acknowledge the customer's presence. At other times, telling the customer how long he or she will have to wait is sufficient reassurance that the wait at some point will end. Signs can serve this purpose as well. As you approach the Port Aransas, Texas, ferry landing, for example, you see signs posted along the road noting the number of minutes you have left to wait if you are stopped in line at that point.

When appropriate, scheduling appointments is one strategy to reduce waiting time, but it is not foolproof. Unforeseen events might interfere, or prior appointments might require more time than expected. If the appointed time comes and goes, the anxiety of not knowing how long the wait will be sets in—along with some measure of irritation at the "insult" of being stood up. A simple explanation and apology for the delays, however, usually will go a long way in reestablishing goodwill.

Excuse Me, but I Was Next

Uncertain and unexplained waits create anxieties and, as noted above, occasionally some resentment in customers. The moment a customer sees a later arrival being served first, however, anxiety about how long the wait will be is transformed into anger about the unfairness of it all. This can lead to a testy—if not explosive—situation, and the service provider is just as likely as the usurper to be the target of the anger.

A simple strategy for avoiding violations of the first-come, first-served (FCFS) queuing policy is the take-a-number arrangement. For example, customers entering a meat market take a number from a dispenser and wait for it to be called. The number currently being served may be displayed so that the new customer can see how long the wait will be. With this simple measure, management has relieved the customer's anxiety over the length of the wait—and the possibility of being treated unfairly. As an ancillary benefit, it also encourages "impulse buying" through allowing the customer to wander about the shop instead of needing to protect a place in line. As equitable as it is, however, this system is not totally free from producing anxiety; it does require the customer to stay alert for the numbers being called or risk losing his or her place in line.

Another simple strategy for fostering FCFS service when there are multiple servers is use of a single queue. Banks, post offices, and airline check-in counters commonly employ this technique. A customer who enters one of these facilities joins the back of the line; the first person in line is served by the next available server. Anxiety is relieved, because there is no fear that later arrivals will "slip" ahead of their rightful place.[3] Often, customers who have been "guaranteed" their place in this way will relax and enjoy a few pleasantries with others in the line. Note that such camaraderie also occupies the customer's empty time and makes the waiting time seem shorter. Queue configurations are examined in more detail later in this chapter.

Not all services lend themselves to such a straightforward prioritization, however. Police service is one example; for obvious reasons, an officer on the way to a call about a "noisy dog next door" will change priorities when told to respond to a "robbery-in progress." In this case, the dispatcher can ameliorate the "noisy-dog" caller's wait anxiety by explaining the department's response policy and providing the caller with a reasonable expectation of when an officer will arrive.

Other services may wish to give preferential treatment to special customers. Consider the express check-in for "high rollers" at Las Vegas hotels, or for first-class passengers at airline check-in counters. Keep in mind, however, that such special "perks" also can engender irritation among the unfavored who are standing in long lines nearby. A management sensitive to the concerns of all its customers will take measures to avoid an image of obvious discrimination. In the example just mentioned, one solution might be to "conceal" the preferential treatment by locating it in an area that is separate from the regular service line.

Principles of Waiting Line Management

The management of queues at Burger King represents an evolving process of refinement. When these stores first opened, a "conventional" lineup was used that required customers to arrange themselves in single file behind a single cash register, where orders were taken. Assemblers prepared the orders and presented them to customers at the far end of the counter. This conventional style of line-up often is called the "snake," as mentioned in the following *Wall Street Journal* article.[4]

Louis Kane hates snakes.

The restaurant executive means the single lines that feed customers one at a time to a group of cashiers. He thinks snakes are much too "institutional." Besides, he says, he would rather try to guess which line will move the fastest. But surveys show that customers prefer snakes to multiple lines because they hate "getting stuck behind some guy ordering nine cappuccinos, each with something different on top," says Mr. Kane, co-chairman of the Boston-based Au Bon Pain soup-and-sandwich chain.

The customers have won. Over the past couple of years, Au Bon Pain has instituted snakes at every restaurant that has enough room. But the debate lives on. "We talk about this a great deal," Mr. Kane says.

The issue is queues. Experts suggest that no aspect of customer service is more important than the wait in line to be served. The act of waiting—either in person or on the phone—"has a disproportionately high impact" on customers, says David Maister, a Boston consultant who has studied the psychology of waiting. "The wait can destroy an otherwise perfect service experience."

A customer waiting in line is potentially a lost customer. According to one study, up to 27% of customers who can't get through on the telephone will either buy elsewhere or skip the transaction altogether, says Rudy Oetting, a senior partner at Oetting & Co., a New York company that consults on telephone use. Adds Russell James, an official at Avis Rent a Car Inc.: "You can't be out-lined by a competitor or you will lose business."

Today's customers are also more demanding than ever. "The dramatic difference between 1980 and 1990 can be described in one word: speed," says N. Powell Taylor, manager of GE Answer Center, a General Electric Co. operation that fields three million calls a year. "People expect quicker answers. No one has the time any more."

In the past few years particularly, many companies have stepped up efforts to shorten waits—or at least make them more tolerable. Here are some of the methods they are trying:

Animate

Some contend that a wait isn't a wait if it's fun. At Macy's in New York now, the line to see Santa Claus wends its way through displays of dancing teddy bears, elves and electric trains. "It's part of the adventure of going to see Santa Claus," says Jean McFaddin, a vice president at the big department store, where 300,000 people see Santa in 30 days.

At Disneyland and Walt Disney World, the waits—which can be up to 90 minutes long—are planned along with the attractions themselves. Visitors waiting for rides that board continuously pass animated displays that are designed to be viewed as people walk along. Waits for theater shows include such attractions as singers and handicraft displays aimed at audiences that will be waiting in one place as long as 30 minutes. Indeed, the waits themselves are called "preshows." Says Norman Doerges, executive vice president of Disneyland, "that's what makes the time pass, it's the entertainment."

At the Omni Park Central Hotel in New York, when a line exceeds six people, assistant managers are dispatched to the hotel restaurant to bring out orange and grapefruit juice to serve to the people in line. "We are trying to tell the guest 'we know you are here,'" says Philip Georgas, general manager and regional vice president.

Still, not all diversions are suitable. Many callers don't like listening to recordings while they're on hold. GE plays its corporate theme for customers while they wait, but it draws the line at playing recorded advertising. "We tend to stay away from commercials," says Mr. Taylor, because of the fear that customers will think company employees "are probably sitting there doing nothing," making customers wait so they will have to listen to the commercials.

Discriminate

"The key thing is not just moving people out of the line," says Mr. James at Avis. "The key is who you move out of the line." For the past two years, high-volume renters at Avis have been able to sign a permanent rental agreement in advance and be driven directly to their cars when they arrive at many Avis locations. Somewhat less-frequent renters check in at a kiosk near the car park. Other car rental concerns are offering similar preferential services.

Such service is increasingly common in the travel, banking and credit-card industries. But "one needs a great deal of creativity in this area" lest less-favored customers be offended, says Mr. Maister. "Those businesses that want to serve priority customers faster are best advised to do it out of sight of the regular customers." He cites some airlines that locate first-class check-in counters away from the economy counters. "You don't want to rub the noses of the economy passengers in it."

Automate

While assembly-line techniques can accelerate manufacturing operations, they often slow the delivery of services. When callers must speak to several different people to get a complete answer, "crew interference" sets in, says Warren Blanding, editor of Customer Service Newsletter in Silver Spring, Md. "The most efficient way to do a job is to have one person do it." So Employers Health Insurance, Green Bay, Wis., has assembled a complex computer database of scripts that employees can read to customers on the telephone. The employee keys in the caller's name, location and type of health insurance question. The computer then pops up a question-and-answer format that can be read verbatim.

"We know that 75% of the calls we get in are standard questions," says Sterling L. Phaklides, an assistant vice president in the claims division. "Because people are sticking to the scripts, they are giving up-to-date information" without consulting technicians, he says. But callers who ask questions that aren't covered in the scripts can be referred to specialists at any point. "It does save telephone time," the official says. The claims area handles 3,700 calls a day; only about 1% of callers hang up before they are connected—which is better than average, he says.

Obfuscate

Mr. Maister says the perceived wait is often more important than the actual wait. In a paper on the psychology of waiting, he notes that some restaurants deliberately announce longer waiting times, thus pleasing customers when the wait is actually shorter. At Disneyland in Anaheim, Calif., lines snake around corners, Mr. Maister says. Thus people focus more on how fast the line is moving than on how long the line is.

Disneyland says its aim isn't to deceive. It posts waiting times at the start of each line. "A big danger in disguising a line is that people don't know what they are getting into," says Mr. Doerges. "If you do it without proper preparation, people get frustrated."

Still, some think that even that information will be too depressing. Technology is available that will announce a caller's place in line, but Penny Rhode, vice president, customer service, at First Gibralter Bank in Dallas, chose not to use it. "I felt like . . . focusing on the positive, rather than perhaps saying that there are 14 callers ahead of you."

Under First Gibralter's system, after 12 minutes a phone voice offers the caller the option of continuing to wait or leaving a message. Since it started the system in October, the bank has averaged about 100 messages a day out of between 3,000 and 3,200 calls.

Dissatisfaction with the slowness of a single-line arrangement led Burger King to try the "hospitality" line-up, in which cash registers are evenly spaced along the counter and customers select a line (in effect betting on which of several will move the fastest). In this arrangement, the cashier who takes an order also assembles the order. Although the hospitality line-up proves to be very flexible in meeting peak-period demand, it does tend to be more labor-intensive than the conventional line-up. Consequently, Burger King made yet another change, this time to what is called a "multiconventional" line-up, which is a hybrid of both earlier systems. The restaurant returned to a single line, but a new cash register now allows up to six orders to be recorded at the same time. Assemblers prepare the orders and distribute them at the end of the counter. Returning to a single line has guaranteed fairness, because customers are served in the order of their arrival. In addition, customers have enough time to make their meal selection without slowing the entire order-taking process.

Burger King's concern with reducing customer waiting time represents a trend toward providing faster service. In many cases, speed of delivery is viewed as a competitive advantage in the marketplace. For example, many hotels today will total your bill and slide it under your room door during the last night of your stay, thereby achieving "zero waiting time" at the check-out counter.

FIGURE 12.1
Queuing System
Schematic

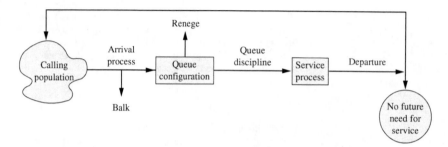

Fluctuations in demand for service are difficult to cope with because the consumption and production of services occur simultaneously. Customers typically arrive at random and place immediate demands on the available service. If service capacity is fully utilized at the time of his or her arrival, then the customer is expected to wait patiently in line. Varying arrival rates and service time requirements result in the formation of queues (i.e., lines of customers waiting their turn for service). The management of queues is a continuing challenge for service managers.

Essential Features of Queuing Systems

Figure 12.1 depicts the essential features of queuing systems. These are (1) calling population, (2) arrival process, (3) queue configuration, (4) queue discipline, and (5) service process.

Services obtain customers from a *calling population*. The rate at which they arrive is determined by the *arrival process*. If servers are idle, then the customer is immediately attended; otherwise, the customer is diverted to a queue, which can have various configurations. At this point, some customers may *balk* when confronted with a long or slow-moving waiting line and seek service elsewhere. Other customers, after joining the queue, may consider the delay to be intolerable, and so they *renege,* which means that they leave the line before service is rendered. When a server does become available, a customer then is selected from the queue, and service begins. The policy governing the selection is known as the *queue discipline*. The service facility may consist of no servers (i.e., self-service), one or more servers, or complex arrangements of servers in series or in parallel. After the service has been rendered, the customer departs the facility. At that time, the customer may either rejoin the calling population for future return or exit with no intention of returning.

We shall now discuss in more detail each of these five essential features of queuing systems.

Calling Population

The calling population need not be homogeneous; it may consist of several subpopulations. For example, arrivals at an outpatient clinic can be divided into walk-in patients, patients with appointments, and emergency patients. Each class of patient will place different demands on services, but more important, the waiting expectations of each will differ significantly.

In some queuing systems, the source of calls may be limited to a finite number of people. For example, consider the demands on an office copier by a staff of three secretaries. In this case, the probability of future arrivals depends on the number of persons who currently are in the system seeking service. For instance, the probability of a future arrival becomes zero once the third secretary joins the copier queue. Unless the population is quite small, however, an assumption of independent arrivals or infinite population usually suffices. Figure 12.2 shows a classification of the calling population.

Arrival Process

Any analysis of a service system must begin with a complete understanding of the temporal and spatial distribution of the demand for that service. Typically, data are collected

FIGURE 12.2
Classification of Calling Population

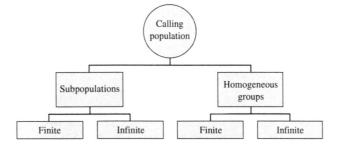

by recording the actual times of arrivals. These data then are used to calculate interarrival times. Many empirical studies indicate that the distribution of interarrival times will be exponential, and the shape of the curve in Figure 12.3 is typical of the *exponential distribution*. Note the high frequency at the origin and the long tail that tapers off to the right. The exponential distribution also can be recognized by noting that both the mean and the standard deviation are theoretically equal ($\mu = 2.4$ and $\sigma = 2.6$ for Figure 12.3).

The exponential distribution has a continuous probability density function of the form

$$f(t) = \lambda e^{-\lambda t} \qquad t \geq 0 \tag{1}$$

where λ = average arrival rate within a given interval of time (e.g., minutes, hours, days)

t = time between arrivals

e = base of natural logarithms (2.718 . . .)

mean = $1/\lambda$

variance = $1/\lambda^2$

The cumulative distribution function is

$$F(t) = 1 - e^{-\lambda t} \qquad t \geq 0 \tag{2}$$

Equation (2) gives the probability that the time between arrivals will be t or less. Note that λ is the inverse of the mean time between arrivals. Thus, for Figure 12.3, the mean time between arrivals is 2.4 minutes, which implies that λ is $1/2.4 = 0.4167$ arrival per

FIGURE 12.3
Distribution of Patient Interarrival Times for a University Health Clinic

Source: E. J. Rising, R. Baron, and B. Averill, "A Systems Analysis of a University Health-Service Outpatient Clinic." Reprinted with permission from *Operations Research* 21, no. 5, September–October 1973, p. 1038, Operations Society of America. No further reproduction permitted without the consent of the copyrighted owner.

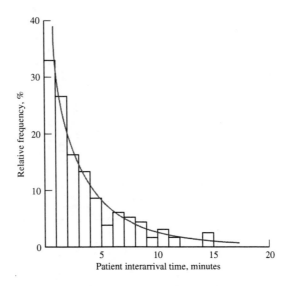

minute (i.e., an average rate of 25 patients per hour). Substituting 0.4167 for λ, the exponential distribution for the data displayed in Figure 12.3 is

$$f(t) = 0.4167 \, e^{-0.4167t} \qquad t \geq 0$$

with a cumulative distribution of

$$F(t) = 1 - e^{-0.4167t} \qquad t \geq 0$$

The cumulative distribution above can be used to find the probability that if a patient has already arrived; another will arrive in the next 5 minutes. We simply substitute 5 for t, and so

$$F(5) = 1 - e^{-0.4167(5)}$$
$$= 1 - 0.124$$
$$= 0.876$$

Thus, there is an 87.6 percent chance that another patient will arrive in the next 5 minute interval. Test this phenomenon the next time you are waiting in a physician's office.

Another distribution, known as the *Poisson distribution*, has a unique relationship to the exponential distribution. The Poisson distribution is a discrete probability function of the form

$$f(n) = \frac{(\lambda t)^n e^{-\lambda t}}{n!} \qquad n = 0, 1, 2, 3, \ldots \tag{3}$$

where λ = average arrival rate within a given interval of time (e.g., minutes, hours, days)

t = number of time periods of interest (usually $t = 1$)

n = number of arrivals $(0, 1, 2, \ldots)$

e = base of natural logarithms $(2.718\ldots)$

mean = λt

variance = λt

The Poisson distribution gives the probability of n arrivals during the time interval t. For the data of Figure 12.3, substituting for $\lambda = 25$ and $t = 1$, an equivalent description of the arrival process is

$$f(n) = \frac{[(25)(1)]^n e^{-(25)(1)}}{n!} \qquad n = 0, 1, 2, 3, \ldots$$

This gives the probability of $0, 1, 2, \ldots$ patients arriving during any 1-hour interval. Note that we have taken the option of converting $\lambda = 0.4167$ arrival per minute to $\lambda = 25$ arrivals per hour. This function can be used to calculate the interesting probability that no patients will arrive during a 1-hour interval by substituting 0 for n as shown below:

$$f(0) = \frac{[(25)(1)]^0 e^{-(25)(1)}}{0!} = e^{-25} = 1.4 \times 10^{-11}, \text{ a very small probability}$$

Figure 12.4 shows the relationship between the Poisson distribution (i.e., arrivals per hour) and the exponential distribution (i.e., minutes between arrivals). As can be seen,

FIGURE 12.4
Poisson and Exponential Equivalence

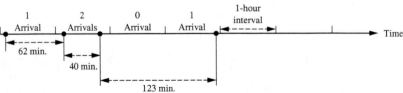

Poisson distribution of number of arrivals per hour (top view)

Exponential distribution of time between arrivals in minutes (bottom view)

FIGURE 12.5
Ambulance Calls by Hour of Day

Source: Reprinted with permission from James A. Fitzsimmons, "The Use of Spectral Analysis to Validate Planning Models," *Socio-Economic Planning* 8, no. 3, June 1974, p. 127. Copyright © 1974, Pergamon Press Ltd.

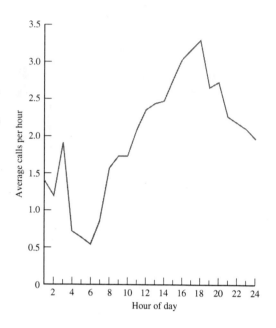

FIGURE 12.6
Patient Arrivals at Health Clinic by Day of Week

Source: E. J. Rising, R. Baron, and B. Averill, "A Systems Analysis of a University Health-Service Outpatient Clinic." Reprinted with permission from *Operations Research* 21, no. 5, September–October 1973, p. 1035, Operations society of America. No further reproduction permitted without the consent of the copyrighted owner.

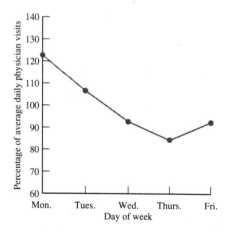

they represent alternative views of the same process. Thus, an exponential distribution of interarrival times with a mean of 2.4 minutes is equivalent to a Poisson distribution of the number of arrivals per hour with a mean of 25 (i.e., 60/2.4).

Service demand data often are collected automatically (e.g., by trip wires on highways), and the number of arrivals over a period of time is divided by the number of time intervals to arrive at an average rate per unit of time. The demand rate during the unit of time should be stationary with respect to time (i.e., lambda [λ] is a constant); otherwise, the underlying fluctuations in demand rate as a function of time will not be accounted for. This dynamic feature of demand is illustrated in Figure 12.5 for hours in a day, in Figure 12.6 for days of the week, and in Figure 12.7 for months of the year.

Variation in demand intensity directly affects the requirements for service capacity. When possible, service capacity is adjusted to match changes in demand, perhaps by varying the staffing levels. Another strategy is to smooth demand by asking customers to make appointments or reservations. Differential pricing is used by the telephone company to encourage callers to use off-peak hours, and movie theaters provide ticket discounts for patrons arriving before 6 PM. Figure 12.8 presents a classification of arrival processes.

310 Part Three *Managing Service Operations*

FIGURE 12.7

Airline Passenger Travel between U.S. and the World, 1994

Source: http://www.bts.gov/oai/international/table1.txt

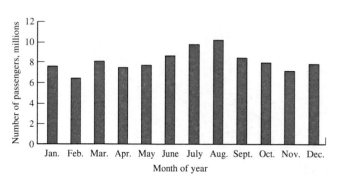

FIGURE 12.8

Classification of Arrival Process

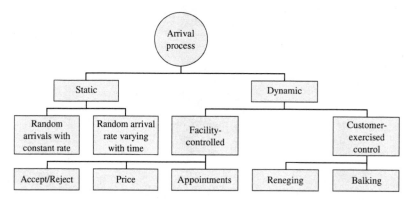

Our discussion has focused on the frequency of demand as a function of time, but the spatial distribution of demand also may vary. This is particularly true of emergency ambulance demand in an urban area, which has a spatial shift in demand resulting from the temporary movements of population from residential areas to commercial and industrial areas during working hours.

Queue Configuration

Queue configuration refers to the number of queues, their locations, their spatial requirements, and their effects on customer behavior. Figure 12.9 illustrates three alternative waiting configurations for a service, such as a bank, a post office, or an airline counter, where multiple servers are available.

For the multiple-queue alternative shown in Figure 12.9*a*, the arriving customer must decide which queue to join. The decision need not be irrevocable, however, because one may switch to the end of another line. This line-switching activity is called *jockeying*. In any event, watching the line next to you moving faster than your own is a source of aggravation, but the multiple-queue configuration does have the following advantages:

1. The service provided can be differentiated. The use of express lanes in supermarkets is an example. Shoppers with small demands on service can be isolated and processed quickly, thereby avoiding long waits for little service.
2. Division of labor is possible. For example, drive-in banks assign the more experienced teller to the commercial lane.
3. The customer has the option of selecting a particular server of preference.
4. Balking behavior may be deterred. When arriving customers see a long, single queue snaked in front of a service, they often interpret this as evidence of a long wait and decide not to join that line.

Figure 12.9*b* depicts the common arrangement of brass posts with red velvet ropes strung between them, forcing arrivals to join one sinuous queue. Whenever a server

FIGURE 12.9
Alternative Waiting-Area Configurations

Multiple Queues

(a)

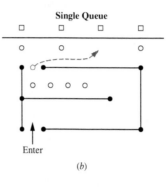

Single Queue

Enter

(b)

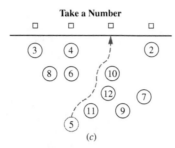

Take a Number

(c)

becomes available, the first person in line moves over to the service counter. This is a popular arrangement in bank lobbies, post offices, and amusement parks. Its advantages are:

1. The arrangement guarantees fairness by ensuring that a first-come, first-served rule (FCFS) applies to all arrivals.
2. There is a single queue; thus, no anxiety is associated with waiting to see if one selected the fastest line.
3. With only one entrance at the rear of the queue, the problem of cutting-in is resolved and reneging made difficult.
4. Privacy is enhanced because the transaction is conducted with no one standing immediately behind the person being served.
5. This arrangement is more efficient in terms of reducing the average time that customers spend waiting in line.

Figure 12.9c illustrates a variation on the single queue in which the arriving customer takes a number to indicate his or her place in line. When using such numbers to indicate positions in a queue, there is no need for a formal line. Customers are free to wander about, strike up a conversation, relax in a chair, or pursue some other diversion. Unfortunately, as noted earlier, customers must remain alert to hear their numbers being called or risk missing their turns for service. Bakeries make subtle use of the "take-a-number" system to increase impulse sales. Customers who are given the chance to browse among the tantalizing pastries often find that they purchase more than just the loaf of fresh bread for which they came.

The "virtual queue" is perhaps the most frustrating of all because there is no visible indication of your position in line. When placed on hold while trying to reach a business, a caller is reluctant to hang up because the call might be answered momentarily but is also frustrated by losing productive use of this waiting time. Some call centers have addressed this problem by periodically reporting the caller's position in line.

If the waiting area is inadequate to accommodate all customers desiring service, then they are turned away. This condition is referred to as a *finite queue*. Restaurants with limited parking may experience this problem to a certain extent. A public parking garage is a classic example because, once the last stall is taken, future arrivals are rejected with the word *FULL* until a car is retrieved.

Finally, concealment of the waiting line itself may deter customers from balking. Amusement parks often process waiting customers by stages. The first stage is a line outside the concession entrance, the second is the wait in an inside vestibule area, and the final stage is the wait for an empty vehicle to convey a party through the attraction. Figure 12.10 shows a classification of queue configurations.

FIGURE 12.10
Classification of Queue Configurations

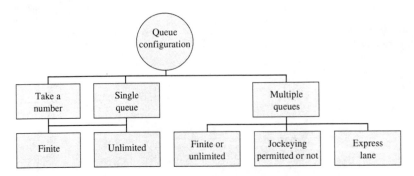

Queue Discipline

The *queue discipline* is a policy established by management to select the next customer from the queue for service. The most popular service discipline is the first-come, first-served (FCFS) rule. This represents an egalitarian approach to serving waiting customers, because all customers are treated alike. The rule is considered to be static because no information other than position in line is used to identify the next customer for service.

Dynamic queue disciplines are based on some attribute of the customer or status of the waiting line. For example, consider a professor who has a queue of students outside his or her door during office hours might select the next student based on a probable short activity time (e.g., turn in a paper). This shortest-processing-time (SPT) rule has the property of minimizing the average time that customers spend in the system (i.e., both waiting and being served). This rule is seldom used in its pure form, however, because customers who require long service times would continually be pushed to the back of the queue for more recent arrivals requiring shorter times.

A more sophisticated dynamic queue discipline is the $c\mu$ priority rule where "*c*" is a linear delay cost rate and "μ" is the rate of customers served per unit time. This priority rule has the social optimization objective of maximizing the sum of benefits for customer plus provider. The rule assigns priority to customers in increasing order of their $c\mu$ index (i.e., high cost and short service time moves one to the front of the queue). Note how this addresses the shortcoming of the SPT rule by combining the cost of delay with the service processing time $1/\mu$. This priority rule is ideal for servicing customers within the same organization because the value of c is easily determined.

Typically, arrivals are placed in priority classes on the basis of some attribute, and the FCFS rule is used within each class. An example is the express check-out counter at supermarkets, where orders of 10 or fewer items are processed. This allows large stores to segment their customers and, thereby, compete with the neighborhood convenience stores that provide prompt service.

In a medical setting, the procedure known as *triage* is used to give priority to those who would benefit most from immediate treatment. The most responsive queue discipline is the preemptive priority rule. Under this rule, the service currently in process for a person is interrupted to serve a newly arrived customer with higher priority. This rule usually is reserved for emergency services, such as fire or ambulance service. An ambulance that is on the way to a hospital to pick up a patient for routine transfer will interrupt this mission to respond to a suspected cardiac-arrest call.

Creative dynamic queue disciplines take advantage of the status of the queue. Consider the concept of round-robin service as used by a dentist with multiple examination rooms. For example, a patient is given a local anesthetic before a tooth extraction. While the anesthetic takes effect, the dentist moves onto another patient who requires x-rays. Thus, customers share the service provider by alternating between waiting and being served. When the number of customers in the queue becomes large, the option of using the SPT rule within a FCFS discipline may be acceptable in a socially agreeable queue. Note that for multiple queues, when jockeying is permitted, the FCFS rule cannot be guaranteed. Figure 12.11 shows a classification of queue disciplines.

FIGURE 12.11

Classification of Queue Discipline

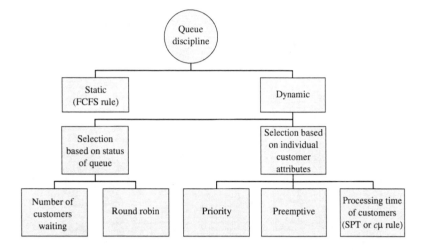

Service Process

The distribution of service times, arrangement of servers, management policies, and server behavior all contribute to service performance. Figure 12.12 contains histograms of several service time distributions in an outpatient clinic with $\bar{x} = 1/\mu$. As the figure shows, the distribution of service times may be of any form. Conceivably, the service time could be a constant, such as the time to process a car through an automated car wash; however, when the service is brief and simple to perform (e.g., preparing orders at a fast-food restaurant, collecting tolls at a bridge, or checking out items at a supermarket), the distribution of service times frequently is exponential (*see* Figure 12.3). The histogram for second-service times, Figure 12.12c, most closely approximates an exponential distribution. The second-service times represent those brief encounters in which, for example, the physician prescribes a medication or goes over your test results with you. The distribution of service times is a reflection of the variations in customer needs and server performances.

FIGURE 12.12

Histograms of Outpatient-Clinic Service Times

Source: E. J. Rising, R. Baron, and B. Averill, "A Systems Analysis of a University Health-Service Outpatient Clinic." Reprinted with permission from *Operations Research* 21, no. 5, September–October 1973, p. 1039, Operations Society of America. No further reproduction permitted without the consent of the copyrighted owner.

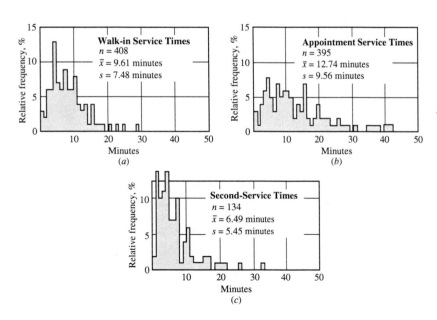

314   Part Three *Managing Service Operations*

TABLE 12.1
**Service Facility
Arrangements**

Service Facility	Server Arrangement
Parking lot	Self-service
Cafeteria	Servers in series
Toll booths	Servers in parallel
Supermarket	Self-serve, first stage; parallel servers, second stage
Hospital	Services in parallel and series, not all used by each patient

FIGURE 12.13
**Classification of Service
Processes**

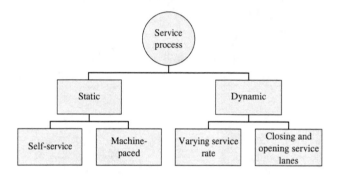

Table 12.1 illustrates the variety of service facility arrangements that are possible. With servers in parallel, management gains flexibility in meeting the variations in demand for service. Management can vary the service capacity effectively by opening and closing service lines to meet changes in demand. At a bank, additional teller windows are opened when the length of queues becomes excessive. Cross-training employees also adds to this flexibility. For example, at supermarkets, stockers often are used as cashiers when lines become long at the check-out counters. A final advantage of parallel servers is that they provide redundancy in case of equipment failures.

The behavior of service personnel toward customers is critical to the success of the organization. Under the pressure of long waiting lines, a server may speed up and spend less time with each customer; unfortunately, a gracious and leisurely manner then becomes curt and impersonal. Sustained pressure to hurry may increase the rate of customer processing, but it also sacrifices quality. This behavior on the part of a pressured server also can have a detrimental effect on other servers in the system. For example, a busy emergency telephone operator may dispatch yet another patrol car before properly screening the call for its critical nature; in this situation, the operator should have spent more time than usual to ensure that the limited resources of patrol cars were being dispatched to the most critical cases. Service processes are classified in Figure 12.13.

Summary

An understanding of the queuing phenomenon is necessary before creative approaches to the management of service systems can be considered. An appreciation of the behavioral implications of keeping customers waiting reveals that the perception of waiting often is more important than the actual delay. Waiting also has economic implications for both the service firm and its customers.

A schematic queuing model identified the essential features of queuing systems: calling population, arrival process, queue configuration, queue discipline, and service process. An understanding of each feature provides insights and identifies management options for improving customer service.

Service Benchmark

FIVE MINUTES IN LINE IS LONGER THAN FIVE MINUTES AT HARD LABOR

Time goes slowly when you're in line, that's a law. The Disney theme parks are evading that law as much as they can and defying it when they can't.

Disney instituted "Fast Pass," a computerized ticketing system that allows customers to get on certain rides with little or no waiting in line. To get a Fast Pass, a customer inserts a regular admission ticket into a turnstile and a computer inside the turnstile prints out a ticket with a designated one-hour period. When the customer arrives at the ride during the designated time, he or she is allowed to go right in, usually with no wait time at all.

Another way that Disney tries to alleviate the pain of waiting in lines is to allow overnight guests of Walt Disney World Resort hotels to enter any Disney park 90 minutes before regular day visitors are permitted to enter. Hotel guests who have multiday tickets get special after-hours admission, and entertainment, such as musical groups, is provided at some attractions to ease the wait time. Tip boards in each park display wait times of all of the attractions so guests can plan their visits.

Most airlines now have kiosks at some airports that allow passengers to check in without standing in the customary lines. There is also talk of issuing computerized identification to prescreened passengers that would allow them to bypass the usual lines for security screening into the passenger boarding concourses.

Key Terms and Definitions

Balk occurs when an arriving customer sees a long queue and decides not to seek service. *p. 306*
Calling population source of service customers from a market area. *p. 306*
Exponential distribution the continuous distribution that describes the time between arrivals or service times. *p. 307*
Jockeying the practice of customers in a multiple-queue system leaving one queue to join another. *p. 310*
Poisson distribution the discrete distribution that describes random arrivals or departures from a busy server per time interval (e.g., hour). *p. 308*
Queue discipline a rule for selecting the next customer in line to be served (e.g., FCFS). *p. 312*
Reneging occurs when a customer in queue departs before obtaining service. *p. 306*

Topics for Discussion

1. Suggest some strategies for controlling the variability in service times.
2. Suggest diversions that could make waiting less painful.
3. Select a bad and a good waiting experience, and contrast the situations with respect to the aesthetics of the surroundings, diversions, people waiting, and attitude of servers.
4. Suggest ways that service management can influence the arrival times of customers.
5. When the line becomes long at some fast-food restaurants, an employee will walk along the line taking orders. What are the benefits of this policy?

Interactive Exercise

The class breaks into small groups with at least one international student in each group, if possible. Based on overseas travel, each group reports on observations of waiting behavior from a cultural perspective.

Solved Problems

Problem Statement

A fast-food restaurant is interested in studying its arrival of customers. During the busy lunch period they have observed an average of 20 customers arriving per hour Poisson distributed.

a. If a customer has just entered the store, what is the probability of another arrival in the next 10 minutes?

b. What is the probability of two customers arriving in a five minute window?

Solution

a. We use Equation (2) with a $\lambda = 20/60 = 1/3$ arrival per minute because our focus is on the next $t = 10$-minute time interval.

$$F(t) = 1 - e^{-\lambda t} = 1 - e^{-(1/3)(10)} = 0.96 \text{ almost a certainty}$$

b. We use Equation (3) with a $\lambda = 20/60 = 1/3$ arrival per minute because our focus is on the next $t = 5$-minute time interval.

$$f(n) = \frac{\lambda t^n e^{-\lambda t}}{n!} = \frac{[(1/3)(5)]^2 e^{-(1/3)(5)}}{2!} = 0.26$$

Exercises

12.1. You show up early in the morning to buy tickets for a concert but you find a long line and are told that the average time between arrivals has been about 15 minutes.

a. What is the chance you will loose my place at the end of the line, if after just arriving, you leave for 5 minutes to use the restroom?

b. What is the probability that zero, one, or two arrivals will come during your five minute rest break?

12.2. Create a Poisson histogram in the range from zero to nine arrivals per hour for a distribution with mean of 4 arrivals per hour. Is your distribution symmetrical about the mean?

12.3. Using Equation (2) prepare the cumulative exponential distribution for the patient interarrival times shown in Figure 12.3 with a mean of 0.4167 arrivals per minute. Plot your distribution over a range of zero to ten minutes in increments of one minute. What is the upper limit of your distribution?

Selected Bibliography

Cayirli, Tugba; Emre Veral; and Harry Rosen. "Assessment of Patient Classification in Appointment System Design." *Production and Operations Management* 17, no. 3 (May–June 2008), pp. 338–53.

Chambers, Chester, and Panagiotis Kouvelis. "Modeling and Managing the Percentage of Satisfied Customers in Hidden and Revealed Waiting Line Systems." *Production and Operations Management,* 15, no. 1 (Spring 2006), pp. 103–16.

Conway, R. W.; W. L. Maxwell; and L. W. Miller. *Theory of Scheduling.* Reading, MA: Addison-Wesley, 1967.

Davis, Mark M., and Janelle Heineke. "How Disconfirmation, Perception and Actual Waiting Times Impact Customer Satisfaction." *International Journal of Service Industry Management* 9, no. 1 (1998), pp. 64–73.

———, and Michael J. Maggard. "An Analysis of Customer Satisfaction with Waiting Times in a Two-Stage Service Process." *Journal of Operations Management* 9, no. 3 (August 1990), pp. 324–34.

Durrande-Moreau, Agnes. "Waiting for Service: Ten Years of Empirical Research." *International Journal of Service Industry Management* 10, no. 2 (1999), pp. 171–89.

———, and Jean-Claude Usunier. "Time Styles and the Waiting Experience: An Exploratory Study." *Journal of Service Research* 2, no. 2 (November 1999), pp. 173–86.

Evangelist, Shane; Badger Godwin; Joey Johnson; Vincent Conzola; Robert Kizer; Stephanie Young-Helou; and Richard Metters. "Linking Marketing and Operations: An Application at Blockbuster, Inc." *Journal of Service Research* 5, no. 2 (November 2002), pp. 91–100.

Hassin, R., and M. Haviv. *To Queue or Not to Queue.* Boston: Kluwer, 2003.

Jones, Peter, and Emma Peppiatt. "Managing Perceptions of Waiting Times in Service Queues." *International Journal of Service Industry Management* 7, no. 5 (1996), pp. 47–61.

Katz, K. L.; B. M. Larson; and R. C. Larson. "Prescription for the Waiting-in-Line Blues: Entertain, Enlighten, and Engage." *Sloan Management Review* 32, no. 2 (Winter 1991), pp. 44–53.

Larson, Richard C. "Perspectives on Queues: Social Justice and the Psychology of Queuing." *Operations Research* 35, no. 6 (November–December 1987), pp. 895–905.

Maister, D. H. "The Psychology of Waiting Lines." In *The Service Encounter,* eds. J. A. Czepiel, M. R. Solomon, and C. F. Surprenant. Lexington, Mass.: Lexington Press, 1985, pp. 113–23.

Mondschein, Susana V., and Gabriel Y. Weintraub. "Appointment Policies in Service Operations: A Critical Analysis of the Economic Framework." *Production and Operations Management* 12, no. 2 (Summer 2003), pp. 266–86.

Nie, Winter. "Waiting: Integrating Social and Psychological Perspectives in Operations Management." *Omega* 28, 2000, pp. 611–29.

Rafaeli, Anat; Greg Barron; and Keren Haber. "The Effects of Queue Structure on Attitudes." *Journal of Service Research* 5, no. 2 (November 2002), pp. 125–39.

Schultz, Carl R. "Economic Service Quotas." *Journal of Service Research* 5, no. 2 (November 2002), pp. 154–63.

Stidham, S. Jr. "Analysis, Design, and Control of Queuing Systems." *Operations Research* 50, no. 1 (2002), pp. 197–216.

Tansik, David A., and Robert Routhieauz. "Customer Stress-Relaxation: The Impact of Music in a Hospital Waiting Room." *International Journal of Service Industry Management* 10, no. 1 (1999), pp. 68–81.

Taylor, Shirley. "Waiting for Service: The Relationship between Delays and Evaluations of Services." *Journal of Marketing* 58, April 1994, pp. 56–69.

Van Mieghem, Jan A. "Dynamic Scheduling with Convex Delay Costs: The Generalized $c\mu$ Rule." *Annuals of Applied Probability* 5, no. 3 (1995), pp. 809–33.

Whiting, Anita, and Naveen Donthu. "Managing Voice-to-Voice Encounters: Reducing the Agony of Being Put on Hold." *Journal of Service Research* 8, no. 3 (February 2006), pp. 234–44.

Endnotes

1. Yoram Barzel, "A Theory of Rationing by Waiting," *Journal of Law and Economics* 17, no. 1 (April 1974), p. 74.

2. Adapted from David H. Maister, "The Psychology of Waiting Lines." In J. A. Czepiel, M. R. Solomon, and C. F. Surprenant (eds.), *The Service Encounter.* Lexington, Mass.: Lexington Press, 1985, chap. 8, pp. 113–23.

3. For a discussion of slips and skips, see Richard C. Larson, "Perspectives on Queues: Social Justice and the Psychology of Queuing," *Operations Research* 35, no. 6 (November–December 1987), pp. 895–905.

4. Amanda Bennett, "Their Business Is on the Line," *The Wall Street Journal,* December 7, 1990, p. B1. Reprinted by permission of *The Wall Street Journal,* © 1989, Dow Jones & Company, Inc. All Rights Reserved Worldwide.

5. This case, sad to say, is true in its entirety. The names of the physician and his staff have been omitted, not to protect them but because this kind of treatment of patients is so pervasive in the American health care system that it serves no purpose to identify them. We offer the case for two reasons: first, because it is very instructive regarding important material in this chapter, and second, because it points out that customers and providers must work together in our evolving service society. Service providers must be sensitive to the needs of customers and customers must demand and reward good service.

Chapter

10

Service Facility Location

Learning Objectives

After completing this chapter, you should be able to:

1. Explain the difference between competitive clustering and saturation marketing.
2. Explain the impact of the Internet on location decisions.
3. Describe how a geographic information system is used in service location decisions.
4. Differentiate between a Euclidian and metropolitan metric approach to measuring travel distance.
5. Locate a single facility using the cross-median approach.
6. Use the Huff retail location model to estimate revenue and market share for a potential site.
7. Locate multiple facilities using the set covering model.

From a marketing perspective service location focuses on attracting customers to a site because of convenience (e.g., fast food restaurants located on a high traffic street) or physical attributes (e.g., resort on a beautiful beach). However, location also affects the service delivery design and has an impact on employees. Consider the experience of an insurance firm in Los Angeles.

A study by David A. Lopez and Paul Gray illustrates how an insurance company in Los Angeles decentralized its operations by using telecommunications and strategically locating its satellite offices.[1] An examination was made of the benefits and costs to the insurance firm when work was moved to the workers rather than when workers moved to their work. Insurance companies and other information-based industries are good candidates for employer decentralization, because members of their office staff perform routine clerical tasks using the firm's computer databases. The proposed plan replaced the centralized operation in downtown Los Angeles with a network of regional satellite offices in the suburbs where the workers live.

The analysis also included a location study to determine the size, site, and number of satellites that would minimize the variable costs associated with employee travel and the fixed costs of establishing the satellite offices. The decentralization plan yielded several benefits to the company: (1) reduced staff requirements, (2) reduced employee turnover and training, (3) reduced salaries for clerical employees, (4) elimination of a lunch program, and (5) increased income from lease of the headquarters site. Employees whose travel to work was reduced by at least 5½ miles realized a net benefit over their reduced salary and loss of subsidized lunch. This employee benefit is important in light of increasing energy expenses for transportation.

It was found that underwriting life insurance and servicing insurance policies could be performed at remote locations using online computers. Phone communications usually were sufficient for personal contacts, and few face-to-face meetings were needed. These findings substantiate those of other studies in Britain and Sweden indicating that individuals require face-to-face contacts only for initial meetings and periodic refreshing; they do not require continual face-to-face contact to reach decisions and conduct routine business.

Traditionally, location decisions have been based on intuition and had a considerable range of success. Although site selection often is based on opportunistic factors such as site availability and favorable leasing, a quantitative analysis can be useful to avoid a serious mistake. For example, regardless of how low the rent may be, being the only store in a deserted shopping mall offers no advantage.

Chapter Preview

This chapter begins with a discussion of strategic location considerations. For example, the strategies of competitive clustering or saturation marketing are used to attract customers to a service site. Other service delivery strategies, such as using marketing intermediaries and the Internet, remove the need for customer travel and, thus, a decision on site location can be based on other considerations, such as cost or availability of skilled labor. Geographic information systems (i.e., demand and its characteristics distributed across a market area) are a critical input to location models. The chapter concludes with a discussion of modeling considerations and a review of several facility location techniques for both single- and multiple-facility situations.

Strategic Location Considerations

In a study of La Quinta Motor Inns to learn why some inns were successful and others not, several strategic location dimensions were discovered including flexibility, competitive positioning, demand management, and focus.[2]

Flexibility of a location is a measure of the degree to which the service can react to changing economic situations. Because location decisions are long-term commitments with capital-intensive aspects, it is essential to select locations that can be responsive to future economic, demographic, cultural, and competitive changes. For example, locating sites in a number of states could reduce the overall risk of a financial crisis resulting from regional economic downturns. This portfolio approach to multisite location could be augmented by selecting individual sites near inelastic demand (e.g., locating a hotel near a convention center).

Competitive positioning refers to methods by which the firm can establish itself relative to its competitors. Multiple locations can serve as a barrier to competition through building a firm's competitive position and establishing a market awareness. Acquiring and holding prime locations before the market has developed can keep the competition from gaining access to these desirable locations and create an artificial barrier to entry (analogous to a product patent).

Demand management is the ability to control the quantity, quality, and timing of demand. For example, hotels cannot manipulate capacity effectively because of the fixed nature of the facility; however, a hotel can control demand by locating near a diverse set of market generators that supply a steady demand regardless of the economic condition, the day of the week, or the season.

Focus can be developed by offering the same narrowly defined service at many locations. Many multisite service firms develop a standard (or formula) facility that can be duplicated at many locations. While this "cookie-cutter" approach makes expansion easier, sites that are located in close proximity could siphon business from each other. This problem of demand cannibalization can be avoided if a firm establishes a pattern of desired growth for its multisite expansion.

In the following discussion, we will look at additional strategic location considerations beginning with the concept called competitive clustering, which is used for shopping goods, as well as a strategy called saturation marketing that defies the curse of cannibalization. Other strategies extend the service market beyond the confines of geography using marketing intermediaries, substitution of communication for travel, physical separation of front from back office operations, and finally the use of the Internet to reach a global audience.

Competitive Clustering

Competitive clustering is a reaction to observed consumer behavior when they are choosing among competitors. When shopping for items such as new automobiles or used cars, customers like to make comparisons and, for convenience, seek out the area of town where many dealers are concentrated (i.e., the so-called motor mile).

Motel chains such as La Quinta have observed that inns located in areas with many nearby competitors experience higher occupancy rates than those located in isolation. It is surprising that locating near the competition is a strategy with profitable counterintuitive results for some services.

Saturation Marketing

Au Bon Pain, a café known for its gourmet sandwiches, French bread, and croissants, has embraced the unconventional strategy of *saturation marketing* popularized in Europe. The idea is to group outlets of the same firm tightly in urban and other high-traffic areas. Au Bon Pain has clustered 16 cafés in downtown Boston alone, with many of them fewer than 100 yards apart—in fact, one group of five shops operates on different floors of Filene's department store. Although modest cannibalization of sales has been reported, the advantages of reduced advertising, easier supervision, and customer awareness, when taken together, overwhelm the competition and far outweigh the drawbacks. This strategy works best in high-density, downtown locations, where shops can intercept impulse customers with little time to shop or eat.[3]

The success of this approach became apparent to us during a summer visit to Helsinki, Finland, where we noticed ice cream vendors from the same firm with carts on nearly every corner of the downtown walking streets. The sight of a vendor seems to plant the idea of a treat in the mind of a passerby, who then takes advantage of the next, nearby opportunity.

Auto dealers that locate in clusters attract customers from afar because of the convenience of one-stop comparison shopping. Bob Daemmrich/The Image Works

Marketing Intermediaries

The idea that services are created and consumed simultaneously does not seem to allow for the "channel-of-distribution" concept as developed for goods. Because services are intangible and cannot be stored or transported, the geographic area for service would seem to be restricted. However, service channels of distribution have evolved that use separate organizational entities as intermediaries between the producer and the consumer.

James H. Donnelly provides a number of examples that illustrate how some services have created unlimited geographic service areas.[4] The retailer who extends a bank's credit to its customers is an intermediary in the distribution of credit. That Bank of America is a California bank does not limit use of the Visa card, which is honored worldwide. A health maintenance organization (HMO) performs an intermediary role between the practitioner and the patient by increasing the availability and convenience of "one-stop" shopping, and group insurance written through employers and labor unions is an example of how the insurance industry uses intermediaries to distribute its service.

Substitution of Communication for Travel

An appealing alternative to moving people from one place to another is the use of telecommunications. One proposal that has met with some success is the use of telemetry to extend health care services into remote regions. Sometimes paramedics or nurse practitioners can use communication with a distant hospital to provide health care without transporting the patient. In addition, the banking industry has promoted direct payroll deposit, which permits employees to have their pay deposited directly into their checking accounts. By authorizing employers to deposit salaries, the employees save trips to the bank; bankers also benefit through reduced check-processing paperwork and less congestion at their drive-in teller facilities.

Separation of Front from Back Office

For many services the front and back office need not be co-located (e.g., dry cleaning, shoe repair, banks and ATMs). As shown in Table 10.1, thinking in terms of separating the front from the back office can yield strategic benefits.

If the front office and back office need not be co-located, opportunities exist for creative service design. When you place a drive-in order at a Texas McDonalds, for example, the order taker might be located at a call center in Iowa. Taking orders from several stores at a central location allows the local employees to concentrate on filling the order. Viewing location decisions from both an internal (employee) and external (customer) perspective also highlights opportunities for self-service and substitution of electronic media for physical travel. Notice the strategic role of front office location in creating a barrier to entry and the back office location in achieving cost economies.

TABLE 10.1
Considerations in Locating the Front and Back Office

	Front Office	Back Office
External Customer (consumer)	Is travel out to customer or customer travel to site?	Is service performed on person or property?
	Is location a barrier to entry? Can electronic media substitute for physical travel?	Is co-location necessary? How is communication accomplished?
Internal Customer (employee)	Availability of labor?	Are economies of scale possible?
	Are self-service kiosks an alternative?	Can employees work from home?
		Is offshoring an option?

Impact of the Internet on Service Location

With the introduction of the Internet in the mid-1990s, the potential for electronic commerce has become a reality—customers shop from a desk at home and surf the Web for interesting home pages to visit. A Web site has become the virtual location of pure e-commerce firms (e.g., Amazon.com) or an alternative channel of distribution for established click-and-mortar retailers (e.g., Barnes & Noble). The limits of a market area were once defined by how far a customer would travel to the site, but physical travel is irrelevant in the virtual world of the Internet. Location, however, is still a concern for e-commerce retailers that must ship a product. This aspect of a business is now driven by access to overnight shippers (e.g., locating a warehouse in Memphis for access to FedEx). Internet providers of electronic services, such as brokers (e.g., Fidelity.com), are less reliant on physical offices, and the location of an auction facilitator (e.g., eBay.com) can be based on personal preference of the owners or on access to talented employees. Finally, the Internet facilitates 24/7 access to call centers located strategically around the world. Each center (e.g., India, Ireland, and Jamaica) operates a normal daylight shift staffed with educated English literate low-wage labor.

The concept of *e-distance*, the barrier created by internal and external navigation, arises from the desire to attract customers to a Web site. For example, an undiscovered Web site is infinitely distant and one that is five clicks away might rule out 90 percent of the public. Site navigation is a measure of distance, so Web developers often use a two-click rule, i.e., a customer's destination should be no more than two clicks away from the homepage. Locating and getting to the Web site is another form of distance. If a customer uses a search engine, he or she still needs to read, evaluate, and select a link to follow.

Julie Kendall reports on a study of small off-Broadway theatres in southern New Jersey that are unable to take advantage of the "competitive clustering" strategy because no central theatre district exists.[5] Theaters are scattered across eight counties and getting potential audiences to realize they exist is a challenge. A shared Web site, however, allows a potential patron to browse the available plays with direct links to each theater for ticket purchase and seat selection. The shared Web site reduces the e-distance of theater patrons from that of searching several individual Web sites to visiting a single site. The result is a virtual application of the competitive clustering strategy in which the attraction of patrons is increased for all theaters.

Site Considerations

Available real estate represents a major constraint on the final selection of a site. Moreover, site selection requires a physical visit to assess the local environment (e.g., observing if the locale is upscale enough for a luxury hotel). Table 10.2 contains many physical attributes to consider such as access, visibility, and traffic that are important

TABLE 10.2
Site Selection Considerations

1. *Access:*
   Convenient to freeway exit and entrance ramps
   Served by public transportation
2. *Visibility:*
   Set back from street
   Sign placement
3. *Traffic:*
   Traffic volume on street that may indicate potential impulse buying
   Traffic congestion that could be a hindrance (e.g., fire stations)
4. *Parking:*
   Adequate off-street parking
5. *Expansion:*
   Room for expansion
6. *Environment:*
   Immediate surroundings should complement the service
7. *Competition:*
   Location of competitors
8. *Government:*
   Zoning restrictions
   Taxes
9. *Labor:*
   Available labor with appropriate skills
10. *Complements:*
    Complementary services nearby

to attracting customers to the site. The nearby location of competitors often is desirable as noted in our discussion of competitive clustering. Another consideration is the existence of complementary services, such as locating a restaurant with motels nearby.

If customers do not need to travel to the site, these physical attributes may not be important, but, instead one might consider the availability of skilled labor. For example, we noted that it is common practice for service firms to locate call centers in Bangalore, India, because of the availability of low cost, talented, English-speaking employees.

Regression Analysis in Location Decisions

When a firm with many facilities wants to expand, it can rely on the wealth of statistical information about existing facilities to forecast the performance of a candidate location. A regression model based on several independent variables, such as size, competitors nearby, and traffic, can be constructed to forecast performance (i.e., anticipated revenue).

As an example, the management of La Quinta Motor Inns, a national chain of hotels, commissioned a study to determine the direction of its expansion efforts.[6] It wanted to know which factors determined a profitable hotel location and, thus, would allow management to screen available real estate for new hotel sites. Investigators collected data on many factors at existing locations, such as traffic count, number of competitive rooms nearby, visibility of signs, local airport traffic, types of neighboring businesses, and distance to the central business district. In all, 35 factors, or independent variables, were considered.

The inn's operating margin, obtained by adding depreciation and interest expenses to the profit and then dividing by the total revenue, was chosen as the most reliable measure, or dependent variable Y, on which to base a forecast. A statistical evaluation of the data for all the variables in Table 10.3 allowed the investigators to identify four critical factors—STATE, PRICE, INCOME, and COLLEGE—to be used in the forecast model. The resulting regression model (1) contains several independent variables with negative coefficients that need explanation. The variable STATE, defined as state population per inn, is a measure of brand exposure. A small number for this variable represents a high density of La Quinta Motor Inns in the state and, thus, brand recognition is strong. The variable INCOME, defined as average family income, is a measure of the affluence of the area in which the inn is located. Because La Quinta Motor Inns targets the business traveler, locations in non-residential areas are preferred.

$$\text{Operating margin } Y = 39.05 + (-5.41)\text{STATE} + (5.86)\text{PRICE} +$$
$$(-3.09)\text{INCOME} + (1.75)\text{COLLEGE} \qquad (1)$$

By investigators' collecting data on the independent variables at a proposed hotel site and making appropriate transformations as needed, the operating margin can be forecasted. The results of this study proved the model to be very good in predicting the likelihood of success for a new inn at a proposed location.

Geographic Information System

A new use of an old technology is moving into the professional business arena. Geographic information systems (GIS) are helping to make many business decisions and solving a variety of common business problems. These systems at one time were confined to the provenances of scientists and cartographers. Now, however, the Environmental Research Institute, Inc., has introduced ArcView, a GIS for business applications.[7] This resource, available on a compact disc, can be used for tasks such as mapping customer databases,

TABLE 10.3

Independent Variables for Hotel Location

Source: Reprinted by permission, S. E. Kimes and J. A. Fitzsimmons, "Selecting Profitable Hotel Sites at La Quinta Motor Inns," *Interfaces* 20, no. 2, March–April 1990, p. 14. Copyright 1990, the Operations Research Society of America and The Institute of Management Sciences, 290 Westminster Street, Providence, RI 02903.

Name	Description
Competitive factors	
INNRATE	Inn price
PRICE	Room rate for the inn
RATE	Average competitive room rate
RMS1	Hotel rooms within 1 mile
RMSTOTAL	Hotel rooms within 3 miles
ROOMSINN	Inn rooms
Demand generators	
CIVILIAN	Civilian personnel on base
COLLEGE	College enrollment
HOSP1	Hospital beds within 1 mile
HOSPTOTL	Hospital beds within 4 miles
HVYIND	Heavy industrial employment
LGTIND	Light industrial acreage
MALLS	Shopping mall square footage
MILBLKD	Military base blocked
MILITARY	Military personnel
MILTOT	MILITARY + CIVILIAN
OFC1	Office space within 1 mile
OFCTOTAL	Office space within 4 miles
OFCCBD	Office space in central business district
PASSENGER	Airport passengers enplaned
RETAIL	Scale ranking of retail activity
TOURISTS	Annual tourists
TRAFFIC	Traffic count
VAN	Airport van
Area demographics	
EMPLYPCT	Unemployment percentage
INCOME	Average family income
POPULACE	Residential population
Market awareness	
AGE	Years inn has been open
NEAREST	Distance to nearest inn
STATE	State population per inn
URBAN	Urban population per inn
Physical attributes	
ACCESS	Accessibility
ARTERY	Major traffic artery
DISTCBD	Distance to downtown
SIGNVIS	Sign visibility

determining site locations, analyzing demand, and improving delivery service. It has applications for every area of business, including banking, health care, real estate, and management.

In very simple terms, ArcView translates data, such as demographic information, into a map. Consider, for example, a table that lists street addresses and median home values.

It may be possible to discern a pattern in the list, if the data are for a community of 150 people in central Montana. If the data are for Denver, however, we cannot possibly discern a pattern that might be useful to determine a location for a new high-end specialty shop. ArcView solves our Denver problem by transferring the data to a map base and color-coding the median home values according to different zip codes. We can see immediately which areas are likely to have customers for an expensive store.

Consider another example. Suppose a state agency wants to establish a warehouse to store surplus foods for Meals on Wheels organizations in an 18-county area. Most Meals on Wheels clients are elderly and homebound, so the agency commissioner wants to identify a location that will be most convenient for the Meals on Wheels units that have the highest demand. One solution to this problem is to use ArcView to look at the distribution of the population by age groups. Figure 10.1 shows that the counties on the southeastern perimeter of the area have larger populations in the 55+ age group. Based on this information, the warehouse could be located to serve these counties most conveniently.

Modeling Considerations

Many factors enter into the decision to locate a service facility. Figure 10.2 classifies location issues that will be used to guide our discussion. The broad categories are geographic representation, number of facilities, and optimization criteria.

Geographic Representation

The traditional classification of location problems is based on how the geography is modeled. Location options and travel distance can be represented on either a plane or a network. Location on a plane (i.e., flat surface) is characterized by a solution space that has infinite possibilities. Facilities may be located anywhere on the plane and are identified by an *xy* cartesian coordinate (or, in a global context, by latitudes and longitudes), as shown in Figure 10.3. Distance between locations is measured at the extremes in one of

FIGURE 10.1
Population Density by Age Group

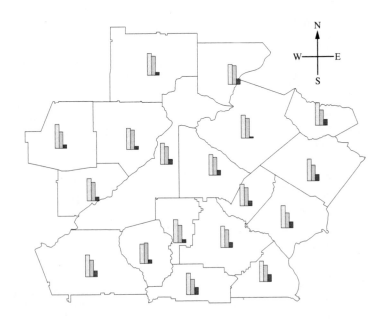

Population Age Groups

0–29   30–54   55+

FIGURE 10.2
Classification of Service
Facility Location Issues

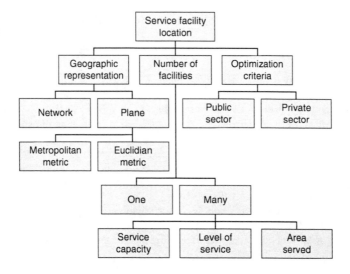

two ways. One method is the *euclidian metric,* or vector, travel distance (remember the Pythagorean theorem), which is defined as

$$d_{ij} = [(x_i - x_j)]^2 + (y_i - y_j)^2]^{\frac{1}{2}} \tag{2}$$

where
  d_{ij} = distance between points i and j

x_i, y_i = coordinates of the ith point

x_j, y_j = coordinates of the jth point

For example, if

  the origin $x_i, y_i = 2,2$ and   the destination $x_j, y_j = 4,4$
then

$$d_{ij} = [(2 - 4)^2 + (2 - 4)^2]^{\frac{1}{2}} = 2.83$$

The other method is the *metropolitan metric,* or rectangular displacement, travel distance (i.e., north-south and east-west travel in urban areas), which is defined as

$$d_{ij} = |x_i - x_j| + |y_i - y_j| \tag{3}$$

FIGURE 10.3
Geographic Structure

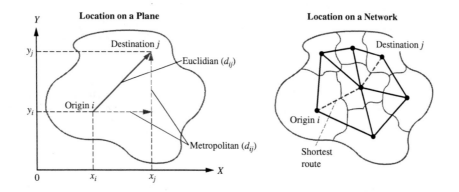

Using the same example from above for the metropolitan metric:

$$d_{ij} = |2 - 4| + |2 - 4| = 4.0$$

Location on a network is characterized by a solution space that is restricted to the nodes of that network. For example, a highway system could be considered a network, with major highway intersections as nodes. The arcs of the network represent travel distance (or time) between pairs of nodes, calculated using the shortest route.

The selection of geographic representation and distance metric often is dictated by the economics of the data collection effort and the problem environment. Networks can represent more accurately the geographic uniqueness of an area (e.g., the travel restrictions caused by a river with few bridges or by mountainous terrain). Unfortunately, the cost of gathering the travel times between nodes can be prohibitive. When locating is done on a plane that represents an urban area, the metropolitan metric often is used, because streets for some cities are arranged in an east-west and north-south pattern. Both the metropolitan and euclidian metrics require an estimate of the average speed to convert distance traveled to time.

Number of Facilities

The location of a single facility generally can be treated mathematically with little difficulty. Unfortunately, the methods used to site a single facility do not guarantee optimal results when they are modified and applied to multisite location problems. Finding a unique set of sites is complicated by assigning demand nodes to sites (i.e., defining service areas for each site), and the problem is complicated further if the capacity at each site varies. In addition, for some services such as health care, a hierarchy of service exists. Private physicians and clinics offer primary care, general hospitals provide primary care plus hospitalization, and health centers add special treatment capabilities. Thus, the selection of services provided also may be a variable in multisite location studies.

Optimization Criteria

Private and public sector location problems are similar in that they share the objective of maximizing some measure of benefit. The location criteria that are chosen differ, however, because the "ownership" is different. Within the private sector, the location decision is governed by either minimization of cost (e.g., in the case of distribution centers) or maximization of profit (e.g., in the case of retail locations). In contrast, we like to think that public facility decisions are governed by the needs of society as a whole. The objective for public decision making is to maximize a societal benefit that may be difficult to quantify.

Private Sector Criteria

Traditional private sector location analysis focuses on a trade-off between the cost of building and operating facilities and the cost of transportation. Much of the literature has addressed this problem, which is appropriate for the distribution of products (i.e., the warehouse location problem). These models may find some applications in services, however, when the services are delivered to the customers (e.g., consulting, auditing, janitorial, and lawn care services).

When the consumer travels to the facility, no direct cost is incurred by the provider. Instead, distance becomes a barrier restricting potential consumer demand and the corresponding revenue generated. Facilities such as retail shopping centers therefore are located to attract the maximum number of customers.

Public Sector Criteria

Location decisions in the public sector are complicated by the lack of agreement on goals and the difficulty of measuring benefits in dollars to make trade-offs with facility investment. Because the benefits of a public service are difficult to define or quantify directly, surrogate (or substitute) measures of utility are used.

The average distance traveled by users to reach the facility is a popular surrogate. The smaller this quantity, the more accessible the system is to its users. Thus, the problem becomes one of minimizing the total average distance traveled, with a constraint on the number of facilities. The problem is additionally constrained by some maximum travel distance for the user. Another possibility is the creation of demand. Here the user population is not considered fixed but is determined by the location, size, and number of facilities. The greater the demand created or drawn, the more efficient the system is in filling the needs of the region.

These utility surrogates are optimized with constraints on investment. Analysis of cost-effectiveness usually is performed to examine trade-offs between investment and utility. The trade-offs for the surrogates are (1) the decrease in average distance traveled per additional thousand-dollar investment and (2) the increase in demand per additional thousand-dollar investment.

Effect of Optimization Criteria on Location

The selection of optimization criteria influences service facility location. For example, William J. Abernathy and John C. Hershey studied the location of health centers for a three-city region.[8] As part of that study, they noted the effect of health-center locations with respect to the following criteria:

1. *Maximize utilization.* Maximize the total number of visits to the centers.

2. *Minimize distance per capita.* Minimize the average distance per capita to the closest center.

3. *Minimize distance per visit.* Minimize the average per-visit travel distance to the nearest center.

The problem was structured so that each city had a population with a different mix of health care consumption characteristics. These characteristics were measured along two dimensions: (1) the effect of distance as a barrier to health care use and (2) the utilization rate at immediate proximity to a health care center. Figure 10.4 shows a map of the three cities and the location of a single health care center under each of the three criteria. These criteria yield entirely different locations because of the different behavioral patterns of each city. For criterion 1 (maximize utilization), the center is located at city C, because this city contains a large number of elderly individuals for whom distance is a strong barrier. City B is selected under criterion 2 (minimize distance per capita), because this city is centrally located between the two larger cities. City A is the largest population center and has the most mobile and frequent users of health care; therefore, criterion 3 (minimize distance per visit) leads to this city being selected.

FIGURE 10.4
Location of One Health Center for Three Different Criteria

Source: W. J. Abernathy and J. C. Hershey, "A Spatial-Allocation Model for Regional Health-Services Planning." Reprinted with permission from *Operations Research* 20, no. 3, 1972, p. 637, Operations Research Society of America. No further reproduction permitted without the consent of the copyright owner.

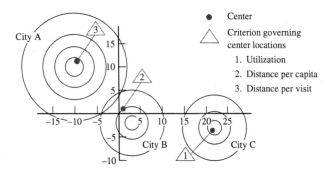

Facility Location Techniques

An understanding of the facility location problem can be gained from the results of locating a single facility on a line. For example, consider the problem of locating a beach mat concession along the beach front at Waikiki. Suppose you wish to find a location that would minimize the average walk to your concession from anywhere on the beach. Further, suppose you have data showing the density of bathers along the beachfront, which is related to the size and location of hotels. This distribution of bathers is shown schematically in Figure 10.5.

The objective is

$$\text{Minimize} \qquad Z = \sum_{i=0}^{s} w_i(s - x_i) + \sum_{i=s}^{n} w_i(x_i - s) \qquad (4)$$

where

w_i = weight of demand (bathers) attached to the ith location on the beach

x_i = location of the ith demand point on the beach in yards from the west end of the beach

s = site of the beach mat concession

The total-distance function Z is differentiated with respect to s and set equal to zero. This yields

$$\frac{dZ}{ds} = \sum_{i=0}^{s} w_i - \sum_{i=s}^{n} w_i = 0 \qquad \text{or} \qquad \sum_{i=0}^{s} w_i = \sum_{i=s}^{n} w_i \qquad (5)$$

This result suggests that the site should be located at the median with respect to the density distribution of bathers. That is, the site is located so that 50 percent of the potential demand is to each side (i.e., 29 in Figure 10.5). We probably should have expected this, because the median has the property of minimizing the sum of the absolute deviations from it.

The result for locating a site along a line can be generalized for locating a site on a plane if we use the metropolitan metric. Total travel distance will be minimized if the coordinates of the site correspond to the intersection of the x and y medians for their respective density distributions. We will refer to this as the *cross-median* approach.

The selection of a solution technique is determined by the characteristics of the problem, as outlined in Figure 10.2. Our discussion of location techniques is not exhaustive, but a few techniques will be discussed to illustrate various approaches to the problem.

FIGURE 10.5
Location of Beach Concession

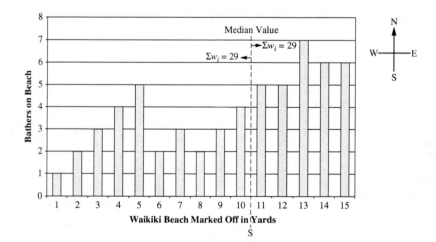

The selected techniques also represent approaches that deal with the various problem characteristics: single-facility versus multiple-facility location, location on a plane or a network, and public versus private optimization criteria.

Cross Median Approach for a Single Facility

Locating a single facility on a plane to minimize the total travel distance Z by means of the metropolitan metric is straightforward using the cross-median approach. The objective is

$$\text{Minimize} \quad Z = \sum_{i=1}^{n} w_i \{ |x_i - x_s| + |y_i - y_s| \} \tag{6}$$

where

$\quad w_i = $ weight attached to the ith point (e.g., trips per month)

$\quad x_i, y_i = $ coordinates of the ith demand point

$\quad x_s, y_s = $ coordinates of the service facility

$\quad n = $ number of demand points served

Note that the objective function may be restated as two independent terms.

$$\text{Minimize} \quad Z = \sum_{i=1}^{n} w_i |x_i - x_s| + \sum_{i=1}^{n} w_i |y_i - y_s| \tag{7}$$

Recall from our beach mat example that the median of a discrete set of values is such that the sum of absolute deviations from it is a minimum. Thus, our optimum site will have coordinates such that (1) x_s is at the median value for w_i ordered in the x direction and (2) y_s is at the median value for w_i ordered in the y direction. Because x_s, y_s, or both may be unique or lie within a range, the optimal location may be at a point, on a line, or within an area.

**Example 10.1
Copying Service**

A copying service has decided to open an office in the central business district of a city. The manager has identified four office buildings that will generate a major portion of its business, and Figure 10.6 shows the location of these demand points on an xy coordinate system. Weights are attached to each point and represent potential demand per month in hundreds of orders. The manager would like to determine a central location that will minimize the total distance per month that customers travel to the copying service.

FIGURE 10.6
Locating a Copying Service Using Cross-Median Approach

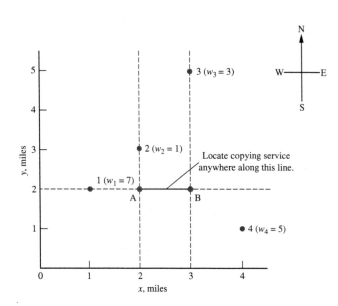

TABLE 10.4
Median Value for x_s

Point i	Location x_i	Σw_i
	Ordering west to east $\longrightarrow$	
1	1	7 = 7
2	②	7 + 1 = 8
3	3	
4	4	
	Ordering east to west $\longleftarrow$	
4	4	5 = 5
3	③	5 + 3 = 8
2	2	
1	1	

Because of the urban location, a metropolitan metric is appropriate. A site located by the cross-median approach will be used to solve this problem. First, the median is calculated using equation (8):

$$\text{Median} = \sum_{i=1}^{n} \frac{w_i}{2} \qquad (8)$$

From Figure 10.6, we find that the median has a value of $(7 + 1 + 3 + 5)/2 = 8$. To identify the x-coordinate median for x_s, we sum the values of w_i in the x direction both west to east and east to west. The top half of Table 10.4 lists in descending order the demand points from west to east as they appear in Figure 10.6 (i.e., 1, 2, 3, 4). The weights attached to each demand point are summed in descending order until the median value of 8 is reached or exceeded. The median value of 8 is reached when the weight of location 2 is added to the weight of location 1: thus, the first x median is established at the value of 2 miles (i.e., the x coordinate of location 2 is circled).

This procedure is repeated with demand points ordered from east to west, as shown in descending order in the bottom half of Table 10.4 (i.e., 4, 3, 2, 1). The second x median is established at the value of 3 miles (i.e., the x coordinate of location 3 is circled).

Table 10.5 illustrates the same procedure for identifying the y-coordinate median for y_s. The top half of Table 10.5 lists in descending order the demand points from south to north as they appear in Figure 10.6 (i.e., 4, 1, 2, 3). In this case, the median value of 8 is first exceeded at location 1 when its weight is added to that of location 4 to yield a total of 12. The y median is established at the value of 2 miles (i.e., the y coordinate of location 1 is circled). At the bottom of Table 10.5, the demand points from north to south are listed in descending order as they

TABLE 10.5
Median Value for y_s

Point i	Location y_i	Σw_i
	Ordering south to north $\uparrow$	
4	1	5 = 5
1	②	5 + 7 = 12
2	3	
3	5	
	Ordering north to south $\downarrow$	
3	5	3 = 3
2	3	3 + 1 = 4
1	②	3 + 1 + 7 = 11
4	1	

appear in Figure 10.6 (i.e., 3, 2, 1, 4). Again, the median value is first exceeded at location 1 when its weight is added to those of locations 3 and 2 to yield a total of 11. Thus, we are left with only one *y* median at 2 miles.

The cross-median approach of determining the median from all four points of the compass ensures that if a range of locations is appropriate, it will be identified readily. In this case, any location on the line segment AB minimizes total travel distance (e.g., coordinates $2 = x_s = 3$ and $y_s = 2$).

Note from Table 10.6 that the total weighted travel distance calculated for point A and point B is equal to 35 miles in both instances; thus, any location at either point A or point B or along the line between them will be acceptable. As this example illustrates, a location solution can be a line (i.e., a city street), a point (i.e., an intersection), or an area (i.e., a city block). Thus, the cross-median approach can result in some site selection flexibility.

Huff Model for Retail Outlet

When locating a retail outlet such as a supermarket, the objective is to maximize profit. In this case, a discrete number of alternative locations must be evaluated to find the most profitable site.

A gravity model is used to estimate consumer demand. This model is based on the physical analog that the gravitational attraction of two bodies is directly proportional to the product of their masses and inversely proportional to the square of the distance that separates them. For a service, the attractiveness of a facility may be expressed as

$$A_{ij} = \frac{S_j}{T_{ij}^{\lambda}} \tag{9}$$

where

A_{ij} = attraction to facility *j* for consumer *i*

S_j = size of the facility *j*

T_{ij} = travel time from consumer *i*'s location to facility *j*

λ = parameter estimated empirically to reflect the effect of travel time on various kinds of shopping trips (e.g., where a shopping mall may have a $\lambda = 2$, convenience stores would have a $\lambda = 10$ or larger)

David L. Huff developed a retail location model using this gravity model to predict the benefit that a customer would have for a particular store size and location.[9] Knowing that customers also would be attracted to other competing stores, he proposed the ratio P_{ij}.

TABLE 10.6   **Total Weighted Distance for Locations A and B**

Location A (2,2)					Location B (3,2)				
Office	**Distance**		**Weight**	**Total**	**Office**	**Distance**		**Weight**	**Total**
1	1	×	7	= 7	1	2	×	7	= 14
2	1	×	1	= 1	2	2	×	1	= 2
3	4	×	3	= 12	3	3	×	3	= 9
4	3	×	5	= 15	4	2	×	5	= 10
				35					35

For n stores, this ratio measures the probability of a customer from a given statistical area i traveling to a particular shopping facility j.

$$P_{ij} = \frac{A_{ij}}{\sum\limits_{j=1}^{n} A_{ij}} \tag{10}$$

An estimate of E_{jk}, the total annual consumer expenditures for a product class k at a prospective shopping facility j, then can be calculated as

$$E_{jk} = \sum\limits_{i=1}^{m} (P_{ij} C_i B_{ik}) \tag{11}$$

where

P_{ij} = probability of a consumer from a given statistical area i traveling to a shopping facility j, calculated by means of equation (10)

C_i = number of consumers at area i

B_{ik} = average annual amount budgeted by consumer at area i for a product class k

m = number of statistical areas

An estimate of M_{jk}, the market share captured by facility j of product class k sales, can be calculated as

$$M_{jk} = \frac{E_{jk}}{\sum\limits_{i=1}^{m} C_i B_{ik}} \tag{12}$$

An exhaustive procedure is used to calculate the expected annual profit of each potential site for various possible store sizes at the site. Net operating profit before taxes is calculated as a percentage of sales adjusted for the size of the store. The result is a list of potential sites with the store size at each that maximizes profit. All that remains is to negotiate a real estate deal for the site that comes closest to maximizing annual profit.

TABLE 10.7
Travel Distance in Miles (T_{ij}) (Using Metropolitan Metric)

	Customer Location (i)			
Site (j)	1	2	3	4
Proposed (3, 2)	2	2	3	2
Existing (2, 2)	1	1	4	3

TABLE 10.8
Attraction (A_{ij})

	Customer Location (i)			
Site (j)	1	2	3	4
Proposed ($S_1 = 2$)	0.5	0.5	0.2222	0.500
Existing ($S_2 = 1$)	1.0	1.0	0.0625	0.111
Total attraction	1.5	1.5	0.2847	0.611

TABLE 10.9
Probability (P_{ij})

	Customer Location (i)			
Site (j)	1	2	3	4
Proposed	.33	.33	.78	.82
Existing	.67	.67	.22	.18

TABLE 10.10
Monthly Expenditures (E_{jk}) and Market Share (M_{jk})

	Customer Expenditures				Monthly Total	Market Share %
Site (j)	1	2	3	4		
Proposed	$2,333	$ 333	$2,340	$4,100	$9,106	0.57
Existing	4,667	667	660	900	6,894	0.43
Totals	$7,000	$1,000	$3,000	$5,000	$16,000	1.00

**Example 10.2
Copying
Service—Huff
Analysis**

Assume that the copying service in Example 10.1 has been established at ($x = 2$, $y = 2$), as shown by location A in Figure 10.6 (on p. 247) at the far left end of the optimal line. Further, assume that each customer order represents an expenditure of approximately $10. Because convenience would be an important customer criterion, assume that $\lambda = 2$. If we wish to open a competing store at location ($x = 3$, $y = 2$) (i.e., at location B on the far right end of the optimal line) but with *twice* the capacity of the existing copy center, how much market share would we expect to capture? Using the travel distances in Table 10.7 as input to the Huff model, the calculations shown in Tables 10.8 to 10.10 are obtained.

This example illustrates the result of an aggressive location strategy as used by well-financed national retail chains. For example, as the name might imply, Blockbuster Video has a reputation of moving into a community with supersized stores and driving out small, locally operated video-rental establishments.

Location Set Covering for Multiple Facilities

The difficulty of evaluating decisions regarding public facility location has resulted in a search for surrogate, or substitute, measures of the benefit of the facility location. One such measure is the distance that the most distant customer would have to travel to reach the facility. This is known as the *maximal service distance*. We want to find the minimum number and location of facilities that will serve all demand points within some specified maximal service distance; this is known as the *location set covering* problem.

**Example 10.3
Rural Medical
Clinics**

A state department of health is concerned about the lack of medical care in rural areas, and a group of nine communities has been selected for a pilot program in which medical clinics will be opened to serve primary health care needs. It is hoped that every community will be within 30 miles of at least one clinic. The planners would like to determine the number of clinics that are required and their locations. Any community can serve as a potential clinic site except for community 6, because facilities are unavailable there. Figure 10.7 shows a network

FIGURE 10.7
Travel Network for a Rural Area

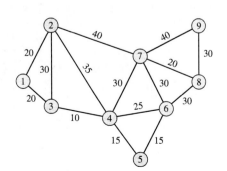

TABLE 10.11

Range of Service for Potential Sites

* Community 6 cannot serve as a clinic site.

† Subsets of potential sites.

Community	Set of Communities Served from Site	Potential Sites That Could Serve the Community*
1	1,2,3,4	1,2,3,4
2	1,2,3	(1,2,3)†
3	1,2,3,4,5	1,2,3,4,5
4	1,3,4,5,6,7	1,3,4,5,7
5	3,4,5,6	(3,4,5)†
6	4,5,6,7,8	4,5,7,8
7	4,6,7,8	(4,7,8)†
8	6,7,8,9	7,8,9
9	8,9	(8,9)†

identifying the cities as numbered circles; lines drawn between the sites show the travel distances in miles.

The problem is approached by first identifying for each community the other communities that can be reached from it within the 30-mile travel limit. Beginning with community 1, we see in Figure 10.7 that communities 2, 3, and 4 can be reached within the 30-mile distance limit. The results of similar inspections for each community are reported in the second column of Table 10.11 as the set of communities served from each site. An equivalent statement could be made that this set, less any communities that could not serve as a site, represents the set of sites that could cover the community in question for service within 30 miles. Thus, for community 5, a clinic located at site 3, 4, or 5 meets the maximal travel limit.

The third column of Table 10.11 represents the set of potential sites that could cover a given community. Several of these sets have been placed in parentheses, however, because they represent subsets of other potential locations. For example, because community 2 can only be served by sites 1, 2, and 3, one of these sites must be selected for a clinic location. Identifying these subsets reduces the problem size while ensuring that restrictions are satisfied.

Note that because of our desire to minimize the number of clinics to cover all the communities, any site common to two or more of these subsets is an excellent candidate for selection. In this case, sites 3, 4, and 8 are candidates. From inspection, we see that if sites 3 and 8 are selected, all subsets are accounted for; thus, all communities can be covered with just these two clinics. We also have identified the service region for each clinic; the clinic located at community 3 will serve communities 1 through 5, and the clinic located at community 8 will serve communities 6 through 9.

The location set covering problem often can yield more than one solution. In this example, if the maximal travel distance were set at 40 miles, the following five pairs of clinic site locations would provide coverage: (3, 8), (3, 9), (4, 7), (4, 8), and (4, 9).

Summary

Facility location plays an important role in the strategy of a service firm through its influence on the competitive dimensions of flexibility, competitive positioning, demand management, and focus. Strategies such as competitive clustering are common for shopping goods, and saturation marketing has been successful for some small retail outlets. In addition, use of marketing intermediaries can decouple the provider from the consumer. If the requirement for face-to-face interaction between server and customer is not necessary, as illustrated by Internet service providers, the substitution of electronic communication for physical transportation becomes possible.

Service Benchmark

HERE A BUN, THERE A BUN, EVERYWHERE A BUN-BUN

The idea of clustering or saturation marketing has come of age and been embraced enthusiastically by many companies such as Au Bon Pain, Benetton, and Starbucks. At first blush, the notion of locating several shops from one company in a small geographical area, sometimes within one block of each other, seems risky. For Au Bon Pain, a chain known for its special sandwiches and baked goods, the advantages have outweighed the disadvantages.

Saturation marketing decreases the need for advertising—why advertise when prospective customers can't walk one block, or sometimes even just one floor in a department store, without passing a Benetton clothing shop or a Starbucks coffee shop? Au Bon Pain has also found that it is easier to supervise the shops when they are located close together. Saturation marketing is most successful in high-density, urban locations, particularly for businesses like Starbucks and Au Bon Pain, which are not destination shops. Customers usually stop at these places on their way to other destinations.

Clustering seems to work better with company-owned outlets rather than with independently-owned franchises. If one company-owned outlet does siphon off a little business from another one, it does not affect the company's bottom line. If one independently-owned franchise siphons business from another one, however, it is of concern to an independent owner who comes out on the shorter end.

The discussion of facility location techniques began with the single-facility problem. The cross-median approach identified an optimal location for minimizing the total distance traveled by customers. The location of a single retail outlet to maximize profit is an important decision that has been studied by David Huff using a gravity model to predict customer attractiveness to a store based on its size and location. For the multiple-facility location problem, the concept of location set covering is central to understanding the many approaches to identifying multiple-site locations.

Key Terms and Definitions

Competitive clustering the grouping of competitors (e.g., automobile dealerships) in close proximity for convenience in comparative shopping by customers. *p. 237*

Cross-median an approach to the location of a single facility using the metropolitan metric to minimize the total weighted distance traveled. *p. 246*

E-distance a barrier found in Web site design created by internal and external navigation. *p. 239*

Huff model a retail location model that is based on an analogy to celestial gravity to measure the attraction of a customer for a facility. *p. 249*

Location set covering an approach to finding the minimum number and location of facilities that will serve all demand points within a specified maximum travel distance. *p. 251*

Marketing intermediaries a business entity in the channel of distribution between the final customer and the service provider (e.g., a bank extending credit to a retailer through a credit card). *p. 238*

Metropolitan metric a measure of distance traveled assuming rectangular displacement (e.g. north-south and east-west travel in urban areas). *p. 243*

Saturation marketing the location of a firm's individual outlets (e.g., ice cream vendors) in close proximity to create a significant presence that attracts customer attention. *p. 237*

254   Part Two *Designing the Service Enterprise*

Topics for Discussion

1. Pick a particular service, and identify shortcomings in its site selection.
2. How would you proceed to estimate empirically the parameter λ in the Huff retail location model for a branch bank?
3. What are the characteristics of a service that would make communication a good substitute for transportation?
4. What are the benefits of using intermediaries in the service distribution channel?
5. Go to http://www.mapinfo.com/ and find the definition of "location intelligence." What use can be made of geographic information?

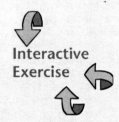

Interactive Exercise

The class discusses the business opportunities of using Google Earth.

Solved Problems

1. Cross-Median Location Problem

    Problem Statement
    A health clinic is being planned to serve a rural area in west Texas. The service area consists of four communities at the following xy coordinate locations in miles: A (6, 2), B (8, 6), C (5, 9), D (3, 4), with populations of 2,000, 1,000, 3,000, and 2,000, respectively. Recommend a "cross-median" location for the health clinic minimizing the total weighted metropolitan distance traveled.

    Solution
    First, calculate the median value in thousands:

    $$\text{Median} = (2 + 1 + 3 + 2)/2 = 4$$

    Second, plot the four communities on a grid with population in thousands as subscripts:

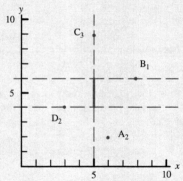

    Third, draw the x-median dotted line (i.e., vertical line) on the plot by moving from left to right, adding the weights until the sum is equal to or exceeds the median (i.e., $D_2 + C_3 = 5$). The result is one vertical line at $x = 5$. Moving from right to left, add the weights until the sum is equal to or exceeds the median (i.e., $B_1 + A_2 + C_3 = 6$). The result is the same vertical line at $x = 5$.

Fourth, draw the y-median dotted line (i.e., horizontal line) on the plot by moving from top to bottom, adding the weights until the sum is equal to or exceeds the median (i.e., $C_3 + B_1 = 4$). The result is a horizontal line at $y = 6$. Moving from bottom to top, add the weights until the sum is equal to or exceeds the median (i.e., $A_2 + D_2 = 4$). The result is another horizontal line at $y = 4$. The recommended location results in a line segment shown as a dark line in the plot with xy coordinates of (5,4 to 5,6).

2.   Retail Location Using the Huff Model

Problem Statement

The west Texas area in the plot above is served by a grocery store in community D. A proposed store with three times the floor space is being considered for location in community C. Assume that monthly expenditures per customer average about $100. Then, using the metropolitan metric for travel and $\lambda = 2$, use the Huff model to estimate the impact on monthly expenditures and market share for the existing store in community D if the proposed store in community C is constructed.

Solution

First, determine the travel distances using the metropolitan metric:

Travel Distance in Miles (T_{ij}) (Using Metropolitan Metric)

	Community (i)			
Site (j)	A (6, 2)	B (8, 6)	C (5, 9)	D (3, 4)
Proposed C (5, 9)	8	6	0	7
Existing D (3, 4)	5	7	7	0

Second, using equation (14), calculate the attraction matrix with $\lambda = 2$. For example, the attraction of community A to the proposed location at C (with $S = 3$ to account for the larger floor space) would be calculated as

$$A_{ij} = \frac{S_j}{T_{ij}^{\lambda}} = \frac{S_1}{T_{11}^2} = \frac{3}{8^2} = \frac{3}{64} = 0.0469$$

Note that the attraction is given a value of ∞ where the store is located in the same community ($T_{ij} = 0$ in the denominator).

Attraction (A_{ij})

	Community Location (i)			
Site (j)	A	B	C	D
Proposed $S_1 = 3$	0.0469	0.0833	∞	—
Existing $S_2 = 1$	0.0400	0.0204	—	∞
Total attraction	0.0869	0.1037		

Third, using equation (15), calculate the probability using the total attraction as the denominator. For example, the probability of residents in community A traveling to the proposed grocery store location at C would be calculated as

$$P_{ij} = \frac{A_{ij}}{\sum_{j=1}^{n} A_{ij}} = \frac{A_{11}}{A_{11} + A_{12}} = \frac{0.0469}{0.0469 + 0.04} = 0.54$$

Probability (P_{ij})

	Community Location (i)			
Site (j)	A	B	C	D
Proposed	.54	.80	1.0	0
Existing	.46	.20	0	1.0

Fourth, using equation (16), the monthly expenditures are calculated, and using equation (17), the market shares are determined. For example, expenditures from residents of community A at the proposed grocery store location at C would be calculated as

$$E_{jk} = \sum_{i=1}^{m} (P_{ij} C_i B_{ik}) = P_{11} C_1 B_1 = (.54)(2000)(100) = \$108,000$$

Monthly Expenditures (E_{jk}) and Market Share (M_{jk})

	Community Expenditures				Monthly Total	Market Share %
Site (j)	A	B	C	D		
Proposed	$108,000	$ 80,000	$300,000	$ 0	$488,000	0.61
Existing	92,000	20,000	0	200,000	312,000	0.39
Totals	$200,000	$100,000	$300,000	$200,000	$800,000	1.00

Exercises

10.1. Revisit the copying service in Example 10.1 and assume that over the years, the monthly demand from the four customers has increased to the following weights: $w_1 = 7$, $w_2 = 9$, $w_3 = 5$, $w_4 = 7$. If we previously located the copying service at point A in Figure 10.6, should we now consider a relocation?

10.2. A temporary-help agency wants to open an office in a suburban section of a large city. It has identified five large corporate offices as potential customers. The locations of these offices in miles on an xy coordinate grid for the area are $c_1 = (4, 4)$, $c_2 = (4, 11)$, $c_3 = (7, 2)$, $c_4 = (11, 11)$, and $c_5 = (14, 7)$. The expected demand for temporary help from these customers is weighted as $w_1 = 3$, $w_2 = 2$, $w_3 = 2$, $w_4 = 4$, and $w_5 = 1$. The agency reimburses employees for travel expenses incurred by their assignments; therefore, recommend a location (i.e., xy coordinates) for the agency that will minimize the total weighted metropolitan distance for job-related travel.

10.3. Four hospitals located in one county are cooperating to establish a centralized blood-bank facility to serve them all. On an xy coordinate grid of the county, the hospitals are found at the following locations: $H_1 = (5, 10)$, $H_2 = (7, 6)$, $H_3 = (4, 2)$, and $H_4 = (16, 3)$. The expected number of deliveries per month from the blood bank to each hospital is estimated at 450, 1,200, 300, and 1,500, respectively. Using the cross-median approach, recommend a location for the blood bank that will minimize the total distance traveled.

10.4. A pizza delivery service has decided to open a branch near off-campus student housing. The project manager has identified five student apartment complexes in the northwest area of the city, the locations of which, on an xy coordinate grid in miles, are $C_1 = (1, 2)$, $C_2 = (2, 6)$, $C_3 = (3, 3)$, $C_4 = (4, 1)$, and $C_5 = (5, 4)$. The expected demand is weighted as $w_1 = 5$, $w_2 = 4$, $w_3 = 3$, $w_4 = 1$, and $w_5 = 5$. Using the cross-median approach, recommend a location for the pizza branch that will minimize the total distance traveled.

10.5. A small city airport is served by four airlines. The terminal is rather spread out, with boarding areas located on an xy coordinate grid at $A = (1, 4)$, $B = (5, 5)$, $C = (8, 3)$, and $D = (8, 1)$. The number of flights per day, of approximately equal capacity, is $A = 28$, $B = 22$, $C = 36$, and $D = 18$. A new central baggage claim area is under construction. Using the cross-median approach, recommend a location for the new baggage claim area that will minimize the total weighted distance from the boarding areas.

10.6. You have been asked to help locate a catering service in the central business district of a city. The locations of potential customers on an xy coordinate grid are $P_1 = (4, 4)$, $P_2 = (12, 4)$, $P_3 = (2, 7)$, $P_4 = (11, 11)$, and $P_5 = (7, 14)$. The expected demand is weighted as $w_1 = 4$, $w_2 = 3$, $w_3 = 2$, $w_4 = 4$, and $w_5 = 1$. Using the cross-median approach, recommend a location for the catering service that will minimize the total weighted distance traveled to serve the customers.

10.7. Revisit the copying service Huff analysis in Example 10.2. Recalculate the monthly customer expenditures and the market share for the proposed copying center at location B if the new store will be *three* times the capacity of the existing store at location A and the new demand weights from Exercise 10.1 above are used.

10.8. A locally owned department store samples two customers in each of five geographic areas to estimate consumer spending in its home appliances department. It is estimated that these customers are a good sample of the 10,000 customers the store serves. The number of customers in each area is $C_1 = 1,500$, $C_2 = 2,500$, $C_3 = 1,000$, $C_4 = 3,000$, and $C_5 = 2,000$. It is found that the two consumers have the following budgets in dollars for home appliances per year: $B_{11} = 100$, $B_{12} = 150$; $B_{21} = 75$, $B_{22} = 100$; $B_{31} = 125$, $B_{32} = 125$; $B_{41} = 100$, $B_{42} = 120$; and $B_{51} = 120$, $B_{52} = 125$.

   a. Using the Huff retail location model, estimate annual home appliance sales for the store.

   b. Bull's-Eye, a chain department store, opens a branch in a shopping complex near by. The Bull's-Eye branch is three times larger than the locally owned store. The travel times in minutes from the five areas to the two stores ($j = 1$ for the locally owned store, $j = 2$ for Bull's-Eye) are $T_{11} = 20$, $T_{12} = 15$; $T_{21} = 35$, $T_{22} = 20$; $T_{31} = 30$, $T_{32} = 25$; $T_{41} = 20$, $T_{42} = 25$; and $T_{51} = 25$, $T_{52} = 25$. Use the Huff retail location model to estimate the annual consumer expenditures in the home appliance section of each store assuming that $\lambda = 1$.

10.9. A community is currently being served by a single self-serve gas station with six pumps. A competitor is opening a new facility with 12 pumps across town. Table 10.12 shows the travel times in minutes from the four different areas in the community to the sites and the number of customers in each area.

   a. Using the Huff retail location model and assuming that $\lambda = 2$, calculate the probability of a customer traveling from each area to each site.

   b. Estimate the proportion of the existing market lost to the new competitor.

TABLE 10.12
Travel Times to
Gas Stations

Area	1	2	3	4
Old station	5	1	9	15
New competitor	20	8	12	6
Number of customers	100	150	80	50

10.10. Recall the rural medical clinics in Example 10.3 and suppose that each community were required to be 25 miles at most from the nearest clinic. How many clinics would be needed, and what would their locations be? Give all possible location solutions.

10.11. A bank is planning to serve the rural communities shown in Figure 10.8 with automated teller machines (ATMs). The travel time in minutes between communities in the service area is shown on the network in Figure 10.8. The bank is interested in determining the number and location of ATMs necessary to serve the communities so that a machine will be within 20 minutes' travel time of any community.

10.12. The volunteer fire department serving the communities in Figure 10.8 has just purchased two used fire engines auctioned off by a nearby city.

    a. Select all possible pairs of communities in which the fire engines could be located to ensure that all communities can be reached in 30 minutes or less.

    b. What additional consideration could be used to make the final site selection from the community pairs found in part a?

FIGURE 10.8
Service Area Network

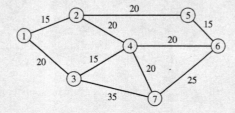

Selected Bibliography

Chhajed, D.; R. L. Francis; and T. J. Lowe. "Contributions of Operations Research to Location Analysis." *Location Science* 1, no. 4 (1993), pp. 263–87.

Craig, C. S.; A. Ghosh; and S. McLafferty. "Models of the Retail Location Process: A Review." *Journal of Retailing* 60, no. 1 (Spring 1984), pp. 5–36.

Fitzsimmons, James A., and B. N. Srikar. "Emergency Ambulance Location Using the Contiguous Zone Search Routine." *Journal of Operations Management* 2, no. 4 (August 1982), pp. 225–37.

Mandell, Marvin B. "Modeling Effectiveness-Equity Trade-offs in Public Service Delivery Systems." *Management Science* 37, no. 4 (April 1991), pp. 467–82.

Min, H. "Location Planning of Airport Facilities Using the Analytic Hierarchy Process." *Logistics and Transportation Review* 30, no. 1 (March 1995), pp. 79–94.

Price, W. L., and M. Turcotte. "Locating a Blood Bank." *Interfaces* 16, no. 5 (1986), pp. 17–26.

Schmenner, Roger W. "The Location Decisions of New Services." In *New Service Development,* eds. J. A. Fitzsimmons and M. J. Fitzsimmons. Thousand Oaks, Calif.: Sage Publications, 2000, pp. 216–38.

Swersey, Arthur J., and Lakshman S. Thakur. "An Integer Programming Model for Locating Vehicle Emissions Testing Stations." *Management Science* 41, no. 3 (March 1995), pp. 496–512.

Endnotes

1. D. A. Lopez and P. Gray, "The Substitution of Communication for Transportation: A Case Study," *Management Science* 23, no. 11 (July 1977), pp. 1149–60.

2. S. E. Kimes and J. A. Fitzsimmons, "Selecting Profitable Hotel Sites at La Quinta Motor Inns," *Interfaces* 20, no. 2 (March 1990), pp. 12–20.

3. Suzanne Alexander, "Saturating Cities with Stores Can Pay," *The Wall Street Journal,* September 11, 1989, p. B1.

4. James H. Donnelly, "Marketing Intermediaries in Channels of Distribution for Services," *Journal of Marketing* 40, January 1976, pp. 55–70.

5. Julie E. Kendall, "E-distance and the Theatres of South Jersey," *Decision Line,* March 2003, pp. 13–15.

6. S. E. Kimes and J. A. Fitzsimmons, "Selecting Profitable Hotel Sites at La Quinta Motor Inns," *Interfaces* 20, no. 2 (March 1990), pp. 12–20.

7. Christian Harder, *ArcView GIS Means Business,* Redlands, Calif.: Environmental Research Systems, Inc., (1997), pp. 125.

8. W. J. Abernathy and J. C. Hershey, "A Spatial-Allocation Model for Regional Health Services Planning," *Operations Research* 20, no. 3 (May–June 1972), pp. 629–42.

9. David L. Huff, "A Programmed Solution for Approximating an Optimum Retail Location," *Land Economics,* August 1966, pp. 293–303.

10. This case was prepared by James H. Vance under the supervision of Professor James A. Fitzsimmons.

Appendix C

Values of L_q for the $M/M/c$ Queuing Model

ρ	$c = 1$	$c = 2$	$c = 3$	$c = 4$	$c = 5$	$c = 6$	$c = 7$	$c = 8$
0.15	0.026	0.001						
0.20	0.050	0.002						
0.25	0.083	0.004						
0.30	0.129	0.007						
0.35	0.188	0.011						
0.40	0.267	0.017						
0.45	0.368	0.024	0.002					
0.50	0.500	0.033	0.003					
0.55	0.672	0.045	0.004					
0.60	0.900	0.059	0.006					
0.65	1.207	0.077	0.008					
0.70	1.633	0.098	0.011					
0.75	2.250	0.123	0.015					
0.80	3.200	0.152	0.019					
0.85	4.817	0.187	0.024	0.003				
0.90	8.100	0.229	0.030	0.004				
0.95	18.050	0.277	0.037	0.005				
1.0		0.333	0.045	0.007				
1.1		0.477	0.066	0.011				
1.2		0.675	0.094	0.016	0.003			
1.3		0.951	0.130	0.023	0.004			
1.4		1.345	0.177	0.032	0.006			
1.5		1.929	0.237	0.045	0.009			
1.6		2.844	0.313	0.060	0.012			
1.7		4.426	0.409	0.080	0.017			
1.8		7.674	0.532	0.105	0.023			
1.9		17.587	0.688	0.136	0.030	0.007		
2.0			0.889	0.174	0.040	0.009		
2.1			1.149	0.220	0.052	0.012		
2.2			1.491	0.277	0.066	0.016		
2.3			1.951	0.346	0.084	0.021		
2.4			2.589	0.431	0.105	0.027	0.007	
2.5			3.511	0.533	0.130	0.034	0.009	
2.6			4.933	0.658	0.161	0.043	0.011	
2.7			7.354	0.811	0.198	0.053	0.014	

(continued)

ρ	$c = 1$	$c = 2$	$c = 3$	$c = 4$	$c = 5$	$c = 6$	$c = 7$	$c = 8$
2.8			12.273	1.000	0.241	0.066	0.018	
2.9			27.193	1.234	0.293	0.081	0.023	
3.0				1.528	0.354	0.099	0.028	0.008
3.1				1.902	0.427	0.120	0.035	0.010
3.2				2.386	0.513	0.145	0.043	0.012
3.3				3.027	0.615	0.174	0.052	0.015
3.4				3.906	0.737	0.209	0.063	0.019
3.5				5.165	0.882	0.248	0.076	0.023
3.6				7.090	1.055	0.295	0.091	0.028
3.7				10.347	1.265	0.349	0.109	0.034
3.8				16.937	1.519	0.412	0.129	0.041
3.9				36.859	1.830	0.485	0.153	0.050
4.0					2.216	0.570	0.180	0.059
4.1					2.703	0.668	0.212	0.070
4.2					3.327	0.784	0.248	0.083
4.3					4.149	0.919	0.289	0.097
4.4					5.268	1.078	0.337	0.114
4.5					6.862	1.265	0.391	0.133
4.6					9.289	1.487	0.453	0.156
4.7					13.382	1.752	0.525	0.181
4.8					21.641	2.071	0.607	0.209
4.9					46.566	2.459	0.702	0.242
5.0						2.938	0.810	0.279
5.1						3.536	0.936	0.321
5.2						4.301	1.081	0.368
5.3						5.303	1.249	0.422
5.4						6.661	1.444	0.483
5.5						8.590	1.674	0.553
5.6						11.519	1.944	0.631
5.7						16.446	2.264	0.721
5.8						26.373	2.648	0.823
5.9						56.300	3.113	0.939
6.0							3.683	1.071
6.1							4.394	1.222
6.2							5.298	1.397
6.3							6.480	1.598
6.4							8.077	1.831
6.5							10.341	2.102
6.6							13.770	2.420
6.7							19.532	2.796
6.8							31.127	3.245
6.9							66.055	3.786
7.0								4.447
7.1								5.270
7.2								6.314
7.3								7.675
7.4								9.511
7.5								12.109
7.6								16.039
7.7								22.636
7.8								35.898
7.9								75.827

Appendix D

Equations for Selected Queuing Models

Definition of Symbols

n = number of customers in the system

λ = [lambda] mean arrival rate (e.g., customer arrivals per hour)

μ = [mu] mean service rate per busy server (e.g., service capacity in customers per hour)

ρ = [rho] (λ/μ) mean number of customers in service

N = maximum number of customers allowed in the system

c = number of servers

P_n = probability of exactly n customers in the system

L_s = mean number of customers in the system

L_q = mean number of customers in queue

L_b = mean number of customers in queue for a busy system

W_s = mean time customer spends in the system

W_q = mean time customer spends in the queue

W_b = mean time customer spends in queue for a busy system

I. Standard $M/M/1$ Model ($0 < \rho < 1.0$)

$$P_0 = 1 - \rho \tag{I.1}$$

$$P(n \geq k) = \rho^k \tag{I.2}$$

$$P_n = P_0\rho^n \tag{I.3}$$

$$L_s = \frac{\lambda}{\mu - \lambda} \tag{I.4}$$

$$L_q = \frac{\rho\lambda}{\mu - \lambda} \tag{I.5}$$

$$L_b = \frac{\lambda}{\mu - \lambda} \tag{I.6}$$

$$W_s = \frac{1}{\mu - \lambda} \tag{I.7}$$

$$W_q = \frac{\rho}{\mu - \lambda} \tag{I.8}$$

$$W_b = \frac{1}{\mu - \lambda} \tag{I.9}$$

II. Standard *M/M/c* Model ($0 < \rho < c$)

$$P_0 = \frac{1}{\left(\displaystyle\sum_{i=0}^{c-1} \frac{\rho^i}{i!}\right) + \dfrac{\rho^c}{c!(1 - \rho/c)}} \tag{II.1}$$

$$P_n = \begin{cases} \dfrac{\rho^n}{n!} P_0 & \text{for } 0 \le n \le c \\[2ex] \dfrac{\rho^n}{c! \, c^{n-c}} P_0 & \text{for } n \ge c \end{cases} \tag{II.2}$$

$$P(n \ge c) = \frac{\rho^c \, \mu c}{c!(\mu c - \lambda)} P_0 \tag{II.3}$$

$$L_s = \frac{\rho^{c+1}}{(c-1)!(c-\rho)^2} P_0 + \rho \tag{II.4}$$

$$L_q = L_s - \rho \tag{II.5}$$

$$L_b = \frac{L_q}{P(n \ge c)} \tag{II.6}$$

$$W_s = \frac{L_q}{\lambda} + \frac{1}{\mu} \tag{II.7}$$

$$W_q = \frac{L_q}{\lambda} \tag{II.8}$$

$$W_b = \frac{W_q}{P(n \geq c)} \tag{II.9}$$

III. Standard $M/G/1$ Model ($V(t)$ = service time variance)

$$L_s = L_q + \rho \tag{III.1}$$

$$L_q = \frac{\rho^2 + \lambda^2 V(t)}{2(1 - \rho)} \tag{III.2}$$

$$W_s = \frac{L_s}{\lambda} \tag{III.3}$$

$$W_b = \frac{L_q}{\lambda} \tag{III.4}$$

IV. Self-Service $M/G/\infty$ Model ($e = 2.718$, the base of natural logarithms)

$$P_n = \frac{e^{-\rho}}{n!}\rho^n \quad \text{for } n \geq 0 \tag{IV.1}$$

$$L_s = \rho \tag{IV.2}$$

$$W_s = \frac{1}{\mu} \tag{IV.3}$$

V. Finite-Queue $M/M/1$ Model

$$P_0 = \begin{cases} \dfrac{1 - \rho}{1 - \rho^{N+1}} & \text{for } \lambda \neq \mu \\[2mm] \dfrac{1}{N + 1} & \text{for } \lambda = \mu \end{cases} \tag{V.1}$$

$$P(n > 0) = 1 - P_0 \tag{V.2}$$

$$P_n = P_0\rho^n \quad \text{for } n \leq N \tag{V.3}$$

$$L_s = \begin{cases} \dfrac{\rho}{1 - \rho} - \dfrac{(N + 1)\rho^{N+1}}{1 - \rho^{N+1}} & \text{for } \lambda \neq \mu \\[3mm] \dfrac{N}{2} & \text{for } \lambda = \mu \end{cases} \tag{V.4}$$

$$L_q = L_s - (1 - P_0) \tag{V.5}$$

$$L_b = \frac{L_q}{1 - P_0} \tag{V.6}$$

$$W_s = \frac{L_q}{\lambda(1 - P_N)} + \frac{1}{\mu} \tag{V.7}$$

$$W_q = W_s - \frac{1}{\mu} \tag{V.8}$$

$$W_b = \frac{W_q}{1 - P_0} \tag{V.9}$$

VI. Finite-Queue *M/M/c* Model

$$P_0 = \frac{1}{\left(\displaystyle\sum_{i=0}^{c} \frac{\rho^i}{i!}\right) + \left(\dfrac{1}{c!}\right)\left(\displaystyle\sum_{i=c+1}^{N} \frac{\rho^i}{c^{i-c}}\right)} \tag{VI.1}$$

$$P_n = \begin{cases} \dfrac{\rho^n}{n!} P_0 & \text{for } 0 \leq n \leq c \\[3mm] \dfrac{\rho^n}{c!c^{n-c}} P_0 & \text{for } c \leq n \leq N \end{cases} \tag{VI.2}$$

$$P(n \geq c) = 1 - P_0 \sum_{i=0}^{c-1} \frac{\rho^i}{i!} \tag{VI.3}$$

$$L_s = \frac{P_0\rho^{c+1}}{(c - 1)!(c - \rho)^2}\left[1 - \left(\frac{\rho}{c}\right)^{N-c} - (N - c)\left(\frac{\rho}{c}\right)^{N-c}\left(1 - \frac{\rho}{c}\right)\right] + \rho(1 - P_N) \tag{VI.4}$$

518 Appendix D *Equations for Selected Queuing Models*

$$L_q = L_s - \rho(1 - P_N)$$
(VI.5)

$$L_b = \frac{L_q}{P(n \geq c)}$$
(VI.6)

$$W_s = \frac{L_q}{\lambda(1 - P_N)} + \frac{1}{\mu}$$
(VI.7)

$$W_q = W_s - \frac{1}{\mu}$$
(VI.8)

$$W_b = \frac{W_q}{P(n \geq c)}$$
(VI.9)